Benjamin Franklin
and
American Foreign Policy

Benjamin Franklin
and
American Foreign Policy

By
GERALD STOURZH

SECOND EDITION

THE UNIVERSITY OF CHICAGO PRESS
CHICAGO AND LONDON

Library of Congress Catalog Card Number: 54–9355

THE UNIVERSITY OF CHICAGO PRESS, CHICAGO 60637
The University of Chicago Press, Ltd., London W.C. 1

TO MY MOTHER

TABLE OF CONTENTS

PREFACE TO SECOND EDITION

Since the first publication of this book in 1954, the major event in the field of Franklin scholarship has been the launching of the definitive edition of *The Papers of Benjamin Franklin* by the American Philosophical Society and by Yale University under the editorship of Leonard W. Labaree and his associates. Beginning in 1959, eleven volumes of the *Papers* have appeared so far, supplemented in 1964 by a new scholarly edition of *The Autobiography of Benjamin Franklin*, prepared by the editors of the *Papers* and published also by Yale University Press. Among the great accomplishments of these definitive editions, I would like to refer the reader to the important critical introductions by the editors to a number of Franklin's writings analysed in this book, particularly those concerning the Albany Plan of 1754 and Franklin's "Canada Pamphlet" of 1760.

Although the method of reproduction used for the present edition has not allowed changing all quotations and references to the new edition of the *Papers*, the text established by the Yale Edition of the *Papers* (and the *Autobiography*) has been taken into account wherever changes, additions, omissions or substitutions of words or phrases, or changes of dates, were involved.

The literature on problems discussed in this book has been enriched in the last years by several significant contributions. I would like to single out Julian P. Boyd's series of articles on Silas Deane in *William and Mary Quarterly,* 3rd series, vol. 16 (1959); Felix Gilbert's *To the Farewell Address* (1961); William S. Hanna's *Benjamin Franklin and Pennsylvania Politics* (1964); Richard W. Van Alstyne's *Empire and Independence* (1965); Richard B. Morris' *The Peacemakers* (1965); and Max Savelle's *The Origins of American Diplomacy* (1967). It has not seemed necessary, however, to change any of the facts or interpretations as I presented them in the original edition of this book.

G. S.

Free University of Berlin

PREFACE

THIS study is concerned with interpretation rather than with narrative, with the concepts, objectives, and motivations underlying political action rather than with action itself. To relate political action with political thought, to examine the intricate interplay of ideas and interests, presents one of the most promising, if difficult, tasks of historical and political analysis. It is a task which has been particularly neglected in the realm of international relations. This book, then, is a study neither in diplomatic history nor in political theory. It endeavors to analyze systematically the principles of Franklin's approach to foreign policy by probing into his actions as well as into his expressions of opinion concerning international politics.

Is it legitimate to address one's self to the study of Benjamin Franklin in this way? Do not the astounding many-sidedness of his career, the practical mind, and the empiric temper of this most graceful of all utilitarians, as Sainte-Beuve called him, defy any attempt at "systematic analysis"? Has not everything been said about Franklin? Although the history of Franklin scholarship is long and various and the history of Franklin hagiography even longer, it has been only within the last twenty-five years that syntheses like Carl Becker's and Carl Van Doren's—to which we soon shall have to add the one by Verner W. Crane—have removed the manyfold clichés of the Franklin legend. But the richness and subtlety of Franklin's personality have not been exhausted. In spite of appearances to the contrary, Franklin remains the most enigmatic and least accessible of the Founding Fathers. And, if this study confirms anything, it confirms Carl Becker's conclusion that Franklin, "genuine, sincere, loyal as he surely was, . . . is nevertheless not wholly committed; some thought remains uncommunicated; some penetrating observation is held in reserve." It is this detachment, so conspicuously lacking in John Adams or even in Jefferson, which makes the study of Franklin so fascinating and yet so perplexing.

However, a study of the kind presented here, not bound by the strictly chronological and descriptive arrangement of Van Doren's work, or by the scarcity of space available to Carl Becker in the *Dictionary of American Biography,* might perhaps help to uncover some significant and recurrent traits of Franklin's attitude to politics, which otherwise would run the danger of being lost in the overwhelming diversity of his concerns. I believe that there was more unity of purpose and coherence of underlying principles in Franklin's approach to politics in general and to international politics in particular than the widely held view of the "pragmatic" and "opportunistic" Franklin would lead one to suspect.

This study has not been limited to the period after 1776, in which year American foreign policy proper begins. American foreign policy, though depending upon the birth of the United States as a sovereign nation, did not emerge from a *tabula rasa*. Attitudes, opinions, and prejudices of the preceding decades colored the approach of the new nation to foreign affairs; and Franklin, who had passed his seventieth year when he signed the Declaration of Independence, by that time had accumulated more experiences and ideas concerning foreign relations than any of his younger colleagues. Franklin, indeed, provides the best proof for the importance of tracing the origins of American foreign policy farther back than the year 1776.

A purely topical arrangement might do injustice to the complexity of historic development as it unfolded during the eighty-four years of Franklin's crowded life. A combination of topical and chronological treatment has therefore been chosen. The first chapter examines some fundamental principles characteristic of Franklin's political outlook in general. The second chapter discusses the state of international relations at the middle of the eighteenth century, when Franklin first had to face the menace of involvement in the Franco-British struggle for preponderance in North America, and carries the analysis of Franklin's reaction to this challenge to the end of the Seven Years' War in 1763. The third chapter investigates Franklin's conception of British-American relations up to the outbreak of the Revolution, as far as it is relevant to the development of his ideas on international affairs. The fourth chapter deals with the problem of "isolationism" and "entangling alliances" until the conclusion of the French alliance in 1778, and the fifth chapter inquires into Franklin's attitude toward the French alliance from 1778 onward. The sixth chapter discusses Franklin's ideas on the settlement with England after the Declaration of Independence, while the seventh chapter analyzes Franklin's role in the attempts of the Age of Reason to subdue the evils of international power politics.

While writing this book, I have incurred a heavy debt of gratitude. Above all, my thanks are due to Professor Hans J. Morgenthau, of the University of Chicago and Director of the Center for the Study of American Foreign Policy, who suggested this study while I was a research associate at the Center for the Study of American Foreign Policy; without his generous support this study could never have been completed. I am very grateful for his advice throughout the whole period of my research. I have had the benefit of a conversation with Professor Verner W. Crane, of the University of Michigan, whose unequaled knowledge of Franklin saved me from several pitfalls which otherwise I would hardly have avoided. Professors Daniel J. Boorstin, William T. Hutchinson, and Robert E. Osgood, of the University of Chicago, and Kenneth W. Thompson, of Northwestern University, have read the manuscript. I wish to express my gratitude to them for many most valuable suggestions as to substance as well as to style and structure. I am greatly indebted to Mrs. Phyllis Maslow, Miss Louise Rhoads, and Miss Elizabeth Sterenberg, of the Center for the Study of American Foreign Policy, for clarifying the style of the manuscript. Many improvements have been suggested by Miss Evi Ellis and Miss Johanna Menzel. In addition, Mrs. Maslow took upon herself the burden of retyping the whole manuscript.

I wish to express my appreciation to Professor William E. Lingelbach, Director of the Library of the American Philosophical Society in Philadelphia; Mr. Colton Storm, Director *ad interim* of the William L. Clements Library in Ann Arbor, Michigan; and Mr. William H. Ewing, Curator of Manuscripts in the William L. Clements Library, for their advice and assistance. The Collection of Transcripts Relative to the Peace Negotiations of 1782 and 1783, compiled by the late Randolph G. Adams, while he was Director of the William L. Clements Library, has been most useful for my research. It is a pleasant duty to acknowledge the unfailing courtesy and help of the staffs of the Library of the American Philosophical Society, the Library of the Historical Society of Pennsylvania, the Library of Congress, the Mason-Franklin Collection of Yale University Library, and the University of Chicago Library. I am also very grateful to the University of Chicago Press for help in preparing the manuscript for publication.

G. S.

CHICAGO, ILLINOIS
November 14, 1953

ACKNOWLEDGMENTS

CHAPTER I of this book is based in large part on material previously published in the December, 1953, issue of the *American Political Science Review* under the title "Reason and Power in Benjamin Franklin's Political Thought." Permission to quote passages from copyrighted material has also been given by the following: The Pennsylvania Company for Banking and Trusts as Trustee under the Will of Howard C. Myers, Beneficiary under the Will of Albert Henry Smyth, editor of *The Writings of Benjamin Franklin;* the American Historical Association for S. F. Bemis, *The Diplomacy of the American Revolution;* the American Philosophical Society, Philadelphia, for the *Letters and Papers of Benjamin Franklin and Richard Jackson, 1753–1785,* edited by Carl Van Doren, for *The Letters of Benjamin Franklin & Jane Mecom,* edited by Carl Van Doren, and for the *Letters of Benjamin Rush,* edited by L. H. Butterfield; the Citadel Press, New York, for *The Complete Writings of Thomas Paine,* edited by Philip Foner; the editors of *World Politics* for the article, "The 'New Diplomacy' of the Eighteenth Century," published in *World Politics,* October, 1951; the University of North Carolina Press for *Benjamin Franklin's Letters to the Press, 1758–1775,* edited by Verner W. Crane; the Yale University Press for Charles M. Andrews, *The Colonial Period of American History,* and Carl Becker, *The Heavenly City of the Eighteenth Century Philosophers.* I am also grateful for the permission to quote from unpublished material to the following: American Philosophical Society, Philadelphia; William L. Clements Library, Ann Arbor, Michigan; Library of Congress, Washington, D.C.; Public Record Office, London; and Yale University Library, New Haven, Connecticut.

CHAPTER I

REASON AND POWER IN FRANKLIN'S
POLITICAL THOUGHT

THE BASIC PROBLEM: COERCION, REASON, AND HUMAN NATURE

THE fundamental problem of politics is the problem of coercion. Experience has taught man that he must restrain the freedom of action or sometimes even destroy the existence of some of his fellowmen in order to secure his own life and the life of others for whom he is responsible. But civilized man has ever yearned for a time when co-operation rather than competition, love rather than fear and hatred, generosity rather than egotism, mercy rather than retaliation, and enlightened reason rather than selfish passion would govern the affairs of humanity. In the midst of horrors and trials of every kind, man has not given up the dream of a time when swords would be beaten into plowshares. In other words, man eternally strives to replace discord by harmony and present imperfection by lasting perfection.

Often man has imagined this perfect state to have existed at the beginning of creation. While some have despaired of re-establishing this perfect state here and now and have put their hope in the Kingdom of God, which is not of this world, others—whose ranks and activities have increased particularly within the last two hundred years—have been busy proving that ultimate harmony is possible on earth and have endeavored to find devices for insuring it. Both the old Christian Fathers and modern liberals have agreed, however, in regarding politics as a competitive rather than a co-operative process and the coercive machinery of the state as the consequence of human selfishness and imperfection. There is no essential difference between the Church Fathers' definition of the state as *poena et remedium peccati*—as punishment for, but at the same time protection against, sin—and Thomas Paine's famous dictum that

society is produced by our wants and government by our wickedness; the former promotes our happiness *positively* by uniting our affections, the latter *negatively* by restraining our vices. . . . Society in every state is a blessing, but government,

1

even in its best state, is but a necessary evil. . . . Government, like dress, is the badge of lost innocence. . . . For were the impulses of conscience clear, uniform and irresistibly obeyed, man would need no other law-giver.[1]

Consequently, it has been the tendency of those who believed that they had found the clue to the achievement of harmony and perfection to advocate the abolishment of politics and the replacement (in Friedrich Engels' words) of the government of men by the administration of things.

This confidence in the ultimate possibility of banishing strife and co-ercion from this world presupposes belief either in the goodness or in the malleability of human nature. In the first case, the assumed socia-bility and innate sympathy of man for his fellow-men is to facilitate greatly the removal of misunderstandings and obstacles for a more perfect world. In the second case, the progress of enlightenment and reason is expected to exclude those atavisms incompatible with the advanced state of human knowledge. Reason, endowed with the ability to discern scientific truth and to apply its insights to social relation-ships, is thus to assume its role as the antagonist of power politics. Political power, defined as "capacity to impose one's will on others by reliance on effective sanctions in case of non-compliance,"[2] is a com-pound of persuasion and coercion: coercion is an intrinsic particular of "power." The belief in the possibility of abolishing coercion, there-fore, implicitly and sometimes explicitly includes the elimination of power politics. What remains is persuasion pure and simple; that is, rational argument and scientific theories are deemed sufficient ultimate-ly to govern social relationships.

On the other hand, those who hold that there is an ineradicable element of selfishness, pride, and corruption in human nature will obviously refuse to concede to human reason and to "scientific prin-ciples" such a paramount role in political things. They believe that persuasion and rational argument are not sufficient to check evildoers, that men will ever oppose their fellow-men in clashes of interest or of ambition, and that the law of self-preservation will ever require balancing and checking strength with strength, power with power, and violence with violence. This belief does not, however, contradict the view that moderation and prudence in the use of power will always distinguish reasonable policies from the disastrous follies of "power politics" run wild.

Obviously, then, man's understanding of political phenomena, international as well as domestic, is inseparable from his conception of human nature. It is impossible to isolate a systematic discussion of ideas on international relations from those on domestic politics or on human nature. Therefore we deem it essential to subject Benjamin Franklin's views of human nature to a close scrutiny and to confront them with some of the dominant trends of his time. This is all the more indispensable in view of the truly universal range of his mind. Diplomacy, after all, was only one of his many-fold activities.[3]

Franklin as the Embodiment of the Age of Enlightenment

Franklin was the very incarnation, it seems, of a new and enlightened spirit which, with the War of Independence, suddenly illuminated the international scene. He was one of the most famous personalities of the Age of Reason, whose reputation, according to John Adams, "was more universal than that of Leibnitz or Newton, Frederick or Voltaire, and his character more beloved and esteemed than any or all of them."[4] The elder Pitt, defending Franklin against attacks in the House of Lords, referred to him as one "whom all Europe held in high Estimation for his Knowledge and Wisdom, and rank'd with our Boyles and Newtons; who was an Honour, not to the English Nation only, but to Human Nature."[5]

Indeed, Franklin seemed to many of his contemporaries the very personification of the Age of Reason. Condorcet, who had known him personally, summed up his description of Franklin's political career in these words: "In a word, his politics were those of a man who believed in the power of reason and the reality of virtue."[6] In Germany an admirer used even more enthusiastic words: "Reason and virtue, made possible through reason alone, consequently again reason and nothing but reason, is the magic with which Benjamin Franklin conquered heaven and earth."[7] After his death in 1790 Franklin became a veritable saint of the French Revolution. On the boulevards of Paris a play entitled *L'Imprimeur ou la fête de Franklin* by Desfontaines was produced. The play ends with these lines:

> If you would say who among men
> Upheld the torch of honor,
> Who, like Rousseau, showed us how
> To become what we are,
> Ah! It is Franklin, ever Franklin,
> Whose name shall be our song![8]

To posterity as well as to his contemporaries, Franklin has remained the embodiment of the Age of Reason. "His mind was in complete harmony with . . . his age," Ralph Barton Perry writes; "his many years of residence in England and France . . . enabled him to be, no less than Paine, an embodiment of the cosmopolitan spirit of the Enlightenment. . . . Nothing could more perfectly express the optimism of the Enlightenment than his affirmation of the harmony between prudence and benevolence."[9] Charles A. Beard, in his Introduction to Bury's *The Idea of Progress,* explicitly refers to Franklin as an outstanding example of American writers on progress.[10] Henry Steele Commager says that it was the faith in reason which gave unity to Franklin's life.[11] Similar statements could be multiplied without end. Unanimous agreement seems to exist that Franklin was "in tune with his time."[12]

This raises, of course, the question of the essential characteristics of Franklin's time. Perhaps no period of modern history has suffered more from facile generalization than the Age of Enlightenment. Many of these stereotypes have automatically been transferred to Benjamin Franklin, who has become the symbol of everything which was "typical" of the eighteenth century. The worship of reason and progress, optimism, faith in the perfectibility of the human race, and belief in natural law and humanitarianism are most commonly associated with the eighteenth-century climate of opinion. These easy generalizations with sometimes ill-defined terms let us forget the important modifications of these concepts which actually determined the intellectual evolution of the century. We shall show presently that these generalizations, instead of illuminating the essence of Franklin's moral and political thought, obscure rather some of the mainsprings of his thought and action.

Moreover, many of the notions which are commonly applied to the eighteenth century, as, for instance, the belief in progress, in the essential goodness and perfectibility of human nature, while significant chiefly in respect to the currents of thought and action connected with the American and French Revolutions, do little to deepen our understanding of earlier developments. However, it is to the first half of the eighteenth century that we must now turn. We are prone to overlook the extraordinary difference of age which separated Franklin from the other Founding Fathers of the Republic. He was born in 1706, twenty-six years before George Washington, twenty-nine years before John Adams, thirty-seven years before Thomas Jefferson, thirty-nine years before John Jay, forty-five years before James Madison, and fifty-one years before Alexander Hamilton.

THE "GREAT CHAIN OF BEING"

Franklin's fame rests chiefly on the achievements of his middle and later years. *Poor Richard's Almanack* (begun 1732), the *Advice to a Young Tradesman* (1748), and *The Way to Wealth* (1757), as well as the *Autobiography,* established his reputation as the high priest of business morality, as the expert guide to success and wealth in the world of commerce. "Frugality," "industry," and "thrift" are the inevitable words which appear to be the very essence of Benjamin Franklin's "homespun" teachings.

In the world of the eighteenth-century philosophers, Franklin was accepted and celebrated first as a natural philosopher and then as the great statesman and founder of American independence: *Eripuit coelo fulmen et sceptrum tyrannis.*[13] John Adams commented on the growing myth surrounding the heroes of American independence rather sarcastically: "The history of our Revolution will be one continued Lye from one end to the other. The essence of the whole will be *that Dr. Franklin's electrical Rod, smote the Earth and out sprung General Washington. That Franklin electrified him with his rod—and thence forward these two conducted all the Policy, Negotiations, Legislatures and War.*"[14] Franklin started his study of electricity in 1746, and his *Experiments and Observations on Electricity,* which made him famous in Europe, appeared five years later.

However, one needs to remember that Franklin was a moral philosopher long before he became a natural philosopher and before he advised his fellow-men on the way to wealth. In fact, even after having achieved world-wide fame as a natural philosopher, he wrote to a dear friend: "The Knowledge of Nature may be ornamental, and it may be useful; but if, to attain an Eminence in that, we neglect the Knowledge and Practice of essential Duties, we deserve Reprehension."[15] Long before taking part in politics himself, Franklin, at the age of twenty-two, formed a "club for mutual improvement,"[16] the Junto, where great emphasis was laid on moral or political problems. Whether self-interest was the root of human action, whether man could attain perfection, whether "encroachments on the just liberties of the people"[17] had taken place—all these things were a matter of discussion at Franklin's club.[18] Already at the age of nineteen, during his first stay in London, he had printed his first independent opus, *A Dissertation on Liberty and Necessity, Pleasure and Pain*.[19] This piece showed that no trace was left of his Presbyterian family background. The secularization of Franklin's thought had been completed.[20] Gone were the Puritan belief in revelation and the Christian conception of human nature, which, paradoxically, included the notion of the depravity of man as well as of his uniqueness among all created beings.[21] Franklin's *Dissertation* shows him thoroughly acquainted with the leading ideas of his time.

The early decades of the eighteenth century were characterized by a climate of opinion which aptly has been called "Cosmic Toryism."[22] Pope's *Essay on Man* and many pages of Addison's *Spectator*—both of which Franklin admired—most perfectly set forth the creed of a new age. Overshadowing everything else, there was joy about the discoveries of the human mind which had solved the enigma of creation:

> Nature and Nature's Laws lay hid in Night:
> GOD said, *Let Newton be,* and all was Light.[23]

The perfection of that great machine, the Newtonian universe, filling humanity with admiration for the Divine Watchmaker, seemed to suggest that this world was indeed the best of all possible worlds. Everything, then, was necessary, was good. Pope's "Whatever is, is right," is the key phrase of this period. The universe had been made in "order that all possible forms of beings might manifest themselves after their kinds."[24] The goodness of the Creator revealed itself in his giving existence to all possible creatures. By necessity, then, anything less than God "must be imperfect, and, in its degree of imperfection, evil."[25] In other words, the universe "presented the spectacle of a continuous scale or ladder of creatures, extending without a break from the worm to the seraph."[26] Somewhere in this scale, or, to use a favorite phrase of that period, the "Great Chain of Being," there must be a place for man. Man, as it were, formed the "middle link" between lower and higher creatures. No wonder, then, that Benjamin Franklin chose as motto for his *Dissertation* the following lines of Dryden:

> Whatever is, is in its Causes just,
> Since all Things are by Fate; but purblind Man
> Sees but a part o' th' Chain, the nearest Link,
> His Eyes not carrying to the equal Beam
> That poises all above.[27]

The consequences of the conception of the universe as a "Great Chain of Being" for Franklin's understanding of human nature are highly significant. To be sure, man had liberated himself from the oppression of original sin, and in his newly established innocence he hailed the Creator and praised the Creation. But, if the depravity of human nature had been banished, so had man's striving for redemption, man's aspiration for perfection. There was nothing left which ought to be redeemed. Indeed, in the new rational order of the universe, it would not seem proper to long for a higher place in the hierarchy of beings. Man's release from the anguish of original sin was accompanied by a lowering of the goals of human life. "The imperfection of man is indispensable to the fullness of the hierarchy of being."[28] Man had, so to speak, already attained the grade of perfection which belonged to his station. From the point of view of morality, then, what this amounted to was a "counsel of imperfection —an ethics of prudent mediocrity."[29] It meant a morality of contentment. There was no room for either enthusiasm or fanaticism. Sobriety, in some cases mixed with complacency, was the prevailing mood. The pride of man to transcend his station by reason is frowned upon: "In Pride, in reas'ning Pride, our error lies."[30]

This sort of quiet contentment with, and enjoyment of, one's place in the "Great Chain of Being" must have been a comforting creed for the wealthy and educated classes of the Augustan Age.[31] For them, nothing unpleasant could be hidden in that perfect defense of cosmic as well as earthly conservatism:

> ORDER is Heav'n's first law; and this confest,
> Some are, and must be, greater than the rest,
> More rich, more wise.[32]

This was not the optimism of progress, which we usually associate with the eighteenth century. It was an optimism of acceptance,[33] perfectly satisfactory for those who had nothing of which to complain. For the rich and complacent, the real and the good seemed indeed to coincide.

Not so for Benjamin Franklin. Late in his life, in 1771, he referred to "the poverty and obscurity in which I was born and bred."[34] His innate desire for justice and equality, his keen awareness of existing conditions of injustice and inequality, his own experience of things which he could not possibly call just or good—for instance, he tells us that his brother's "harsh and tyrannical treatment of me might be a means of impressing me with that aversion to arbitrary power that has stuck to me through my whole life"[35]—all this revolted against the facile optimism of the Augustan Age.

Franklin, indeed, accepted the cosmological premises of his age (as witness the above-quoted motto of his *Dissertation*). But he decidedly refused to accept the shallow optimism surrounding these premises. Franklin's youthful desire for logical consistency drove him to conclusions which make the edifice of "Cosmic Toryism"—so imposing in Pope's magnificent language—appear a mockery and an absurdity. Franklin's argumentation, in fact, was simple enough: God being all-powerful and good, man could have no free will, and the distinction between good and evil had to be abolished. He also argued that pain or uneasiness was the mainspring of all our actions and that pleasure was produced by the removal of this uneasiness. It followed that *"no State of Life can be happier than the present, because Pleasure and Pain are inseparable."*[36] The most significant passage, for our purposes, is the conclusion. The unintentional irony of this brand of optimism cannot be better expressed than in the words of young Franklin:

> I am sensible that the Doctrine here advanc'd, if it were to be publish'd, would meet with but an indifferent Reception. Mankind naturally and generally love to be flatter'd: Whatever sooths our Pride, and tends to exalt our Species above the rest of the Creation, we are pleas'd with and easily believe, when ungrateful Truths shall be with the utmost Indignation rejected. "What! bring ourselves down to an Equality with the Beasts of the field! With the *meanest* part of the Creation! 'Tis insufferable!" But, (to use a Piece of *common* Sense) our *Geese* are but *Geese* tho' we may think 'em *Swans;* and Truth will be Truth tho' it sometimes prove mortifying and distasteful.[37]

The dilemma which confronted Franklin at the age of nineteen is indeed characteristic of all eighteenth-century philosophers. Carl Becker has made it the central theme of his famous book:

> There it was then—the ugly dilemma, emerging from the beautiful premises of the new philosophy: if nature is good, then there is no evil in the world; if there is evil in the world, then nature is so far not good. How will they meet it, the enlightened ones? . . . Will they, closing their eyes to the brute facts, maintain

that there is no evil in the world? . . . We know what the philosophers did in this emergency. They found, as we all find when sufficiently hard pressed, that reason is amenable to treatment. They therefore tempered reason with sentiment, reasons of the heart that reason knows not of; or held it in leash by experience, the universal judgment of mankind; or induced it to delay its pronouncements in view of the possibility (which in a pinch might be taken as a fact) that the world was after all neither a completed drama nor a perfected machine, but rather something as yet unfinished, something still in the making.[38]

How did Franklin cut that Gordian knot, the dilemma of evil in a supposedly harmonious world? He sacrificed "reason" to "experience." He turned away from metaphysics for the very pragmatic reason that his denial of good and evil did not provide him with a basis for the attainment of social and individual happiness.

I grew convinced that *truth, sincerity* and *integrity* in dealings between man and man were of the utmost importance to the felicity of life. . . . Revelation had indeed no weight with me, as such; but I entertain'd an opinion that, though certain actions might not be bad *because* they were forbidden by it, or good *because* it commanded them, yet probably those actions might be forbidden *because* they were bad for us, or commanded *because* they were beneficial to us.[39]

To achieve useful things rather than doubtful metaphysical speculations, to become a doer of good—these, then, became the principal aims of Franklin's thought and action.[40]

The Age of Reason, then, presents us with a more perplexing picture than we might have supposed. Reason, after all, may mean three different things: reason as a faculty of man; reason as a quality of the universe; and reason as a temper in the conduct of human affairs.[41] We might venture the generalization that the earlier Enlightenment stressed reason as the quality of the Newtonian universe,[42] whereas the later Enlightenment, in spite of important exceptions, exalted the power of human reason to mold the moral and social life of mankind. Franklin's "reason," finally, is above all a temper in the conduct of human affairs.

The chorus of those who asserted the compatibility of human imperfection and general harmony was joined by Bernard Mandeville, a personal acquaintance of Franklin. In his famous *Fable of the Bees* Mandeville argued that men are actuated by self-interest and that this self-interest even contrives to establish the prosperity of society as a whole; nevertheless, he declared those acts alone to be virtuous "by which Man, contrary to the impulse of Nature, should endeavour the Benefit of others, or the Conquest of his own Passions out of a Rational Ambition of being good."[43] The very rigor of his ethical demands in contrast to his practical devices suggests that Mandeville lacked "idealism." This was not the case, however, with Benjamin Franklin. The consciously paradoxical Mandeville could offer no salvation for young Franklin caught on the horns of his dilemma. Shaftesbury, Mandeville's bête noire, promised better help. Franklin's option for Shaftesbury was made clear from his reprinting two dialogues—until recently held to have been his own—in the *Pennsylvania Gazette*. He also composed two pieces himself; in his first piece, a dialogue, Franklin asserted that the "SCIENCE OF VIRTUE" was "of more worth, and of more consequence" to one's happiness than all other knowledge put together. Moreover, in his second piece Franklin combated the (Mandevillean) idea that "the greater the *Self-Denial* the greater the Virtue."[44]

FRANKLIN AND "PROGRESS"

The restraining influence of the idea of the "Great Chain of Being" retained its hold on Franklin after his return to a more conventional recognition of good and evil. In his "Articles of Belief" of 1728 he said that "Man is not the most perfect Being but one, rather that as there are many Degrees of Beings his Inferiors, so there are many Degrees of Beings superior to him."[45] Franklin presented the following questions and answers to the discussions in the Junto:

Can a man arrive at perfection in this life, as some believe; or is it impossible, as others believe?

Answer. Perhaps they differ in the meaning of the word *perfection*. I suppose the perfection of anything to be only the greatest the nature of that thing is capable of. Different things have different degrees of perfection, and the same thing at different times. Thus, a horse is more perfect than an oyster, yet the oyster may be a perfect oyster, as well as the horse a perfect horse. And an egg is not so perfect as a chicken, nor a chicken as a hen; for the hen has more strength than the chicken, and the chicken more life than the egg; yet it may be a perfect egg, chicken, and hen.

If they mean a man cannot in this life be so perfect as an angel, it may be true; for an angel, by being incorporeal, is allowed some perfections we are at present incapable of, and less liable to some imperfections that we are liable to. If they mean a man is not capable of being so perfect here as he is capable of being in heaven, that may be true likewise. But that a Man is not capable of being so perfect here, as he is capable of being here; is not sense. . . . In the above sense, there may be a perfect oyster, a perfect horse, a perfect ship; why not a perfect man? That is, as his present nature and circumstances admit.[46]

Man's necessarily "imperfect" state of perfection is here acknowledged. However, it is very striking to see that Franklin refused to employ this theory as a justification of the status quo. Within certain bounds, change, or progress for the better, was possible. "If they mean a man . . . is not capable of being so perfect here," as might be possible, this is nonsense, Franklin declares. Many years later he used exactly the same argument in the debate on the status of America within the British Empire. A pro-English writer had presented the familiar argument of "Cosmic Toryism" (and of conservatism in general, of course): "To expect perfection in human institutions is absurd." Franklin retorted indignantly, "Does this justify any and every Imperfection that can be invented or added to our Constitution?"[47]

This attitude differs from the belief in moral progress and perfectibility. There are, however, some passages in Franklin's later writings, more frequently quoted than the preceding ones, which seem to suggest his agreement with the creed of moral progress and perfectibility. Two years before his death, looking with considerable satisfaction upon the achievements of his country[48] and his own life,[49] Franklin replied to the letter of a Boston clergyman:

I have been long impressed with the same sentiments you so well express, of the growing felicity of mankind, from the improvements in philosophy, morals, politics, and even the conveniences of common living, by the invention and acquisition of new and useful utensils and instruments, that I have sometimes almost wished it had been my destiny to be born two or three centuries hence. For invention and improvement are prolific, and beget more of their kind. The present progress is rapid. Many of great importance, now unthought of, will before that period be produced; and then I might not only enjoy their advantages, but have my curiosity gratified in knowing what they are to be.[50]

However, he immediately added: "I see a little absurdity in what I have just written, but it is to a friend, who will wink and let it pass."[51]

There remains, then, a wide gulf between this qualified view of human progress and the exuberant joy over the progress of man's rational and moral faculties, an exuberance so perfectly expressed in the lines of a good friend of Franklin's, the British nonconformist clergyman and philosopher, Joseph Priestley: "Whatever was the beginning of this world, the end will be glorious and paradisiacal beyond what our imaginations can now conceive. Extravagant as some people may suppose these views to be, I think I could show them to be fairly suggested by the true theory of human nature and to arise from the natural course of human affairs."[52]

Franklin himself was perfectly aware of the gulf which separated his own conception of human nature from the ideas and hopes of his friends. He distinguished sharply between man's intellectual progress and the steadily increasing power of man over matter, on the one hand, and the permanency of moral imperfection, on the other. He wrote to Priestley:

> I should rejoice much, if I could once more recover the Leisure to search with you into the Works of Nature; I mean the *inanimate,* not the *animate* or moral part of them, the more I discover'd of the former, the more I admir'd them; the more I know of the latter, the more I am disgusted with them. Men I find to be a Sort of Beings very badly constructed, as they are generally more easily provok'd than reconcil'd, more disposed to do Mischief to each other than to make Reparation, much more easily deceiv'd than undeceiv'd, and having more Pride and even Pleasure in killing than in begetting one another.[53]

He had begun to doubt, Franklin continued, whether "the Species were really worth producing or preserving. . . . I know, you have no such Doubts because, in your zeal for their welfare, you are taking a great deal of pains to save their Souls. Perhaps, as you grow older, you may look upon this as a hopeless Project."[54]

One is struck by the remarkable constancy and consistency of Franklin's views on human nature. In 1735, in his Preface to that year's *Poor Richard,* Franklin proclaimed much the same truth, only in less philosophic language: "Whatever may be the Musick of the Spheres, how great soever the Harmony of the Stars, 'tis certain there is no Harmony among the Stargazers; but they are perpetually growling and snarling at one another like strange Curs."[55] Fifty-one years later Franklin tried to dissuade the author of a work on natural religion from publishing it. In this famous letter we may find the quintessence of his concept of human nature. It is not too cheerful. We discover little of the trust in human reason which is so generally supposed to be a mark of Franklin's moral teachings.

> You yourself may find it easy to live a virtuous Life, without the Assistance afforded by Religion; you having a clear perception of the Advantages of Virtue, and the Disadvantages of Vice, and possessing a Strength of Resolution sufficient to enable you to resist common Temptations. But think how great a Proportion of Mankind consists of weak and ignorant Men and Women, and of inexperienc'd, and inconsiderate Youth of both Sexes, who have need of the Motives of Religion to restrain them from Vice, and support their Virtue, and retain them in the Practice of it till it becomes *habitual,* which is the great Point for its Security. . . . If men are so wicked as we now see them *with religion,* what would they be *if without it?*[56]

One cannot help being reminded of Gibbon's approval of conditions in the Rome of the Antonines, where all religions were considered equally false by the wise, equally true by the people, and equally useful by the magistrates.

THE BELIEF IN "REASON"

Reason, as a temper in the conduct of human affairs, counted much with Franklin, as we shall see later. Reason, as a faculty of the human mind stronger than our desires or passions, counted far less. Often Franklin candidly and smilingly referred to the weakness of reason. In his *Autobiography* he tells us of his struggle "between principle and inclination," when, on his first voyage to Philadelphia, his vegetarian principles came into conflict with his love of eating fish. Franklin, remembering that greater fish ate the smaller ones, did not see any reason why he should not eat fish: "So convenient a thing it is to be a *reasonable creature,* since it enables one to find or make a reason for every thing one has a mind to do."[57] Consequently, it was more than a phrase created by the mere desire of reconciliation when Franklin wrote after the War of Independence to his Loyalist son William, who had been governor of New Jersey: "I ought not to blame you for differing in Sentiment with me in Public Affairs. We are Men, all subject to Errors. Our Opinions are not in our own Power; they are form'd and govern'd much by Circumstances, that are often as inexplicable as they are irresistible."[58]

Reason as a guide to human happiness was recognized by Franklin only to a limited degree. "Our Reason would still be of more Use to us, if it could enable us to *prevent* the Evils it can hardly enable us to *bear.*—But in that it is so deficient, and in other things so often misleads us, that I have sometimes been almost tempted to wish we had been furnished with a good sensible Instinct instead of it."[59]

Trial and error appeared to Franklin a better guide to public and private felicity than abstract reasoning. "We are, I think, in the right Road of Improvement, for we are making Experiments. I do not oppose all that seem wrong, for the Multitude are more effectually set right by Experience, than kept from going wrong by Reasoning with them."[60] Another time Franklin had been even blunter: "What Assurance of the *Future* can be better founded than that which is built on Experience of the *Past?*"[61] In the following quotation he acknowledges the weakness of reason by the use of a pungent folk saying: "An Answer now occurs to me, for that Question of Robinson Crusoe's Man Friday, which I once thought unanswerable, *Why God no kill the Devil?* It is to be found in the Scottish Proverb, *'Ye'd do little for God an the De'el were dead.'* "[62]

Franklin's skepticism about the efficacy of "reason" also becomes apparent in his opinion that "happiness in this life rather depends on internals than externals; and that, besides the natural effects of wisdom and virtue, vice and folly, there is such a thing as being of a happy or an unhappy constitution."[63] In 1786 he described the growing welfare of America to an English friend and concluded that "all among us may be happy, who have happy dispositions; such being necessary to happiness even in Paradise."[64]

There remains one problem with regard to Franklin's denial of moral progress and his rather modest view of the power of human reason in moral matters: his serenity—some might call it "complacency" —in spite of his awareness of the disorder and imperfection of human life. Sometimes, it is true, he was uneasy:

> I rather suspect, from certain circumstances, that though the general government of the universe is well administered, our particular little affairs are perhaps below notice, and left to take the chance of human prudence or imprudence, as either may happen to be uppermost. It is, however, an uncomfortable thought, and I leave it.[65]

But, on another occasion, Franklin felt obliged to quiet the anxieties of his sister, who had been upset by his remark that men "are devils to one another."[66]

> I meant no more by saying Mankind were Devils to one another, than that being in general superior to the Malice of the other Creatures, they were not so much tormented by them as by themselves. Upon the whole I am much disposed to like the World as I find it, & to doubt my own Judgment as to what would mend it. I see so much Wisdom in what I understand of its Creation and Government, that I suspect equal Wisdom may be in what I do not understand: And thence have perhaps as much Trust in God as the most pious Christian.[67]

Indeed, Franklin's philosophy does not contain that quality of the tragic sense of life which inevitably presents itself wherever a recognition of the discrepancy of man's actual depravity and the loftiness of his aspirations exists.

We suggest a threefold explanation for this phenomenon. First of all, as has been pointed out above, the complex of ideas associated with the concept of the "Great Chain of Being," predominant at the time of Franklin's youth, worked in favor of bridging this gulf by lowering the goals of human endeavor. Second, the success story of his own life taught him that certain valuable things in human life can be achieved. Third, we cannot help thinking that Franklin himself was endowed with a "happy constitution" which he deems a requisite for true happiness in this life.

The Passion of Pride

Having discovered that Franklin acknowledged the imperfection of human reason and consequently the existence and importance of the passions to a greater degree than one might have supposed, let us specify in greater detail his insight into the nature of the two outstanding passions of social life, the desire for wealth and the desire for power—avarice and ambition. "That I may avoid Avarice, Ambition. . . . —Help me, O Father," was Franklin's prayer in the "Articles of Belief" of 1728.[68]

The universal fame of Poor Richard and the description of Franklin's own "way to wealth" in his *Autobiography* (his account of his life ends with his arrival in London in 1757 for the first of his three great public missions in Europe) have led many people to see in him only the ingenious businessman who pursues thrift for thrift's sake and money for money's sake. Franklin, as symbol of the spirit of capitalism, of middle-class virtues, is often supposed to have subordinated all other considerations to the desire for more gain, more wealth. Nothing could be further from the truth than this assertion. To be sure, he recognized the existence and the nature of avarice in unequivocal terms: "The Love of Money is not a Thing of certain Measure, so as that it may be easily filled and satisfied. Avarice is infinite; and where there is not good Oeconomy, no Salary, however large, will prevent Necessity. He that has fixed and what others may think a competent Income, is often as much to be byassed by the Expectation of more, as if he had already none at all."[69] Franklin denied, however, that desire for more wealth actuated his work. His early retirement from business (1748) to devote himself to the higher things of life, to public service, scientific research, or reading, seems to confirm this point.

Franklin, then, considered wealth essentially as means to an end. He knew that it was not easy "for an empty sack to stand upright." He looked upon his fortune as an essential factor to his not having succumbed to corruption, so universal in the England of his time and wholeheartedly detested by him. "What in my younger days enabled me more easily to walk upright, was, that I had a trade, and that I knew I could live upon little; and thence (never having had views of making a fortune) I was free from avarice, and contented with the plentiful supplies my business afforded me."[70] In a famous and often-quoted letter to his mother, Franklin said that at the end of his life he "would rather have it said, *He lived usefully* than *He died Rich*."[71] About the same time (two years after his retirement) he wrote to his printer friend, William Strahan, in England: "Your sentiments of the general foible of mankind in the pursuit of wealth to no end are expressed in a manner that gave me great pleasure in reading. . . . London citizens, they say, are ambitious of what they call *dying worth* a great sum. The very notion seems to me absurd."[72]

On the other hand, the motive of power and prestige, as we would say today, not only found much earlier recognition in Franklin's writings, but he also confessed candidly that he himself was not free from this desire and the feeling of being superior to his fellow-men. At the age of sixteen, in his first secret contributions to his brother's *New-England Courant* (young Franklin wrote under the pseudonym of "Mrs. Dogood"), he gave a satisfactory definition of what we nowadays would call lust for power and what was in the eighteenth century called Pride.

> Among the many reigning Vices of the Town which may at any time come under my Consideration and Reprehension, there is none which I am more inclin'd to expose than that of *Pride*. It is acknowledged by all to be a Vice the most hateful to God and Man. Even those who nourish it in themselves, hate to see it in others. The proud Man aspires after Nothing less than an unlimited Superiority over his Fellow-Creatures.[73]

And "Mrs. Dogood" added a special warning: " 'Tis not inconsistent with Charity to distrust a Religious Man in Power, tho' he may be a good Man; he has many Temptations 'to propagate *public Destruction* for *Personal Advantages* and *Security*.' "[74]

As Arthur O. Lovejoy has pointed out, the idea of pride was very frequently contemplated during the earlier half of the eighteenth century.[75] There are two different, though not unrelated, conceptions of pride. First of all, it means "the most powerful and pervasive of all passions" which manifests itself in two forms: self-esteem and desire

for the admiration of others. The second conception is closely connected with the idea of the "Great Scale of Being"; it then means
the generic pride of man as such, the sin against the laws of order, of
gradation, the revolt of man against the station which has been allotted
to him by the Creator. Again, Pope is the spokesman of his age:

> The bliss of Man (could Pride that blessing find)
> Is not to act or think beyond mankind.[76]

These different conceptions of pride are indeed inseparable. In Franklin's own writings the accent is on the first rather than on the second
meaning of the term. This topic runs through his work like a red
thread. In 1729, at the age of twenty-three, he wrote that "almost every
Man has a strong natural Desire of being valu'd and esteem'd by the
rest of his Species."[77] In 1751 he penned some observations to a friend
which testify to the keen psychological insights of their author:

What you mention concerning the love of praise is indeed very true; it reigns
more or less in every heart; though we are generally hypocrites, in that respect,
and pretend to disregard praise. . . . Being forbid to praise themselves, they learn
instead of it to censure others; which is only a roundabout way of praising themselves. . . . This fondness for ourselves, rather malevolence to others, I take to be
the general source of censure. . . .[78]

Very revealing with regard to our discussion is Franklin's well-
known account of his project of an "Art of Virtue." His list of
virtues to be practiced contained at first only twelve. "But a Quaker
friend having kindly informed me that I was generally thought proud
. . . I added *Humility* to my list. . . . I cannot boast of much success
in acquiring the *reality* of this virtue, but I had a good deal with regard
to the *appearance* of it."[79]

Franklin's account of his rise in Pennsylvania's public life and politics
reflects his joy and pride about his career. In 1737 he was appointed
postmaster of Philadelphia and justice of the peace; in 1744 he established the American Philosophical Society; in 1748 he was chosen member of the Council of Philadelphia; in 1749 he was appointed provincial
grandmaster of the Colonial Masons; 1750 brought his appointment as
one of the commissioners to treat with the Indians in Carlisle; and
in 1751 he became a member of the Assembly of Pennsylvania. Franklin was particularly pleased with the latter appointment, and he "conceiv'd my becoming a member would enlarge my power of doing
good. I would not, however, insinuate that my ambition was not

flatter'd by all these promotions; it certainly was; for, considering my low beginning, they were great things to me; and they were still more pleasing, as being so many spontaneous testimonies of the public's good opinion, and by me entirely unsolicited."[80]

There is no change of emphasis with respect to pride during Franklin's long life. The old man of seventy-eight denounces the evil of pride with no less fervor, though with more self-knowledge, than the boy of sixteen:

> In reality, there is, perhaps, no one of our natural passions so hard to subdue as *pride*. Disguise it, struggle with it, beat it down, stifle it, mortify it as much as one pleases, it is still alive, and will every now and then peep out and show itself; you will see it, perhaps, often in this history; for even if I could conceive that I had compleately overcome it, I should probably by [be] proud of my humility.[81]

The idea of pride with which Franklin had been imbued in his youth accompanied him through all his long life. His candor was too great to let him gloss over the pride of his own nature. Furthermore, and this point will be elaborated in one of the following chapters, his experience of English political life which he acquired during his two protracted stays in England (from 1757 to 1762 and from 1765 to 1775) made an indelible impression on his mind. The corruption and venality in English politics and disastrous blunders of English politicians which Franklin traced back to this cause[82] probably were the main reasons for which he advocated what he himself said some might regard as a "Utopian Idea": the abolition of salaries for the chief executive at the Federal Convention of 1787. The reason he gave for advocating such a step has hitherto not been appreciated as being of crucial importance for an understanding of his political thought:

> There are two Passions which have a powerful Influence in the Affairs of Men. These are *Ambition* and *Avarice;* the Love of Power and the Love of Money. Separately, each of these has great Force in prompting Men to Action; but when united in View of the same Object, they have in many minds the most violent Effects. Place before the Eyes of such Men a Post of *Honour,* that shall at the same time be a Place of *Profit,* and they will move Heaven and Earth to obtain it.[83]

It has never been pointed out that this idea had ripened in Franklin's mind for several years. The first expression of it is to be found early in 1783.[84] In 1784 he mentioned this idea several times, and here we find one of the few allusions to a concept of checks and balances in Franklin's thought. He recommended making "every place of *honour* a place of *burthen.* By that means the effect of one of the passions above-mentioned would be taken away and something would he added to counteract the other."[85] At another time Franklin suggested that these two passions should be "separated and made to act one against the other."[86] Again in another letter he speaks of ambition "being to some degree ballanced by *Loss*"[87] in his new scheme of the "separation of passions."

We hope to have produced sufficient evidence for our contention that Franklin's views on human nature, and in particular his views on the nature of political man, do not quite fit into the pattern of rationalism and belief in moral progress which is usually associated with the Enlightenment. Obviously, the next step in our investigation leads us to the question of how Franklin applied his concept of human nature to the analysis of political phenomena. The two crucial points of interest are his attitude toward the phenomenon of political factions, parties, or interest groups, on the one hand, and toward democracy, on the other.

The Nature of Politics

Franklin's frequent praise of the general welfare did not blind him to the fact that most other people had a much narrower vision than his own. "Men will always be powerfully influenced in their Opinions and Actions by what appears to be their particular Interest," he wrote in his first tract on political economy, at the age of twenty-three.[88] Fortunately, one of the very few memoranda and notes dealing with the studies and discussions of young Franklin which have come to our knowledge directly concerns our problem. He himself, in his *Autobiography,* gives us the text of *"Observations* on my reading history, in Library, May 9th, 1731," which, in his words, had been "accidentally preserv'd":

That the great affairs of the world, the wars, revolutions, etc., are carried on and effected by parties.

That the view of these parties is their present general interest, or what they take to be such.

That the different views of these different parties occasion all confusion.

That while a party is carrying on a general design, each man has his particular private interest in view.

That as soon as a party has gain'd its general point, each member becomes intent upon his particular interest; which, thwarting others, breaks that party into divisions, and occasions more confusion.

That few in public affairs act from a mere view of the good of their country, whatever they may pretend; and, tho' their actings bring real good to their coun-

try, yet men primarily considered that their own and their country's interest was
united, and did not act from a principle of benevolence.

That fewer still, in public affairs, act with a view to the good of mankind.[89]

These lines do not mirror Shaftesbury's benevolent altruism; Franklin's contention that men act primarily from their own interest "and
did not act from a principle of benevolence," "tho' their actings bring
real good to their country," strongly suggests the general theme of *The
Fable of the Bees,* the work of Bernard Mandeville, Shaftesbury's antagonist, whom Franklin had met in London: "Private vices, public
benefits."

Many decades later, after the Federal Convention, Franklin wrote
to the French physiocrat, Dupont de Nemours (who had suggested
that the convention be delayed until the separate constitutions of the
member-states be corrected—according to physiocratic principles, of
course) :

> We must not expect that a new government may be formed, as a game of chess
> may be played, by a skilful hand, without a fault. The players of our game are
> so many, their ideas so different, their prejudices so strong and so various, and
> their particular interests, independent of the general, seeming so opposite, that not
> a move can be made that is not contested; the numerous objections confound the
> understanding; the wisest must agree to some unreasonable things, that reason-
> able ones of more consequence may be obtained, and thus chance has its share
> in many of the determinations, so that the play is more like *tric-trac* with a box
> of dice.[90]

Only three years earlier, Franklin had observed melancholically "how
preposterously the affairs of this world are managed. . . . We assemble
parliaments and councils, to have the benefit of their collected wisdom;
but we necessarily have, at the same time, the inconvenience of their
collected passions, prejudices, and private interests."[91]

In public, and in the service of his country, Franklin played down
the evils of party strife, which he himself was the first to regret. This
becomes particularly obvious in a pamphlet on *The Internal State of
America,* written in France after the conclusion of the peace treaty
with England, in order to attract European emigrants to America. His
argument sounds somewhat apologetic:

> It is true, that in some of the States there are Parties and Discords; but let us look
> back, and ask if we were ever without them? Such will exist wherever there is
> Liberty; and perhaps they help to preserve it. By the Collision of different Senti-
> ments, Sparks of Truth are struck out, and Political Light is obtained. The differ-
> ent Factions, which at present divide us, aim all at the Publick Good; the Differ-
> ences are only about the various Modes of promoting it. . . . Parties are therefore the

common lot of Humanity; and ours are by no means more mischievous or less beneficial than those of other Countries, Nations, and Ages, enjoying in the same degree the great Blessing of Political Liberty.[92]

In private, Franklin did not conceal his suspicions that "unity out of discord" was not so easily and naturally achieved as his just-quoted method of obtaining "political light" might suggest. But he certainly did not believe that passions and prejudices always overrule enlightened self-interest. He held that "there is a vast variety of good and ill Events, that are in some degree the Effects of Prudence or the want of it."[93] Toward the end of his life, Franklin had come to the conclusion that, in order "to get the bad Customs of a Country chang'd, and new ones, though better, introduc'd, it is necessary first to remove the Prejudices of the People, enlighten their Ignorance, and convince them that their Interest will be promoted by the propos'd Changes; and this is not the Work of a Day."[94] As early as 1751 he had expressed the opinion that "reasonable sensible Men, can always make a reasonable scheme appear such to other reasonable Men, if they take Pains, and have Time and Opportunity for it." However, this hope is severely limited by the conclusion: ". . . unless from some Circumstances their Honesty and Good Intentions are suspected."[95] That Franklin thought those circumstances to exist frequently, we learn from a famous message to George Washington, written in France in 1780. He told Washington how much the latter would enjoy his reputation in France, "pure and free from those little Shades that the Jealousy and Envy of a Man's Countrymen and Cotemporaries are ever endeavouring to cast over living Merit."[96] Although he talked so much about "common interests" himself, Franklin could be impatient when others built their arguments on this point. This may be seen with rare clarity in marginal notes in a pamphlet whose author argued that "if the Interests of Great Britain evidently raise and fall with those of the Colonies, then the Parliament of Great Britain will have the same regard for the Colonists as for her own People." With sharp words, which he would never use in public, where he had learned to speak with "modest diffidence," Franklin retorted:

All this Argument of the Interest of Britain and the Colonies being the *same* is fallacious and unsatisfactory. Partners in Trade have a *common* Interest, which is the same, the Flourishing of the Partnership Business: But they may moreover have each a *separate* Interest; and in pursuit of that *separate* Interest, one of them may endeavour to impose on the other, may cheat him in the Accounts, may draw to himself more than his Share of the Profits, may put upon the other more than an equal Share of the Expence and Burthen. Their having a common Interest is no Security against such Injustice. . . . The Majority in Parliament being favoured in the Proportion will never confer to do Justice to the Minority by a mere equal Assessment.[97]

FRANKLIN AND DEMOCRACY

It is fair to ask how Franklin's views on the above matters square with Franklin's avowal of radically democratic views after 1775. In view of the foregoing, he would not, it seems, agree with the underlying assumptions of Jeffersonian democracy, stated by Jefferson himself: "Nature hath implanted in our breasts a love of others, a sense of duty to them, a moral instinct, in short, which prompts us irresistibly to feel and to succor their distresses."[98] It was also Jefferson who believed that "man was a rational animal, endowed by nature with rights, and with an innate sense of justice."[99] On this faith in the rationality and goodness of man, the theory of Jeffersonian democracy has been erected. Franklin, for different reasons, has often been included in the broad group of "Jeffersonians," with their common sympathy for the French Enlightenment, for physiocratic ideas, for "useful knowledge." The American Philosophical Society, founded by Franklin, formed indeed a sort of center for Jeffersonian philosophy. Vernon L. Parrington said of Franklin that "he was a forerunner of Jefferson, like him firm in the conviction that government was good in the measure that it remained close to the people."[100] Charles A. Beard, discussing the members of the Federal Convention, tells us that Benjamin Franklin "seems to have entertained a more hopeful view of democracy than any other member of that famous group."[101] All this must seem rather strange in view of the none-too-cheerful conception of human nature which we have found in Franklin. His radically democratic views after 1775—before that time his outlook seemed essentially conservative—have baffled contemporary observers as it has later students.

There is, as a matter of fact, plenty of evidence for Franklin's sincere devotion to monarchy during the greater part of his life. It was the most natural thing for him to assure his friend, the famous Methodist preacher, George Whitefield, that a settlement of colonies on the Ohio would be blessed with success "if we undertook it with a sincere Regard to . . . the Service of our gracious King, and (which is the same thing) the Publick Good."[102] Seven years later Franklin tried to calm the pessimistic apprehensions of his printer friend, William Strahan, about the corrupt political life in England by referring to the young king, in whom Franklin had set many hopes: "And as to their Quantity of Virtue, it bids fair for Increasing; if the old saying be true, as it certainly is, Ad exemplum Regis, etc."[103] Franklin loved to contrast the corruption of Parliament and the virtues of George III. In very enthusiastic terms Franklin told an American friend of his that he could "scarcely conceive a King of better Dispositions, of more exemplary virtues, or more truly desirous of promoting the Welfare of all his Subjects."[104] One year later he exhorted the Americans again: "Let us, therefore, hold fast our Loyalty to our King, who has the best Disposition towards us, and has a Family Interest in our Prosperity; as that steady Loyalty is the most probable means of securing us from the arbitrary Power of a corrupt Parliament, that does not like us, and conceives itself to have an Interest in keeping us down and fleecing us."[105]

Another indication of Franklin's antiradical attitude before 1775 were the indignant terms in which he expressed his horror at the excitement over the famous case of John Wilkes: "Even this capitol, the residence of the King, is now daily a scene of lawless riot and confusion. Mobs patrolling the streets at noonday, some knocking all down that will not roar for Wilkes and liberty."[106]

Another "conservative" aspect of Franklin which cannot be glossed over lightly is his acceptance of the Puritan and mercantilistic attitude toward the economic problems of the working class. All his life he was critical of the English poor laws. He deplored "the proneness of human nature to a life of ease, of freedom from care and labour,"[107] and he considered that laws which *compel the rich to maintain the poor*" might possibly be "fighting against the order of God and Nature, which perhaps has appointed want and misery as the proper punishments for, and cautions against, as well as necessary consequences of, idleness and extravagance."[108] This was written in 1753. But as late as 1789, long after Franklin had come out for the political equality of the poor and for a radical theory of property, he still confirmed to an English correspondent that "I have long been of your opinion, that your legal provision for the poor is a very great evil, operating as it does to the encouragement of idleness."[109]

Where does Franklin's indorsement of democracy emerge most clearly? It is made most emphatically in his advocacy of a unicameral legislature for the Commonwealth of Pennsylvania as well as for the United States.

The issue of unicameral versus bicameral legislative bodies—an issue much discussed in the latter decades of the eighteenth century—reflected faithfully, as a rule, the clash of views of two different theories of human nature and of politics. The bicameral system was based on the principle of checks and balances: a pessimistic view of human nature naturally would try to forestall the abuse of power in a single and all-powerful assembly. On the other hand, most of those who trusted in the faculties of human reason did not see the necessity for a second chamber to check and harass the activities of a body of reasonable men.

In the case of Franklin, however, one does not find this correspondence of political convictions with views on human nature.

Franklin was the president of the Pennsylvania Convention of 1776, which set up—almost uniquely among the American states—a unicameral system.[110] This, of course, filled many of the French *philosophes* with great joy. Franklin, they supposed, had secured a triumph of enlightened principles in the New World. Condorcet, in his "Éloge de Franklin," had this to say:

Franklin's voice alone decided this last provision. He thought that as enlightenment would naturally make rapid progress, above all in a country to which the revolution had given a new system, one ought to encourage the devices of perfecting legislation, and not to surround them with extrinsic obstacles. He knew that a complex constitution might fit a people driven through passing circumstances toward liberty, while neither cherishing nor understanding it; but that a simple constitution alone was good enough for a people where the love of liberty is the principal sentiment of all citizens and the study of its principles the main occupation of their reason. . . . The opinion contrary to his stands for that discouraging philosophy which considers error and corruption as the habitual state of societies and the development of virtue and reason as a kind of miracle which one must not expect to make enduring. It was high time that a philosophy both nobler and truer should direct the destiny of mankind, and Franklin was worthy to give the first example of it.[111]

As a matter of fact, it has since been shown that Franklin, who at the time of the Pennsylvania Convention also served in the Continental Congress, played a minor role in the actual adoption of the unicameral system. The unicameral legislature was rooted in the historical structure of Pennsylvania's proprietary government.[112] However, this is irrelevant from our point of view, since Franklin indorsed and defended the unicameral system in his *Queries and Remarks respecting Alterations in the Constitution of Pennsylvania* written in November, 1789.

From his point of view, John Adams was certainly justified in seeing in Franklin and Turgot the roots of that terrible evil, a unicameral legislature. Adams referred to them and their friends as "the school of folly, but alas, Franklin, Turgot, Rochefoucauld and Condorcet, under Tom Paine, were the great masters of that Academy."[113]

In his opposition to checks and balances and a second chamber, Franklin's most famous companion was Thomas Paine, the author of *The Age of Reason*. This similarity of views between Franklin and possibly the most vocal spokesman of the creed of reason and the perfectibility of man perhaps contributes to the misinterpretation of Franklin's position among the eighteenth-century philosophers. Paine's arguments against the system of checks and balances and for a single house were characteristic of the later Enlightenment:

It is the nature of freedom to be free. . . . Freedom is the associate of innocence, not the companion of suspicion. She only requires to be cherished, not to be caged, and to be beloved is, to her, to be protected. Her residence is in the undistinguished multitude of rich and poor, and a partisan to neither is the patroness of all. She connects herself with man as God made him, not as fortune altered him.[114]

This argument, of course, presupposes the rationality and goodness of human nature. We might perhaps agree with Thomas Paine that "no man was a better judge of human nature than Franklin,"[115] but Paine certainly did not have Franklin's conception of human nature.

Let us turn back to Franklin's own writings to try to find out the reasons for his almost radical attitude in 1776 and 1787. We may first state what is *not* at the root of his democratic faith: belief in the goodness and the wisdom of the people. This idea is quite foreign to Franklin. Discussing the question of electing the officers of the militia of Pennsylvania in 1755, he said that "if all officers appointed by governors were always men of merit, and fully qualified for their posts, it would be wrong ever to hazard a popular election."[116] In an often-quoted letter to Governor Shirley concerning the Albany Plan of union (published during Franklin's lifetime), Franklin thought that "it is very possible, that this general government might be as well and faithfully administered without the people, as with them."[117] Nor did he fundamentally change his view in the last years of his life. "Popular favour is very precarious, being sometimes *lost* as well as *gained* by good actions."[118] On February 17, 1788, Franklin wrote to his French friend and translator of his *Autobiography,* Le Veillard: "Though there is a general dread of giving too much power to our *governors,* I think we are more in danger from too little obedience in the *governed.*"[119] In the same year Franklin wrote publicly that "popular Opposition to a public Measure is no Proof of its Impropriety."[120] What a strange democrat it was who told the Federal Convention that "there is a natural Inclination in Mankind to kingly Government."[121] The most plausible and popular reason for belief in democracy, then, is eliminated.

On the other hand, neither did Franklin believe in the intrinsic goodness of the wealthy or the wisdom of the powerful. As a matter of fact, he never did believe in aristocratic government, be it by an aristocracy of wealth or a hereditary aristocracy. He threw all his scorn on the House of Lords and thought "Hereditary Professors of Mathematicks" preferable to hereditary legislators because they could do less mischief.[122]

It is noteworthy that in the whole of Franklin's work only one reference to Montesquieu can be found: it concerns his ideas on criminal law. The separation of powers, the role of the aristocracy in a healthy society—these are doctrines which never took possession of Franklin's mind.

The antithesis between Adams, under the influence of Harrington, and Franklin, chiefly influenced by his own experience, is remarkably complete. Adams wrote that "it must be remembered that the rich are *people* as well as the poor; that they have rights as well as others; that they have as clear and as *sacred* a right to their large property as others have to theirs which is smaller; that oppression to them is as possible and wicked as to others."[123] Franklin mounts a formidable counterattack:

And why should the upper House, chosen by a Minority, have equal Power with the lower chosen by a Majority? Is it supposed that Wisdom is the necessary concomitant of Riches, and that one Man worth a thousand Pounds must have as much Wisdom as Twenty who have each only 999; and why is Property to be represented at all? . . . The Combinations of Civil Society are not like those of a Set of Merchants, who club their Property in different Proportions for Building and Freighting a Ship, and may therefore have some Right to Vote in the Disposition of the Voyage in a greater or less Degree according to their respective Contributions; but the important ends of Civil Society, and the personal Securities of Life and Liberty, these remain the same in every Member of the society; and the poorest continues to have an equal Claim to them with the most opulent.[124]

It is this very strong objection against the attempt to use—openly or covertly—a second chamber as a tool of class rule which seems to lie at the bottom of Franklin's disapproval of the bicameral system. Franklin, we ought to point out, was aware of the necessity and inevitability of poises and counterpoises. This is shown by his attempt, referred to above, to create a sort of balance of passions, playing off avarice against ambition. We shall meet some, though very rare, allusions to a balance-of-power concept in Franklin's utterances on imperial and international relations. The most pointed and direct reference to the idea of checks and balances, however, may be found in a so far unpublished letter to a well-known figure of Pennsylvania politics, Joseph Galloway. In 1767 Franklin discussed and welcomed a new circuit bill for the judges of Pennsylvania. He suggested and encouraged an increase of the salaries to be granted by the Assembly for the judges to match the nominating and recalling powers of the Proprietor: "From you they should therefore receive a Salary equal in Influence upon their Minds, to be held during your Pleasure. For where the Beam *is moveable,* it is only by equal Weights in opposite Scales that it can possibly be kept even."[125]

Consequently, the arguments of Thomas Paine or the French *philosophes,* which derive their validity from assumptions about the goodness or rationality of human nature, do not hold in the case of Franklin. In view of our discussion of Franklin's theory of human nature, it seems an oversimplification to suggest, as has recently been done, that, for instance, Madison, "like Adams and Jefferson, and unlike Paine and Franklin, . . . never believed that we can put our confidence in any group of elected officials."[126] Another brilliant essay on American political thought fails to capture the essential quality of Franklin's political thought by saying that, "despite the European flavor of a Jefferson or a Franklin, the Americans refused to join in the great Enlightenment enterprise of shattering the Christian concept of sin, replacing it with an unlimited humanism, and then emerging with an earthly enterprise as glittering as the heavenly one that had been destroyed."[127] Our essay attempts precisely to make the point that the alternatives of Calvinist pessimism or the "unlimited humanism" of the later Enlightenment are not present in Franklin's political thought. His thought is rooted in a climate of opinion which combined the rejection of the doctrine of original sin with a rather modest view of human nature.

It seems, then, that the desire for equality rather than any rationalistic concepts offers the clue to an adequate understanding of all those elements in Franklin's political thought which at first sight would appear inconsistent with his not too cheerful view of human goodness. His striving for equality also offers a solution to a very thorny problem: his apparently very late conversion to democracy—which came rarely into the open before his decision for American independence in 1775—and his faithful loyalty to the Crown before that date. The American interest obliged him to fight against Parliament—an aristocratic body in those days—while remaining loyal to the king; in recognizing the king's sovereignty while denying Parliament's rights over the colonies, Franklin by necessity was driven into a position which, historically speaking, seemed to contradict his Whig principles. The complaining Americans spoke, as Lord North rightly said, the "language of Toryism."[128] During the decade before 1775 Franklin fought for the equal rights of England and the colonies under the Crown. But his desire for equality went deeper than that. In his *Some Good Whig Principles,* while conceding that the government of Great Britain ought to be lodged "in the hands of King, Lords of Parliament, and Representatives of *the whole body* of the freemen of this realm,"[129] he took care to affirm that "every man of the commonalty (excepting infants, insane persons, and criminals) is, of common right, and by the laws of God, *a freeman*" and that "the poor man has an *equal* right, but *more* need, to have representatives in the legislature than the rich one."[130] Equality, then, is not incompatible with monarchy.

Franklin's previously quoted speech in the Federal Convention provides us with an essential insight. He expressed the belief in "a natural Inclination in Mankind to kingly Government."[131] But why? His reasons are very revealing: "It sometimes relieves them from Aristocratic Domination. They had rather one Tyrant than 500. It gives more of the Appearance of Equality among Citizens; and that they like."[132] It seemed to require the foolhardiness of George III to alienate the monarchical feelings of Franklin. But he never showed signs of being greatly impressed with the English aristocracy. The man whom he admired most among all British statesmen was not an aristocrat but Pitt, "the great Commoner." Above all, Franklin knew from his own experience that wisdom, reasonableness, and public spirit could grow among the poor. He was proud of his origin and his career.[133]

From all this we may draw a significant conclusion. It is too simple to speak of Franklin's "conservatism" before 1775 and of his "radicalism" after 1775. R. M. MacIver illustrates the conservative character of the first stage of American political thought preceding the appeal to natural rights by reference to Benjamin Franklin, who, in spite of his later attacks on the Order of the Cincinnati, "nevertheless clung to the principle of a hereditary, though constitutional monarchy, until the tide of revolution rendered it untenable."[134] The term "conservative" does not do justice to the possibility of paying faithful allegiance to a monarchy and still disliking aristocracies of heredity or wealth. Because of his innate desire for equality as well as his defense of the American cause against the encroachments of Parliament, Franklin found it much easier to be a monarchist. Monarchy, rather than aristocracy, was compatible with those elements of his thought which after 1775 made him a democrat.

Another of these factors which, while not incompatible with monarchical feelings, contributed greatly to Franklin's acceptance of democracy is the belief which he shared with David Hume that power, in the last analysis, is founded on opinion. "I wish some good Angel would forever whisper in the Ears of your great Men, that Dominion is founded in Opinion, and that if you would preserve your Authority among us, you must preserve the Opinion we us'd to have of your Justice."[135]

Franklin's voyage from London to Philadelphia had given occasion for the following remark: "I own, indeed, that if a commander finds he has not those qualities in him that will make him beloved by his people, he ought, by all means, to make use of such methods as will make them fear him, since one or the other (or both) is absolutely necessary."[136] "Government must depend for it's Efficiency either on Force or Opinion."[137] Force, however, is not so efficient as opinion: "Alexander and Caesar . . . received more faithful service, and performed greater actions, by means of the love their soldiers bore them, than they could possibly have done, if, instead of being beloved and respected, they had been hated and feared by those they commanded."[138] Efficiency, then, became an argument for democracy. "Popular elections have their inconveniences in some cases; but in establishing new forms of government, we cannot always obtain what we may think the best; for the prejudices of those concerned, if they cannot be removed, must be in some degree complied with."[139] The same pragmatic measure was applied in an already-quoted letter to Governor Shirley, where, speaking of popular government, Franklin advises that "where heavy burthens are to be laid on them, it has been found useful to make it, as much as possible, their own act; for they bear better, when they have, or think they have some share in the direction."[140]

It has rarely been noticed how detached Franklin, the greatest champion of democracy in the Federal Convention, was from the problem of the best government. The following sentence may offer us a clue to the perplexing problem of why he gave comparatively little attention to the theoretical questions of political philosophy and devoted almost all his time to the solution of concrete issues: In his speech at the conclusion of the deliberations of the Federal Convention he stated his disagreement with several points of the Constitution, nevertheless urging general allegiance and loyalty to its principles. Asking his colleagues to doubt a little their feeling of infallibility, and again mentioning that "much of the strength and efficiency of any government, in procuring and securing happiness to the people, depends on opinion," Franklin summed up the experience of his life: "I think a general Government necessary for us, and there is no *form* of government but what may be a blessing to the people, if well administered."[141] Perhaps Franklin, when he spoke those words, was thinking of one of the favorite writers of his youth, Alexander Pope:

> For Forms of Government let fools contest;
> Whate'er is best administer'd is best.[142]

THE DUAL CHARACTER OF FRANKLIN'S POLITICAL THOUGHT

There are two outstanding and sometimes contradictory features in Franklin's political thought. On the one hand, we found a very acute comprehension of the power factor in human nature and, consequently, in politics. On the other hand, Franklin always during his long life revolted in the name of equality against the imperfections of the existing order. He himself stated the basic antithesis of his political thought: power versus equality.

Fortunately, Franklin's notes on the problem at hand have been preserved; they are to be found in his marginal comments to Allen Ramsay's pamphlet, *Thoughts on the Origin and Nature of Government,* which presents the straight view of power politics. Franklin revolted against the rationalization and justification of the power factor.[143] "THE NATURAL WEAKNESS OF MAN IN A SOLITARY STATE," Ramsay proclaimed, "PROMPTS HIM TO FLY FOR PROTECTION TO WHOEVER IS ABLE TO AFFORD IT, THAT IS TO SOMEONE MORE POWERFUL, THAN HIMSELF; WHILE THE MORE POWERFUL STANDING EQUALLY IN NEED OF HIS SERVICE, READILY RECEIVES IT IN RETURN FOR THE PROTECTION HE GIVES." Franklin's answer is unequivocal: *"May not Equals unite with Equals for common Purposes?"*[144]

In the last analysis, Franklin looked upon government as the trustee of the people. In his very first publication as a sixteen-year-old boy, he had stated this Whig principle,[145] from which he never deviated. In opposition to Ramsay's doctrine, according to which the governed have no right of control whatsoever, once they have agreed to submit themselves to the sovereign, Franklin declared the accountability of the rulers:

If I appoint a Representative for the express purpose of doing a Business for me that is for *my Service* and that of others, & to consider what I am to pay as my Proportion of the Expence necessary for accomplishing that Business, I am then tax'd by my own Consent.—A Number of Persons unite to form a Company for Trade, Expences are necessary, Directors are chosen to do the Business & proportion those Expences. They are paid a Reasonable Consideration for their Trouble. Here is nothing of weak & strong, Protection on one hand, & Service on the other. The Directors are the Servants, not the Masters; their Duty is prescrib'd, the Power they have is from the members & returns to them. The Directors are also accountable.[146]

Franklin refused to recognize that power alone could create right. When Ramsay declared that according to nature's laws every man "IN SOCIETY SHALL RANK HIMSELF AMONGST THE RULING OR THE RULED, ALL EQUALITY AND INDEPENDENCE BEING BY THE LAW OF NATURE STRICTLY FORBIDDEN,"[147] Franklin rejoined indignantly: "I do not find this Strange Law among those of Nature. I doubt it is forged."[148] Franklin summarized Ramsay's doctrine as meaning that "He that is strongest may do what he pleases with those that are weaker,"[149] and commented angrily: "A most Equitable Law of Nature indeed."[150] Franklin's belief in the accountability of government, together with his more pragmatic conviction that force alone cannot solve the great problems of politics, produced his declaration of faith that "Government is not establish'd merely by *Power;* there must be maintain'd a general Opinion of its *Wisdom* and *Justice,* to make it firm and durable."[151]

The study of Franklin's political thought and foreign policy derives its particular flavor from the peculiar contradiction that existed in his own mind. This strange antagonism becomes perfectly clear in a statement on the Anglo-American conflict three years before the Declaration of Independence; Franklin had this to say on England's prospects: *"Power* does not infer *Right;* and, as the *Right* is nothing, and the *Power,* (by our Increase,) continually diminishing, the one will soon be as insignificant as the *other*."[152] Franklin, in fact, tried to make the best of both worlds. This curious interdependence of moral with power-political considerations will be the main topic of the succeeding chapters.

CHAPTER II

THE QUEST FOR SECURITY AND THE
DREAM OF EMPIRE

The Primacy of Foreign Policy and the Age of Mercantilism

IT HAS been said that "the foreign policy of a state or nation necessarily pre-supposes its existence as a political body."[1] Although this statement is substantially true, it would be fallacious to draw the conclusion that the formation of American foreign policy began in 1776 on a *tabula rasa*. Colonial Americans, even if they did not have any previous experience in the conduct of foreign affairs, were not at all unfamiliar with the problems of foreign policy as such. They had actively taken part in an international contest which is gradually coming to be recognized as "perhaps the most momentous event in the life of the English-speaking people in the New World,"[2] that is, the decisive struggle between Great Britain and France for dominion in the New World, commonly referred to as the French and Indian War or the Seven Years' War but in recent years much more appropriately named "the Great War for the Empire."[3]

American historians are paying increasing attention to a phenomenon which for a long time played an important role in European historiography: the primacy of foreign over domestic affairs in a world of sovereign national states. The idea of the primacy of foreign policy has found its classical expression in Leopold von Ranke's "Dialogue on Politics." Ranke said: "The position of a state in the world depends on the degree of independence it has attained. It is obliged, therefore, to organize all internal resources for the purpose of self-preservation. This is the supreme law of the state."[4]

The discovery and realization of the fact that isolation from international power politics was only a temporary and passing phase of American history during a part of the nineteenth century has contributed to the present tendency to view the evolution of American history in a world setting. Frederick Jackson Turner has noted that "so long as the Mississippi valley was menaced, or in part controlled,

33

by rival European states, just so long must the United States be a part of the state system of Europe, involved in its fortunes."[5] He has also recommended the incorporation of the terminology of European expansion—expressions such as "colonization," "sphere of influence," "hinterland"—into American historiography.[6]

Recently the question has been raised "whether the Revolution with its empire-building objectives ought not to be set squarely within the frame of reference of the Seven Years' War. The dynamics of American imperialism belong to the pre-Revolution years."[7] This has been answered in the affirmative: The Revolution has been described as an "aftermath of the Great War for the Empire," and it has been said that the British victory over France in 1763 "opened up . . . the prospect, if given freedom of action, of a vast growth of power and wealth with an amazing westward expansion."[8] The victory of 1763 decided indeed what kind of civilization was destined to dominate the North American continent.

Before examining Franklin's attitude to this development of gigantic dimensions, it is essential to discuss first some relevant aspects of the prevailing theory of international relations that provided the framework for his thought on foreign affairs: the doctrine of mercantilism. We shall then point out the origin of his interest in foreign affairs in his quest for security of the American colonies. Finally, we shall discuss how Franklin, going far beyond the mere quest for security, developed his views on the expansion of the British Empire in America —views which, though rooted in the theories of mercantilism, contained much that was explosive and which were finally to destroy the dream of a powerful and self-contained empire in his own mind.

Mercantilism, as is well known, means many things to many people. Differences of opinion have been so considerable that one would do well to guard against the conception of mercantilism as a rigid and logically consistent economic or political doctrine. Among the mercantilists themselves, agreement existed chiefly in regard to two features of economic doctrine: the importance of trade and a favorable balance of trade, on the one hand, and, in view of the fact that the export of manufactures was more desirable than the export of raw materials, the importance of the laborer, on the other. Mercantilists, furthermore, confronted with the spectacle of a world of nation-states just then in the process of consolidation, a world where the struggle for self-preservation and the struggle for preponderance were at times scarcely distinguishable, quite naturally drew an analogy between military power and wealth. With the aid of the assumption of a close relationship between "balance of power" and "balance of trade," they were easily led to the conclusion that "wealth, like power, also was only a relative matter, a matter of proportion between countries, so that a loss inflicted on a rival country was as good as an absolute gain for one's own country."[9]

The existence of international power conflicts, together with the doctrine that the amount of trade and wealth in the world was limited, produced the view that one nation, commercially as well as politically, could gain only at the expense of the others. In recognizing this, Thomas Hobbes and John Locke, usually considered as standing at opposite poles of political thought, both join in proclaiming the primacy of foreign policy. Said Hobbes, speaking of the importance of population for the commonwealth: "The multitude sufficient to confide in for our security, is not determined by any certain number, but by comparison with the enemy we feare."[10] Locke, discussing the other pillar of power, money, asserted that "Riches do not consist in having more Gold and Silver, but in having more in proportion, than the rest of the World, or than our Neighbours."[11]

The awareness of international rivalry and the quest for security in the face of constant danger of war go far to explain, in the case of England, the adoption of mercantile principles and measures, even though such measures were opposed to the agricultural interests still prevailing in the seventeenth century.[12] What has been so aptly called the "law of the lowest level"[13] operated in international affairs in 1650 or 1750 just as much as in 1950. A mercantilist writer puts the argument very well:

I shall not now dispute, whether the World might not have been happier by its continuance under Confinement and stak'd down to Agriculture, and those Mechanick Arts that are needful to the Conveniences of Life, (without purveying for our Pride and Sensuality) than it is by launching out into that Measure and degree of Mercantile Commerce which has excited our Lusts as well as fed them, and given Provocation to Vice by yielding Fewel to it. But some Nations have departed from the ancient simplicity of Living contented with Productions of their own Countries and having by Navigation and Trade, raised themselves to Wealth, Power and Increase of inhabitants; it thereupon grew necessary for other Nations to fall into like Methods, lest otherwise they should have been a Prey, as well as a Derision to them whom Trade hath rendered Mighty and Opulent.[14]

Here we have, then, a close connection of political and economic considerations. In view of the confusion which exists regarding the problem of political versus economic motivation, it seems necessary, before further progressing with our discussion, to establish a framework within which this problem of the relationship between politics and economics can be analyzed and judged. It seems to us that there exist five basic approaches, which are not mutually exclusive but rather reflect complementary aspects of one underlying phenomenon.

First of all, the issue may be looked upon in the light of divergent theories of human nature. It may be contended that either the love of power or the love of riches is the predominant factor in man's social life. Nineteenth-century liberals, and, in particular, Marxists, have been prone to disregard the possibility of a strong power drive in human nature; and, in their assumption that the love of riches could ultimately be satisfied by the harmony of interests or through social engineering, they have concentrated almost exclusively on purely economic problems. On the other hand, a more recent school of thought has attributed quite extraordinary importance to the will to power which pervades relationships that are ordinarily referred to as economic.[15]

Second, the problem may be seen as one involving different groups of people or different classes. We are told that "colonization appealed to many classes. Patriots believed colonies could serve as a base for war with Spain. The religiously inclined thought of the Indians awaiting conversion. Philanthropists found in expansion a solution for England's surplus population. Merchants foresaw new markets, naval leaders an increase of shipping and mariners, and a new source for naval supplies."[16] In different people different urges and motives may be potent. In all ages the motives, interests, and abilities of merchants and statesmen could differ widely. Nobody grasped this more clearly than the author of a pamphlet written in answer to one of Franklin's most important pronouncements on foreign policy. In this context we refer only to one magnificent passage, which deserves to be quoted in full:

I proceed to mention one argument used by the more moderate for relinquishing Guadaloupe, and it is thus; That we may depend upon its being given up to France, because the merchants of England, who are the best judges of its national interest, have shewn no anxiety about Guadaloupe, or expressed any inclination to have it kept. To which I answer, . . . I can by no means admit that the merchants are the best judges of national measures, I shall not say they are just the worst, but sure I am they are far from being the best; nor can it be otherwise; . . . Their heads and thoughts are entirely fixed upon the present times, where and how to make the greatest gain to themselves, in which some can take more liberties than others.

But how widely different is this from those who are formed to conduct the helm of state, those who must study the philosophy and policy of government, which teaches them to look back as far as authentic histories can conduct them with certainty, to mark the causes of the rise and decline of ancient states, to study the passions and designs of the great men of those times, which were productive of such events; to compare the passions and operations of the human mind in the present times, with those that are past; to carry on those observations to future times, to mark where the state may be ship-wrecked, and avoid those dangers; to observe what may aggrandize her in future times, and take measures to secure that, before her cotemporaries or enemies can discover the danger, or prevent the effect.

When these two, the merchant and the minister, are thus briefly compared, how widely different are they; in reality almost as wide as east from west; let us not deceive ourselves then in these notions, that the merchants are, or can be, the best judges of the philosophy of government, or the interest of a state.[17]

A third approach attributes paramount importance to geographic factors. Whereas security, that is, a political factor, is regarded as the supreme "reason of state" of French foreign policy, British foreign policy is said to have placed commercial considerations above political ones. As Montesquieu put it in regard to England: "Other nations have subordinated commercial interests to political interests; this nation has always subordinated her political interests to her commercial interests."[18] However, as we shall see presently, this view is correct only as far as it goes. Taken as the absolute rule of foreign policy at the expense of other important factors, it leads to an over-simplification (and that means a falsification) of history.

In discussions on mercantilism a fourth approach to the relationships of politics and economics is even more significant. The economic motive is said to predominate in one age, the pursuit of power in another period of history. For example, it has been asserted that mercantilism considered power as an end in itself, whereas the succeeding era of free trade, beginning with Adam Smith, subordinated considerations of power to considerations of wealth and plenty.[19] Other scholars have put the matter somewhat differently:

By the end of the seventeenth and the beginning of the eighteenth centuries the balance of trade had become, in the eyes of the growing body of merchants, the very *raison d'être* of the balance of power, and behind every diplomatic, military, and naval operation a trade motive could generally be found. To statesmen, merchants, and planters trade leadership had become a mainspring of policy and one of the necessary accompaniments of national prosperity, wealth, and power.[20]

By some students of mercantilism the primacy of political over economic considerations is stressed as the hallmark of mercantilist thought. Other scholars seem to emphasize the motive force of commerce. The most satisfactory explanation of this puzzle has been given by Professor Viner. He has pointed out how important it is to distinguish "between the official and the unofficial expositions of the doctrine, between the actual policies and the reasoning by which they were supported, and between continental and English mercantilism."[21] Following this advice, one would easily find that all the above-mentioned approaches contain certain truths but that none of them has the right to claim exclusive validity. In this respect it is essential to keep in mind that "English mercantilist doctrine was the product of merchants to an extent without parallel on the Continent."[22] It therefore seems that, first of all, English mercantilist doctrine stressed the acquisition of wealth as an end in itself more than Continental writers and, second, that references to the fact that wealth was also conducive to power seem "often to have been intended to win the support of the less commercial-minded official and landed classes for the proposals of the 'merchants' or business men."[23] On the other hand, government policy in England was never solely guided by economic considerations,[24] and Viner expresses the opinion that the "trade wars" of the seventeenth and eighteenth centuries "were such more in the imagination of the mercantile writers than in the intent of the governing classes who embarked upon them."[25]

However, this does not yet penetrate to the root of the matter. A fifth approach seems to offer a more comprehensive explanation. It is certainly possible that different people are motivated by different interests, caused either by their character or by their occupation or both. It is also possible that at different times and in different countries for a variety of reasons one set of interests—for instance, "economic" interests—will exert more influence than another set of interests, "political" interests, for example. Accordingly, states have been divided into "power states" and "welfare states."[26] "Welfare arguments are 'economic'; power arguments are 'political.' "[27]

At this stage of the argument the elusive character of the word "political" presents us with serious difficulties. There seem to be three dimensions of political power, which, although in practice inextricably interrelated, ought to be separated in theoretical discussions.

First of all, power is desired for self-preservation and security. Second, having assured these minimum requirements of individual as well as social life (which are, of course, always liable to rather elastic interpretations), men and states may still strive for greater power; power then may become—and this is the second dimension—an end in itself, sought for its own sake. Third, power may be used for the purpose of gaining certain positive objectives or goals of social life: liberty, democracy, the public welfare, or a life of plenty.

The essential fact is that self-preservation and the quest for security always and anywhere take precedence over considerations of welfare.[28] We do not always have a choice between power and welfare, or power and wealth, but we must possess a minimum of power in order to be able to acquire wealth or to erect the welfare state. "Economic" or "philosophic" considerations may exert greater influence on social life only when the basic need for security has been satisfied.

With regard to this aspect of the problem, even Adam Smith was prepared to concede the primacy of politics over economics or, what amounts in this respect to the same thing, the primacy of foreign over domestic policy. The quest for security is at the root of his famous defense of the Navigation Laws: "The act of navigation is not favourable to foreign commerce or the growth of that opulence which can arise from it. . . . As defence, however, is of much more importance than opulence, the act of navigation is, perhaps, the wisest of all the commercial regulations of England."[29]

Consequently, neither an interpretation claiming power as the ultimate goal of mercantilism nor an interpretation suggesting commerce as the ultimate goal of mercantilism tells the whole story. Power (whether for the sake of security, for its own sake, or for the sake of some ultimate economic or religious ideal) and wealth were both valued by different people as ultimate ends. However, whereas mercantilist as well as postmercantilist thought assumed that wealth bred power, during the postmercantilist period "there was an increasing tendency to assume that power was largely attained at the expense of wealth. . . . Considerations of power, though necessary in the interest of national self-preservation, conflicted with considerations of plenty."[30]

In conclusion, we believe that many of the frequent contrasts of "power" versus "plenty" miss the point. The basic problem is not whether "power" is the ultimate goal of one historic era or of one group of people or of one country in contrast to the cherishing of "plenty" or "welfare" by other ages, peoples, or countries. For all alike, the degree of security, or, in Ranke's words, "the degree of independence," is the measuring rod with the help of which "political" and "economic" actions may be evaluated.

Only those states whose security is sufficiently protected by their favorable geographic position or those who have otherwise accumulated an overwhelming preponderance of power can afford seemingly benevolent attitudes in foreign policy. Consequently, it is again for political reasons—that is, for reasons of sufficient security—that in countries like Great Britain and the United States economic considerations seemingly could determine foreign policy. This "primacy of economics" and of domestic issues over foreign issues, proclaimed with regard to the United States with particular fervor by Charles A. Beard, rests on the presupposition—not always explicitly stated—of political security. Shifts in the world power situation have again and again destroyed this comfortable situation, lowered the "degree of independence," and drawn those favored countries into the turmoil of international politics.

THE FEAR OF ENCIRCLEMENT IN THE AMERICAN COLONIES

We may suggest that this fifth approach is helpful for an understanding of the historic situation in which the British colonies found themselves when Franklin began to express himself on foreign affairs. The mid-eighteenth century was precisely a time when guns began to take precedence over butter, when, in other words, the security of the British colonies had reached such a low degree as to make imperative the subordination of narrowly "mercantilistic" commercial considerations to political strategy. Why was it that after 1748—the year in which the Peace of Aix-la-Chapelle had brought to a close the War of the Austrian Succession (King George's War)—imperial policy shifted "its emphasis from the commercial to factors of power and protection"? How did it happen that, again in the words of Professor Gipson, "the 'commercial' Empire after this date seems to have taken a secondary place in the evolving British policy to the 'power' Empire"?[31] The obvious answer is that during the first half of the eighteenth century the British continental colonies were still separated from French territory by a wide security belt of hinterland inhabited by the Indians.[32] However, at mid-century most of the desirable lands "in the old colonies had been engrossed and newcomers were forced to cross the Appalachian divide in search of farms."[33] Land speculators and settlers began to be interested in the land south and west of the Alleghenies, and from 1750 onward a steady and uncontrollable flow of people moved into what had formerly been considered as the security belt. On the other hand, the French were desirous of enhancing the security of their continental possessions centered around the St. Lawrence and the Mississippi and consequently attempted to establish a barrier against English advancement south of the Great Lakes and in the Ohio Valley.

The clash of British and French expansionism represented a deep sociological conflict.[34] It could not possibly be avoided after the geographic security factors had been removed. Although in retrospect one may say that, broadly speaking, the British expansion had much more vitality than the French movement and that France, because of her engagements on the continent of Europe, was constantly faced with the problem of readjusting her often conflicting European and imperial policies,[35] it can by no means be asserted that the British victory was inevitable.[36] The progress of the French west of the Alleghenies and their successful Indian policy presented a very real threat in the eyes of farseeing Colonials. On both sides the gradual removal of the security belt beyond the Alleghenies caused the breakdown of a "system that looked to immediate commercial gains" and gave way "to a system that sacrificed these to long range policy of power consolidation in North America."[37]

Farseeing Englishmen or those Colonials whose view transcended intercolonial rivalries and jealousies could not help being concerned about the encirclement of the British settlements on the continent.[38] In 1732 the well-known Pennsylvania statesman, James Logan, composed a memorial, which has been preserved for us in a copy written by Benjamin Franklin. Logan put the core of the Colonial anxieties in one sentence:

Tho' Canada as an Encroachment has always given uneasiness to the English Colonies, yet as it is generally a very Cold and not very fruitful Countrey, there never appeared any great Probability of its being very considerable, 'till the Sieur la Salle about the year 1680 discovered the great River Missisippi to which the English notwithstanding had a Prior pretence. In this the French made no progress 'till since the peace of Utrecht, but *now they Surround all the British Dominions on the Main.*[39]

Logan was not unaware of "geopolitical" considerations which might cause the French to look with envious eyes on the British colonies:

> But to all this Vast Tract, the French have no other Inlet from the Sea, than by the Mouths of those two great Rivers Saint Lawrence and Messisippi both of which are Tedious and Dangerous, the one by Rocks and the other by Shoals. They cannot therefore but be very Sensible that a nearer Access to some parts of it by the Ocean is requisite and would Extreamly well Suit them.[40]

About twenty years later the apprehension of the colonies about the French encirclement was voiced much more urgently by men associated with Franklin either by friendship or by the common concern for the safety of the colonies. Archibald Kennedy, collector of customs and receiver-general of the Province of New York, wrote several pamphlets, one of them prefaced by Franklin, and attempted to drive home to his fellow-Colonials the fact that "the *French* are now drawing a Line along the Borders of our Settlements in every Province, from the mouth of the *St. Lawrence,* to the Mouth of the *Mississippi.*"[41] In a book printed by Franklin, the well-known Pennsylvania mapmaker, Lewis Evans, pointed out that the possession of the land between the colonies and the Mississippi would decide the fate of the southern British colonies; in case of a French settlement, the English would be forced to submit, "or have their Throats cut, and loose all their Slaves."[42] Responsible people in the northern colonies were no less concerned, particularly Governor Shirley of Massachusetts, with whose unwavering efforts for Colonial union Benjamin Franklin was closely connected at the time of the Albany Congress. All colonies, Shirley wrote in 1748, "may in Process of time be equally indangered by the spreading and Growth of the French upon our Borders."[43] William Clarke, a citizen of Boston, well acquainted with Governor Shirley, expressed the fear of encirclement in a pamphlet which was published together with an essay by Franklin, as follows:

> That the French have had this [dispossessing the English] in view from the beginning of their Settlements in North America, seems clear from their surrounding the English Colonies, and building Forts upon the Lakes, and most convenient rivers on the back of the English settlements from St. Lawrence River to Missisippi, and claiming an exclusive navigation in those lakes and rivers, and the property of all that part of the Continent.[44]

On the other hand, the French showed no less apprehension of the dynamic forces which around mid-century began to emanate from the English colonies in a westward direction. In a famous memoir the returning French governor of Canada, the Marquis de la

Galissonnière, emphatically stressed the need for sacrificing "immediate financial gain" to security considerations.

> Whilst peace appeared to have lulled the jealousy of the English in Europe, this bursts forth in all its violence in America; and if barriers capable of staying its effects be not opposed at this very moment, that nation will place itself in a condition to completely invade the French Colonies at the opening of the first war.[45]

> It cannot be denied that this Colony [Canada] has been always a burthen to France, and it is probable that such will be the case for a long while; but it constitutes, at the same time, the strongest barrier that can be opposed to the ambition of the English.[46]

Canada alone, de la Galissonnière continued, was able to wage war against all the English possessions on the continent—possessions, he added, "which are as dear to them as they are precious in fact, whose power is daily increasing, and which, if means be not found to prevent it, will soon absorb not only all the Colonies located in the neighbouring islands of the Tropic, but even all those of the Continent of America."[47]

This evidence sufficiently illustrates the growing urgency with which observers on both sides recognized the fact that the stability of the American balance of power was breaking down. The dynamics of the two opposing expanding powers gained momentum during the interval between the War of the Austrian Succession (King George's War), the last war which in its imperial aspects had been fought largely for commercial issues, and the Great War for the Empire, which was a much more serious matter, where the future of a continent stood at stake.

FRANKLIN AND THE DEFENSE OF PENNSYLVANIA

When, in 1747, Franklin for the first time spoke out on matters of foreign policy, these larger aspects of the conflict had not yet become as apparent as they were to become three or four years later. Nevertheless, it is significant that his concern with international relations did not originate in issues of commerce or foreign trade, which still loomed so large in the international affairs of that time. It was a threat to the security of Philadelphia toward the close of King George's War which called forth Franklin's first statement on foreign policy. The appearance in July, 1747, of French and Spanish privateers in Delaware Bay, capturing a ship coming from Antigua and murdering its captain, as well as rumors from the West Indies in the fall of that

year that French privateers planned to sack Philadelphia, aroused
the anxiety of responsible Philadelphia citizens, particularly of Franklin, who had already achieved a position of great prominence and
respectability in the city and who at that time, in his own words,
"had, on the whole, abundant reason to be satisfied with my being
established in Pennsylvania."[48] However, he added, "there were two
things which I regretted, there being no provision for defense, nor for
a compleat education of youth; no militia, nor any college."[49]

The menace of French and Spanish privateers afforded an opportunity
for Franklin to compose his first political tract.[50] The general ineffectiveness of the colonies with regard to efficient defense—owing to their
preoccupation with local affairs and their unwillingness to put aside
petty jealousies and quarrels—was increased in the case of Pennsylvania by its comparatively favorable geographic situation (protected
from the French by the northern colonies and from the Spanish by
the southern colonies) and, above all, by the tortuous efforts of the
Quakers to combine strict adherence to their pacifist beliefs with governmental responsibilities. Franklin's first political pronouncement, therefore, was formulated as an intentional repudiation of Quaker pacifism.
In *Plain Truth, or, Serious Considerations on the Present State of the
City of Philadelphia, and Province of Pennsylvania,* published under
the pseudonym "a Tradesman of Pennsylvania," he struck a note which
was to mark his political writings and speeches until the very end
of his life: the plea for unity as the indispensable prerequisite for
power and efficiency. "At present we are like the separate Filaments of
Flax before the Thread is form'd, without Strength, because without
Connection; but UNION would make us strong, and even formidable."[51]
This being the keynote of Franklin's appeal to his fellow-Pennsyl-
vanians, he proceeded to explain to his fellow-Philadelphians the
significant changes which had occurred in the international position
of Pennsylvania.

> The Length and Difficulty of our Bay and River have been thought so effectual
> a Security to us, that hitherto no Means have been entered into that might dis-
> courage an Attempt upon us, or prevent its succeeding.
> But whatever Security this might have been while both Country and City were
> poor, and the Advantage to be expected scarce worth the Hazard of an Attempt,
> it is now doubted whether we can any longer safely depend upon it. Our Wealth,
> of late years much encreas'd, is one strong Temptation, our defenceless State
> another, to induce an Enemy to attack us.[52]

The reference to wealth as a source of temptation for foreign aggressors was, of course, an almost self-evident argument in the age of mercantilism. But, more particularly, Franklin was addressing a very commercially minded community. After dealing briefly with another danger which might threaten from the opposite direction—the Indians —he turned again to his main argument, the menace to the commercial interests of the Philadelphians:

> But whatever different Opinions we have of our Security in other Respects, our TRADE, all seem to agree, is in Danger of being ruin'd in another Year. The great Success of our Enemies, in two different Cruizes this last Summer in our Bay, must give them the greatest Encouragement to repeat more frequently their Visits, the Profit being almost certain, and the Risque next to nothing. . . . Will not the Consequences be, a discouraging of many of the Vessels that us'd to come from other Places to purchase our Produce, and thereby a Turning of the Trade to Ports that can be entered with less danger, and capable of furnishing them with the same Commodities, as *New York*, &c?[53]

After attempting to frighten his countrymen with the prospect of losing many of their trading opportunities to rival colonies and rival ports and having faced them with the danger of commercial decay and decline, Franklin supported and surrounded his discussion of the material interests with the powerful rhetoric of patriotism. Moral arguments had to supplement his appeal to self-interest. He scornfully attacked the selfishness of the big merchants opposed to the Quakers and the other groups of the community, comparing them to one who "refused to pump in a sinking Ship, because one on board, whom he hated, would be saved by it as well as himself."[54] Franklin's indignation with these people could rise to great heights of eloquence:

> Yet the Quakers have *Conscience* to plead for their Resolution not to fight, which these Gentlemen have not. *Conscience* with you, Gentlemen, is on the other Side of the Question: Conscience enjoins it as a DUTY on you (and indeed I think it such on every Man) to defend your Country, your Friends, your aged Parents, your Wives, and helpless Children: And yet you resolve not to perform this duty, but act *contrary* to *your own* Consciences, because the Quakers act *according to theirs*. . . . But such, it seems, is the Unhappiness of human Nature, that our Passions, when violent, often are too hard for the united force of Reason, Duty, and Religion.[55]

Having railed at the narrow-mindedness of the big merchants, justified neither by enlightened self-interest nor by moral commands, Franklin turned to one decisive obstacle to an efficient enforcement of security measures which was peculiar to Pennsylvania among all the other colonies: the religious pacifism of the Quakers. The actual responsibilities of government had involved some sacrifice of principle and of nonviolence even in internal affairs. The dilemma between political responsibility and religious principle evidently presented itself in particular sharpness in the realm of defense or foreign affairs.

Franklin devotes some pages of his *Autobiography* to this question. He describes the difficulties and inconsistencies of the Quakers in a very good-natured and inoffensive way, but one cannot help feeling that he sometimes relishes his account when he finds them caught in the pitfalls of hypocrisy. Franklin tells how his long service in the Pennsylvania Assembly gave him "frequent opportunities of seeing the embarrassment given them by their principle against war, whenever application was made to them, by order of the crown, to grant aids for military purposes."[56] He does not hesitate to point out that they employed "a variety of evasions to avoid complying, and modes of disguising the compliance when it became unavoidable." The common mode at last was "to grant money under the phrase of its being *'for the king's use,'* and never to inquire how it was applied."[57] Franklin, in fact, had come to the conclusion that "the defense of the country was not disagreeable to any of them, provided they were not requir'd to assist in it. And I found that a much greater number of them than I could have imagined, tho' against offensive war, were clearly for the defensive."[58]

The refusal of the Quakers to face straightforwardly the implications of governmental responsibilities with regard to security afforded an opportunity for Franklin to set forth, with a bluntness which rarely appears in his later writings, his views on the necessity of "power":

> Should we intreat them to consider, if not as Friends, at least as Legislators, that *Protection* is as truly due from the Government to the People, as *Obedience* from the People to the Government; and that if on account of their religious Scruples, they themselves could do no Act for our Defence, yet they might retire, relinquish their Power for a Season, quit the Helm to freer Hands during the present Tempest, to Hands chosen by their own Interest too, whose Prudence and Moderation, with regard to them, they might safely confide in, secure, from their own native Strength, of resuming again their present Stations, whenever it shall please them.[59]

Franklin's demand that the Quakers relinquish political power in emergency situations was fulfilled only nine years later, when the pressure of the Great War for the Empire finally induced ten Quakers to resign in order to avoid unnecessary trouble for the Assembly.[60]

Franklin contrasted the theorics of the Quakers with the views of the "very great part of the People"[61] and added significantly an allusion to the materially favorable situation of the Quakers, who, after all, had their brethren in England who would always stand by and help out.

Tho' *they* themselves may be resigned and easy under this naked, defenceless State of the Country, it is far otherwise with a very great Part of the People,—with *us,* who can have *no Confidence that God will protect those that neglect the use of rational Means for their Security;* nor have any Reason to hope, that our Losses, if we should suffer any, may be made up by Collections in our Favour at Home.[62]

The plea for unity in the face of danger, the demand for common effort, and the appeal to overcome the sectional jcalousies and selfish interests which tore Pennsylvania were the core of Franklin's argument. In *Plain Truth* one may see perhaps even more clearly than in any of his later writings how his call for harmony, for the "common good," on the domestic scene is tied up with considerations of safety from external interference. From *Plain Truth* onward, this line of argument accompanies most of Franklin's political writings.

Perhaps some in City, Towns and Plantations near the River, may say to themselves, *An* Indian *War on the Frontiers will not affect us; the Enemy will never come near our Habitations; let those concern'd take Care of themselves.* And others who live in the Country, when they are told of the Danger the City is in from Attempts by Sea, may say, *What is that to us? The Enemy will be satisfied with the Plunder of the Town, and never think it worth his while to visit our Plantations: let the Town take care of itself. . . .* But are these the Sentiments of true *Pennsylvanians,* of Fellow-Countrymen, or even of Men that have Common Sense or Goodness. . . . Are not the People of City and Country connected as Relations both by Blood and Marriage, and in Friendships equally dear? Are they not likewise united in Interest, and mutually useful and necessary to each other? . . .
. . . The very Fame of our Strength and Readiness would be a Means of Discouraging our Enemies; for 'tis a wise and true Saying, that *One Sword often keeps another in the Scabbard.* The Way to secure Peace is to be prepared for War. They that are on their Guard, and appear ready to receive their Adversaries, are in much less Danger of being attack'd, than the supine, secure and negligent.[63]

No clearer statement of that tragic paradox of political life, *Si vis pacem, para bellum,* could be found. In spite of the fact that Franklin during the War of Independence frequently repeated that "there was never a good war nor a bad peace"—often quoted as proof of his "pacifism"—and allowing for the fact that the paragraph above occurs in a tract written for public consumption, painting the seriousness of the situation in particularly strong colors, it may be justifiable to say that *Si vis pacem, para bellum,* presents Franklin's ultimate wisdom with regard to international politics. It has been contradicted by none of his actions. It would be a mistake to see in those words the expression of a warlike or ambitious spirit. We ought to note, however, that the emphasis in his writings lies on the prevention of war as well as on the importance of prestige or reputation for power. For Franklin there is nothing desirable in war itself. Unlike many other men of good will, he knew perfectly well, at any time of his life, how to distinguish the desirable, the possible, and the necessary.[64] Recognition of certain unpleasant facts did by no means imply of them moral approval. Franklin knew that the price of peace might be heavy but was worth paying.

Plain Truth, then, although called forth (as were all Franklin's political writings) by a special occasion, represents in some respects the most basic statement of his attitude toward international affairs. His concern for unity in Pennsylvania had to a large extent been caused by his clear recognition of threats from abroad. This time the foreign danger had come from the sea, and the city of Philadelphia had been menaced most directly. However, in *Plain Truth* Franklin did not fail to give warning of future conflicts in the West:

> And is our *Country,* any more than our City, altogether free from Danger? Perhaps not. We have, 'tis true, had a long Peace with the *Indians:* But it is a long Peace indeed, as well as a long Lane, that has no Ending. The *French* know the Power and Importance of the *Six Nations,* and spare no Artifice, Pains or Expence, to gain them to their Interest. . . . When They [the Indians] consider these Things, is there no Danger that, thro' Disgust at our Usage, joined with Fear of the *French* Power, and greater Confidence in their Promises and Protection than in ours, they may be wholly gained over by our Enemies, and join in the War against us?[65]

SECURITY THROUGH UNITY: FRANKLIN'S EFFORTS
FOR INTERCOLONIAL UNION

The next stage of Franklin's thought on foreign affairs was to a large extent determined by developments in the West. The continental struggle between the British and the French empires was to enter its decisive stage ofter 1750. The magnitude of the threat to the security of the British colonies induced Franklin to carry his call for unity one step further. His vision of political affairs transcended the limits of Pennsylvania and embraced the whole of the British colonies.

The westward movement, which gained momentum during the "truce" that separated King George's War from the Great War for the Empire, while encouraged by the British government in some cases, as in the Ohio Valley, was on the whole the result of private enterprise and initiative.[66] It was largely a migration of people "moving by small advances, motivated largely by their own personal desires."[67] This disorganized and competitive rather than co-operative way of moving westward, in striking contrast to the centralized and state-controlled expansion of the French Empire, was bound to lead to a disastrous deterioration of the relationship of the Colonials with the Indians, who more and more tended to succumb to the influence of the rationally planned French Indian policy.

The situation was further aggravated by intercolonial rivalry with regard to the West, whether trade or land speculation, "the major get-rich-quick activity of eighteenth century planters, merchants, and politicians, was concerned."[68] This rivalry was dominated by the fact that some of the colonies—particularly the middle colonies of Pennsylvania, Maryland, Delaware, and New Jersey—had definite western boundaries, limiting the opportunities for speculation, whereas other colonies, above all, Virginia, claimed territory from sea to sea.[69] It was only natural that the first concerted undertaking in western land speculation should come from Virginia: the Ohio Company, organized in 1747. The activities of the company were jealously watched in other less fortunately situated colonies, and particularly in Philadelphia, whose merchants felt a threat to their western trade.[70] In the landless colonies two devices were to be developed to check the exploitation of the West by one colony to the detriment of others: first, there was the idea of reducing the boundaries of colonies extending to the South Sea "to dimensions more convenient for the common purposes of government,"[71] as Franklin was to put it at Albany; and, second, the establishment of new colonies west of Pennsylvania.[72] The quarrels of competing land companies and colonies over conflicting charter claims and royal grants, however, were to develop fully only after the end of the war in the sixties and seventies.[73] In the fifties the Ohio Company found no substantial rival in Pennsylvania, torn by the conflict of the Proprietary and the Quaker parties, and these issues were overshadowed by troubles with the Indians and the clash with France.

Unity as a necessity of survival had already been called for by

James Logan in his memoir of 1732, which Franklin probably had read and copied before he began, in 1751, to write down his thoughts and ideas on matters of continental, even imperial, concern. The relationship with the Indians, of course, had always to be seen in the context of the gigantic continental empire of the French. Contrasting the salient features of the British and French regimes in North America, Logan said:

The whole Countrey [Canada] is further under one general Command which the People obey with such Alacrity that in case of any Attack they all fly on the first Notice to the Place of Danger as readily as in a Garrison on beating and Sounding a Call. They Fortify also wherever they come. But above all they are now Masters of almost all the Indians on the Eastern part of the main. . . . Thus the Indians are endeared and are very true to them, tho' were proper means used, it would not be very difficult to gain them by the Force of Interest, to which, tho' these People have no Estates, they are very much Attach'd. This is the present Condition of the French, while that of the British Colonies is too much the reverse. Each of them is a distinct Government wholly independent of each other, pursuing its own Interest and Subject to no General Command.[74]

Early in 1751 Franklin indorsed Archibald Kennedy's call for intercolonial management and control of Indian affairs. The printer James Parker, Franklin's business partner in New York, had sent him the manuscript of Kennedy's *The Importance of Gaining and Preserving the Friendship of the Indians to the British Interest, Considered*. Franklin replied to Parker on March 20, 1751:

I have, as you desire, read the Manuscript you sent me; and am of Opinion, with the publick-spirited Author, that securing the Friendship of the *Indians* is of the greatest Consequence to these Colonies; and that the surest means of doing it, are, to regulate the *Indian* Trade, so as to convince them, by Experience, that they may have the best and cheapest Goods, and the fairest Dealing from the *English;* and to unite the several Governments, so as to form a Strength that the *Indians* may depend on for Protection in Case of a Rupture with the *French;* or apprehend great Danger from, if they should break with us.[75]

Again, foreign affairs—the threat of the French in the background— loom larger than any other consideration in Franklin's mind. Again, as in *Plain Truth,* his stress lay on the importance of reputation for strength rather than on advocacy of the actual use of force except in emergency cases. "Every Thing relating to Indian Affairs and the Defence of the Colonies"[76] were the only two items which "might be properly put" under the management[77] of the General Council, which was to be formed by all the colonies and to be presided over by a governor-general appointed by the Crown.

Franklin's outline sheds a revealing light on his conception of politics. It throws into sharp relief two outstanding traits of his political thought which have been discussed in the preceding chapter: his grasp of power relationships, on the one hand, and his appreciation of reason as a temper in the conduct of human affairs,[78] on the other. These two traits, each of them taken alone, might lead to dangerous extremes. Power politics without "reasonableness" might lead to overambitious policies. Reasonableness alone might produce an easygoing optimism bound to be cruelly disappointed sooner or later. The common denominator of these two features of Franklin's political thought is "enlightened self-interest." His arguments for avoiding the pitfalls of intercolonial and intersectional jealousies and conflicts are a masterpiece of political reasoning:

> This Union of the Colonies, however necessary, I apprehend is not to be brought about by the Means that have hitherto been used for that Purpose. A Governor of one Colony, who happens from some circumstances in his own Government, to see the Necessity of such an Union, writes his Sentiments of the Matter to the other Governors, and desires them to recommend it to their respective Assemblies. . . . But Governors are often on ill Terms with their Assemblies, and seldom are the Men that have the most Influence among them.[79]

Instead, Franklin suggested that, for instance, the colony of New York might send "Ambassadors" to the other colonies to discuss the matter with leading Colonials and to bring about co-operation and union by the initiative of the Colonial assemblies themselves rather than on the initiative of officers of the Crown. Furthermore, he argued against imposing union on the colonies by Act of Parliament. "Enlightened self-interest" ought to overcome petty suspicions and conflicts:

> A voluntary Union entered into by the Colonies themselves, I think, would be preferable to one impos'd by Parliament; for it would be perhaps not much more difficult to procure, and more easy to alter and improve, as Circumstances should require and Experience direct. It would be a very strange Thing, if *Six Nations* of ignorant Savages should be capable of forming a Scheme for such an Union, and be able to execute it in such a Manner, as that it has subsisted Ages, and appears indissoluble; and yet that a like Union should be impracticable for ten or a Dozen *English* Colonies, to whom it is more necessary, and must be more advantageous; and who cannot be supposed to want an equal Understanding of their Interests.[80]

Another basic idea of Franklin's political thought, the idea of equality, is introduced into the discussion for an eminently practical purpose:

Perhaps if the Council were to meet successively at the Capitals of the several Colonies, they might thereby become better acquainted with the Circumstances, Interests, Strength, or Weakness, &c., of all, and thence be able to judge better of Measures propos'd from time to time: At least it might be more satisfactory to the Colonies, if this were propos'd as a Part of the Scheme; for a Preference might create Jealousy and Dislike.[81]

The appeal to expediency rather than right in measures advocating the greatest possible equality well illustrates Franklin's constant preoccupation with the psychology of politics.[82]

The gradual deterioration of relations with the Indians and with the French in the years after 1751 was to give Franklin another opportunity to demand united efforts of all colonies for their common security. In the *Pennsylvania Gazette* of May 9, 1754, after the French had taken possession of the forks of the Ohio, there appeared a woodcut of a snake separated into parts, representing the colonies, with the motto beneath it: "Join or Die." This woodcut illustrated an article which was probably written by Franklin and which in any case represented his feelings:

The confidence of the French in this undertaking seems well grounded in the present disunited state of the British colonies, and the extreme difficulty of bringing so many different governments and assemblies to agree to any speedy and effectual measures for our common defense and security; while our enemies have the great advantage of being under one direction, with one council, and one purse.[83]

This article preceded the Albany Congress by only a few weeks. For our purposes it will not be necessary to go into the details of the negotiations and to discuss to what extent the plan finally adopted embodied features of the different proposals which were laid before the assembly.[84] We shall content ourselves with an analysis of some relevant points of the *Short Hints towards a Scheme for Uniting the Northern Colonies,* which contains a sketch of the ideas Franklin submitted to the Congress, and then proceed to discuss Franklin's *Reasons and Motives on Which the Plan of Union Was Formed,* which he appended to the plan after it had been accepted for transmission to the respective assemblies, with the intention of justifying his action before the Pennsylvania Assembly.[85]

Franklin's Introduction to his *Reasons and Motives* succinctly sums up the core of the argument for union which he had made his own in 1751:

The commissioners from a number of the northern colonies, being met at Albany, . . . considering . . . that one principal encouragement to the French, in invading and insulting the British American dominions, was their knowledge of our disunited state, and of our weakness arising from such want of union; . . . the said commissioners, considering also the present encroachments of the French, and the mischievous consequences that may be expected from them, if not opposed with our force, came to an unanimous resolution; *That a union of the colonies is absolutely necessary for their preservation.*[86]

So far Franklin's reasoning presents nothing new. However, his papers relating to the Albany Plan are the first political writings in which his vision of political unity transcends the limits of the English colonies in two directions. In his letter to James Parker on Colonial union, Franklin had contented himself with the plea for closer Colonial union and defense, but a closer relationship with England through establishing the projected union by Act of Parliament had been explicitly rejected. The possibility or necessity of westward expansion had not been mentioned at all. This time, Franklin included an area of gigantic dimensions in the political unit which he thought essential for security and prosperity.

In striking contrast to his outline of 1751, Franklin now advocated in his *Short Hints* the establishment of the Colonial union by Act of Parliament,[87] a novelty which was adopted by the Albany Congress. His new attitude revealed that he recognized the failure of his appeal to the "enlightened self-interest" of the colonies. Now he looked to London for help and for authority.

The second new feature of Franklin's schemes for Colonial union is the very extensive interpretation which he gave to the meaning of "safety and defense." In his *Short Hints* he included the "Duty and Power of the Governor-General and Grand Council" to "make and support new settlements," to build forts, and to do "everything that shall be found necessary for the defence and support of the colonies in general, and increasing and extending their settlements, &c."[88] In the *Reasons and Motives* he considerably elaborated on his *Short Hints:*

The establishing of new colonies westward on the Ohio and the Lakes, a matter of considerable importance to the increase of British trade and power, to the breaking that of the French, and to the protection and security of our present colonies, would best be carried on by a joint union.[89]

A particular colony has scarce strength enough to extend itself by new settlements, at so great a distance from the old; but the joint force of the Union might suddenly establish a new colony or two in those parts, or extend an old colony to particular passes, greatly to the security of our present frontiers, increase of trade and people, breaking off the French communication between Canada and Louisiana, and speedy settlement of the intermediate lands.[90]

This program indeed opens new perspectives. The quest for security, the common-sense argument of strength through unity which, we must add, betrays clearly the Pennsylvanian's desire for curbing the claims of Virginia, is joined by a much larger vision of a powerfully expanding empire. Expansion is, to a very large extent, still a function of security: The joint colonies might be able to establish western settlements "suddenly," that is, they might act by surprise and antici-pate French advance movements or even forestall French counter-movements. More important, Franklin envisages "breaking off the French communication between Canada and Louisiana." It is interest-ing to remember that Logan's memoir, which was probably known to Franklin by this time, described Canada as "being considerable" and pointed out the great danger to the British colonies arising from the connection of Canada with Louisiana.[91]

Franklin's outline for increasing the security of the colonies, then, takes on enormous dimensions. Not content to unite the colonies only for the purpose of defense against the French, and convinced that the trans-Appalachian "security belt" had gone beyond recall, he proposed to reduce French power on the continent of America with radical means. Obviously, we have now reached a point in Franklin's thought where the mere concern for security, without losing its sincerity or its urgency, becomes blurred by and scarcely distinguishable from the dream of a powerful realm, offering millions of people of future generations safety and prosperity.

THE BEGINNINGS OF FRANKLIN'S EXPANSIONISM[92]

It has been said that Franklin at the Albany Congress "began to think of the founding of new colonies at the western frontier."[93] This is correct in so far as Franklin's papers relating to the Albany Con-gress contain his first explicit statement proposing new colonies in the West. Nevertheless, his proposals of 1754 must be seen in the context of an earlier paper of his which he had withheld from publica-tion since its composition in 1751. The first proof of Franklin's burning interest in westward expansion is to be found in his *Observations concerning the Increase of Mankind, Peopling of Countries, Etc.* The immediate occasion for writing the *Observations* was an Act of Parliament of 1750 which restricted, on the complaint of British ironmasters, the manufacturing of iron in Pennsylvania.[94] This gave Franklin an opportunity to take a position with regard to several important aspects of mercantilism. Before giving an account of his thoughts on this subject, we will have to mention very briefly some important modifications which were taking place in mercantilist colonial theories during the first half of the eighteenth century.

Colonial plantations had only gradually come to occupy an important place in English mercantilist thought. Even trade was not the first consideration when England began to protect herself with navigation laws. The political basis of mercantilism may be seen in the fact that "the first object even of the navigation acts was navigation not trade; and the building of ships, the breeding and increase of seamen, and the preservation and defense of the kingdom preceded trade, just as trade preceded plantations in the general scheme of things."[95]

From the middle 1680's onward, the value of the colonies received increasing attention from English mercantilist writers, who also pointed out how much more valuable the West Indies were compared with the continental colonies. It was axiomatic in this period of mercantilist thought that colonies ought to be situated in a climate different from that of the mother-country in order to furnish commodities which the mother-country itself could not produce. The West Indies, then, were a tremendous source of wealth to their respective European possessors and loomed large in the international politics of the eighteenth century. They fitted perfectly into the idea of a self-sufficient commercial empire. Some colonies in more northern regions, such as Newfoundland, were always highly appreciated because of their fisheries, which were a "nursery of seamen" and a source of naval strength. The continental possessions between Maryland and Nova Scotia, however, were considered a nuisance rather than an asset.[96] They were looked upon as competitors in the production of foodstuffs, in fisheries, in shipbuilding, and in the carrying trade. Colonies, according to the prevailing opinion at the turn of the century (1700), had to fulfil their main function as sources of supply rather than as markets for British manufactures.[97]

However, several factors contributed to a shift in emphasis. First of all, the War of the Spanish Succession enhanced the importance of naval stores relative to other Colonial products, like sugar and tobacco, which previously had been most valued.[98] Consequently, the northern colonies rose in significance for the mother-country. Furthermore, the increase of population of the northern colonies during the first half of the eighteenth century offered a new and rapidly expanding market for the growing British manufactures. The new tendency in mercantilism was well expressed by its first notable exponent, William Wood: The colonies "are of the utmost concern for us to preserve and encourage, and if we take care to preserve them from foreign insults and invasions they will, as they increase in people, probably consume much more of our manufactures than at present they do."[99]

This argument is the starting point from which Franklin develops his ideas on American expansion and attempts to combine his defense of Pennsylvanian and Colonial interests with mercantilist theories which, by definition, regarded colonies only in respect to their usefulness for the mother-country.

In his *Observations* Franklin disposes of the idea that American manufactures might become a threat to the mother-country by pointing out that manufactures could develop only in a densely populated country; the "natural livelyhood" of a country with a "middle population,"[100] that is, the American colonies, was agriculture. This generalization is indeed "one of the central ideas in Franklin's theory of population."[101] With its help, Franklin goes on to exploit the argument first proposed by Wood:

> But notwithstanding this Increase, so vast is the Territory of *North America,* that it will require many Ages to settle it fully; and, till it is fully settled, Labour will never be cheap here, where no Man continues long a Labourer for others, but gets a Plantation of his own, no Man continues long a Journeyman to a Trade, but goes among those new Settlers, and sets up for himself, &c. Hence Labour is no cheaper now in *Pennsylvania,* than it was 30 years ago, tho' so many Thousand labouring People have been imported.
>
> The Danger therefore of these Colonies interfering with their Mother Country in Trades that depend on Labour, Manufactures, &c., is too remote to require the attention of *Great Britain.*
>
> But in Proportion to the Increase of the Colonies, a vast Demand is growing for British Manufactures, a glorious Market wholly in the Power of *Britain,* in which Foreigners cannot interfere, which will increase in a short Time even beyond her Power of supplying, tho' her whole Trade should be to her Colonies: Therefore *Britain* should not too much restrain Manufactures in her Colonies. A wise and good Mother will not do it. To distress, is to weaken, and weakening the Children weakens the whole Family.[102]

In this passage we find in a nutshell the central idea of Franklin's concept of empire. He modifies the mercantilist concept of empire by insisting that the colonies ought not to be "distressed" by restraint and unconditional subordination to the mother-country.

Even more significant, however, is Franklin's elaboration of another cardinal point of mercantilist doctrine: the emphasis on population rather than territory as a source of wealth and power.[103] As Sir William Petty wrote in 1662 in a book which was known to Franklin: "Here in England is a false opinion that our Country is fully peopled . . . and a mistake, that the greatness and glory of a Prince lyeth rather in the extent of his Territory, then [sic] in the number, art, and industry of his people."[104] Numbers alone, of course, did not make up a country's wealth. Mercantilists were interested in a large number of working people. They abhorred idleness and frowned upon unjustified support for the poor which might encourage their unwillingness to work. Furthermore, mercantilists laid particular stress on the desirability of a dense rather than a large population; both these features of mercantilist thought are connected with their preference for manufactures as against agriculture. Franklin, in advocating American expansion, had to combat two mercantilist apprehensions: first of all, their distrust of the acquisition of large territories overseas and, second, the fear of some, though by no means of all, mercantilist writers that emigration to the colonies would result in depopulating and consequently mortally wounding the mother-country.[105]

Franklin attempts to dissipate mercantilist doubts about the expediency of acquiring large territories by elaborating on his theory that an increasing colonial population, if it finds an outlet in new territory, is not only not dangerous but, quite the contrary, even conducive to the greatness of the mother-country. However, it always is clear that, in developing his theory of population, Franklin's most personal interest concerns the prosperity and security of British North America in particular.

Franklin's theory is this: The essential point for the increase of people is the encouragement of marriages. Here the outstanding factor is the need for cheap and plentiful land which renders possible early and frequent marriages. The growth of population, consequently, proceeds at a much higher pace in America than in Europe. In fact, Franklin contended that, whereas in Europe there might be one marriage per year among one hundred people, in America there would be two; whereas European marriages would, on the average, have only four children, the possibility of young marriages in America would produce an average of eight children. He concluded that the American population ought to be doubled every twenty-five years. Franklin then went on to point out detrimental factors which would check the increase of population and which ought to be prevented: conquest by a foreign nation, loss of territory, loss of trade, loss of food, bad government and insecure property, and the introduction of slaves. His reasoning on the importance of trade and food follow well-known mercantilist lines.[106] Especially remarkable is his insistence on the importance of exports, which strongly betrays his concern with the relative power position of the British Empire; again it becomes apparent that at the time Franklin wrote the *Observations* he had already very much in mind the larger issue of the approaching continental struggle between British and French power.

> Foreign Luxuries and needless Manufactures, imported and used in a Nation, do, by the same Reasoning, increase the People of the Nation that furnishes them, and diminishes the People of the Nation that uses them. Laws, therefore, that prevent such Importations, and on the contrary promote the Exportation of Manufactures to be consumed in Foreign Countries, may be called (with the Respect to the People that make them) *generative Laws,* as, by increasing Subsistence they encourage Marriage. Such Laws likewise strengthen a Country, doubly, by increasing its own People and diminishing its Neighbours.
>
> Some *European* Nations prudently refuse to consume the Manufactures of *East-India:*—They should likewise forbid them to their Colonies; for the Gain to the Merchant is not to be compar'd with the Loss, by this Means, of People to the Nation.[107]

Very explicitly, then, Franklin puts political before economic considerations.

From Franklin's particular point of view, the question of territory is even more important. He refers, as he does frequently, to history in order to prove his point and tells how the Celtic Britons, driven into Wales by the conquering Saxons, and "crowded together in a barren Country insufficient to support such great Numbers, diminish'd 'till the People bore a Proportion to the Produce."[108] It is not unfair to suggest what Franklin had in mind when he wrote these lines: the feeling of encirclement, the fear of suffocation by the gigantic French Empire in the back of the colonies, which had been so eloquently expressed in James Logan's memoir and in the writings of other farsighted Colonials. Franklin's arguments all pile up until he finally breaks out into a cry for "living space," which may truly be said to represent the first conscious and comprehensive formulation of "Manifest Destiny":

> Hence the Prince that acquires new Territory, if he finds it vacant, or removes the Natives to give his own People Room; the Legislator that makes effectual Laws for promoting of Trade, increasing Employment, improving Land by more or better Tillage, providing more Food by Fisheries; securing Property, &c. and the Man that invents new Trades, Arts, or Manufactures, or new Improvements in Husbandry, may be properly called *Fathers* of their Nation, as they are the Cause of the Generation of Multitudes, by the Encouragement they afford to Marriage.[109]

Franklin's primary concerns, now as ever, were the security and the welfare of the colonies. However, he does not fail to link American and British interests together. The growth of America and the advantage of England are forged together:

> Thus there are suppos'd to be now upwards of One Million *English* Souls in *North-America,* (tho' 'tis thought scarce 80,000 have been brought over Sea,) and yet perhaps there is not one the fewer in *Britain,* but rather many more, on Account of the Employment the Colonies afford to Manufactures at Home. . . .
> In fine, a Nation well regulated is like a Polypus; take away a Limb, its Place is soon supply'd; cut it in two, and each deficient Part shall speedily grow out of the Part remaining. Thus if you have Room and Subsistence enough, as you may by dividing, make ten Polypes out of one, you may of one make ten Nations, equally populous and powerful; or rather increase a Nation ten fold in Numbers and Strength.[110]

This powerful vision of an expanding empire which in its great emphasis on the settling of new land and new territory goes considerably beyond the usual mercantilist ideas and envisages new notions of empire, even more, of "Manifest Destiny," is nevertheless set squarely within the framework of the basic assumptions of the age of mercantilism; that is, it takes into account the anarchy prevailing in international society, and there is as yet no trace of an ultimate harmony of interests which was to become the salient point in the thought of a suceeding age. Franklin never ceases to see expansion within the wider context of the international rivalry for survival and for predominance. Estimating that the one million colonists of 1751 would double every twenty-five years, he foresees the time when "the greatest Number of *Englishmen* will be on this Side the Water."[111]

> What an Accession of Power to the British Empire by Sea as well as Land! What Increase of Trade and Navigation! What Numbers of Ships and Seamen!

We have been here but little more than 100 years, and yet the force of our Privateers in the late War, united, was greater, both in Men and Guns, than that of the whole *British* Navy in Queen *Elizabeth's* Time. How important an Affair then to *Britain* is the present Treaty for settling the Bounds between her Colonies and the *French,* and how careful should she be to secure Room enough, since on the Room depends so much the Increase of her People.[112]

In his little work of 1751 we have, then, the first systematic expression of Franklin's expansionism. From this time onward, much of his thinking on foreign affairs, particularly during the Great War for the Empire, was in some respects a reiteration and elaboration of ideas which he had first developed in the *Observations* of 1751. This paper is of particular interest because in it one may discern those elements of Franklin's thought which were eventually to undermine many current notions of the mercantilist theory of international relations.

Franklin accepts many of the fundamental tenets of mercantilism. First of all, he accepts the fundamental assumption of international rivalry and anarchy; consequently, he is fully aware of the paramount significance of sea power for Great Britain, which appears above all in his reference to the increase of navigation and the number of ships and seamen. He also shares the crucial mercantilist idea of the importance of exports, and he is in tune with his time in frowning upon luxury and "unnecessary manufactures." Franklin's American environment and experience and his fervent interest in the security and the well-being of the colonies now lead him to stress and develop some mercantilist ideas out of proportion to the general mercantilist scheme of things. He shared with most mercantilists a belief in strength through numbers. However, with Franklin the "increase of mankind" becomes almost an obsession; it is the central point of his expansionism and the very core of his faith in the inescapable growth of American power, either within the framework of the British Empire or without and even against it.

Prompted by his desire to make the needs and interests of North America acceptable to the British mercantilists, Franklin also worked out a theory of agriculture which would fit into the mercantilist pattern. The opinion which condemned the mercantilist disregard for agriculture, and which was given currency by Adam Smith, has more recently been revised.[113] It has been pointed out that, in spite of the fact that the mercantilists were chiefly concerned with manufactures, they did not neglect the place which agriculture was to take in a self-contained empire. Franklin's stress on the importance of agriculture, then, was not unrelated to general mercantilist ideas. It was his position as an American which was to lead him toward an ever greater appreciation of agriculture and which was eventually to push him to a sweeping condemnation of mercantilism and to the acceptance of the physiocratic doctrine (of which more will be said later).

In the *Observations* there is comparatively little on the need for security, except in rather general terms. What impresses one in reading the *Observations* is the tremendously dynamic conception of the future development of British North America. Expansion is clearly "Manifest Destiny," even without and apart from the French menace which might justify expansion for purely strategic reasons, with the aim of erecting new bastions in defense of the old colonies. The dynamics of expansion override more humanitarian considerations even in the case of Franklin. With great candor and, which is even more interesting, without the slightest attempt for an "ideological pretext," he proclaimed that a prince "that acquires new Territory, if he finds it vacant, or *removes the Natives to give his own People Room*"[114] may properly be called the father of his nation.

The scant attention given to security considerations in the narrower sense in the *Observations* does not mean that Franklin underestimated their urgency. In 1751 he wrote a letter to James Parker in which he advocated Colonial union for the promotion of more efficient defense; and at the time of the Albany Congress the two great themes of Franklin's thought on international affairs—security and expansion—are combined in a powerful appeal for unity and co-ordinated advance toward the west. Furthermore, he had learned the lessons of intercolonial quarrels and discord, and he understood that survival and development depended upon the united effort of the whole British Empire.

From the time of the Albany Congress onward, these three concepts—security, expansion, and imperial unity—are almost inextricably interwoven as Franklin's thought developed along ever bolder lines. The ideas embodied in his remarks on the Albany Plan of Union were spelled out in greater detail and underpinned with much more subtle reasoning in his *Plan for Settling Two Western Colonies in North America, with Reasons for the Plan* written apparently soon after the Albany Congress. The idea of establishing new colonies reflects the desire of the landless colonies to circumvent the claims of the other colonies. However, there is no reason to depreciate the urgency of Franklin's concern for common defense because of these second thoughts. Discussing the project of a Philadelphia merchant whom he thought unequal to the task of setting up a settlement west of Pennsylvania—a project based on the *Plan*, drawn up by Franklin "to divert the Connecticut Emigrants from their design of Invading this Province" —he still insisted on the necessity of "a strong English Settlement or two in those Parts. I wish to see it done, and am almost indifferent how or by whom it is done."[115]

In Franklin's remarks on the Albany Plan, the main emphasis quite naturally had been on the strategic need for new settlements as outposts of the old. In the new project for the settling of western colonies there is for the first time an entirely candid avowal of the pressure of population which around mid-century broke through the traditional limits in the west and flowed over into the regions south and west of the Alleghenies.

> Our people, being confined to the country between the sea and the mountains, cannot much more increase in number; people increasing in proportion to their room and means of subsistence. . . .[116]

> And as there are already in the old colonies many thousands of families that are ready to swarm, wanting more land, the richness and natural advantage of the Ohio country would draw most of them thither, were there but a tolerable prospect of a safe settlement.[117]

The theory developed four or five years earlier in the *Observations concerning the Increase of Mankind* is now applied to the concrete problem of the Anglo-French contest for dominion in North America. The struggle over the "security belt" between the Appalachian range and the Mississippi is much more than merely a strategic affair. It is a struggle for "living space," to use this rather discredited term in its valid meaning.

> The great country back of the Appalachian Mountains, on both sides the Ohio, and between that river and the Lakes is now well known, both to the English and French, to be one of the finest in North America, for the extreme richness and fertility of the land; the healthy temperature of the air, and mildness of the climate; the plenty of hunting, fishing, and fowling; the facility of trade with the Indians; and the vast convenience of inland navigation or water-carriage by the Lakes and great rivers, many hundred of leagues around.
> From these natural advantages it must undoubtedly (perhaps in less than

another century) become a populous and powerful dominion; and a great accession of power either to England or France.[118]

The attraction of a fertile and healthy country and the pressure of settlers and traders from the old colonies toward the west are now tied up with the threat of the growing French power, with the fear of encirclement; but British mercantile interests are not forgotten:

If we longer delay to settle that country, and suffer them to possess it, . . . the French will increase much more, by that acquired room and plenty of subsistence, and become a great people behind us. . . . They will cut us from all commerce and alliance with the Western Indians, to the great prejudice of Britain, by preventing the sale and consumption of its manufactures.[119]

In a passage entirely characteristic of Franklin's vision of the "increase of mankind" which occupies such a fundamental place in his thought, he stretches "security considerations" very far indeed:

They [the French] will both in time of peace and war (as they have always done against New England) set the Indians on to harass our frontiers, kill and scalp our people, and drive in the advanced settlers; and so, in preventing our obtaining more subsistence by cultivating of new lands, they discourage our marriages, and keep our people from increasing; thus (if the expression may be allowed) killing thousands of our children before they are born.[120]

Franklin, in these words, proclaims the right of expansion as a good thing in itself. There is no "ideological disguise." He had only briefly dealt with the fact that "the French are now making open encroachments on these territories, in defiance of our known rights." He disdains to elaborate on these "known rights." Furthermore, he transcends the notion of expansion as mere defense for the old colonies, although he never loses sight of this vital aspect of the matter. Franklin, in fact, posits the right of the British people to increase and to accumulate wealth without any further justification. Expansion for defense and expansion for its own sake are merged into one powerful case for the immediate settlement of the western country.

If two strong colonies of English were settled between the Ohio and Lake Erie, in the places hereafter to be mentioned, these advantages might be expected:

1. They would be a great security to the frontiers of our other colonies, by preventing the incursions of the French and French Indians of Canada, on the back parts of Pennsylvania, Maryland, Virginia, and the Carolinas; . . .

2. The dreaded junction of the French settlements in Canada with those of Louisiana would be prevented.

3. In case of a war, it would be easy, from those new colonies, to annoy Louisiana, by going down the Ohio and Mississippi; and the southern part of Canada, by sailing over the Lakes, and thereby confine the French within narrower limits.

4. . . . . By means of the Lakes, the Ohio, and the Mississippi, our trade might be extended through a vast country, among many numerous and distant nations, greatly to the benefit of Britain.

5. The settlement of all the intermediate lands, between the present frontiers of our colonies on one side, and the Lakes and Mississippi, on the other, would be facilitated and speedily executed, to the great increase of Englishmen, English trade, and English power.[121]

Franklin goes still one step further and does not hesitate to reveal the ultimate consequences and goals of his proposals. Saying that the recovery of the Indian trade from the French would greatly weaken French power, he continues by pointing out that *"it seems highly probable, that in time they must be subjected to the British crown, or driven out of the country."*[122]

In conclusion one might observe two remarkable features of Franklin's reasoning in this *Plan for Settling Two Western Colonies.* Again, as four years before in the letter to James Parker on Colonial union, the appeal to the enlightened self-interest of the colonists seems to provide the core of Franklin's argument:

The difficulty of settling the first English colonies in America, at so great a distance from England, must have been vastly greater, than the settling these proposed new colonies; for it would be the interest and advantage of all the present colonies to support these new ones; as they would cover their frontiers, and prevent the growth of the French power behind or near their present settlements.[123]

Another outstanding trait is his pronounced emphasis on foresight as the mark of true statesmanship. Looking beyond immediate issues and prejudices to one's true interests distinguished Franklin from the majority of his contemporaries in Pennsylvania and in intercolonial politics. Again, he raises his warning voice and declares that to prevent evil is better than to cure it.

Such settlements may better be made now, than fifty years hence; because it is easier to settle ourselves, and thereby prevent the French settling there, as they seem now to intend, than to remove them when strongly settled.

If these settlements are postponed, then more forts and stronger, and more numerous and expensive garrisons must be established, to secure the country, prevent their settling, and secure our present frontiers; the charge of which may probably exceed the charge of the proposed settlements, and the advantage nothing near so great.[124]

However, Franklin knew very well that the intelligent comprehension of one's interest, which he himself constantly endeavored to practice, was not too common a virtue. His first great disappointment in this respect had been the unwillingness of the colonies to form a voluntary union without an Act of Parliament. The second disappointment was the failure of all concerned to bring the Albany Plan or a similar scheme into life. This gave Franklin an opportunity to indulge in melancholy meditations on the imperfection of human nature.

> But such mistakes are not new; history is full of the errors of states and princes.
> > "Look round the habitable world, how few
> > Know their own good, or, knowing it, pursue!"
> Those who govern, having much business on their hands, do not generally like to take the trouble of considering and carrying into execution new projects. The best public measures are therefore seldom *adopted from previous wisdom, but forc'd by the occasion*.[125]

Imperialism and the Great War for the Empire

Franklin's arguments in the *Plan*[126] still present the whole problem of territorial expansion very much from an American angle. However, the imperial point of view—in other words, seeing, without betrayal of American interests, the developments in North America under the perspective of the interests of the whole British Empire—from now onward takes on ever greater importance in Franklin's thought. The beginning of the decisive struggle, the Great War for the Empire, was, of course, instrumental in this shift of emphasis. He had faced squarely the imperial issues as early as 1751 in his *Observations,* which, however, were not published at that time. Now, in 1755, Governor Shirley of Massachusetts urged Franklin to consent to the publication of his tract.[127] The *Observations concerning the Increase of Mankind* appeared anonymously as an appendix to the already-mentioned pamphlet of William Clarke of Boston, *Observations on the Late and Present Conduct of the French.* The "division of labor" between Clarke and Franklin is highly interesting. It was left to Clarke to enumerate "his Majesty's undoubted Right to those Territories that the French have been and are now invading,"[128] whereas Franklin, who was never very legally minded (as John Jay was to discover to his dismay in 1782), contented himself with the sociological aspects of the matter.

In 1756 Franklin wrote a letter to George Whitefield, whom he held in high esteem, in which he indulged a little in daydreaming:

I sometimes wish that you and I were jointly employ'd by the Crown, to settle a Colony on the Ohio. I imagine we could do it effectually, and without putting the Nation to much expence. But I fear we shall never be called upon for such a service. What a glorious Thing it would be, to settle in that fine Country a large strong Body of Religious and Industrious People! What a security to the other Colonies; and Advantage to Britain, by Increasing her People, Territory, Strength and Commerce.[129]

The order in which Franklin enumerates his desiderata is very significant. Safety comes first; and his preoccupation with "the increase of Mankind" clearly appears in his estimation that people and territory were first among the advantages to Great Britain. New territory and more people would, so runs Franklin's familiar argument, create strength and encourage commerce.

Above all, the struggle for North America was viewed by Franklin in its imperial significance. This afforded him another opportunity to combat the mercantilist doctrine of the subordination of the colonies to the mother-country. "The British colonies bordering on the French are properly frontiers of the British empire,"[130] Franklin wrote to Governor Shirley, and he added forcefully that Colonials could not conceive that "by hazarding their lives and fortunes, in subduing and settling new countries, extending the dominion, and increasing the commerce of their mother nation, they have forfeited the native rights of Britons, which they think ought rather to have been given them, as due to such merit, if they had been before in a state of slavery."[131] There is almost a veiled threat in this passage: there is no respect for the letters of a law which does not correspond to the demands of equity. This foreshadows the revolutionary appeal to natural rights two decades later.

Even more remarkable is the facility with which Franklin propagates the *subduing*[132] and settling of new countries and the extension of dominion as a good thing. It seems almost more than a strange coincidence that on the very same day he wrote his letter to Governor Shirley there appeared in the *Pennsylvania Gazette* his *Dialogue between X, Y, & Z concerning the Present State of Affairs in Pennsylvania,* in which Franklin proclaimed that to die for our country's cause "is the sweetest of all deaths."[133]

The Great War for the Empire indeed marks the high tide of Franklin's "nationalism."[134] Even more revealing than his utterances made at the beginning of that great contest are his writings on the peace settlement which was to guarantee the durability of the gains of that war, bought at such a high price. Strangely enough, biographers of Franklin or analysts of his political ideas, while often referring to his famous Canada pamphlet, nevertheless have failed to give it that careful analysis which would be warranted in view of the fact that Franklin's *The Interest of Great Britain Considered with Regard to Her Colonies and the Acquisitions of Canada and Guadaloupe* presents his most systematic statement on international politics. On the other hand, those historians who have investigated most thoroughly the pamphlet war which was waged in England toward the end of the Great War for the Empire over the relative advantages of retaining either Canada or Guadeloupe, conquered from the French, do not see Franklin's arguments in the context of his earlier and later thought on the same subject. Furthermore, it seems that, in spite of the four most important examinations of the Canada-Guadeloupe controversy,[135] some points might legitimately be raised which have not sufficiently been made explicit in these four works and which take on a special meaning on the basis of our previous discussion of the issue "politics versus economics."

Earlier students have stressed the role of two colonial theories, the older one holding that colonies were chiefly or solely useful as a source of raw material, whereas the later view looked upon colonies above all as new markets for expanding British manufactures.[136] It has been said that "this more recent conception of dependencies won a notable victory in the treaty of peace."[137] Modern scholarship has come to the conclusion that by 1760 the emphasis on the value of colonies as more than merely sources of supply was not a novelty and that "a balanced opinion had long embraced both aspects."[138]

In contrast to the preceding War of Jenkins' Ear with Spain, which had largely been a contest of conflicting mercantile interests, the Great War for the Empire against France was "what the Spanish war was not, a matter of life and death."[139] The French were to be driven out of Canada "in order to cut off the root of all future wars. The statesmen and the mob alike believed this to be the real object of the struggle and the most necessary."[140]

Although the latest editor of Franklin's collected writings took over the traditional opinion of Franklin admirers that "the ingenuity and dexterity of the argument in this able and admirable pamphlet had much to do with the retention of Canada by Great Britain,"[141] there is no reason to believe that the pamphlet war greatly influenced or shaped ministerial decisions. However, the public controversy provides us with an admirable summary of theories and views on international relations at a crucial period of change. In many respects it can be said that in this controversy one may find the last great and most explicit defense of the mercantilist theory of international relations.

The controversy began with the *Letter Addressed to Two Great Men,* generally ascribed to John Douglas, later Bishop of Salisbury. The *Letter,* addressed to Newcastle and Pitt, discussed the over-all conditions of a stable peace. While not failing to point out the advantages of the expanding market on the North American continent, it squarely put the main issue before the readers in these words: "You must keep *Canada,* otherways you lay the Foundation of another War."[142] Douglas was anxious to point out that the acquisition of Canada, although no original war aim, was "besides being so reasonable in itself . . . perfectly agreeable to that Moderation expressed by his Majesty, in his Speech, of *not having entered into the War with Views of Ambition.* The Possession of *Canada,* is no View of Ambition; it is the only Security the *French* can give us, for their future Regard to Treaties."[143]

This statement called forth a series of vigorous counterattacks[144] which comprised all the typical arguments of the old mercantilist theories. Particularly remarkable among these writers is the distrust of "purely political" measures which are taken in violation of time-honored maxims supposed to satisfy commercial and political reasoning all at once. As this aspect of the controversy has been rather neglected, some characteristic quotations might here be given.

"Advantages of a merely political Kind," argued a writer who was possibly William Burke, a cousin of Edmund Burke, against the acquisition of Canada,

will be always more or less problematical; their exact Value can hardly ever come to be estimated; and the political System is itself subject to such Fluctuation, that what at one Time we may have sought with infinite Eagerness, and bought at an enormous Expence, by a Change, owing perhaps to the Death or Deposition of a foreign Prince, to a Love Intrigue, to personal Resentment, or possibly to mere Inconstancy and Caprice in those who govern, may be rendered in a Moment insignificant or useless, and even sometimes dangerous; but *there is no Situation in which Wealth is not Strength, and in which Commerce is not Wealth.* If Commerce is our Object, we know, and in all other cases we can at best only guess, what we acquire.[145]

This passage reveals a deep suspicion of commercially minded people against the "irrational" and often arbitrary measures of dynastic politics, as well as the search for a scheme which might lead politics into more rational channels. In the same mood the projects for Canada were attacked as irrational manifestations of giddy minds: the same writer speaks of the "passion of boundless Empire" which might be "flattered" by the acquisition of vast but unprofitable forests, and he conceded that there might perhaps be "something magnificent in such a Delusion."[146] Finally, the writer wants to debunk the hypocritical "security considerations" of the pro-Canada people: "Under the name of Security, we sought with Eagerness extensive and unprofitable Empire, and rejected moderate but lucrative Acquisition."[147]

But not only commercially minded people like the writer of the foregoing passages attacked the project to keep Canada. A man who put politics far above economics, whose views on the political ineptitude of merchants we have quoted in the introduction to this chapter, nonetheless came out against Canada and in favor of Guadeloupe. The anonymous author of *Reasons for Keeping Guadaloupe at a Peace, Preferable to Canada, Explained in Five Letters from a Gentleman in Guadaloupe to His Friend in London,* a writer who professed to look "upon Machiavel, or cardinal Richlieu, as much better patterns to follow in state affairs than Don Quixote,"[148] this author also admonished his readers "to leave the false and destructive ambition of extent of territory, to the more deluded part of the world to whom it may better agree."[149] "The having all North-America to ourselves, by acquiring Canada, dazzles the eyes, and blinds the understanding of giddy and unthinking people, as it is natural for the human mind to grasp at every appearance of wealth and grandeur."[150] This author spoke of Canada as "gilded pills of destruction"[151] and called his countrymen to reason and moderation.

In an earlier pamphlet William Burke also laid more stress upon political arguments. How little, Burke complained, do people "attend to Reason, or Justice, and often to their own most important Interests"[152] in the hour of success. He attacked the security concept put forward in Douglas' pamphlet by saying that to desire the Enemies whole Country upon no other Principle but that otherwise you cannot secure your own, is turning the Idea of mere Defence into the most dangerous of all Principles. It is leaving no Medium between Safety and Conquest. It is to suppose yourself never safe, whilst your Neighbour enjoys any Security.[153]

. . . Our real Dependence for keeping *France,* or any other Nation, true to her Engagements, must not be in demanding Securities, which no Nation whilst independent can give, but on our own Strength and our own Vigilance.[154]

Burke forcefully said that "the Genius and Dispositions of Nations, as well as Men, is best discerned by the use they make of Power."[155] Therefore he counseled that the "utmost rational Aim of our Ambition" should be directed to make the power of the nation "respectable rather than terrible."[156] Burke did not fail to refer to Montesquieu, who had given the most famous expression to the doctrine of the danger of large territories prevailing in his day. Burke warns the British not to follow the example of the Romans, the French, and the Spanish, who decayed because "they had attained a greater Power than they had wisdom sufficient to direct; for the sake of gratifying the passion of the Day, they lost sight of their lasting Interest."[157]

It was Burke's pamphlet which called forth Franklin's detailed refutation of the old mercantilist views.[158] *The Interest of Great Britain Considered with Regard to Her Colonies and the Acquisitions of Canada and Guadaloupe* appeared anonymously in London in 1760. Right at the beginning there are two reflections which are quite characteristic of Franklin. Again he thinks that foresight is a very commendable thing: "But as a peace, when it is made, may be made hastily; and as the unhappy continuance of the war affords us time to consider, among several advantages gain'd or to be gain'd, which of them may be most for our interest to retain, if some and not all may possibly be retained; I do not blame the public disquisition of these points, as premature or useless."[159] He expresses his belief in the virtues of discussion in a phrase very similar to the one used many years later in apologizing for party strife "in some American states":[160] "Light often arises from a collision of opinions, as fire from flint and steel; and if we can obtain the benefit of the *light,* without danger from the *heat* sometimes produc'd by controversy, why should we discourage it?"[161]

Burke had made a sharp distinction between acquisition based on "an original Right," on the one hand (meaning acquisition of "those Objects for which a Country went to War"), and on security, on the other.[162] He had come to the conclusion that the pro-Canada authors (in this case, Douglas) did "not claim *Canada* on a Principle of Right"[163] and that even "on the Principle of Security" the acquisition of all Canada was not necessary, as a more favorable boundary in North America comprising "all those important Posts and Communications by which alone *Canada* became in any Degree dangerous to us"[164] would eliminate all serious threats from this quarter of the world.

Franklin did not at all recognize this sharp distinction of right and security. He combats Burke's opinion that England ought to confine herself to those regions only that "were the objects for which we began the war."[165] Franklin retorts that "we did not make those claims because they were large enough for security, but because we could rightfully claim no more. Advantages gain'd in the course of this war may increase the extent of our rights. Our claims before the war contain'd some security; but that is no reason why we should neglect acquiring more when the demand of more is become reasonable."[166]

The startling statement of this passage is that "advantages gain'd in the course of this war may increase the extent of our rights." Franklin's use of the word "rightful" has nothing to do with a legalistic notion of rights confirmed by formal documents: the right is seen in the context of the power relationship with the enemy. Furthermore, the meaning of "reasonable" as used by Franklin is miles apart from that which we would expect to come from one of the reputedly most typical representatives of the Age of Reason. A "demand of more" becomes reasonable when it is backed by sufficient power; "reasonable" policy as seen by Franklin corresponds to the demands of a modern student of foreign policy that "commitments and power [ought to be] brought into balance."[167]

Franklin does not leave the matter at this point; he becomes still more specific when he attacks Burke's dictum that one ought not to require securities which "no nation while independent can give."[168] "No nation," Franklin rejoins, "that has carried on a war with disadvantage, and is unable to continue it, can be said, under such circumstances, to be *independent*."[169] This definitely amounts to the recognition of a fact of paramount importance which has been emphasized at the beginning of this chapter: that independence and dependence of a country do not depend so much on the letter of the law, on the existence of legal sovereignty, but that there are "degrees of independence," that independence is a relative matter contingent on the ever changing international power constellation.

Respect for the "independence" of one's enemy, so we may paraphrase Franklin's argument, never did and never will restrain any country from demanding additional security if it is in a power position to do so. "Farther security has always been deemed a motive with a conqueror to be less moderate; and even the vanquish'd insist upon security as a reason for demanding what they acknowledge they could not otherwise properly ask."[170] Franklin mentions several examples of recent history in order to drive home his point and, more particularly, in order to prove that France would be the last country to act with exaggerated respect for the independence of others. Franklin refers, among other examples, to the War of the Polish Succession of 1733, which France "commenced with declarations of her having no ambitious views, and which finished by a treaty at which the ministers of *France* repeatedly declared that she desired nothing for herself, in effect gained for her *Lorrain,* an indemnification ten times the value of all her *North American* possessions."[171] He puts his case in terms so outspoken as to leave no doubt whatsoever that the quest for security is at least as good a justification for conquest as legal rights based on hereditary or other titles confirmed by treaties. In other words, the quest for security itself becomes a right:

> In short, security and quiet of princes and states have ever been deemed sufficient reasons, when supported by power, for disposing of rights; and such disposition has never been looked on as want of moderation. It has always been the foundation of the most general treaties. The security of *Germany* was the argument for yielding considerable possessions there to the *Swedes:* and the security of *Europe* divided the *Spanish* monarchy by the partition treaty, made between powers who had no *other* right to dispose of any part of it. There can be no cession that is not supposed at least to increase the power of the party to whom it is made. It is enough that he has a right to ask it, and that he does it not merely to serve the purposes of a dangerous ambition.[172]

Franklin's sharp distinction between conquest for security's sake and conquest for the sake of ambition stands indeed in contrast to the opinion of Burke, who had pointed, not unreasonably, to the fallacy of making clear-cut distinctions between the drive for security and the drive for ambition. Burke pushed his argument to its logical extreme and complained that the sort of security asked for by the pro-Canada authors "is a Demand that extends infinitely in its Consequences, extends . . . to the utter Destruction of Mankind."[173] Upon this principle, Burke argued, there would remain the same disputes and the same wars "as long as we have any Nation near us."[174]

Franklin, however, had striking propositions at hand. The kind of reasoning which he developed here for the first time in refuting Burke's "debunking" of the security concept, we might mention in passing, was to play a great role in Franklin's negotiations with the British during and at the end of the War of Independence. Franklin now for the first time indicates that he did not believe that peace is unlimited; instead he held the view that the removal of certain concrete stumbling blocks and points of conflict once and for all could be conducive to peace and eventually even to good will. Franklin found Burke's universal extension of the security concept quite preposterous. Mockingly, Burke had said that the principle of the pro-Canadians applied to Europe would give the European powers a right to demand the surrender of French independence and sovereignty. Franklin, disgusted with such abstract reasoning, replied that of course "the circumstances of the two cases are widely different."[175] In Europe, he said,

we are separated by the best and clearest of boundaries, the ocean, and we have people in or near every part of our territory. Any attempt to encroach upon us, by building a fort, even in the obscurest corner of these islands, must therefore be known and prevented immediately. . . . In *America* it is quite otherwise. A vast wilderness thinly or scarce at all peopled, conceals with ease the march of troops and workmen. . . . But what is still worse, the wide-extended forests between our settlements and theirs are inhabited by barbarous tribes of savages, that delight in war, and take pride in murder, subjects properly neither of the *French* nor *English,* but strongly attach'd to the former by the art and indefatigable industry of priests, similarity of superstitions, and frequent family alliances. These are easily, and have been continually, instigated to fall upon and massacre our planters, even in times of full peace between the two crowns, to the certain diminution of our people and the contraction of our settlements. . . . Surely circumstances so widely different, may reasonably authorize different demands of security in *America,* from such as are usual or necessary in *Europe.*[176]

It has been seen that Franklin did not refrain from describing the sorry state of Indian affairs in, to say the least, one-sided terms, and he conspicuously failed to say anything about the misdeeds on the British frontier, about which he had been the first to complain when confronted with the problem of uniting and organizing Indian affairs on an intercolonial basis. On the other hand, his argument of the significance which "natural frontiers" do have for the degree of security of different states is unimpeachable. Franklin, as a matter of fact, used the same argument which was advanced by one of his adversaries with the intention of combating British expansion on the continent of North America; Franklin's opponent said:

> If this mother-country should be an island, and sensible that the greatest share of the blessings she enjoys are owing to her being an island, disengaged from the quarrels of the continent, then any colonies she could establish upon any large continent, might have the disadvantage of robbing her in a great measure of her natural and happy state of being an island, and engaging her in continental quarrels.[177]

This is an argument for isolationism. However, Franklin's anonymous opponent strives to avoid sources of conflict by withdrawing from the American continent (not altogether justly drawing a parallel with "European entanglements"), whereas Franklin attempts to eliminate conflict by the opposite policy of envisaging the gradual removal of the few foreign powers from the American continent. More particularly, he does not fail to draw his reader's attention to the healthy effects of the removal of the Dutch from the North American mainland: "Happy it prov'd to both nations" that Holland ceded the New Netherlands to England in 1674; peace has ever since continued between these two countries which would "have been frequently disturbed, if they had retained the possession of that country, bordering several hundred miles on our colonies of *Pensilvania* westward, *Connecticut* and the *Massachusetts* eastward."[178]

Franklin's ideas boil down to this: in the case of another armed conflict between England and France, England could avoid a two-front war. "We shall then, as it were, have our backs against a wall in America, the seacoast will be easily protected by our superior naval power."[179] He took care to make his argument as specific as possible:

> The security desirable in *America* may be considered as of three kinds. 1. A security of possession, that the *French* shall not drive us out of the country. 2. A security of our planters from the inroads of savages, and the murders committed by them. 3. A security that the *British* nation shall not be obliged, on every new war, to repeat the immense expence occasion'd by this, to defend its possessions in *America*.[180]

According to this pattern, Franklin took up Burke's suggestion that a strategically favorable boundary with forts in the most vital places would reduce French power in Canada to impotence. Franklin was willing to concede that Burke's proposal might be valuable as to the first kind of security, that is, it might be sufficient to stave off French attempts to invade the colonies; however, he immediately pointed out the costliness of such a procedure. As for the second point, protection against the Indians, Franklin rightly said that only "a wall like that of *China*" would be a sufficient security against Indian attacks instigated by the French. The third kind of security obviously could be achieved only by removing the source of the evil, that is, by keeping Canada.

Cutting off the roots of future conflict this way was indeed a much more radical device than relying on strength and vigilance as recommended by Burke. In masterly fashion Franklin counters Burke's apparently so "realistic" appeal to moderation united with strength. There may be administrations that would be less wise and prudent. Franklin combines the praise of the present regime and of "the best of kings" with the warning that "we cannot, we ought not to promise ourselves the uninterrupted continuance of those blessings."[181] "The safety of a considerable part of the state, and the interest of the whole are not to be trusted to the wisdom and vigor of future administrations, when a security is to be had more effectual, more constant, and much less expensive."[182]

Having established the gist of his argument, Franklin devotes the remaining thirty pages of the pamphlet to establishing American expansion in its own right, transcending the security appeal. He does so by refuting two other points which had been raised against the acquisition of Canada: the theory that the French in America were acting as a check upon the Colonial striving for independence and the old mercantilist doctrine that colonies with large territories and with an economic structure similar to the mother-country are undesirable.

With regard to the latter point, Franklin adds little new to the theories he had advanced as early as 1751 in his *Observations concerning the Increase of Mankind,* a work which was also published as an appendix to the Canada pamphlet. The writer of the Canada pamphlet relied heavily on the theories of "a very *able pen*"[183] on the demographic conditions of manufacturing and agricultural countries; Franklin, of

course, was referring to his own earlier work. However, this time he
devoted more space to his earlier arguments. New territory and westward expansion are represented by him as the only way to prevent the
growth of competitive American manufactures. Only very dense populations, Franklin repeated, are capable of producing many manufactures. Franklin does not hesitate to state his adherence to this theory in
somewhat brutal terms:

> Manufactures are founded in poverty. It is the multitude of poor without land
> in a country, and who must work for others at low wages or starve, that enables
> undertakers to carry on a manufacture, and afford it cheap enough to prevent the
> importation of the same kind from abroad, and to bear the expence of its own
> exportation.
> But no man who can have a piece of land of his own, sufficient by his labour
> to subsist his family in plenty, is poor enough to be a manufacturer, and work
> for a master. Hence while there is land enough in *America* for our people, there
> can never be manufactures to any amount or value.[184]

Franklin conceded to the frightened British mercantilists that the
population of the colonies increases much faster than that of the mother-
country. However, "the increase within the mountains only, would evidently make the comparative population equal to that of *Great Britain.*"[185] To limit the territorial expansion of the continental colonies
was the worst device which the English mercantilists could propose.
For some centuries, Franklin ventured to prophesy, the American
people would "spread through the whole tract of country, on this side
the *Mississippi,* and secured by *Canada* in our hands,"[186] and find its
occupation in agriculture.

Franklin did not leave it at that. He hastened to add political to
economic arguments. British trade, he pointed out, ought to keep
increasing for centuries to come, until America would be as densely
peopled as England, and so would British naval power, "because the
ocean is between us and them, and our ships and seamen must increase as that trade increases."[187]

Franklin now was back at his favorite theme: the increase of mankind. Again he points out, as he had done in the *Observations,* that
the increased demand for British manufactures would produce an
augmentation of the population of Britain itself. In a way entirely
characteristic of Franklin, he throws into relief the political implications of his theory: "Reflect how much greater our strength may be,
if numbers give strength, when our manufacturers shall occupy every

part of the island where they can possibly be subsisted."[188] We may remember Franklin's metaphor of the polypus-like growth of nations, that a limb taken away is soon supplied by a new one. This time he replaced this metaphor by a comparison: "The human body and the political differ in this, that the first is limited by nature to a certain stature, which, when attain'd, it cannot, ordinarily, exceed; the other by better government and more prudent police, as well as by change of manners and other circumstances, often takes fresh starts of growth, after being long at a stand; and may add tenfold to the dimensions it had for ages been confined to."[189]

Franklin now turns to the chief political argument of the anti-Canada writers, their apprehension that the continental colonies, unchecked by the fear of a French invasion, might be less in need of the mother-country and more ready to become independent. James Logan had recognized this argument as early as 1731 and had achieved a remarkable degree of objectivity for a Colonial when he said that "in Time it will Probably be the true Interest of both Britain and France to have each other's Colonies on the Continent Supported as the most Effective Check that could be thought of, to retain them on both sides in a sight of their Duty."[190] Franklin ingeniously countered this argument by pointing to the fact that in the case of Colonial aspirations for independence nothing could be more dangerous than "the neighbourhood of foreigners at enmity with the sovereign government, capable of giving either aid or an asylum, as the event shall require."[191]

However, as Logan himself did not fail to mention, the danger of revolution and independence was remote, provided that "the Colonies are treated with Tenderness and Humanity and not Considered only as Slavishly Subservient to the Interest of the Countrey they came from."[192] Now Franklin in the Canada pamphlet attached a strikingly similar condition to his assurance that a union of the colonies against the mother-country "is not merely improbable, it is impossible. . . . When I say such an union is impossible, I mean without the most grievous tyranny and oppression."[193]

Except for this—as Logan and Franklin hoped—unlikely emergency, there seemed to Franklin not the slightest chances for Colonial union and independence dreaded by the mercantilists.

Their jealousy of each other is so great, that however necessary an union of the colonies has long been, for their common defence and security against their enemies, and how sensible soever each colony has been of that necessity, yet they have never been able to effect such an union among themselves, nor even to agree in requesting the mother country to establish it for them. Nothing but the immediate command of the crown has been able to produce even the imperfect union, but lately seen there, of the forces of some colonies. If they could not agree to unite for their defence against the *French* and *Indians,* who were perpetually harassing their settlements, burning their villages, and murdering their people; can it reasonably be supposed there is any danger of their uniting against their own nation, which protects and encourages them, with which they have so many connections and ties of blood, interest and affection, and which 'tis well known they all love much more than they love one another?[194]

Franklin refers to the lessons of Roman history and praises the Roman *divide et impera* in order to prove his point. The Roman example taught the "security arising to the chief government from separate states among the governed." Roman policy in Greece, where autonomy was restored to the several states, ought to be pursued by England with regard to her colonies: *"Independence of each other, and separate interests,* tho' among a people united by common manners, language, and I may say religion, inferior neither in wisdom, bravery, nor their love of liberty, to the *Romans* themselves, was all the security the sovereigns wished for their sovereignty."[195]

This is one of the few allusions Franklin makes to the concept of a balance of power and must be taken with a grain of salt. Characteristically, he does not conceive or advocate a system of "checks and balances" of completely independent units. He does qualify his concept of separate interests by emphasis on the allegiance to certain common values, manners and religion, for instance. Furthermore, Franklin, who had a more grandiose vision of the American future than any other man of his generation, and who in his writings so explicitly envisaged the growth of America as a whole, and who had already devoted so much zeal and enthusiasm to the cause of Colonial union, could not think of pushing his suggestion, written for an English public, to an extreme and of supporting or propagating wholeheartedly a policy of playing off the different colonies against each other. The very idea of "checks" on the development of the colonies— and the policy of *divide et impera* inevitably would imply this—produced outcries of indignation from Franklin's pen (outcries which, incidentally, foretell his outrage about the British atrocities during the War of Independence which was to play such a decisive role at the peace negotiations of 1782). Burke's suggestion that the increase of Colonial population should be "checked" by leaving the French in Canada brought down the wrath of Franklin: "We have already seen in what manner the *French* and their *Indians check the growth* of our colonies. 'Tis a modest word, this, *check,* for massacring men, women and children."[196] The crime against the "increase of mankind" is the most horrible of all crimes in Franklin's imagination. Scornfully he suggests that

if it be, after all, thought necessary to *check* the growth of our colonies, give me leave to propose a method less cruel. . . . The method I mean is that which was dictated by the *Egyptian* policy, when the "infinite increase" of the *children of Israel* was apprehended as dangerous to the state. Let an act of parliament then be made, enjoining the colony midwives to stifle in the birth every third or fourth child. By this means you keep the colonies to their present size.[197]

More than ever, the manifest destiny of westward expansion appears as the ultimate goal of Franklin's political thought. New country for settlement is his outstanding concern, and, although he confesses to be far from thinking that "we have sugar-land enough," he objects to Guadeloupe for the reason that "a country *fully inhabited* by any nation is no proper possession for another of different language, manners and religion."[198] Only a few pages before this Franklin had made reference to Machiavelli with respect to the same point: "To this I shall add only the observation of *Machiavel,* in his *Prince,* that a government seldom long preserves its dominion over those who are foreigners to it; who, on the other hand, fall with great ease, and continue inseparably annexed to the government of their own nation, which he proves by the fate of the *English conquests* in *France.*"[199]

All this throws into relief the striking contrast which exists between European eighteenth-century diplomacy, paying little regard to peoples and nationalities, motivated either by dynastic considerations or by rational calculations of the balance of power, and Franklin's conception of foreign policy, based on his all-powerful desire of living space for a rapidly increasing people. His ideas must indeed be measured by the dimensions of the new continent from which they came. The dynamics of his expansionism cannot be equaled by any tendency of European diplomacy in the eighteenth century before the French Revolution.

The controversy about Canada versus Guadeloupe, seen from Franklin's point of view, indeed takes on much greater significance than it had for most of the English protagonists of the acquisition of Canada. For them, security rather than expansion for its own sake was influential in determining their preference for Canada. When Franklin concluded his argument that Guadeloupe was only a small addition to Britain's West Indian possessions, whereas "the value of *North America* is capable of an immense increase,"[200] much more was at stake for him than most of his British readers realized.

In view of this overriding objective, all "pacifism," to give that word a very broad meaning, vanished. As a matter of fact, between 1758 and 1761, Franklin was engaged in war propaganda. While the Canada pamphlet is the most serious and systematic statement of his views, he attempted to serve the same purpose by writing humorous or satirical pieces for the press, advocating the vigorous prosecution of the war until worth-while peace terms would be guaranteed.[201] At the end of 1758 Franklin endeavored to convince the public that the tremendous sum of twelve million pounds, the military costs for the coming year, was rightly spent "in pursuance of this just war."[202] Almost one year later he sent to the *London Chronicle* a "Description of Those Who, at Any Rate, Would Have a Peace with France." These people he stigmatized as actuated either by lust for power or by self-interest, that is, either as being jealous of the glorious deeds of Pitt's administrations or as putting commercial interests before the public good.[203] In December, 1759, Franklin published *Humorous Reasons for Restoring Canada,* in which he anticipated the arguments of his Canada pamphlet, presenting them in ironic form.[204] The best-known piece of Franklin's war propaganda appeared in August, 1761. This hoax purported to be a chapter of Tommaso Campanella's *De monarchia hispanica,* "Of the Meanes of Disposing the Enemie to Peace."[205] In this chapter Franklin-Campanella recommended the use of what we would call "psychological warfare." Spain should use English intellectuals "in low Estate, and pinched by Fortune,"[206] and employ their pens to weaken the courage and endurance of the British people:

Let them magnifie the Blessings of Peace, and enlarge mightily thereon, which is not unbecoming grave Divines and other Christian Men. Let them expatiate on the Miseries of Warre, the Waste of Christian Blood, the growing Scarcitie of Labourers and Workmen . . . the Increase and great Burthen of Taxes, and the impossibilitie of supplying much longer the expence of the contest; let them ticulars only, (thereby to excite Envie against those, who manage and provide for the same) while so prejudicial to the Commonweale and People in general . . . in this Warre of Wordes, the Avarice and Ambition, the Hopes and Fears, and all the Crowd of Human Passions will, in the minds of our enemies, be raised, armed, and put in array to fight for your Interests against the reall and substantiall Interest of their own Countries.[207]

So far could Franklin go in order to combat the defeatism and pacifism of those whose attitude might put into jeopardy the glorious acquisitions on the continent of North America.

Franklin's letters concerning the conquest and acquisition of Canada betray an excitement and enthusiasm which contrast strongly with the usual picture of the opportunistic and detached Franklin. The conquest of Canada inspired him to one of his most grandiose visions. His highest hopes seemed finally to be within his grasp. Franklin wrote to his friend, Lord Kames, the Scottish philosopher:

No one can more sincerely rejoice than I do, on the reduction of Canada; and this not merely as I am a colonist, but as I am a Briton. I have long been of opinion, that the *foundations of the future grandeur and stability of the British empire lie in America;* and though, like other foundations, they are low and little seen, they are, nevertheless, broad and strong enough to support the greatest political structure human wisdom ever yet erected. I am therefore by no means for restoring Canada. If we keep it, all the country from the St. Lawrence to Mississippi will in another century be filled with British people. Britain itself will become vastly more populous, by the immense increase of its commerce; the Atlantic sea will be covered with your trading ships; and your naval power, thence continually increasing, will extend your influence round the whole globe, and awe the world! If the French remain in Canada, they will continually harass our colonies by the Indians, impede if not prevent their growth; your progress to greatness will at best be slow, and give room for many accidents that may for ever prevent it. But I refrain, for I see you begin to think my notions extravagant, and look upon them as the ravings of a mad prophet.[208]

Poor Richard dreaming of greatness and glory rather than the way to wealth—it is an unusual, but nonetheless true, image of Franklin. Only rarely did he abandon himself so completely to the power of a vision, but the glorious results of the Great War for the Empire filled him with boundless joy. After the definite conclusion of the Treaty of Paris in 1763, which confirmed England's gain on the American continent, Franklin, who had in the meantime returned to Philadelphia, hastened to write a letter to his friend Strahan in London, "just to congratulate you on the glorious Peace you have made, the most advantageous for the British nation, in my Opinion, of any your Annals have recorded."[209] Significantly, Franklin in this moment of greatest satisfaction did not for a moment forget to look forward to still more grandiose victories: "As to the places left or restored to France, I conceive our strength will now soon increase to so great a degree in North America that in any future war we may with ease reduce them all; and therefore I look upon them as so many hostages or pledges of good behaviour from that perfidious nation."[210]

With the conclusion of the Great War for the Empire and the total reduction of French power on the continent, the quest for security had been fulfilled, the dream of empire had come true. From 1763 onward, foreign affairs naturally vanish from the horizon of the Colonials, and until 1775 there are only occasional references to affairs in Europe. However, it was in these years that Franklin, in innumerable painful attempts to conciliate the interests of England and America, developed ideas and experienced situations which were to determine his outlook on politics in general and foreign affairs in particular when, in 1776, he was called upon to assume a leading position in the United States first adventures in world politics. In the next chapter, therefore, we shall first discuss how there evolved in Franklin's thought a particular concern for the interest of America which, being at first compatible with, and almost indistinguishable from, the interests of the British Empire as a whole, gradually took shape and by 1776 was well able to exist independently from, and even in opposition to, the latter.

CHAPTER III

ENLIGHTENED SELF-INTEREST

THE AMBIGUITY OF NATIONAL INTEREST

AT THE age of twenty-three Franklin had already plunged into the controversies of politics with these words: "There is no Science, the Study of which is more useful and commendable than the Knowledge of the true Interest of one's Country."[1] The phrase "national interest," which has been called "a newcomer among diplomatic formulas,"[2] first achieved prominence in the England of the eighteenth century. It replaced earlier formulas, like the religious slogans of the wars of the Reformation and Counter Reformation, or terms like "national honor," the "king's honor," or "reason of state," which had been discredited by the whims and abuses of dynastic policies. The search for the "true interest" of a country betrays the quest for a rational policy, which marked the age of mercantilism and which found its expression in attempts to lay down mechanical laws of politics, like the balance of trade and the balance of power. Furthermore, the concern for the "national interest" rather than the glory of God or the king's honor was bound to be most prominent in a country which had overcome to a greater degree than most other nations the threat of religious or dynastic absolutism and in which economic interest groups had more influence on government affairs than they had in most Continental countries.

What content did Franklin give to his notion of "the true Interest of one's Country"? The first great crisis of the British Empire in which he was involved, the beginnings of the Seven Years' War and the Albany Plan of Union, gave him an opportunity to spell out his views on the subject: "It is, I suppose, agreed to be the general interest of any state, that its people be numerous and rich; men enough to fight in its defence, and enough to pay sufficient taxes to defray the charge; for these circumstances tend to the security of the state, and its protection from foreign power."[3]

In the doctrine of strict mercantilism the state was the uncontested unit of domestic as well as international politics. The national interest, therefore, had an unequivocal meaning. In the case of Franklin, however, his concept is complicated by the emergence of two factors which take away much of the sharpness and absoluteness of the mercantilist idea of the sovereign nation. As a matter of fact, his concept becomes so much blurred that we shall have to postpone the answer to a question which now might be raised, namely: To what sort of unit did Franklin refer when he spoke of "his country's interest" before 1776? Was it the sovereign kingdom of Great Britain? Was it not rather North America? Or possibly even Pennsylvania?

With this question we have already hinted at one of those two factors which complicate a mercantilist theory of politics in the case of Franklin: the fact that he learned to look upon politics not from one of the capitals of sovereign nation states, not from Paris or London, but from provincial or colonial centers like Philadelphia or Albany. The very fact that Franklin, the Colonial, in defense of his local interests, was forced to revolt against the prevalent opinion that the sovereign nation, the mother-country, alone was entitled to political decisions contributed to shake the compactness of "the sovereign state" in his thought.

This was also effected by a second factor: Franklin was a Whig, and the Whig state, as the forerunner of the liberal "night watchman" state, did not recognize the absolutist "L'État c'est moi," which was passing into oblivion, and it knew nothing of the state idolatry of ages to come. The body politic, so we discovered in the first chapter, ought, according to Franklin, to be founded on the principle of accountability. The state was no end in itself; the national interest could never become an absolute, because security, the ultimate goal of national interest, was only a purpose for which "equals united with equals."[4] The national interest, for Franklin, was not an abstraction; it was the common denominator for many personal needs. The political community was not a monolithic structure; it was designed to serve mutual security, advantages, and interests. At the bottom of Franklin's concept of every group interest—whether national, intra-, or supra-national—is this: "In every fair Connection, each Party should find its own Interest."[5] Mutuality and equality were the measuring rods which determined the value of political connections on every level, provincial, colonial, imperial, or even international. This principle runs through the whole of Franklin's political thought, and it has for him a fourfold importance. First of all, it was the fundamental rule of all business relations; second, it lay at the root of his theory of state; third, it was a defensive weapon of the Colonials against the encroachments of a mercantilistic mother-country, presuming on its right to subordinate the interests of the colonies to her own; and, fourth, it underlay, sometimes implicitly more than explicitly, Franklin's concept of international relations during his mission as America's first ambassador abroad. The first point cannot concern us in this study. The second aspect we have treated in the first chapter. Before analyzing the principles of Franklin's diplomatic mission in France, we must deal with the third point: Franklin's hope of bringing England to a more enlightened conception of her tasks and his final bitter disillusionment and disappointment.

Redressing the Balance: The Fight for Colonial Equality

Not the slightest attempt can be made here even to summarize the history of Franklin's unavailing efforts to establish a more satisfactory relationship between England and America.[6] In particular, we cannot touch at all upon the different constitutional devices which he suggested at different times for this purpose. Franklin's initial projects of including Colonials in the British Parliament, his subtle distinction between internal and external taxes, his final resort to the dominion theory (England and the colonies united in common allegiance to the Crown but not to Parliament)—these lie completely outside the scope of this study. However, if we leave the constitutional issues aside, there still remains the domain of Franklin's basic assumptions about the relationship between Great Britain and the American colonies. We shall endeavor to crystallize some of the fundamental principles which emerged in the course of time and which largely determined his attitude in 1776 when he embarked upon his new task as envoy to France.

We have already intimated that the peculiar quality of Franklin's thought on imperial and international relations derives from the contradiction which seems to be implied in the term "colonial mercantilist." Naturally, he was not willing to sacrifice the needs and interests of Pennsylvania or America to the demands of the mother-country. But Franklin always refused to think only in extreme alternatives. The alternative to subordination was not to fight: it was the attempt to make a fair bargain; it was to appeal to enlightened self-interest; it was to experiment with a "rational policy." A rational policy in the case of Franklin, and in contrast to many other figures of the Enlightenment, does not mean a blueprint for perfection. For Franklin it signifies this: "There is no human Scheme so perfect, but some Inconveniences may be objected to it: Yet when the Conveniences far exceed, the Scheme is judg'd rational, and fit to be executed."[7] Accordingly, he sets out in search of schemes which would bring conveniences to all participants. Franklin, in spite of many bitter disappointments, and sometimes against the inner voice of his experience and knowledge of human nature, never abandoned his hope that "reasonable sensible Men, can always make a reasonable Scheme appear such to other reasonable Men."[8] He believed that a rational policy might be devised "if People from the Knowledge of a Man's Interest do sometimes make a true Guess at his Designs; for *Interest,* they say, *will not Lie.*"[9]

In his first tract on political economy, *A Modest Enquiry into the Nature and Necessity of a Paper Currency,* written in 1729 at the age of twenty-three, Franklin already combined mercantilist analysis with the appeal to mutual interest. He argued that a plentiful currency would be "a means of making the Balance of our Trade more equal than it now is, if it does not give it in our Favour."[10] At the same time Franklin took pains to offer a consolation to the mother-country which to Englishmen, frightened by the decline of population, must have sounded rather doubtful:

And since a Plentiful Currency will be so great a Cause of advancing this Province in Trade and Riches, and increasing the Number of its People; which, tho' it will not sensibly lessen the Inhabitants of *Great Britain,* will occasion a much greater Vent and Demand for their Commodities here; and allowing that the Crown is the more powerful for its Subjects increasing in Wealth and Number, I cannot think it the Interest of *England* to oppose us in making as great a Sum of Paper Money here.[11]

From 1729 to the very eve of American independence, Franklin never failed to preach "what ought to be the Intention of both Countries, viz, mutual Strength, and mutual Advantage."[12] In 1751 he thought that it could not be the interest of England to oppose measures which would help the colonies: "A wise and good Mother will not do it. To distress, is to weaken, and weakening the Children weakens the whole Family."[13] The same argument reappears even more forcefully in one of Franklin's famous letters to Governor Shirley of Massachusetts after the Albany Congress: "The strength and wealth of the parts," he wrote in December, 1754, "is the strength and wealth of the whole; what imports it to the general state, whether a merchant, a smith, or a hatter, grow rich in Old or New England?"[14] Franklin repeated the theme "Let not *private Interests* obstruct *publick* Utility"[15] in hundreds of variations. But his lofty language about the general harmony and the public welfare[16] should not deceive us. Franklin's emphasis on the interests of the whole always implies the redressing of the balance in favor of the colonies, the establishment of truly "mutual" relationships.[17] The argument of 1729 and of 1754 is not changed in 1769 when he dealt with the effects of the American non-importation movement on the British Empire: "But I think, if the Union of the two Countries continues to subsist, it will not hurt the *general* Interest; for whatever Wealth Britain loses by the Failing of its Trade with the Colonies, America will gain; and the Crown will receive equal Aids from its Subjects upon the whole, if not greater."[18] In 1774 Franklin was still preaching the same story; only his words had become more embittered and threatening:

The ordaining of laws in favour of *one* part of the nation, to the prejudice and oppression of *another,* is certainly the most erroneous and mistaken policy. An *equal* dispensation of protection, rights, privileges, and advantages, is what every part is entitled to, and ought to enjoy; it being a matter of no moment to the state, whether a subject grows rich and flourishing on the Thames or the Ohio, in Edinburgh or Dublin. These measures never fail to create great and violent jealousies and animosities between the people favoured and the people oppressed; whence a total separation of affections, interests, political obligations, and all manner of connexions, necessarily ensue, by which the whole state is weakened, and perhaps ruined forever![19]

In view of the frequently stressed "opportunism" and the "pragmatic" attitude of Franklin, it seems essential to show how he insisted on the cardinal point of his ideas on imperial relations—equality of opportunity and mutuality of advantages—in almost the same words, in spite of occasional shifts in tactics, from 1729 until 1774, that is, until the very eve of his conversion to the advocacy of complete independence for the colonies.

Franklin did not fail to be specific about the needs which, in his opinion, were to provide the basis of a lasting and fruitful "fair connection":

No one doubts the Advantage of a strict Union between the Mother Country and the Colonies, if it may be obtain'd and preserv'd on equitable Terms. In every fair Connection, each Party should find its own Interest. Britain will find hers in our joining with her in every War she makes, to the greater Annoyance and Terror of her Enemies; in our Employment of her Manufactures, and Enriching of her Merchants by our Commerce; and her Government will feel some additional Strengthening of its Hands by the Disposition of our profitable Posts and Places. On our side, we have to expect the Protection she can afford us, and the Advantage of a common Umpire in our Disputes, thereby preventing Wars we might otherwise have with each other; so that we can without Interruption go on with our Improvements, and increase our Numbers. We ask no more from her, and she should not think of forcing more from us.[20]

This passage, written in 1773, actually presents the summing-up of Franklin's thought on imperial relations, stripped of the embellishments of moralizing phrases. These are the essentials of everything which had been building up in his mind during many decades, in which triumph had followed disappointments, and disillusion had come after the hour of greatest glory. This detailed exposition of reciprocal advantages fits exactly Franklin's definition of the national interest of 1754. Mutual security is the basic aim. The colonies expected protection; and they, in turn, were willing to contribute their share to imperial defense. Riches and numbers, Franklin had said, were the chief guarantees of strength and security. Britain will increase her wealth by the expanding market which continental America would offer for her manufactures and by the growing Atlantic commerce which would follow; as for the increase in numbers, Franklin's most cherished desideratum, America would take care of that. America could follow her path of westward expansion, and she could go on with her "improvements" only when she was undisturbed by "interruptions" from abroad. In Franklin's vision, Great Britain was destined to be America's shield.

However, not merely his apprehension of foreign danger but also the challenge of Colonial dissensions contributed to Franklin's conviction of the virtues of a "strict Union" between England and America. Although an elaboration of this point would go beyond the purpose of this essay, it must be mentioned that he apparently believed in Britain's role not only as the shield but also as the balancer of the colonies. The reader will recall that Franklin's first statement on intercolonial co-operation in 1751 did not advocate British interference.[21] The failure of this first appeal to the enlightened self-interest of the colonies caused him to look for more realistic devices to insure Colonial union. Disillusioned, but not less determined, Franklin at the Albany Congress gave his support to the idea of establishing Colonial union by an Act of the British Parliament, and he justified his change of attitude by the fact that "the colonies were seldom all in equal danger at the same time, or equally near the danger, or equally sensible of it; that some of them had particular interests to manage, with which a union might interfere; and that they were extremely jealous of each other."[22] The same lament about the hopeless disunity of the colonies occurs, as we have seen, in Franklin's Canada pamphlet of 1760. The sincerity of his argument in the Canada pamphlet, which excluded the possibility of Colonial union and rebellion against the mother-country except in case of extreme oppression, has sometimes been questioned.[23] However, the honesty of Franklin's reasoning seems established when seen in the light of his earlier bitter disappointment about the utter failure of the colonies to comprehend their own interests. Further evidence corroborates this point of view. During the conspiracy of Pontiac in 1763, which followed the end of the hostilities with the French, Franklin again had an occasion to complain. The colonies might ruin the Indians "in one Summer, and forever deter & disable them from future Attempts against us, yet we see & know that such Union is impracticable. . . . Thus, tho' strong, we are in Effect weak; and shall remain so, till you take some Measures at home to unite us."[24] Franklin's idea of Great Britain's acting as an umpire in Colonial disputes, even after he had given up the idea of British legislation for the colonies, consequently must be taken more seriously than it might appear on first sight.

THE CONCEPT OF THE COMMON GOOD

That the advantages of a "consolidating union," of strength through unity, were worthy of the greatest efforts, Franklin never failed to proclaim and to act accordingly. As a matter of fact, he took considerable pride in his exertions to mediate and to bring about unity on the provincial, the colonial, and the imperial level. Compromise and reconciliation were raised by Franklin to the high honor of political virtues. His comment on the sad fate of the Albany Plan is characteristic: "Its fate was singular: the assemblies did not adopt it, as they all thought there was too much *prerogative* in it, and in England it was judg'd to have too much of the *democratic*. . . . The different and contrary reasons of dislike to my plan makes me suspect that it was really the true medium."[25]

With regard to Anglo-American relationships, Franklin adopted the same attitude. In 1774, when his position in England had been shaken by the famous affair of the Hutchinson letters, which had resulted in his dismissal as deputy postmaster-general of the colonies, he wrote a paper in his own defense in which he explicitly tried to "explain the Principles on which I have acted."

> It has long appeared to me, that the only true British Politicks were those which aim'd at the Good of the *Whole British Empire,* not that which sought the Advantage of *one Part* in the Disadvantage of the others; therefore . . . every Abridgment of the Power of the Mother Country, where that Power was not prejudicial to the Liberties of the Colonists, and every Diminution of the Privileges of the Colonists, where they were not prejudicial to the Welfare of the Mo. Country, I, in my own Mind, condemned as improper, partial, unjust, and mischievous; tending to create Dissensions, and weaken that Union, on which the Strength, Solidity, and Duration of the Empire greatly depended; and I opposed, as far as my little Powers went, all Proceedings, either here or in America, that in my Opinion had such Tendency. Hence it has often happened to me, that while I have been thought here too much of an American, I have in America been deem'd too much of an Englishman.[26]

Franklin's constant admonitions to sacrifice selfish and petty jealousies on the altar of the common good, his ever recurring appeal for the equalization of burdens and profits, seem to introduce a strong moralistic flavor into his reasoning. To serve the public welfare, to further the commonweal, appears sometimes as a high achievement of generosity and altruism. Franklin himself is at times, rather misleadingly, given to this interpretation of the common good. In the Canada pamphlet he was anxious to depict American participation in the Great War for the Empire in this light. That this was not a war waged for the cause of the colonies only, Franklin replied angrily and with full justification to English critics who tried to represent the conquest of Canada as a gratuitous act of satisfying Colonial ambitions without materially promoting England's interest. By a curious twist of the argument, he himself finishes by falling into the error with which he so vehemently reproaches his adversaries:

It will not be a conquest for them, nor gratify any vain ambition of theirs. It will be a conquest for the whole; and all our people will, in the increase of trade, and the ease of taxes, find the advantage of it. . . . I hope it will appear before I end these sheets, that if ever there was a *national war,* this is truly such a one: a war in which the interest of the whole nation is directly and fundamentally concerned. *Those who would be thought deeply skilled in human nature, affect to discover self-interested views everywhere at the bottom of the fairest, the most generous conduct.*[27]

In his eagerness to prove the altruism of the British Colonials in fighting the Seven Years' War, Franklin sometimes went amazingly far beyond his own basic principle that "in every fair connection each party should find its own interest." In the Canada pamphlet, in fact, he represents Colonial participation in the war as an act of self-denial.

The inhabitants of them are, in common with the other subjects of *Great Britain,* anxious for the glory of her crown, the extent of her power and commerce, the welfare and future repose of the whole *British* people. They could not, therefore, but take a large share in the affronts offered to *Britain,* and have been animated with a truely *British spirit* to exert themselves beyond their strength, and *against their evident interest.*[28]

Franklin, it must be said, contradicted his own conviction, expressed in private letters[29] as well as by the fact of his pamphleteering for the cause of a "glorious peace." He falsified history and did much less than justice to his own course of action when he continued in the years to follow to present an altruistic picture of American motivation in the war. In 1766, in his famous interrogation in the House of Commons concerning the merits and demerits of the Stamp Act, which contributed to the repeal of the act, Franklin also presented his theory of empire in moralistic dress. The mutuality which in fact was for him the only sound principle of "common interests" and which openly appears in his private letters is in public clouded by the moralistic contrast of egoistic selfish interests versus the altruistic "common good."

I know the last war is commonly spoke of here, as entered into for the defence, or for the sake, of the people of North America. I think it is quite misunderstood. It began about the limits between Canada and Nova-Scotia; about territories to which the Crown indeed laid claim, but were not claimed by any British Colony; none of the lands had been granted to any colonist; we had therefore no particular concern or interest in that dispute. As to the Ohio, the contest there began about your right of trading in the Indian country. . . . The colonies . . . were . . . in perfect peace with both French and Indians; the troops were not, therefore, sent for their defence.

The trade with the Indians, though carried on in America, is not an American interest. The people of America are chiefly farmers and planters. . . . The Indian trade is a British interest . . . therefore the war, as it commenced for the defence of territories of the Crown the property of no American, and for the defence of a trade purely British, was really a British war, and yet the people of America made no scruple of contributing their utmost towards carrying it on, and bringing it to a happy conclusion.[30]

This statement must have startled the House of Commons, and Franklin, asked whether he really thought that "the taking possession of the King's territorial rights, and strengthening the frontiers, is not an American interest"—which was, of course, precisely the gist of Franklin's original reasoning—was forced to retract somewhat his all-too-pointed contention; but, still, he only conceded that it was not "particularly" an American interest but "conjointly a British and an American interest."[31] Yet in the next year he wrote in an article that it was "a British interest, that was to be defended and secured by that war."[32] One begins to wonder what had happened to Franklin's holy fervor for the increase of mankind and his vision of "Manifest Destiny" when he—under the disguise of an anonymous Englishman—rather disingenuously declares it "a certain truth that we went to war with the French in America, merely on a dispute between the two Crowns, concerning the bounds of wilderness lands, belonging to no American, and to secure the Indian trade carried on there with our manufactures, and therefore *solely an interest of ours.*"[33]

One wonders whether Franklin himself finished by believing this new theory of the Great War for the Empire. In or shortly after 1770 he countered the argument of an English pamphleteer that through England's action in the war the colonies "are not apprehensive *now* of the French, nor Indians"[34] with this astonishing comment: "Never were apprehensive of the Indians, nor much of the French. As much expos'd to Danger from the Indians now as ever."[35] Possibly this exaggeration is partly due to Franklin's anger about the opposite error —that England displayed sheer altruism in her Great War for the Empire—which was advanced by Wheelock and many other English writers. Their contention was that "Great Britain has been so generous as to spend an infinite quantity of blood and treasure, to procure them [the colonists] secure settlements in America."[36] Franklin found this pretension "most iniquitous" and noted down that the moving force in the war was rather to be seen in the "clothiers of Yorkshire & the West, or the Smiths & Cutlers of Sheffield, or the Button-makers of

Birmingham." "Was it not to secure & extend their Trade & the Vent
for their Manufactures, that you fought in America; and did not the
Colonies raise and maintain Man for Man with you to fight these
Battles."[37] This marginal note is directly contradicted by Franklin's
exclamation in his Canada pamphlet: "Would it be fair to represent
such a war merely as blood and treasure spent in the cause of the
weavers of *Yorkshire, Norwich,* or the *West,* the cutlers of *Sheffield,*
or the button-makers of *Birmingham?*"[38]

The thesis of England's "selfish" and largely mercantile purposes
in the Great War for the Empire has finally become a part of the
American tradition, to the formation of which Tom Paine's *Common
Sense* greatly contributed. Paine's argument that America had lost
rather than gained by her entanglement in "British" wars may, of
course, partly be explained by the peculiar circumstances and objectives at the time of its publication (January, 1776). But this does
not help us to understand Franklin's about-face. L. H. Gipson has suggested the original reasons for the emergence of this strange theory.
Partly, he argues, it arose from "Pitt's zealous efforts to energize the
colonies to prosecute the war most actively." Another important
element, however, was the fact that before the conclusion of the war
in 1763 certain powerful commercial interests, situated mainly in
Newport, Rhode Island, Boston, and New York, and to a lesser extent in Philadelphia, wanted to carry on a very profitable trade with
the French West Indies and therefore began to speak about the war
in terms which depicted it as a purely English affair, whereas the
French were supposed to be quite friendly to the desires of the
British Colonials.[39]

It seems to us, however, that it must remain a matter of speculation
how profoundly, if at all, Franklin was convinced of this new theory.
It appears strange that Franklin would have been capable of such an
extraordinary act of self-delusion. After all, as late as February, 1765,
he still praised the benefits of the war: "The French being now totally
remov'd from North America, we may, I think, expect the Indians will
be more manageable for the future."[40] And even in 1775 Franklin still
was prepared to concede that "in the last war, it is true, Britain sent a
fleet and army, who acted with an equal army of ours, in the reduction
of Canada; and perhaps thereby did more for us, than we in the preceding wars had done for her."[41]

The contention that the Great War for the Empire was solely an English affair indeed presents a strange extreme of Franklin's position. But the altruistic hue which he gave to his customary utterances on the common good or the general welfare, the scorn which he pours on those pessimistic and defeatist people who explain every action as caused by the wicked motive of self-interest and who ridicule nobler and more generous urges in human nature, is very characteristic of his way of expression, although it may somewhat distort his true reasoning. Franklin basically did not argue for generosity instead of self-interest but rather for a rational, enlightened conception of true long-term interests instead of unenlightened views of seeming immediate self-interest blurred by the irrational factors of passion and pride. In public, he usually found it appropriate to use the language of moral admonition, of indignation, but at times he thought that blunt talk could do a better job. In 1770, for instance, Franklin talked with a frankness which contradicted his more edifying words of years past: "It is an Insult on common Sense to affect an Appearance of Generosity in a Matter of obvious Interest. Is it Generosity that prompts the Rustick to feed his Cow, which yields him milk? Could we have been enriched by our Colonies, if we had not defended them from the common Enemy?"[42]

On the one hand, Franklin held that policies founded on generosity were nonsense. On the other hand, he combated—one is almost inclined to say "fanatically"—the opposite and much more common error of building political structures on the dangerously unstable pillars of honor and pride. Franklin knew perfectly well that, in order to guarantee mutual long-term interests, adjustments had to be made with regard to nonessentials. He was driven to spell out his views on this subject by the reluctance of the British administration to repeal completely the duties offensive to the colonies and to abandon the right to legislate for the colonies. British statesmen sometimes were hesitant to repeal those which they had recognized as detrimental to a solution of the Anglo-American conflict because of the great value which they—in principle not unjustly—attributed to reputation and prestige.

They cannot bear the Denial of the Right of Parliament to make them, tho' they acknowledge they ought not to have been made. They fear being despis'd by all the Nations around if they repeal them; and they say it is of great Impor-

tance to this Nation that the World should see it is Master of its Colonies, otherwise its enemies on a Conceit of its weakness, might be encourag'd to insult it.
On the other hand, they are really afraid of provoking the Colonies too far, lest
a Rupture should become inevitable, and the old Enemies of the Nation take
Advantage of it.[43]

Franklin never tired of driving home to the British leaders that
"the Honour of Parliament and of the Nation, is best maintain'd by
rectifying what it has done improperly as soon as it can be convinc'd
of it, and not by being obstinate in the Wrong."[44] While he was working toward the repeal of the Stamp Act, he was particularly insistent
on this point; he thought "it a mistaken opinion, that the honour
and dignity of government is better supported by persisting in a wrong
measure once entered into, than by rectifying an error as soon as it is
discovered."[45] This opinion may undoubtedly be taken as truly representative of Franklin's innermost thought. He revealed, probably
unintentionally, how worldly he considered his own wisdom to be
when he tried to counter the prestige considerations of British statesmen not with appeals to Christian self-sacrifice and generosity but
with the appeal to "the wisdom of the serpent." Franklin's two strains
of thought, his belief in the realities of power as well as his striving
for equality, although often contradictory, this time are joined in
one very characteristic statement:

Mankind have so far learned the wisdom of the serpent, as, I believe, to prefer
interest to a point of honour, especially when, as in this case, the interest is very
considerable. Whatever the private opinions of Gentlemen may be on this head,
the Trustees of the People, for such every Member of Parliament is, should here
consider the real interest of that people, and be determined by it.[46]

Franklin sincerely believed that enlightened self-interest could provide a firm basis for mutual understanding. America herself would
probably profit more from such a basis of mutual good will than from
the principle of *divide et impera*. "The internal Divisions of this Kingdom, tho' bad in themselves, may perhaps produce some Advantage to
us, or at least lessen the Mischiefs some threaten us with;—but it is
rather to be wish'd Government would relieve & treat us fairly
from Principles of Wisdom and Equity."[47]

One may be sure that this phrase, written in a private letter to an
American who as ardently as Franklin worked for some kind of
reconciliation, presents Franklin's true desire. Because he was deeply
convinced that England's real interests were on the side of mutual

understanding, he could not but see in the factional strife which divided England and in her failure to come to grips with the American problem the sad signs of a nation which passion and pride had pushed near an abyss.

England's Pride

The realization that relations between England and America had to be settled by force rather than good will was a slow and painful process in Franklin's mind. There is much evidence that Franklin, who intellectually and culturally was an Englishman and who occasionally contemplated settling down in England in the midst of admiring friends,[48] was emotionally deeply upset by the approaching break. Furthermore, we ought to consider that the failure of Anglo-American understanding in the 1760's and 1770's was already the second instance in his political experience where his faith in man's capacity to recognize his own true interests had been profoundly shattered; Franklin's increasing bitterness about the disastrous course of British politics must also be seen against the background of his first disappointment with regard to the discords and jealousies of the British colonies in the 1750's and early 1760's, when he had addressed himself for help to Great Britain.

"The pride of this people cannot bear the thought" of a *"Consolidating Union,"* Franklin wrote in exasperation to his philosopher friend in Scotland, Lord Kames; "every man in England seems to consider himself as a piece of a sovereign over America; seems to jostle himself into the throne with the King, and talks of *our subjects in the Colonies."*[49] Franklin could reach great heights of eloquence when he uttered his Cassandra-like warnings: "Providence will bring about its own ends by its own means; and if it intends the downfall of a nation, that nation will be so blinded by its pride and other passions, as not to see its danger, or how its fall may be prevented."[50] The "internal dissension" of England, the state of English politics at the time of Franklin's mission in London, thoroughly disgusted him. He knew that strength could come only through unity as well as that the passions of party strife necessarily clouded the perception of one's true interests.[51] Franklin wrote to Joseph Galloway:

A melancholy thing it is to consider, that, instead of employing the present leisure of peace in such measures as might extend our commerce, pay off our debts, secure allies, and increase the strength and ability of the nation to support a future war, the whole seems to be wasted in party contentions about places of power and profit, in court intrigues and cabals, and in abusing one another.[52]

At another time he referred to the precarious economic situation in England in 1773 as the "blessed Effects of Pride, Pique, and Passion in Government, which should have no Passions."[53] "Passion governs, and she never governs wisely"[54]—this was the conclusion which a sadder and disillusioned Franklin drew from the failure of his mission at the eve of his departure for America.

Franklin's exasperation, bitterness, and disillusionment about Britain's folly have found their best-known expression in two satirical pieces published in September, 1773, *An Edict by the King of Prussia* and *Rules by Which a Great Empire May Be Reduced to a Small One*. In the first hoax, he threw into relief the absurdities of Great Britain's claims on the American colonies by depicting them as demands of Frederick the Great upon the British people, demands which were allegedly justified by the assertion, "well known to all the world, that the first German settlements made in the Island of Britain, were by colonies of people, subject to our renowned ducal ancestors, and drawn from their dominions."[55]

More serious and for our purposes more important was Franklin's own favorite, the *Rules*. Here he showed how Great Britain's policy toward her colonies had in every respect been the exact opposite of statesman-like action. Franklin here summed up several of his more important political maxims which we have already discussed. As early as 1754 he had insisted that the colonies ought to merit the special consideration of England and to receive equal rights with the mother-country in view of the services they had done for her. Franklin's political mercantilism as late as 1773 appears strikingly in his remark in the *Rules* that the settlers of those colonies—if this settlement "should happen to increase her *strength*, by their growing numbers, ready to join in her wars; her *commerce*, by their growing demand for her manufactures; or her *naval power*, by greater employment for her ships and seamen"[56] —might suppose some merit in all this, entitling them to some favor. According to the satirical intention of the *Rules*, Franklin now advised the British statesmen "to *forget it all, or resent it,* as if they had done you injury."[57] We may by-pass most of his twenty rules castigating Britain's pride and folly, so far as they concern the famous issues of taxation and representation. Franklin, however, never forgot the all-important aspect of foreign policy. Bitterly and in despair he exhorted England's rulers: "If you see *rival nations* rejoicing at the prospect of your disunion with your provinces, and endeavouring to promote it; if they translate, publish, and applaud all the complaints of your discontented colonists, at the same time privately stimulating you to severer measures, let not that *alarm* or offend you. Why should you, since you all mean *the same thing?*"[58] It is interesting that all Franklin's rules accept expediency as their guiding criterion.[59]

For Franklin the time had finally come when he decided that the inconveniences of America's connection with Britain were more numerous than the conveniences, where the damage done by the British to American interests exceeded the advantages which were derived from America's protection by British power. He indicated his change of mind in a characteristic mixture of moralistic and realistic arguments: "When I consider the extream Corruption prevalent among all Orders of Men in this old rotten State, and the glorious publick Virtue so predominant in our rising Country, I cannot but apprehend more Mischief than Benefit from a closer Union."[60]

America's Strength

As a matter of fact, during all his constant efforts for reconciliation, Franklin had always been strengthened by his profound conviction of America's inevitable growth. The belief in "Manifest Destiny" had been his greatest support, morally and from the point of view of power considerations. With the consciousness of this faith, Franklin's utterances at times take on an almost threatening undertone, as in this letter to Lord Kames:

> As to America, the advantages of such a union to her are not so apparent. She may suffer at present under the arbitrary power of this country; she may suffer for a while in a separation from it, but these are temporary evils that she will outgrow. Scotland and Ireland are differently circumstanced. Confined by the sea, they can scarcely increase in numbers, wealth and strength, so as to overbalance England. But America, an immense territory, favoured by Nature with all the advantages of climate, soil, great navigable rivers, and lakes, &c. must become a great country, populous and mighty; and will, in less time than is generally conceived, be able to shake off any shackles that may be imposed on her, and perhaps place them on the imposers.[61]

In this instance Franklin minimized America's interests in a union with Britain purposely in order to frighten his English interlocutors; but, on the other hand, there is not the slightest doubt of his invulnerable faith in America's growth. He continues to threaten that "every act of oppression will . . . hasten their final revolt; for the seeds of liberty are universally found there, and nothing can eradicate them."[62]

Franklin curiously mixes moral and power considerations. The seeds of liberty definitely meant for him seeds of power also. He once spoke of "that enthusiasm for liberty, which in other countries and ages has supplied all deficiencies, and enabled a weak people to baffle the efforts of the stronger."[63] At the occasion of the lowering of the tea duty for the American colonies, Franklin, full of moral indignation, wrote that the English "have no Idea that any People can act from any other Principle but that of Interest; and they believe, that 3d in a lb of Tea, of which one does not perhaps drink 10 in a year, is sufficient to overcome all the Patriotism of an American."[64] Franklin here employs the word "interest" in a purely materialistic sense which does not square with his frequent use of the term in a political context.

In any case, Franklin's reference to the "seeds of liberty" and the scorn he throws on "material interest" cannot obliterate the fact that Franklin also speaks the language of power politics. Not only the spirit of liberty but also "an immense territory," favored with all sorts of natural advantages, and the "increase of mankind" in America would substantially transform America's role in the scale of power. Even more explicit than in his previously quoted letter to Lord Kames is Franklin's report about his journey to Ireland which he sent to America: "I found them dispos'd to be friends of America, in which I endeavoured to confirm them, with the Expectation that our growing Weight might in time be thrown into their Scale, and, by joining our Interest with theirs might be obtained for them as well as for us, a more equitable Treatment from this Nation."[65] In a similar vein, he assured his American correspondent that "our great Security lies, I think, in our growing Strength, both in Numbers and Wealth; that creates an increasing Ability of assisting this Nation in its Wars, which will make us more respectable, our Friendship more valued, and our Enmity feared; thence it will soon be thought proper to treat us not with Justice only, but with Kindness, and thence we may expect in a few Years a total Change of Measures with regard to us."[66] This passage reveals strikingly Franklin's capacity to recognize the dependence of the moral behavior of states toward each other upon their mutual power relationships. Justice or kindness becomes a function of the changing patterns of power.

But much more has been revealed. Franklin, although speaking of national or imperial and not of international relations, uses a language, particularly from about 1768 onward, which resembles strongly the terminology of international politics. Long before he had actually decided upon independence, he spoke of two countries, England and America. We may remember that as early as 1760 Franklin had hypothetically expressed similar views. Arguing against the assertion of his opponents in the Canada-Guadeloupe controversy that the removal of the French from the continent would deprive the British of an essential check against Colonial aspirations toward independence, he had replied that, quite on the contrary, the proximity of foreigners "at enmity with the sovereign government" would greatly stimulate these aspirations by providing either aid or asylum.[67] About six years later Franklin continued this argument in words which clearly document how far he had progressed in viewing America as a unit in the international balance of power, even if he at the same time still ardently strove for a modus vivendi within the British Empire. In marginal notes on a pamphlet by the British clergyman and economist, Josiah Tucker, Franklin again took issue with the contention that the removal of the French threat on the continent produced or contributed to the American resistance against British demands. This time he referred particularly to the Stamp Act controversy:

> It seems a prevailing Opinion in England, that Fear of their French Neighbours would have kept the Colonies in Obedience to the Parliament; and that if the French Power had not been subdu'd, no Opposition would have been made to the Stamp Act. A very groundless Notion. On the contrary, had the French Power continued, to which the Americans might have had Recourse in case of Oppression from Parliament, Parliament would not have dared to oppress them.[68]

THE VISION OF AMERICA'S INTERESTS BEFORE 1775

Perhaps we may now be in a better position to assess the frame of reference of Franklin's thought on imperial and international relations. At the outset we must establish the fact that his thought on "national interest" defies analysis in terms of the standards of international law. There is a bewildering diversity of references to "interests" on a variety of levels. Franklin's first call to consider the science of one's country's true interest as the most important subject of study had closed with the exhortation that "it would be highly commendable in every one of us, more fully to bend our Minds to the Study of *What is the true Interest of Pennsylvania.*"[69] Twenty-five years later we find him expressing the hope that "the people of Great Britain, and the people of the colonies, would learn to consider themselves, as not belonging to a different community with different interests; but to one community with one interest."[70] Only a few years after Franklin had proclaimed that the Great War for the Empire was a truly "national war" —the term this time including the American colonies—he told an English correspondent that "Interest with you we have but little."[71] In 1766, however, he assured the House of Commons that the colonies would be ready to grant aids to the Crown for European wars, "for any thing that concerned the general interest. They consider themselves a part of the whole."[72] In the early 1770's, no less than during the heyday of his imperialism during the Seven Years' War, Franklin could still call the good of the whole British Empire "the true political Idea, that every Writer on these Subjects should have in View. Most of them think only of *a Part,* Britain."[73] This did not, however, prevent him from pointing out on the same occasion that the phrase "British Empire" was "a vague Expression," and he voiced his criticism that almost all the writers on this subject "confound themselves & Readers with the Idea that the British Empire is but ONE State; not considering or knowing that it consists of many States under one Sovereign."[74]

However, there is greater unity in Franklin's thought than the shifts of emphasis in his terminology of imperial relations would suggest. His insistence on true mutuality and equality in the relationship of England and America in almost the same words for many decades, his efforts to "redress the balance," his emphasis on reciprocal advantages even in his loftiest praise of the common welfare—all this seems to indicate conclusively that Franklin did not, for one moment, lose sight of what he considered to be the true interests of British America.

It is certainly correct to say that, within the framework of the common good of the British Empire, the emphasis on the "common interest" was greater during the decade from 1754 to 1763 than in later years when Franklin's thought shifted from Colonial home rule to imperial federation. We are far from denying the difference which does exist between the Franklin of the year 1754, frightened by the French and Indian danger, who asked an English friend "to whisper my sentiments in a private letter," saying that "Britain & her Colonies should be considered as one Whole, and not as different States with separate Interests,"[75] and the Franklin of 1767 who threatened coldly that "if *Force* [against the colonies] is used, . . . a total separation of interests will be the final consequence."[76] Apart from all other considerations, it was only natural for him to raise his voice for unity to a higher pitch in the hour of greatest danger and to lay greater stress on particular interest at a time when the colonies were comparatively secure from foreign menace. And Franklin was no less insistent on the equal rights of Americans in 1754 than in the late 1760's or early 1770's. We therefore agree with Professor Crane when he says that "the fluctuations of Franklin's imperial planning between colonial home-rule and imperial federation . . . reflect no real instability of purpose."[77]

This purpose, it seems, was primarily expressed in the desire to secure conditions under which "we can without Interruption go on with our Improvements, and increase our Numbers."[78] In other words, Franklin strove for the security, prosperity, and expansion of British America. This was his concept of America's interest, and we shall now attempt to give a systematic exposition of it as it evolved until the eve of his decision for complete independence in 1775.

1. *Security.*—The quest for security, we found out, lay at the very roots of Franklin's political thoughts and actions from 1747 until 1763, when the greatest stumbling block in the way of America's growth, the French rule in Canada, was removed. But the concern for security continued to form the very foundation of his constant efforts for reconciliation and unity. The protection of America from foreign danger remained until 1775 the principal motive of his imperialism. This was never more apparent than in 1768 when Franklin, in a well-known letter to his son, finally repudiated the right of the British Parliament to legislate for the colonies and recognized the king as the only legal link between Great Britain and the colonies:

Supposing that doctrine established, the colonies would then be so many separate states, only subject to the same king, as England and Scotland were before the union. And then the question would be, whether a union like that with Scotland would or would not be advantageous to *the whole*. I should have no doubt of the affirmative, being fully persuaded that it would be best for *the whole,* and that though particular parts might find particular disadvantages in it, *they would find greater advantages in the security arising to every part from the increased strength of the whole.*[79]

In 1771 Franklin also pointed to security as the common denominator of England and America. In the case of an imperial federation, he said, both countries would be "more secure by their united strength, and more formidable to their common enemies."[80]

Not only did Franklin always keep in mind the importance of unity toward foreign powers in time of war but he was also keenly aware of the significance of prestige for power in peacetime and was willing to concede certain sacrifices for the sake of a strong foreign policy.

> There is an Apprehension lest a too sudden yielding to all our Claims should be deem'd the Effect of Weakness, render the British Court contemptible in the Eyes of Foreigners. . . . You may judge whether it will not be prudent in us to indulge the Mother Country in this Concern for her own Honour, so far as may be consistent with the Preservation of our essential Rights, especially as that Honour may in some Cases be of Importance to the General Welfare.[81]

Franklin was always prepared to give shadow for substance, particularly when the matter was of substantial importance with regard to foreign affairs. In a conversation with Lord Egmont in 1769 about the condition of removing the causes of American discontent, the discussion turned to the loss of prestige which would accompany the explicit renouncement of parliamentary rights to legislate for America. Franklin did not insist on this point too much: "If continuing the Claim pleases you, continue it as long as you please, provided you never attempt to execute it; We shall consider it in the same Light with the Claim of the Spanish Monarch to the Title of King of Jerusalem."[82]

Security first was Franklin's invariable watchword. But this negative content of the concept of national interest was supplemented by more positive ideas.

2. *Prosperity and expansion.*—Under the shield of Britain's naval power, the American colonies in Franklin's time offered a picture of unprecedented growth and prosperity.[83] Plenty of free land attracted immigrants who achieved prosperity as independent farmers.[84] The agricultural character of America's prosperity was one of Franklin's

basic convictions, which he laid down on paper for the first time in 1751 in the *Observations concerning the Increase of Mankind*. Personal liberty and independence were open to the farmer but not to the industrial worker, and this possibility of liberty and independence appealed strongly to Franklin, who estimated "honest Subsistence with Independence" as one of the highest goods.[85]

Franklin's pride and joy about what was to him America's true greatness, the enjoyment of prosperity and personal independence, came never more to the fore than on the occasion of his visit to Ireland in 1771. He contrasts the conditions of Irish peasants and American farmers:

> I have lately made a Tour thro' Ireland and Scotland. In those Countries a small Part of the Society are Landlords, great Noblemen, and Gentlemen, extreamly opulent, living in the highest Affluence and Magnificence: The Bulk of the People Tenants, extreamly poor, living in the most sordid Wretchedness, in dirty Hovels of Mud and Straw, and cloathed only in Rags.
>
> I thought often of the Happiness of New England, where every Man is a Freeholder, has a Vote in publick Affairs, lives in a tidy, warm House, has plenty of good Food and Fewel, with whole cloaths from Head to Foot, the Manufacture perhaps of his own Family. Long may they continue in this Situation![86]

Franklin wanted for himself and for his fellow-Americans honest subsistence with independence. And he knew that in an industrial country this was not possible. "Manufactures are founded in poverty,"[87] Franklin said in 1760. The vision of an agricultural America, then, necessarily, engendered the desire for territorial expansion. The greater the density of population, so ran Franklin's theory, the more manufactures and the more poverty for a large part of the population would ensue. Expansion was the essential condition for the growth and prosperity of America.

THE TRANSITION FROM MERCANTILISM TO PHYSIOCRACY AND FREE TRADE: FRANKLIN'S AMBIGUOUS POSITION

Franklin's belief that "the economic prosperity of his country was largely dependent on the promotion of its agriculture"[88] undermined his originally wholly mercantilistic outlook. He abandoned the theory which he had taken from Sir William Petty and defended in 1729, namely, that labor is the true source of wealth, and came to the conclusion that agriculture is the only creative source of new wealth. This conviction, foreshadowed in Franklin's glorification of American agricultural economy in 1751, drove him naturally into the hands of the French physiocrats. In 1767 he spent five weeks in Paris, where he came into personal contact with leading physiocrats like Quesnay and the elder Mirabeau. Only a few months afterward, we see Franklin writing his now theoretically confirmed views to a friend in America:

> After all, this Country is fond of manufactures beyond their real value, for the true source of riches is husbandry. Agriculture is truly *productive of new wealth;* manufactures only change forms, and, whatever value they give to the materials they work upon, they in the mean time consume an equal value in provisions, &c. So that riches are not *increased* by manufacturing; the only advantage is, that provisions in the shape of manufactures are more easily carried for sale to foreign markets.[89]

A more systematic exposition of these views may be found in Franklin's *Positions To Be Examined, concerning National Wealth,* dated April, 1769. He here developed the theory that the export of manufactures rather than raw materials was advantageous not so much because of "their highly advancing the value of rough materials"[90] (which had been the orthodox mercantilist explanation), but because in buyer countries new and cheap methods of production of the export countries were not known and because, accordingly, "our traders may more easily cheat strangers."[91] Franklin therefore comes to a conclusion which is highly significant for our purposes:

> There seem to be but three ways for a nation to acquire *wealth.* The first is by *war,* as the Romans did, in plundering their conquered neighbours. This is *robbery.* The second by *commerce,* which is generally *cheating.* The third by *agriculture,* the only *honest* way, wherein man receives a real increase of the seed thrown into the ground, in a kind of continual miracle, wrought by the hand of God in his favour, as a reward for his innocent life and his virtuous industry.[92]

The strength of the British Empire for the protection of an agricultural and expanding America: in this formula is the core of Franklin's political aspirations before 1775. From the point of view of the theoretical analysis of international relations, however, this formula poses one perplexing problem, namely, Franklin's relationship to the body of mercantilist doctrines. The praise of agriculture as early as 1751, in 1760, and more elaborately after 1767 does certainly represent a repudiation of the mercantilist predilections for manufactures. Even more important, Franklin's condemnation of wars for wealth and mercantilist methods of commerce (i.e., stress on the export of manufactures) shows that by 1769 he seemed to be in disagreement with some fundamental tenets of mercantilist doctrine. Wars for wealth—even if wealth was ultimately rationalized or actually intended as a means for power and strength—had certainly played a prominent role in the century between 1650 and 1750; the War of Jenkins' Ear, which ran largely parallel to the War of the Austrian Succession (King George's War), could be called the last commercial war of this kind. Franklin believed that there were wars with pre-dominantly economic motivations. We have even seen that he, mostly for polemic reasons, chose to give an economic interpretation to the Great War for the Empire, going so far as to pretend that the war was fought solely in order to create a new expanding market for certain English manufacturers. Following the same line of reasoning, Frank-lin considered low wages for workers as a lesser evil than wars for compelling "other nations to buy our goods, whether they will or no, which some have been mad enough at times to propose."[93] More-over, he did think that wealthy regions attracted foreign conquerors. He once remarked that "as our Country is not wealthy enough so as to afford much ready Plunder, the Temptation to a foreign Invasion of us is the less."[94]

Franklin's condemnation of wars for wealth and his denouncement of the "wicked" mercantilist commerce were only the counterparts of his increasing demands for the removal of trade restrictions. In a fa-mous letter to David Hume he wrote as follows: "I have lately read with great pleasure, as I do everything of yours, the excellent Essay on the *Jealousy of Commerce*. I think it cannot but have a good effect in promoting a certain interest, too little thought of by selfish man, and scarce ever mentioned, so that we hardly have a name for it; I mean the *interest of humanity,* or common good of mankind."[95] This last sen-tence is often quoted as it stands here, and so it takes on an air of abso-luteness which, however, is only a part of the picture. Franklin, when he celebrated the interest of mankind, never forgot the interest of America, and so we ought not to wonder at the immediately following reflection that he hoped, "particularly from that Essay, an abatement of the jealousy, that reigns here, of the commerce of the colonies, at least so far as such abatement may be reasonable."[96] Franklin, ever in the greatest sincerity, tried to make the best of both worlds, and the example given in the letter to Hume was followed in another well known letter to Dupont de Nemours, the famous physiocrat whom he had missed on the occasion of his visit to Paris in 1767.

> We are so far from conceiving that what is best for mankind, or even for Europe in general, may be best for us, that we are even studying to establish and extend a separate interest of Britain, to the prejudice of even Ireland and our colonies. . . . It is from your philosophy that the maxims of a contrary and more happy conduct are to be drawn, which I therefore sincerely wish may grow and increase till it becomes the governing philosophy of the human species, as it must be that of superior beings in better worlds.[97]

In 1764 Franklin expressed the hope that "in time perhaps Mankind may be wise enough to let Trade take its own Course, find its own Channels, and regulate its own Proportions, etc. At present, most of the Edicts of Princes, Placaerts, Laws & Ordinances of Kingdoms & States for that purpose, prove political Blunders."[98] Two years later he wrote that "it seems contrary to the Nature of Commerce, for Government to interfere in the Prices of Commodities. Trade is a voluntary thing between Buyer and Seller, in every Article of which each exercises his own Judgement, and is to please himself."[99]

How do these remarks, which stress the autonomy of the economic sphere, square with the reference, made as late as 1770, to "our brave Colonists, the Discoverers and Settlers of a new World, from whence, as from an inexhaustible Source of Wealth and Plenty, the Means of Power, Greatness, and Glory, inconceivable to our Ancestors, have been pouring into this Kingdom for Ages past"?[100]

The final surprise seems to come when we find that in 1774 Franklin staunchly upheld the wisdom of the Navigation Acts. During his last negotiations in London he defended himself and the Americans against the opinion that they advocated the abolition of the Navigation Acts. In a conversation with Chatham, Franklin observed that the "main material Part" of the Navigation Acts, the trade monopoly of British and colonial ships, was as acceptable to the colonies as to Britain and that the colonies did not object to the regulation of commerce by Parliament, provided the laws were "*bonâ fide* for the Benefit of the *whole Empire,* not for the small Advantage of one Part to the great Injury of another."[101]

In view of these inconsistencies, there have been contradictory opinions among students of Franklin's politics as to his attitude toward mercantilism and laissez faire. An analyst of his economic thought says that "long before he met members of this school [the physiocrats] he had come to believe in international free trade and in the unwisdom and injustice of the British government's regulation of economic activities of the American colonies which were in many ways hampered and restrained from complete and normal growth."[102] Two other observers more cautiously point out that "at least by 1767 he was to become an exponent of agrarianism and free trade."[103] A student of Franklin's political philosophy, on the contrary, stresses the fact that as late as 1774, in view of his approval of the Navigation Acts, Franklin's political concept still could be described as mercantilism minus the discrimination against the colonies.[104]

All these critics are partly justified. The opinion that Franklin was converted to free trade long before his acquaintance with the physiocrats finds its strongest evidence in his cordial indorsement in 1760 of David Hume's essay *Of the Jealousy of Trade*. Hume's essay, written in 1752, is one of the better-known and most concise statements of the antimercantilist point of view before Adam Smith's *Wealth of Nations*.[105] Hume opposed the mercantilist doctrine which considered "all trading states as their rivals" and asserted "in opposition to this narrow and malignant opinion . . . that the encrease of riches and commerce in any one nation, instead of hurting, commonly promotes the riches and commerce of all its neighbours."[106] It is also true that Franklin's insistence on the virtue of agriculture became more systematic after his acquaintance with the physiocrats in 1767; on the other hand, the evidence of his basic agreement with the Navigation Acts as late as 1774 is irrefutable.[107]

We suggest that Franklin's adherence to two apparently conflicting theories may be reduced to a common denominator when we remember that even Adam Smith defended the Navigation Acts because they were essential to the defense of the realm and because defense preceded opulence. In other words, the puzzle disappears when we cease to discuss the transition of Franklin's thought from mercantilism to free trade and physiocracy as a purely economic affair and see it in the context of politics.

On the one hand, Franklin transcended mercantilist doctrine on three points. First of all, he opposed the maxim of the subordination of Colonial interests to those of the mother-country. Second, his knowledge of and concern for the interests of America led him to stress the virtues of agriculture and to deprecate the mercantilist methods of the export of manufactures. Third, and possibly from the point of view of economic doctrine most important, Franklin's political conviction of the mutuality of interests between England and America and his philosophic conviction that enlightened self-interest included a large degree of co-operation rather than competition contributed to permitting him to indorse Hume's ideas that the flourishing of one country does not necessarily mean the ruin of another. There is a striking parallel between Franklin's earliest work on political economy, the otherwise strictly mercantilist character of which has rightly been stressed, and Hume's attack on mercantilism in his essay *Of the Jealousy of Trade*. Franklin said in 1729: "As Providence has so ordered it, that not only different Countries, but even different Parts of the same Country, have their peculiar most suitable Productions; and likewise that different Men have Geniuses adapted to Variety of different Arts and Manufactures, Therefore *Commerce,* or the Exchange of one Commodity or Manufacture for another, is highly convenient and beneficial to Mankind."[108] This stress on exchange of commodities rather than the orthodox mercantilist emphasis on the accumulation of money or bullion was, at that time, of course, prompted by America's need for paper money, and it foreshadowed Franklin's later arguments that the needs of America and England were complementary rather than competitive. But his practical experience was strikingly similar to Hume's theoretical discussion: "Nature, by giving a diversity of geniuses, climates, and soils, to different nations, has secured their mutual intercourse and commerce, as long as they all remain industrious and civilized."[109]

On the other hand, Franklin's objectives sometimes coincided with mercantilist concerns, and this explains why at times he used a language strongly reminiscent of mercantilism. First of all, his intense zeal for the "increase of mankind" in America corresponded perfectly well to the mercantilists' great emphasis on numbers as a source of riches and of strength. That numbers give strength was one of Franklin's favorite and most often recurring arguments. Second, the fact that he was very much concerned with strength and not only with the accumulation of wealth perhaps presents the most important clue to the understanding of his "inconsistencies." The Great War for the Empire was for Franklin not a commercial war, which he would have condemned as a "political blunder,"[110] but a struggle of life and death, a war for security of life in the truest sense of the term. Defense comes before opulence—Franklin never formulated this idea as pointedly as the more theoretically minded Adam Smith did, but Smith's formula helps us to grasp how Franklin was able, without being logically inconsistent, to voice his warm agreement with Hume's essay at the very same time that he wrote the Canada pamphlet, full of "power politics" and mercantilist arguments. Furthermore, it contributes toward understanding Franklin's indorsement of the basic features of the Navigation Acts until the very end of his efforts for the unity of the British Empire. Modern scholarship has shown that the Navigation Laws proper never were a real cause of grievance for the colonists and that one has to be careful to distinguish between these and other restrictions after 1763 which caused Colonial unrest.[111] But in the case of Franklin's thought regarding the British Empire, which was more articulate than that of most of his contemporaries, the Navigation Laws definitely took on political importance as the shield from foreign menace—the shield which would provide the strength necessary to protect the growth and prosperity of the empire. Franklin, in pointing out that he did not object to the monopoly of British and Colonial ships in the Colonial trade, was aware of its consequences for the strength of British Naval power. That this concern for power and protection was clearly in his mind is confirmed by a conversation he had during his last negotiations for reconciliation in London:

> I observ'd, we were frequently charg'd with Views of abolishing the Navigation Act. That in truth, those Parts of it which were of most Importance to Britain, *as tending to increase its naval strength,* viz. those restraining the Trade, to be carried on only in Ships belonging to British Subjects, navigated by at least ¾ British or Colony Seamen, &c., were as acceptable to us as they could be to Britain, since we wish'd to employ our own Ships in preference to Foreigners, and had no Desire to see foreign Ships enter our Ports. That indeed the obliging us to land some of our Commodities in England before we could carry them to foreign Markets, and forbidding our Importation of some Goods directly from foreign Countries, we thought a Hardship, and a greater Loss to us than Gain to Britain, and therefore proper to be repeal'd: But as Britain had deem'd it *an equivalent for her Protection,* we had never apply'd, or propos'd to apply for such Repeal.[112]

Franklin's Concept of International Politics in 1776

At the outbreak of the War of Independence, Franklin had definite ideas on problems of international politics. The increase of power for reasons of security, even through war and conquest, was legitimate. "There can be no cession that is not supposed at least to increase the power of the party to whom it is made. It is enough that he has a right to ask it, and that he does it not merely to serve the purposes of a dangerous ambition."[113] Thus Franklin had written in the Canada pamphlet. Sixteen years later he found himself fighting for the security of America against Great Britain.

On July 30, 1776, three months before setting out on his mission to France, Franklin summed up his conception of international politics. He wrote to Lord Howe: "Long did I endeavour, with unfeigned and unwearied Zeal, to preserve from breaking that fine and noble China Vase, the British Empire; for I knew, that, being once broken, the separate Parts could not retain even their Shares of the Strength and Value that existed in the Whole, and that a perfect Reunion of those Parts could scarce ever be hoped for."[114] Again he castigated the "abounding Pride and deficient Wisdom" of England and raised his voice in a powerful indictment of her:

> Her Fondness for Conquest, as a warlike Nation, her lust of Dominion, as an ambitious one, and her wish for a gainful Monopoly, as a commercial one, (none of them legitimate Causes of war), will all join to hide from her Eyes every view of her true Interests, and continually goad her on in those ruinous distant Expeditions, so destructive both to Lives and Treasure, that must prove as pernicious to her in the End, as the Crusades formerly were to most of the Nations in Europe. . . .
>
> The well-founded Esteem, and permit me to say, Affection, which I shall always have for your Lordship, makes it Painful to me to see you engaged in conducting a War, the great Ground of which, as expressed in your Letter, is "the necessity of preventing the American trade from passing into foreign Channels." To me it seems, that neither the Obtaining or Retaining of any Trade, how valuable soever, is an Object for which men may justly spill each other's Blood; that the true and sure Means of extending and securing Commerce is the goodness and Cheapness of Commodities; and that the profit of no trade can ever be equal to the Expence of compelling it, and of holding it, by Fleets and Armies.
>
> I consider this War against us, therefore, as both unjust and unwise.[115]

Franklin firmly places the onus of war guilt on Great Britain. More explicit than usual, he here expressed his views on international politics. But he makes—perhaps unconsciously—one very important omission: he fails to mention his own belief that wars in which the life or death of a country is at stake might be legitimate; and Franklin himself had given to this legitimate motive a rather extensive interpretation during the Great War for the Empire. He held to the letter rather than the spirit of Lord Howe's message when he classified this war as a "war for gainful monopoly" and refused to admit—possibly even to himself—that in this war, from the point of view of people in England, more might be at stake than gainful monopoly or lust of conquest and dominion. This letter, with what it says as well as what it omits, provides the setting for the character of Franklin's concept of foreign policy in the years to follow.

CHAPTER IV

NO ENTANGLEMENTS

NORTH AMERICA AND THE BALANCE OF POWER

FROM the age of Louis XIV to Waterloo, France was Great Britain's archenemy. Mutual suspicions of the "perfidious" adversary were deeply ingrained in the public opinion of both countries. Each hurled violent accusations of sinister schemes for world dominion at the other. The Anglo-French contest for preponderance had its origins in the European balance of power; but, with the growing importance of commerce and naval strength as elements of national power and their recognition in the theories of mercantilism, public opinion and leading men in France, England, and America realized, in the words of Franklin's opponent in the Canada-Guadeloupe controversy, William Burke, that "there is a Balance of Power in *America* as well as in *Europe*."[1] By the middle of the eighteenth century "responsible statesmen had gone so far as to believe that the balance of power in Europe rested ultimately upon the balance of power in the colonial world."[2] In December, 1750, Marquis de la Galissonnière, the returning governor of Canada, wrote that Canada, in spite of heavy financial burdens, ought to be retained and defended against the English at all costs, "inasmuch as that is the only way to wrest America from the ambition of the English, and as the progress of their empire in that quarter of the globe is what is most capable of contributing to their superiority in Europe."[3] In the midst of the Great War for the Empire the Duke of Choiseuil pleaded for Spanish aid with the following words: "The King [of France] believes, Monsieur, that it is possessions in America that will in the future form the balance of power in Europe, and that, if the English invade that part of the world, as it appears they have the intention of doing, it will result therefrom that England will usurp the commerce of the nations, and that she alone will remain rich in Europe."[4]

On the other side, British Americans were no less aware of the larger issues at stake. Anxious to secure British support, they also tied the question of Colonial defense to the repercussions which the breakdown of the Colonial balance of power would have in Europe; in 1755 William Clarke closed his *Observations on the . . . Conduct of the French . . . in North America*[5] with the urgent warning that, should England lose the continental colonies "and the French gain them, Great Britain herself must necessarily be reduced to an absolute subjection to the French Crown, to be nothing more than a Province of France."[6]

The outcome of the Great War for the Empire did not change sentiments on either side. France's defeat in the New World was accompanied by a low ebb of her prestige in the Old; her reputation for power reached unprecedented depths at the time of the first partition of Poland in 1772. It was only natural that Choiseuil should watch the development of the British-American disputes with an extremely attentive eye. It was his conviction, addressed to Louis XV, that

England is the declared enemy of your power and of your state, and she will be so always. Many ages must elapse before a durable peace can be established with this state, which looks forward to the supremacy in the four quarters of the globe. *Only the revolution which will occur some day in America, though we shall probably not see it, will put England back to that state of weakness in which Europe will have no more to fear of her.*[7]

FRANKLIN AND FRANCE BEFORE 1775

From 1764 on Choiseuil even sent observers to the colonies who were instructed to find out the mood of the colonies with respect to independence, loyalty to Great Britain, and feelings toward France.[8] In 1769 one of them, Kalb, brought back a rather discouraging report: the Colonials were "free and enterprising"; however, basically they were "but little inclined to shake off the English supremacy with the aid of foreign powers . . . such an alliance would appear to them to be fraught with danger to their liberties; . . . a war with us would only hasten their reconciliation."[9]

Kalb's observations were substantially correct; no better test for this exists than to compare them to Benjamin Franklin's remarks made at about the same time. Franklin told his son about the extreme curiosity shown by Durand, the French minister in London, about "the affairs of America":

He . . . pretends to have a great esteem for me, on account of my abilities shown in my examination; has desired to have all my political writings, invited me to dine with him, was very inquisitive, treated me with great civility, makes me visits, &c. I fancy that intriguing nation would like very well to meddle on occasion, and blow up the coals between Britain and her colonies; but I hope we shall give them no opportunity.[10]

Two years later, back from his second journey to Paris, Franklin reported to his American friend, Samuel Cooper, that "all Europe (except Britain) appears to be on our side of the question. But Europe has its Reasons. It fancies itself in some Danger from the Growth of British Power, and would be glad to see it divided against itself. Our prudence will, I hope, long postpone the Satisfaction our Enemies expect from our Dissensions."[11] Six months later Franklin spoke of Europe's interest in Britain's dissensions in a slightly sharper tone: "I own I have a Satisfaction in seeing, that our Part is taken Everywhere; because I am persuaded, that circumstance will not be without its Effect here in our favour. At the same time the malignant Pleasure, which other Powers take in British Divisions, may convince us on both sides of the Necessity of our uniting."[12] By 1766 or shortly thereafter, Franklin had clearly recognized that the decisive weakening of British power would override all other considerations in the minds of foreign nations. Josiah Tucker argued that, in case of a separation of America from the mother-country, the colonies would "have none to complain to, none to assist you: For assure yourself, that Holland, France, and Spain, will look upon you with an evil Eye; and will be particularly on their Guard against you, lest such an example should infect their own Colonies."[13] Whereupon Franklin observed laconically: "Holland, Fr. & Spain, would also be glad of our Custom. And pleas'd to see the Separation."[14]

All this goes a long way to confirm the observations of Kalb, the French emissary, as do the conclusions which we have drawn in the preceding chapter concerning Franklin's theory of empire. His fight for America's equality and his belief in the eventual superiority of America did not in the least impair his vision of the British Empire as a perpetual alliance against foreign menace, acting as a unit with respect to international affairs. Franklin frequently spoke to Englishmen as well as to his American friends of the necessity for and the willingness of America to contribute to the defense of Britain. In his famous examination before the House of Commons he answered the question whether the colonies would grant aids for the Crown "for a British concern, as suppose a war in some part of Europe, that did not affect them," with the solemn assurance: "Yes, for any thing that concerned the general interest. They consider themselves a part of the whole."[15] The admission that British interests in Europe could be considered as a matter of common concern is remarkable. This official declaration is corroborated by Franklin's private letters to America, in which he praises the importance of a military spirit and a militia for America; he adds: "What a Glory would it be for us to send, on any trying Occasion, ready and effectual Aid to our Mother Country!"[16] And as late as mid-1775, when Franklin drew up one of his last offers for reconciliation, he voiced the same sentiments on common defense against foreign enemies.[17] His appeals for unity and common defense were always written with an eye toward the prospective enemies, France and Spain, particularly the former power, which in the Peace of Paris in 1763 had lost not only Canada to the British but also Louisiana west of the Mississippi to the Spanish. In his press campaign against the taxing of the colonies Franklin once satirically suggested that England ought to tax all Europe, except France, "for it is at our Expence of Men and Money chiefly, that the Balance of Europe has been kept even, and that France has not established her favourite Scheme of universal Tyranny."[18]

COMMERCE VERSUS POLITICAL ENTANGLEMENTS

THOMAS PAINE AND JOHN ADAMS

Back in Philadelphia in May, 1775, Franklin after some weeks of apparent hesitation and evasion disclosed his thoughts to his son William, who was governor of New Jersey, and to his friend Galloway, both of whom were to remain loyal to the British Crown. Franklin had now decided for independence; he "exclaimed against the corruption and dissipation of the Kingdom" and expressed his belief that the colonies would finally prevail,[19] and from this moment on he pursued this aim with an unshakable steadfastness. Accordingly, in July, 1775, we find Franklin writing to his English friends, Priestley and Bishop Shipley, that "we have not yet applied to any foreign power for assistance, nor offered our commerce for their friendship."[20]

This remark immediately strikes the note which was to dominate the diplomacy of the new country in its first stage. The question of commerce had a double significance for the struggle of the united colonies. First of all, the falling-out of the British trade on which the economic structure of the colonies had hitherto rested confronted the Colonials with the question of providing means for successful defense. "Can we hope to carry on war without having trade and commerce somewhere?" a delegate to the Continental Congress wrote on February 14, 1776.[21] Franklin certainly was not the last to grasp the urgency of the situation, and it was he who on February 26, 1776, moved formally in Congress to open the colonies to the commerce and ships of all countries for at least two years from July 20, 1776; but the majority of Congress was not yet prepared for that measure, and only on April 6, 1776, did Congress actually resolve to open the American trade to the world.[22]

Second, however, the proposal to exchange America's commerce for the friendship of Europe could be considered as a virtue as well as a necessity. In January, 1776, Thomas Paine's *Common Sense,* written probably upon Franklin's suggestion,[23] had exploded like a bombshell among the bewildered American people and had pointed the way to the future. "What have we to do with setting the world at defiance?" Paine exclaimed.

Our plan is commerce, and that, well attended to, will secure us the peace and friendship of all Europe; because it is the interest of all Europe to have America a free port. Her trade will always be a protection. . . . As Europe is our market for trade, we ought to form no partial connection with any part of it. It is the true interest of America to steer clear of European contentions, which she never can do, while, by her dependence on Britain, she is made the makeweight in the scale of British politics.[24]

The significance of *Common Sense* for the formation of American foreign policy has always been stressed. It has been duly emphasized that the Colonials did not complain about their involvement in European wars and looked upon this consequence of their membership in the British Empire as a matter of course.[25] It has been further said that only *Common Sense* "awakened American statesmen to a realization that one of the most significant things which they might hope for in independence was comparative disentanglement from European international convulsions."[26] The strongest reason for the influence of Paine's ideas on foreign policy, it has been pointed out, was that they "filled an absolute gap."[27]

Evidently influenced by Paine's *Common Sense,*[28] John Adams, in whose writings we find the most articulate expression of American ideas on foreign policy in the decisive years 1775 and 1776, put down some of his guiding ideas as to the "connection we may safely form with" France: "1. No political connection. Submit to none of her authority; receive no governors or officers from her. 2. No military connection. Receive no troops from her. 3. Only a commercial connection; that is, make a treaty to receive her ships into our ports; let her engage to receive our ships into her ports; furnish us with arms, cannon, saltpetre, powder, duck, steel."[29] Adams followed these precepts when it fell upon him to draft a "Plan of Treaties" in accordance with Richard Henry Lee's triple motion of June 7, 1776, for independence, for confederation, and for taking "the most effectual measures for forming foreign alliances."[30] In his own words:

> When, as it happened, I was appointed to draw the plan of a treaty to be carried to France by Dr. Franklin, and proposed by him, Mr. Deane, and Mr. Lee, to the French court, I carefully avoided every thing that could involve us in any alliance more than a commercial friendship. When this plan was reported to Congress, my own most intimate friends, Samuel Adams and Richard Henry Lee, differed from me in opinion. They thought there was not sufficient temptation to France to join us. They moved for cessions and concessions, which implied warranties and political alliance that I had studiously avoided. My principle was perpetual peace, after that war should be concluded, with all powers of Europe, and perfect neutrality in all their future wars. This principle I was obliged to support against long arguments and able disputants, and, fortunately, carried every point.[31]

This stress on "commerce" and the refusal to accept political and military engagements with European powers raise three problems: first, the question of the meaning of the term "alliance" used in Lee's motion; second, the question whether it was really only *Common Sense* which brought American leaders to a realization of the possibilities of a comparative disentanglement from European affairs; and, third, the problem of whether the statements of men like Paine, Adams, Franklin, and some others on purely commercial foreign relations constitute a declaration of American isolationism, whether, as has recently been advanced, these ideas may not also be interpreted as expressions of an idealistic internationalism, or whether a third interpretation of these ideas, at least as far as Franklin is concerned, is not more appropriate.[32]

As for the first question, abundant evidence has been produced to show that the word "alliance" in the eighteenth century did not have that purely political and military connotation which we associate with it today.[33] The term "commercial alliance" was frequently used.[34]

Franklin inquired in December, 1775, whether "there is any state or power in Europe who would be willing to enter into an alliance with us for the benefit of our commerce,"[35] and three months later he instructed Silas Deane, who was about to leave for France, to find out whether France would be inclined to "enter into any treaty or alliance with them [the United Colonies] for commerce or defense, or both."[36] Even in October, 1776, when Congress had adopted a plan for a treaty with France which carefully avoided any political or military obligations and which had been officially called the "Treaty of Amity and Commerce," the Committee of Secret Correspondence of Congress, in charge of foreign affairs, informed Deane of a "treaty of commerce and alliance" to be proposed to France.[37] The ambiguous meaning of the term "alliance" has to be kept in mind particularly because people who discussed the foreign policy debates of 1775 and 1776 in retrospect, as did John Adams in his *Autobiography* and in the letters of his old age, used a clearer and more modern terminology which separated alliances sharply from commercial agreements.

The second question presents us with a more serious problem. In later years John Adams himself upheld the claim to have frowned upon political relations with Europe even before the appearance of *Common Sense,* which he depicted as merely "a tolerable summary of the arguments which I had been repeating again and again in Congress for nine months."[38] The accuracy of this claim has been differently evaluated by several scholars.[39] But even if we suppose that Adams did not independently evolve his opposition to entanglements in European politics as contrasted with European commerce, there is no necessity to see in Paine the only source among the American leaders who kindled these ideas, even if it is undoubtedly true that Paine was dynamite among the people.

"ISOLATIONISM" BEFORE "COMMON SENSE": FRANKLIN'S ATTITUDE

Franklin had come back from England in May, 1775; during the sixty-nine years of his life which had already passed, he had given more thought to foreign affairs than any of the other Colonial leaders. To be sure, he had come home bitterly disgusted with English politics. On the other hand, there is no reason whatsoever to suppose that Franklin's disillusionment with Great Britain alone would have reversed his feelings about "that intriguing nation," France, and the other Continental enemies of England's power, whose *Schadenfreude* about the Anglo-American conflict he had considerably resented.

Franklin during his protracted stay in England was certainly familiar with some of the numerous pamphlets which had called upon the government to use England's insular situation to its full advantage. One of the best-known pamphlets which advocated this policy had been Israel Mauduit's *Considerations on the Present German War,* which appeared in the midst of the Canada-Guadeloupe controversy only two months after Franklin's Canada pamphlet.[40] Another advocate of this policy "to keep clear of the quarrels among other states" was James Burgh, author of the *Political Disquisitions,* who proudly mentioned in this book his intimacy with Franklin.[41] Franklin himself, finally, under the disguise of an Englishman, told the English public in 1770 how "the enormous Load of Debt, which sinks us almost to Perdition" was brought upon England not by the colonies but "by our romantick European Continental Connections."[42] Shortly before this, Franklin in marginal notes stated that the colonies paid more than their due for imperial defense, *"for the sake of continental Connections in which they were separately unconcerned."*[43]

Five years later Franklin had transferred his argument against "romantick" relationships from the European continent to Great Britain, and this time he did not address an English public but an American politician, Joseph Galloway: "I fear they will drag us after them in all the plundering Wars, which their desperate Circumstances, Injustice, and Rapacity may prompt them to undertake; and their wide-wasting Prodigality and Profusion is a Gulph that will swallow up every Aid we may distress ourselves to afford them."[44]

Very similar ideas are expressed in a little satirical piece of Franklin's, *A Dialogue between Britain, France, Spain, Holland, Saxony and America.* This dialogue has usually been dated 1777, but a recent analysis of internal evidence has suggested that Franklin wrote it early in 1775,[45] at about the time he wrote the preceding passage to Joseph Galloway. In this dialogue America complained to Britain that

when you have quarrell'd with all Europe, and drawn me with you into all your Broils, then you value yourself upon protecting me from the Enemies you have made for me. I have no natural Cause of Difference with Spain, France, or Holland, and yet by turns I have join'd with you in Wars against them all. You would not suffer me to make or keep a separate Peace with any of them, tho' I might easily have done it to great Advantage.[46]

This may well be called isolationism before Thomas Paine. It was not enthusiasm but dire necessity which prompted Franklin to envisage an offer of America's commerce in exchange for the friendship of foreign powers, once he had definitely thrown his lot with the camp of independence. Although Franklin in his letter to Priestley mentioned only commerce as America's price for European friendships, he still added that perhaps America would never make even this offer, "but it is natural to think of it, if we are pressed."[47]

Although it has been suspected that Franklin, when he wrote these words, "seems to have felt that a more substantial inducement in the form of some monopoly must be offered to France,"[48] we do not think that his rather reluctant observation to Priestley carries this implication.[49] It probably means neither more nor less than the opinion that Great Britain's "strength is all artificial, from her trade alone,"[50] as a member of the Continental Congress put it in October, 1775, and that "the best instrument we have, is our opposition by commerce."[51]

From November, 1775, onward, Franklin, being the one member of the newly formed Committee of Secret Correspondence[52] with extensive European connections, chiefly carried on the early correspondence of the committee with possible friends of the American cause. In December 1775, he wrote to an acquaintance of his in Holland, the Swiss man of letters, Charles William Frederick Dumas,[53] asking him to sound out European diplomats in his country as to the dispositions of their respective courts with regard to America. Franklin appealed to disinterested as well as to interested motives:

We wish to know whether any one of them, from principles of humanity, is disposed magnanimously to step in for the relief of an oppressed people, or whether if, as seems likely to happen, we should be obliged to break off all connection with Great Britain, and declare ourselves an independent people, there is any state or power in Europe who would be willing to enter into an alliance with us for the benefit of our commerce, which amounted, before the war, to near seven millions sterling per annum, and must continually increase, as our people increase most rapidly.[54]

Dumas's allegiance to the universal republic of letters did not blind him to the realities of politics, and he answered Franklin accordingly. He hastened to qualify his statement in an earlier letter in which he had told Franklin that all Europe wished well for the American cause; he had meant the unprejudiced, equitable, humane European public; in a word, the citizens of universal society, men in general. You must except from this number the holders of English funds, and those courts of Europe who have an understanding with England; these, far from assisting you, will sacrifice you to their interests or their fears. The allies which, under such circumstances, are suitable for you are France and Spain; for it is their interest that you should be free and independent of England, whose enormous maritime power fills them with apprehensions.[55]

Franklin, of course, had been perfectly aware of the interests of France and of Spain during all the years of his stay in England. Also in December, 1775, Franklin composed a letter to the Spanish Prince Gabriel of Bourbon. In words which reveal the characteristic ring of his style, Franklin told the prince:

Looking forward, I think I see a powerful Dominion growing up here, whose Interest it will be, to form a close and firm Alliance with Spain, (their Territories bordering,) and who, being united, will be able not only to preserve their own people in Peace, but to repel the force of all the other Powers in Europe. It seems, therefore, prudent on both sides to cultivate a good Understanding, that may hereafter be so useful to both.[56]

These letters were meant only to sound out possible channels of negotiation. They were entirely noncommittal, and it was only natural that they should be written with less reserve or emphasis on details than specific instructions; they "suggest no closer connection than commerce and friendship."[57]

The French had already met American aspirations halfway in sending to Philadelphia their agent Bonvouloir, who, in December, 1775, held secret meetings with the members of the Committee of Secret Correspondence—so secret that each member came to the meetings in the dark by a different way. Of course Bonvouloir protested his unofficial status as a private businessman who merely had some governmental connections. He preserved an entirely noncommittal attitude and gave no definite reply to the Americans' inquiries whether, "in case proposals should be made, France would be content with an exclusive trade for a certain period as indemnity for the expense she would be under their account"; the Americans assured him "that they could pay by a neutrality, even with a little help, in case of war between the two nations, and by inviolable attachment, in which they would never fail."[58] Members of the Committee of Secret Correspondence, presumably including Franklin, did discuss, then, the possibility of special commercial privileges for France, but the suggestion of "even a little help" falls far short of any proposal of a political alliance. When, after some heart-searching, the committee finally decided to appoint an American agent for France, the nature of America's compensation for France's friendship (that is, assistance) was specified in unequivocal terms. Franklin wrote the instructions for Silas Deane. Apart from recommending that Deane acquire Parisian French, Franklin instructed him to make clear to the French foreign minister, Vergennes, that

the commercial advantages Britain had enjoyed with the Colonies had contributed greatly to her late wealth and importance. That it is likely great part of our commerce will naturally fall to the share of France, especially if she favours us in this application, as that will be a means of gaining and securing the friendship of the Colonies; and that as our trade was rapidly increasing with our increase of people, and, in a greater proportion, her part of it will be extremely valuable.[59]

The Committee of Secret Correspondence, furthermore, instructed Deane to find out whether France would be willing "to enter into any treaty or alliance with them, for commerce or defense, or both."[60] These instructions were written after *Common Sense* had appeared, and Adams' above-quoted notes, with his insistence on the impropriety of political and military connections with France, were apparently written in connection with them.[61]

CONGRESS PREPARES THE TREATY WITH FRANCE

A further stage was reached when, in accordance with Richard Henry Lee's famous motion of June 7, 1776, for independence, confederation, and foreign alliances, a committee for the drafting of a treaty with France was formed. The best report of its proceedings comes from the pen of John Adams:

The committee for preparing the model of a treaty to be proposed to France, consisted of Mr. Dickinson, Mr. Franklin, Mr. John Adams, Mr. Harrison, and Mr. Robert Morris. When we met to deliberate on the subject, I contended for the same principles which I had before avowed and defended in Congress, namely, that we should avoid an alliance which might embarrass us in after times, and involve us in future European wars; that a treaty of commerce which would operate as a repeal of the British acts of navigation so far as respected us, and admit France into an equal participation of the benefits of our commerce . . . would be an ample compensation to France for acknowledging our independence, and for furnishing us, for our money, or upon credit for a time, with such supplies of necessaries as we should want, even if this conduct should involve her in war. . . . *Franklin,* although he was commonly as silent on committees as in Congress, upon this occasion, *ventured so far as to intimate his concurrence with me in these sentiments;* though, as will be seen hereafter, he shifted them as easily as the wind ever shifted, and assumed a dogmatical tone in favor of an opposite system.[62]

This is the only reference we have to Franklin's attitude in Congress with regard to foreign affairs, except a passage in a letter by Franklin himself. In March, 1777, he declared that "I have never yet chang'd the Opinion I gave in Congress, that a Virgin State should preserve the Virgin Character, and not go about suitoring for Alliances, but wait with decent Dignity for the Applications of others."[63]

Comparing the evidence of Franklin's attitude and role before the publication of *Common Sense* and afterward, one fails to detect any basic change. In England he occasionally was found speaking out against unnecessary involvements in European politics, even if he stood firmly by the concept of an Anglo-American community for security. Both before and after the publication of *Common Sense,* Franklin discussed the possibilities of a political and military connection with France, as appears from Bonvouloir's report about his negotiations in Philadelphia in December, 1775, and from the instructions for Deane in March, 1776. But before January, 1776, as well as afterward, we find Franklin personally, in his letters or in Congress, advocating only commercial relationships with Europe.

Having so far established the attitude of the two protagonists of American foreign policy in its earliest period, we ought to consider briefly the nature of the treaty which was drafted under Adams' direction and which was to be carried to France by Franklin. Adams tells that "Franklin had made some marks with a pencil against some articles in a printed volume of treaties, which he put into my hand." He pays Franklin the compliment that "some of these were judiciously selected, and I took them, with others I found necessary, into the draught."[64]

In one of the most recent and most thorough studies of the "Plan of Treaties"[65] it has been shown that Adams—and, we may add, presumably also Franklin—relied heavily on two treaties: the treaty between James II and Louis XIV of November 16, 1686, concerning the neutrality of the American colonies in case of a conflict between England and France, and the commercial treaty between England and France of 1713, accompanying the Treaty of Utrecht. These two were among the most liberal treaties in an age of extreme political and commercial rivalry, and the contemporary controversy about the treaty of 1713 is one of the more important early debates on the issue of strict protectionism versus more liberal principles. In these debates, incidentally, Daniel Defoe, whose literary work greatly influenced Franklin, excelled as champion of the liberal cause, then associated with the Tory party.

The liberal character of the American "Plan of Treaties" appears particularly in its provisions for commercial reciprocity. French traders in America and Americans in France were to enjoy exactly the same rights and privileges as the natives of the respective countries with regard to duties and imports. The draft treaty contained provisions for the general establishment of free and unhampered trade not only between France and America but also with respect to all other countries.[66] If France would not agree to the American proposals, the American commissioners were instructed to substitute the most-favored nation clause instead.

However, there seems to be a strange discrepancy between the motive of the treaty and the means suggested. This was, after all, no ordinary commercial treaty; it was the outcome of a motion demanding "foreign alliances"; it was the device of a new nation struggling for its very existence. In short, the final goal of the treaty was certainly the "involvement of France in the war against England."[67] There were, consequently, some articles dealing with territorial guarantees with which we shall deal later on. The main point is that, in spite of the urgency of the situation, the treaty simply proposed that "if in Consequence of this Treaty, the King of Great Britain, should declare War, against the most Christian King, the said United States shall not assist Great Britain, in such War, with Men, Money, Ships, nor any of the Articles in this treaty denominated Contraband Goods."[68]

This article, No. VIII of the version finally adopted, was the core of the treaty. America offered nothing but her commerce for the friendship and, as was clearly expected, the military intervention of France. To be sure, Congress felt somewhat uneasy about its immodest demands for French generosity. The members of the Committee of Secret Correspondence who drafted the instructions for the envoys to

France foresaw that this article "will probably be attended with some Difficulty."[69] Furthermore, as we have seen, some of John Adams' radical friends themselves thought the wording of this crucial paragraph self-defeating, and Richard Henry Lee proposed a decidedly political amendment to the instructions: the United States was to oblige itself to carry on the war until France would have acquired the so-called "Neutral Islands" in the West Indies which had been ceded to Great Britain in 1763. However, this amendment was defeated.[70] Commercial instead of political relations with Europe were an ideal of which Franklin and Adams had been the most prominent champions and which now had been accepted by the majority of Congress.

In the analyses of the early diplomacy of Congress, it has hardly ever been made sufficiently clear that there were two distinct issues which separated people like Richard Henry Lee and Samuel Adams from Franklin: the debate on "isolationism" versus "internationalism" and also a debate over the hasty solicitation of recognition by, and economic connection with, as many European powers as possible.[71] It must be pointed out here that, while consenting to "merely commercial relations," the radical group around Richard Henry Lee and Samuel Adams found another device to strengthen foreign help for their cause. What has been called the "militia diplomacy" of Congress began when this group won their case, and Congress on October 16, 1776, adopted additional instructions for the commissioners to be sent to Paris, enjoining them to obtain from other European powers recognition of independence and to conclude with them treaties of peace, amity, and commerce whenever the commissioners should "find occasion fit and convenient" to attempt it.[72] It was apparently with particular reference to this decision that Franklin, later on, repeatedly mentioned his opposition to the tendency of Congress to go about "suitoring for Alliances" instead of decently waiting for the application of others; he was, however, overruled.[73] The "militia diplomats" of Congress gained a further victory when Congress on December 24, 1776, appointed a committee (which included Richard Henry Lee and Samuel Adams) to prepare and report on a plan for obtaining foreign assistance, and on December 30, 1776, Congress resolved to send commissioners to the courts of Vienna, Spain, Prussia, and Tuscany.[74]

POLITICS VERSUS ECONOMICS: MERCANTILISM AND THE
DIPLOMACY OF THE AMERICAN REVOLUTION

The refusal to employ political means in America's relations with foreign countries, the refusal to form "entangling alliances"—a term which has lost much of its value because of the emotional tint it has received in numerous heated controversies—has been the subject of many interpretations. The most concise and penetrating summary of the arguments has been made in a recent scholarly analysis which concludes that the majority of Congress—in contrast to a minority believing that the war made it necessary "to have recourse to all the customary methods of power politics"[75]—did not want to pay with a "political alliance" for France's entrance into the war and desired to limit the "future relations of the United States with outside powers . . . to commercial questions." It is pointed out, however, that an interpretation of this attitude as "isolationism" pure and simple "considers this early period too much from the point of view of later developments.... The colonists in attempting to eliminate power politics and to place the relations among nations on a purely commercial basis acted entirely in accordance with radical eighteenth-century thought. In modern terms, it was no less an internationalist than an isolationist attitude which prompted their action." Isolationist and internationalist trends, it is said, could go hand in hand, "because both placed decisive importance on commerce."[76]

On the one hand, the desire of many Americans from 1776 onward to have no political relations with foreign nations, to consider commerce as America's only business with the outside world—in other words, the desire to keep away from European wars and politics—was very definite and real. A striking example of this early isolationism, besides the works of Thomas Paine, is to be found in some writings of Silas Deane, America's first agent in France and from December, 1776, until the spring of 1778 Franklin's and Arthur Lee's fellow-commissioner in Paris. We refer to Deane for a double reason. First, his statements have not been discussed in the only detailed treatment of early American views on isolation[77] and, second, his isolationist views appear as early as June, 1777, before France and America had concluded their alliance and before France's collaboration with Spain had aroused deep suspicions with regard to France in the minds of many originally pro-French Americans like John Adams and Deane himself. As early as June, 1777, at a time when Deane was regarded by the French as the most reliable and outspokenly pro-French of the three American commissioners,[78] he wrote to Dumas in Holland that "it is my ultimate and early wish that America may forever be as unconnected with the politics or interests of Europe as it is by nature situated distant from it, and that the friendly ties arising from a free, friendly, and independent commerce may be the only ties between us."[79]

On the other hand, one is certainly justified in pointing to the coincidence of views between American emphasis on "mere commerce" and the theories of the French Enlightenment, of the *philosophes* and the physiocrats. Enlightenment and reason would teach the rulers to recognize the true interests of their countries, and, furthermore, it would show them that these interests were "compatible and complementary."[80] Moreover, the school of French physiocrats had elaborated their "economic policy," economics and politics coinciding; "they believed that all political problems would be solved if the right economic principles were followed."[81] Those "right economic principles" taught that it was wrong to believe that one country gained only at the expense of another.

These theories of the French Enlightenment, then, amount to the abolition of power politics and its replacement by commercial intercourse. Obviously, in such a state of affairs "isolationism" is not necessary, because such notions as the balance of power and international rivalry become obsolete. Interestingly enough, we find in Deane's "isolationist letter" quoted above indications which would approach an attitude of the "new internationalism." He speaks in the true fashion of the Declaration of Independence when, with modest pride, he announces to Dumas that "I am not raising my countrymen above every other nation in the world; far from it; but they are a new people, and have certain notions that are either new in the world, or have been so long unpracticed upon and unheard of, except in the speculations of philosophers, that it is difficult, perhaps impossible, to compare them with any other nation."[82] The new mood of the Enlightenment seems to be even more strongly expressed when Deane speaks of England engaging "allies pretendedly to keep *the balance of power in Europe, as it is ridiculously and unintelligibly termed by European politicians.*"[83] In Deane's letter we have a perfect example of the contention that isolationist and internationalist elements could go hand in hand, because "both placed decisive importance on commerce."[84]

However, the emphasis on the replacement of political by economic relations, made equally by those who stress early American isolationism and by those who throw internationalist trends into greater relief, leaves out or does not make explicit a most important consideration: economics may be, and very often is, a tool of politics. The year 1776 is so often considered a "new beginning" in government, political philosophy, economic theory, and diplomacy that it is sometimes not deemed necessary to point out that the United States, after all, made diplomacy in the age of mercantilism and that it had to reckon with the doctrines and the prejudices of that age. We are still at times prone to look upon international relations with the preconceptions of the nineteenth century, with its separation of politics and economics. To employ commercial instead of political means does not mean the absence of political ends; it does not mean the elimination of power politics.

Oddly enough, not even the aversion toward and the lack of comprehension of a term like "balance of power" necessarily means the replacement of politics by economics. Witness Silas Deane's "isolationist" letter. It is true, Deane pointed out that he did not understand the term "balance of power"; it is true that he wanted to place America's relation with the rest of the world on a completely "commercial" footing. But at the same time he elaborated a theory of foreign affairs which, as he himself sadly confessed, would bring to naught his dreams of America's undisturbed and peaceful development. Deane's reading of history taught him, as he told Dumas, that the historical process brought forth a continuous decrease of independent states. He expected the unification of Europe, but he also predicted that Great Britain, by dominating India and forming alliances with Russia and America, would achieve a status in which "the riches, as well as the power, of that kingdom will be unparalleled in the annals of Europe, or perhaps of the world."[85] It was easy to foresee, Deane said, that "Great Britain, America, and Russia united will command not barely Europe, but the whole world united."[86]

It is indeed highly interesting to see that a Yankee businessman from Connecticut, in charge of Franco-American commercial relations, in spite of being strongly imbued with Enlightenment ideas, did not for one moment lose sight of a larger perspective which included politics and economics. He speaks of the power as well as the riches of Great Britain in terms which would have appeared outmoded and reactionary to French radical thinkers of the age. Deane envisages world unity not by voluntary federation but by the power of empire. The big three would command Europe and the world. The notion of a political alliance, frowned upon by the radical champions of a new diplomacy, appears to him as undesirable but inevitable. In spite of America's new principles, in spite of the speculations of philosophers, politics will not be abolished.

These were rather general reflections. But the insights which they reveal guided the American diplomats trying to win France's support in the struggle for independence. Deane's thoughts show clearly enough how certain fundamental principles of the age of mercantilism were at the bottom of his reasoning. Great Britain, as the center of the world's manufactures, was to extend her "mercantile system" through alliances. She would have the tremendous expanding markets of America and Russia, where her raw materials would be secured, and this gigantic economic system would generate the power to give law to the world. Riches, in other words, not only were sought for economic ends alone but were also conducive to political power and preponderance.

In a world dominated by many mercantilistic conceptions, America's commerce presented a tremendous political asset. Possibly the policy of Americans like Franklin and John Adams appears to be less unrealistic when we consider this all-important fact of commerce as a political weapon. In order to win the support of France and the other European powers, it might not be necessary to transfer the monopoly of the American trade from Great Britain to any other single country. The simple fact that England was to be deprived of one of her most important sources of strength and wealth, even if no other power would inherit the whole of it, could be held sufficient to procure the support of powers avidly looking for the enfeeblement of England. Franklin in particular, who had himself actively taken part in the last great public debate on mercantilistic foreign policies, was too well acquainted with the significance of the commercial factor in mercantilistic calculations of the balance of power not to know that the weakening of England alone would increase the prestige and weight of France enough to warrant her support for the revolting colonies. It is in this "political" light that we must see the "purely commercial relations" which a majority of Congress under the leadership of Franklin and John Adams considered as the basis of the proposals to be sent to Europe.

Congress took great pains to make the Treaty of Amity and Commerce look as attractive as possible to the French and empowered the commissioners to admit a provision into the treaty according to which the United States obliged itself never to grant an exclusive trade to Great Britain.[87] Robert Morris, member of the Committee of Secret Correspondence since the end of January, 1776, thought that the commerce of North America would compensate France "for the expense and evil of a war with Britain."[88] More cautious, but no less obvious, was the language with which Franklin and his two fellow-commissioners approached the French foreign minister soon after Franklin's arrival in Paris. "North America now offers to France and Spain her amity and commerce. . . . The interests of the three nations are the same. The opportunity of cementing them and of securing all the advantages of that commerce, which in time will be immense, now presents itself. If neglected, it may never return."[89]

One month later, when alarming news of the military events in America reached the commissioners, they addressed an even more urgent appeal to Vergennes. This message completely illustrates Franklin's pen in its curious mixture of power-political and moral reflections:

We can not on this occasion omit expressing our apprehensions that, if Britain is now suffered to recover the Colonies and annex again their great growing strength and commerce to her own, she will become in a few years the most formidable power by sea and land that Europe has yet seen, and assuredly, from the natural pride and insolence of that people, a power to all the other states the most pernicious and intolerable.

We would, therefore, with all deference, submit it to the wisdom of his majesty and his ministers whether, if the independence of the United States of America, with *the consequent diminution of British power* and the freedom of commerce with them, be an object of importance to all Europe and to France in particular, this is not the proper time for effectual exertions in their favor, and for commencing that war which can scarcely be much longer avoided, and which will be sanctified by this best of justifications, that a much injured and innocent people will thereby be protected and delivered from cruel oppression and secured in the enjoyment of their just rights; than which nothing can contribute more to the glory of his majesty and of this nation.[90]

Franklin repeated these ideas almost literally in a private letter to a Dutch friend, the court physician of the emperor Joseph II, Jan Ingenhousz. Franklin described his task in Europe to "procure aids from European powers"; he thought it in the interest of the European powers to grant aids, "as by that means the great and rapidly growing trade of America will be open to all, and not a monopoly of Great Britain, as heretofore; a monopoly, that, if she is suffered again to possess," might produce such an increase in England's strength as to "make her the most formidable power the world has yet seen."[91]

Do we need more proof for our contention that the Americans, and Franklin in particular, were very well aware of the intimate connection between commerce and power? In the preceding chapter we attempted to make the point that not the least important reason of Franklin's support of the Navigation Acts until 1775 lay in his appreciation of the factor of naval power. This letter, *mutatis mutandis,* is written in the same vein. Franklin's insight into the connection between overseas trade and naval power is further confirmed by his repeated references during the same year (1777) to the paramount importance of sea power. Only four days after his letter to Dr. Ingenhousz, Franklin—who always knew how to make a virtue of necessity—found the following advantage in the fact that France had so far (May, 1777) refused to meet openly the demands of America and to conclude the Treaty of Amity and Commerce with her: "In the meantime America has the whole Harvest of Prizes made upon the British Commerce, a kind of Monopoly that has its Advantages, as by affording greater Encouragement to Cruisers, it increases the Number of our Seamen and thereby augments our naval Power."[92]

FRANKLIN'S EARLY DIPLOMACY IN FRANCE

All during the year 1777 Franklin and his fellow-commissioners in France found themselves in an unenviable position. France showed no particular haste to agree to America's applications to recognize her independence and to conclude the Treaty of Amity and Commerce, which Franklin had brought from America. The inevitable consequence of these acts—a consequence which America, of course, wanted to provoke—would have been a war between France and England. As we shall see presently, the policy of Count Vergennes was war with England; but the American defeat on Long

Island in August, 1776, the reversals American arms suffered during the year 1777, the capture of Philadelphia by the British in September, 1777, and the consequent uncertainty whether the American enterprise was stable enough to warrant open intervention, on the one hand, as well as the extremely reticent attitude of Spain after a change of government at the beginning of 1777 and a new peaceful policy with Portugal, on the other, prompted the French government to maintain its policy of secret aid to America, while at the same time officially preserving all appearances of neutrality toward Great Britain.

Franklin, as will appear below, in accordance with the opinions of his fellow-commissioners and new instructions from Congress, did at times depart from his cautious and reserved policy of "no political and military entanglements." However, his basic opposition to going about soliciting alliances and his reluctance to go beyond the basis of the Treaty of Amity and Commerce in order to win French favor did not change. Fundamentally, Franklin in 1777 was no less "isolationist" than in 1775 or 1776. Three reasons seem to account for his attitude. First of all, as we have already seen, he believed that the fact of America's severance from the British mercantile system with the loss of England's commercial monopoly in America and the diminution of naval power which this implied would be a sufficient inducement for France's armed intervention. Commenting on France's double-faced policy of secret help while protesting officially her neutrality, Franklin in September, 1777, thought that

how long these two parts will continue to be acted at the same time, and which will finally predominate, may be a question. As it is the true interest of France to prevent our being annexed to Britain, that so the British power may be diminished, and the French commerce augmented, we are inclined to believe the sincerity is towards us, more especially as the united bent of the nation is manifestly in our favor.[93]

Franklin believed so strongly that this was the true interest of France that he thought too much impetuosity on the part of the American commissioners in Europe a positive evil. About October 21, 1777, the English intelligence agent, Paul Wentworth, had this to report to his superiors in London:

Franklin, with his usual apathy says, He is not deceived by France.—He dreaded their seizing the opportunity with too much warmth, & by relieving the necessities of America too liberally prevent their Industry, their ingenuity & the discovery of the Resources of a Country intended by Heaven for Independence in its utmost

Latitude. He cannot bear the faintest Idea of reconciliation short of Independency—& is averse, in his Conversations, to the Necessity of incurring obligations from France, which may bind America beyond its true Interests.[94]

Second, Franklin was clearly averse to all overly urgent appeals to France because of his conviction that one ought to negotiate from strength. On November 27, 1777, the distress of the American cause seemed to the commissioners to have reached its height—the news of the surrender of Burgoyne's army on October 17, 1777, at Saratoga had not yet reached Paris. Deane proposed a last desperate action at the French court: the commissioners should provoke a "categorical answer to the proposition of an alliance, or satisfy them that without an immediate interposition, we must accommodate with Great Britain."[95] Franklin, however, was of a quite different opinion: "He could not consent to state that we must give up the contest without their interposition, because the effect of such a declaration upon them was uncertain; it might be taken as a menace, it might make them abandon us in despair or in anger."[96]

Franklin's efforts to show no sign of weakness and to present America's willingness to treat with France as a favor rather than an urgent need appear particularly clearly in a report of a conversation with Franklin by a French nobleman, addressed to Vergennes. This conversation took place in September, 1777. Franklin scoffed at the French reluctance to come to a definite and open agreement with the United States. After some wine had somewhat excited the Doctor, so we are told, he said: "There is nothing better to do here than to drink; how can we flatter ourselves . . . that a monarchy will help republicans, revolted against their monarch? How will your ministers be able to believe what they cannot understand?" So Franklin ridiculed the French, but he immediately became more serious and almost uttered a veiled threat.

They [the French ministers] know we have great needs; we ask for help; they hope to exhaust an old enemy, and prevent a new empire from putting itself in the European balance. I am sorry for it! In order to be more surely, more promptly independent, to guarantee ourselves of obtaining liberty by our own strength, I should have liked that that of France should have prevented us from knowing the whole extent of ours: I should have liked, for the good of the two hemispheres, that we had been connected, from the first, in general commerce, through the interest of France.[97]

It seems unlikely, however, that Franklin's insistence on the maintenance of America's prestige was merely a tool of his diplomacy. As a third reason for Franklin's "show of strength" we find a profound faith in America's ultimate victory, nourished by his conviction of the innate strength of an agricultural society. In the critical days of the autumn of 1777 no less than in 1775, when he first expressed it to Bishop Shipley, Franklin took courage and confidence from his deep belief (recorded in the words of William Carmichael, then connected with the American mission in Paris) that "we shall derive Resources from our Distress, like the Earth-born Giant Antaeus, who derived new Strength from his Falls."[98] A few weeks later Arthur Lee wrote in his diary about Franklin's belief that America did not necessarily need immediate French intervention. Franklin "was clearly of opinion that we could maintain the contest; and successfully too, without any European assistance; he was satisfied, as he had said formerly, that the less commerce or dependence we had upon Europe, the better, for that we should do better without any connection with it."[99] Franklin liked to stress the advantages of America's working out her own salvation.[100] Carmichael went so far as to venture the idea that Franklin actually trembled "for Fear his Propositions should be accepted. He wishes no European Connection—He despises France and he hates England."[101]

We must add another interesting piece of evidence of Franklin's reserved and detached disposition with regard to European entanglements. It comes from a source which was necessarily interested in giving as accurate an appraisal as possible of Franklin's attitude: Count Vergennes. On January 7, 1778, already some time after the good news from Saratoga had been enthusiastically received, Vergennes described Franklin's attitude and pointed to the policies which suggested themselves to France:

We are informed that there is a numerous party in America which is endeavouring to fix as a basis of the political system of the new States that no engagement be contracted with the European powers. Doctor Franklin himself professes this dogma. Necessity alone has prevented its being established; but so soon as that ceases to exist, the insurgents, who will have asserted their independence without our help, will think they do not need it in order to maintain that independence. Then we shall be without any bond with them, exposed to their avidity and perhaps to their resentment.[102]

The Attitude of France: Vergennes's Concept of Foreign Policy

It is, indeed, high time to turn our thoughts to the policies of the power which America's leaders from the outset had singled out as most likely to respond to America's approaches: France. The interesting first stage of French help for the United States—secret aid—need not concern us here; it has been thoroughly dealt with elsewhere. The picturesque personality of the writer of *The Marriage of Figaro* occupies the central role in this story; and, on the American side, Franklin's colleagues, Arthur Lee and Silas Deane, had much more to do with it—to the great detriment of Deane—than Franklin himself. Franklin came to France in December, 1776, in order to demand more: recognition of independence, conclusion of a treaty of amity and commerce, and French entrance into the war. We know already that America, besides her amity and commerce, offered nothing more than the somewhat unsatisfactory assurance not to support England in case of a war between France and England. We also know the kind of political reasoning which lay behind America's seemingly all too modest offers of "purely commercial" relationships. We now must find out the French reaction to the offer which Franklin brought from America.

The French foreign minister, Vergennes, who had received his diplomatic grooming at the courts of Trier, Lisbon, Constantinople, and Stockholm, diplomat and statesman of the age of mercantilism, immediately saw through the appearance of America's "purely commercial" and "liberal" offers. We shall quote Vergennes's report to the French ambassador in Madrid about his first interview with Franklin at some length:

I don't know whether Mr. Franklin told me everything, but what he told me is not very interesting with regard to the situation of his country. The ostensible object of his mission, the only one which he has revealed to me, is a treaty of commerce which he desires to conclude with us; he even left me an outline. . . . Its modesty causes surprise, because they do not demand anything which they do not already enjoy, at least from our side. If it is modesty or fear to be a burden to those powers on whose interest they hope to be able to rely, then these sentiments are very laudable; but could it not be possible that this reserve is the result of a more political consideration? The Americans have felt too much the effects of the jealousy of commerce that animated the English, as not to foresee the consequences which it can and must cause. Firmly convinced that England would not remain tranquil if the two crowns would take over the important commerce which England has carried on with her colonies up to now, they [the Americans] perhaps may consider this motive sufficiently strong to effect a rupture between the three powers. This rupture, by changing the stakes of the war, would naturally lead the English to recognize the independence of the colonies which they still withhold, without the colonies finding themselves burdened with an eventual defensive alliance such as a new nation has to avoid because it can only grow and prosper in a long era of peace. We are led to consider this argument as their basic assumption because, while we are asked to give up every claim to recover or conquer any part of North America and of the adjacent islands which formerly belonged to us, we are offered nothing more than strict neutrality in case we should be attacked on account of this treaty. The colonies can still count on the urgency of the interest of the two crowns who can hardly admit the subjugation of the colonies by their mother country.[103]

One thing is obvious: Vergennes understood the motives of people like John Adams and particularly Franklin perfectly well, probably better than their own radical countrymen like Samuel Adams and Richard Henry Lee. The kind of response which the French would make, however, depended on the objectives and goals which French diplomacy wanted to pursue.

Ironically, a devoutly Catholic career diplomat, rather than the messengers of enlightenment and progress, initiated that vital support for the new republic without which history might have taken a very different turn.[104] What was the fundamental concept of Vergennes's foreign policy? Vergennes's point of departure was the humiliating situation in which France found herself between 1763 and 1774. France had reached a low point of power, influence, and prestige. Vergennes drew his conclusions in a memoir of December, 1774:

Regard for and the influence of every power are measured and regulated by the opinion one has of its intrinsic forces; therefore foresight ought to be exercised in the task of establishing this opinion most advantageously. Every nation is respected which is held to be capable of a vigorous resistance and which, not abusing the superiority of its forces, desires only what is just and useful for everybody: peace and general tranquillity. . . . But there is a truth which never ceases to recommend itself, though it be trivial, namely, the longer a peace lasts, the less it appears that it will last; peace has now existed for twelve years, and this implies a great argument against its further stability.[105]

Two main points emerge: the re-establishment of French prestige and the possibility of an approaching war. The low state of France's actual power made the greatest attention to France's prestige the highest duty and requirement of the moment. Nothing would be more detrimental to French prestige than to embark on a policy of conquest and expansion in the fashion of Louis XIV: "France ought to fear territorial aggrandizements from others much more than to desire them for herself. . . . To increase the territory of the kingdom would mean weakening the center in order to protect the remoter parts."[106]

It is true, Vergennes did renounce territorial ambitions, at least on a large scale. But this does not mean, as some writers imply, that he renounced the game of power politics. The Anglo-American conflict gave Vergennes ample reasons to combine his protestations of disinterestedness toward territorial aggrandizement with efforts to overthrow the status quo:

> In agreeing to the desires of the Colonies, and in supposing that the assistance which we are going to grant them will be efficient, the following advantages seem to result: (1) *The power of England will diminish and our power will increase to the same degree.* (2) *Her commerce will suffer an irreparable loss, whereas ours will increase.* (3) It is very probable that in the course of events we shall recover a part of the possessions which the English have taken from us in America, as the fisheries of Newfoundland, of the Gulf of St. Lawrence, of Isle Royale, etc. We do not speak of Canada.[107]

Vergennes did not deny that, in the case of an accommodation or of a British victory in America, a great amount of British power would be immobilized in North America by the constant possibility of a renewed quarrel; however, he argued that in this case England would "preserve the mercantile benefits which she has so far procured from America and will consequently maintain her manufactures and her navy. She will above all prevent the colonies from throwing a considerable weight in the balance in favor of some other power, which they could do in case of independence."[108]

Would not Vergennes's emphasis on commerce indicate that he meant to embark on a war for economic motives? Vergennes himself has given us the answer. He wrote after the alliance with America had been decided upon:

> They perhaps think at Madrid that the interest of acquiring a new trade had principally decided us. This motive, assessed at its true worth, can be only a very feeble accessory. American trade, viewed in its entirety and subject to the monopoly of the mother country, was undoubtedly a great object of interest to the latter and an important source of the growth of her industry and power. But American trade, thrown open as it is to be henceforth to the avidity of all nations, will be for France a very petty consideration.[109]

What emerges, then, as the principal motive in Vergennes's concept of foreign policy is the "diminution of British power." The enfeeblement of England and the consequent change in the balance of power in favor of France were the fundamental objectives of his American policy. To deprive England of her commercial monopoly in America was a political rather than an economic goal—a goal, however, which Vergennes, diplomat in the age of mercantilism, appreciated very highly.

FRANKLIN NEGOTIATES THE TREATIES OF COMMERCE AND ALLIANCE

We have now gone the full circle, and we arrive again at Franklin's guesses of the true interest of France. They are proved to be correct. We need not concern ourselves with the procrastination of Franco-American negotiations during the year 1777. The news from Saratoga, arriving in Paris on December 4, 1777, changed everything. "Now or never," exclaimed Vergennes.[110] The fear that the United States might now really work out its own salvation, stimulated by Franklin's purposely advertised meetings with English negotiators in Paris, convinced the king and the cabinet of the wisdom of accepting the American proposals for a treaty of amity and commerce and finally caused them to go ahead even when Spain declined. The apprehensions of France of becoming the dupe of an Anglo-American reconciliation overcame all sorts of hesitations.

The French argument was put in a nutshell by the head of the political section of the French Foreign Ministry, Conrad Alexandre Gérard, who was to become France's first minister plenipotentiary in the United States and the first foreign diplomat accredited in this country. We have his narrative of the decisive conversation with the American commissioners on January 8, 1778. Gérard told Franklin, Deane, and Arthur Lee that the king's resolutions "were exempt from all views of ambition and aggrandizement; that he only desired to bring about irrevocably and completely the independence of the United States; that he would find therein his essential interest in the weakening of his natural enemy, and that this important and permanent interest would render the American cause in future common to France."[111]

Gérard then proceeded to inquire about the conditions which the commissioners, Congress, and the American people would consider necessary in order to prevent any agreement with England short of "full and absolute independence." It was Franklin who replied and spoke of France's immediate entrance into the war. Gérard countered by saying that, although the king expected France's involvement in the war as a result of his connection with the Americans, he might attempt to establish independence by peaceful means. After some discussion Franklin finally read a statement "to the effect that the immediate conclusion of a treaty of commerce and alliance would induce the Deputies to close their ears to any proposal which should not have as its basis entire liberty, and independence, both political and commercial."[112] Without any hesitation Gérard told Franklin that this could be done as soon as the Americans wanted to. Franklin, according to Gérard, "already softened by this resolution, which he did not appear to expect, observed that this was what they had proposed and solicited vainly for a year past."[113] When Franklin asked for more details, Gérard explained that the Treaty of Amity and Commerce would be permanent; that the king was "too great, too just and too generous" to profit by the circumstances to gain any advantage from them; that he counted "only on the advantages which would result from mutual interest; that the interest was evident and permanent."[114] With regard to France's renunciation of commercial monopolies—a startling and truly revolutionary innovation in the age of mercantilism—Gérard told the commissioners that the king "was eager to give to Europe as well as America on this occasion an example of disinterestedness, by asking of the United States only such things as it might suit them to grant equally to any other power whatsoever."[115]

In these remarks we easily detect the voice of Gérard's master, Vergennes. The stress on the enfeeblement of England, the sacrifice of commercial to political considerations, the reference to the disinterestedness of the French king—all these precepts were now put into practice. But it is much more exciting to imagine what must have occurred in Franklin's mind when Gérard made these disarmingly liberal overtures. The fact alone that after having waited more than one year the French finally did agree to start negotiations with the Americans on the basis which Franklin had desired must have given him an immense feeling of relief; the French willingness to meet almost unconditionally the terms of the American demands "on the basis of mutual interest"—even more, the fact that the French really seemed to grasp what to Franklin were "their true interests"—must have given Franklin quite extraordinary satisfaction. We must bear in mind the constant bitter disappointments which Franklin's appeal to "enlightened self-interest" and to mutual good will had met in the colonies at the time of the Albany Congress and how his mission to England had ended in total frustration. A man like Franklin, whose work for "reasonable" policies, for reciprocal advantages, had so often been destroyed by pride and passion, must have been deeply moved by such "generosity." Without minimizing Franklin's joy that a decisive step had now been made for the independence of his country, it seems to us that one ought to see Franklin's reaction to the French proposals also as the fulfilment of lifelong and often disappointed hopes for mutual understanding. There is no reason to doubt Franklin's sincerity when he "confessed that he saw in it nothing which was not noble and just and which was not in keeping with the most generous and elevated views."[116]

Accompanying this laudatory statement, Franklin included a new proposal which had come from the French: a political treaty, a treaty of alliance to accompany the Treaty of Amity and Commerce. The need for this treaty was explained by the expectation of French involvement in the war as a consequence of the Treaty of Amity and Commerce. France needed certain guarantees for the eventuality of this involvement, which was taken for granted. The Americans, after all, had now to face "political entanglements."

However, these entanglements contained no more than what had already been contemplated by Congress in 1776. The Treaty of Alliance was to come into force only in the case of an actual outbreak of hostilities between England and France (Article I). Article II declared: "The essential and direct End of the present defensive alliance is to maintain effectually the liberty, Sovereignty, and independance absolute and unlimited of the said united States, as well in Matters of Gouvernement as of commerce."[117]

TERRITORIAL ASPECTS OF THE FRENCH ALLIANCE

The fear at the bottom of the aversion of people like Franklin toward political entanglements was the idea, in Franklin's words, that France might grasp the opportunity of helping America with too much warmth. After all, only thirteen years before the Declaration of Independence, the French had been driven out of the North American continent with the active and willing support of the colonists, among whom Franklin had assumed a most conspicuous role. Accordingly, Congress had inserted in its "Plan of Treaties" an article of territorial guarantee, stipulating that France should never

invade, nor under any pretence attempt to possess himself of Labradore, New Britain, Nova Scotia, Acadia, Canada, Florida, nor any of the Countries, Cities, or Towns, on the Continent of North America, nor of the Islands of Newfoundland, Cape Breton, St. John's, Anticosti, nor of any other Island lying near to the said Continent, it being the true Intent and meaning of this Treaty, that the said United States, shall have the sole, exclusive, undivided and perpetual possession of the Countries, Cities, and Towns, on the said Continent, and of all the Islands near to it, which now are, or lately were under the Jurisdiction of or Subject to the King or Crown of Great Britain, whenever they shall be united or confederated with the said United States.[118]

From the outset Congress was determined to assert its claim to the whole of British North America against France as well as England. France's agreement to renounce any revisionist plans with regard to territorial ambitions in North America turned out to be not quite so complete as Congress had demanded. Article IX of the "Plan of Treaties" was superseded by Article VI of the Treaty of Alliance, according to which

the Most Christian King renounces for ever the possession of the Islands of Bermudas as well as any part of the continent of North america which before the treaty of Paris in 1763, or in virtue of that Treaty, were acknowledged to belong to the Crown of Great Britain, or to the united States heretofore called British Colonies, or which are at this Time or have lately been under the Power of the King and Crown of Great Britain.[119]

The famous Article VIII of the American plan was now transformed into Article VIII of the Treaty of Alliance. It was only natural that France should insist on a formal guarantee against a separate peace treaty. Accordingly, the somewhat vague assurance of the original proposal was converted into the stipulation that "neither of the two Parties Shall conclude either Truce or Peace with Great Britain, without the formal consent of the other first obtain'd; and they mutually engage not to lay down their arms, until the Independence of the united States Shall have been formally or tacitly assured by the Treaty or Treaties that shall terminate the War."[120] This provision was not entirely novel for the American commissioners. On February 2, 1777, the three commissioners, alarmed by the preparation of Burgoyne's expedition in England, had decided to go beyond the instructions of Congress and to offer an alliance to France, that is, to conclude no separate peace

with England if France and Spain would enter the war.[121] Shortly
afterward new instructions from Congress arrived authorizing "any
tenders" necessary to secure the immediate assistance of these two
countries.[122] According to these instructions, Franklin had accepted
the task—which must have been distasteful to him—of making far-
reaching offers to Spain: the United States would assist Spain in the
conquest of Pensacola, provided Spain would grant free navigation on
the Mississippi and the use of the harbor of Pensacola; furthermore,
the United States even offered to declare war against Portugal if this
were agreeable to Spain.[123] However, the shift of Spanish policy toward
Portugal in the direction of a peaceful accommodation and the general
reluctance of both France and Spain at that time to come to the open
support of the United States never let these proposals materialize—
not unlikely to the relief of Franklin.

The urgent instructions of Congress which authorized the commissioners in Paris to make these far-reaching offers and the parallel
resolution of the commissioners themselves to take steps, if necessary,
which would by far exceed the original intentions of Congress as
expressed in the "Plan of Treaties" were made, as it were, under
duress; it was the bleak outlook in the military sector which caused
the Americans both in Baltimore and in Paris, independently of each
other, to go beyond their original intention to establish "merely commercial" relations with France and Spain.[124]

However, it has less often been emphasized that even at that time
the Americans still tried to make a virtue of necessity. They con-
sidered themselves obliged to offer a declaration of war against Portugal; they obliged themselves not to conclude any separate peace.
America offered to assist France in driving the English from the West
Indies, which were to become French, and agreed that half of the
Newfoundland fisheries would also be French. On the other hand, the
French were asked to help the Americans actively in the conquest of
Canada, Nova Scotia, Newfoundland, Saint John's, and the Bermudas.[125] In the hour of greatest need the American commissioners
raised a new demand: active help for the conquest of Canada was now
required. The French guarantee of the United States claim upon the
whole of British North America was no longer deemed sufficient. We
hardly err when we suppose that Franklin in particular backed this

demand; it was the conquest of Canada which would reconcile him to the idea of a political alliance. As we shall see later, all through 1776 and 1777 and until 1782 he mentioned Canada as a favorite condition for reconciliation with Great Britain. We need not repeat what we have heard already about Franklin's exertions to wrest Canada from the French during the Great War for the Empire. In 1777, during the tentative negotiations for a Franco-American alliance, the hope of seeing Canada confederated with the United States was one extenuating circumstance which made the prospect of a political alliance with France more acceptable to Franklin. In the decisive conversation of January 8, 1778, between Gérard and the American commissioners, the former mentioned the possibility of including in the alliance terms which would assure the expulsion of the English from the whole continent of North America. Gérard was most explicit about his secret intentions: "I had dwelt on the conquest of the whole continent, because Mr. Deane had confided to me that this was, according to the Doctor's way of thinking, the most definite reason for forming ties with France, which, he is inclined to think, the United States could otherwise do without."[126]

When it came to the formulation of the Treaty of Alliance, however, the French, far from including in the treaty a provision for a common conquest of British North America, cautiously limited themselves to guaranteeing to the United States "their Possessions, and the additions or conquests that their Confédération may obtain during the war, from any of the Dominions now or heretofore possessed by Great Britain in North america . . . the whole as their Possessions shall be fixed and assured to the said States at the moment of the cessation of their present War with England."[127]

This formulation left the Americans at liberty to hope for French support in this great enterprise. In the secret correspondence of the French diplomats, however, Franklin's wishes for the acquisition of Canada did not receive that favorable attention which Gérard's allusions might have suggested to him. As early as August, 1776, the French chargé d'affaires in London, Garnier, reported to Vergennes about a message from Franklin through the intermediary of Silas Deane. (Garnier had been acquainted with Franklin in the latter's London days.) As Garnier told Vergennes:

I at first suspected and afterwards found out that I owed this letter to the acquaintance which I formerly had here with Dr. Franklin. I admire his vast capacity too much not to be flattered at his remembering me, but I am still more pleased that he has no need of me. I did not wish to know the matters in hand: I do not wish that the Colonies should make us recover Canada, still less that they should acquire it themselves. They will have all the more need of us, when England is in possession of it.[128]

However, these things came into the open only much later. Considered as a whole, the French terms left an amazing degree of freedom of action to the Americans. Their commercial treaty was adopted with but few changes.[129] France never asked for commercial privileges, and she also foreswore territorial ambitions. Motivated above all by the desire for diminishing Britain's power by severing America from the British system, France saw that her interests and those of the United States coincided to an extraordinary degree. Similarity of interests also was demonstrated by the fact that there was no real bargaining about the terms of the treaty.

The first phase of American foreign policy had come to an end. Franklin and his fellow-commissioners were soon presented to Louis XVI as the representatives of a sovereign nation, and a French minister plenipotentiary was appointed to go to Philadelphia. After the conclusion of the two Franco-American treaties, the center of diplomatic interest shifted to Philadelphia and to Madrid. It became the task of the new French envoy in Philadelphia to supervise America's war efforts and diplomacy in agreement with the objectives of French policy. These objectives, as laid down in Vergennes's instructions to Gérard, included the retention of Canada, at least, by the English, because this would be "an element of disquiet and anxiety to the Americans, which will make them feel the more the need they have of the alliance and the friendship of the king, and which it is not his interest to remove."[130] Furthermore, Gérard had to make clear to Congress that the main target which now engaged the greatest efforts of French diplomacy, namely, to bring Spain into the war, would involve certain sacrifices, like the surrender of American claims for the Floridas.[131]

The main concern of American foreign policy for almost four years to follow was its relationship with Spain. However, the vain efforts of the United States to court the favor of Spain (which at times even produced the willingness to surrender America's claims for free navigation on the Mississippi) and John Jay's frustrated stay of thirty months in Spain in order to secure an alliance and a loan do not belong to our story. Until the beginning of serious peace talks with the British in the spring of 1782, Franklin found himself on a side track of the diplomacy of the American Revolution in its political aspect. As to finances, he became the most important man: it was he upon whom fell the task of procuring financial aid from France; it was he to whom all American envoys in Europe constantly appealed for help. It would be outside the scope of this essay to trace the story of French financial aid in the American Revolution. It will be interesting only in so far as it colored Franklin's attitude toward the French alliance, of which more will be said in the following chapter.

CHAPTER V

THE GENEROSITY OF FRANCE

FROM SUSPICION TO CONFIDENCE

FRANKLIN'S and Deane's message to America announcing the good news of the French alliance mirrors the joy and the pride of the Americans over their achievement. Two days after the signing of the treaties, Franklin hastened to tell the president of Congress that

we have found throughout this business the greatest cordiality in this court; and that no advantage has been taken or attempted to be taken of our present difficulties to obtain hard terms from us; but such has been the king's magnanimity and goodness, that he has proposed none which we might not readily have agreed to in a state of full prosperity and established power. The principle laid down as the basis of the treaty being, as declared in the preamble, "the most perfect equality and reciprocity"; the privileges in trade, etc., are mutual, and none are given to France but what we are at liberty to grant to any other nation.

On the whole, we have abundant reason to be satisfied with the good will of this court and of the nation in general, which we therefore hope will be cultivated by the Congress by every means which may establish the Union and render it permanent.[1]

Franklin's emphasis on French "magnanimity" and "goodness" may well be taken as an early expression of a moralistic element which has pervaded American thought on foreign affairs ever since in various degrees.[2] The French alliance seems indeed a turning point in Franklin's way of thinking about American entanglements in Europe. There are many signs which would indicate, at least outwardly, that John Adams was justified in saying that Franklin, in contrast to his utterances in Congress in 1776, came to assume "a dogmatical tone in favor of an opposite system."[3] Franklin's suspicions of France are suddenly superseded by expressions of great confidence, and he could even occasionally hope that the Franco-American alliance would be eternal, although this polite wish, occurring in a letter of thanks to two booksellers in Marseilles who had founded a Society of the Friends of America, should not be taken too seriously.[4] It will now be our task to investigate in greater detail how far the change in Franklin's ways of expression does indeed represent a change of "system."

147

As late as January 6, 1778, Franklin had told an English secret agent—
to whom he had granted an interview with the purpose of frightening
the French into an agreement with the Americans—that the "broad
bottom of reciprocal advantages" could provide the only basis for an
Anglo-American settlement.[5] Two days later he got his "reciprocal
advantages" for the first time in his life, but from France. Oddly
enough, Franklin from this point on rarely mentions the reciprocity of
interests. Gratitude for generosity becomes the keynote of his later
pronouncements on Franco-American relations.

FRANKLIN'S GRATITUDE TO FRANCE IN HIS
NEGOTIATIONS WITH ENGLAND

Only four days after the signing of the treaty, Franklin wrote to an
old English friend of his, David Hartley, son of the well-known philosopher, who was constantly busy seeking some accommodation between
England and America. Franklin, of course, could not yet openly avow
the conclusion of the alliance. But his feelings are transparent:

> America . . . was a dutiful and virtuous daughter. A cruel mother-in-law
> turned her out of doors, defamed her, and sought her life. All the world knows
> her innocence and takes her part, and her friends hope soon to see her honourably
> married. . . . I believe she will make as good and useful a wife as she did a daugh-
> ter, that her husband will love and honour her, and that the family from which
> she was so wickedly expelled will long regret the loss of her.[6]

Some weeks later Franklin wrote to another British agent that, in case
England should begin war with France because of the latter's connection with America, "we are bound by ties stronger than can be formed
by any treaty to fight against you with them as long as the war against
them shall continue."[7]

The culmination of this kind of argumentation came two years
later, in the spring of 1782, when Anglo-American peace negotiations
were already under way in Paris. This time Franklin had to deal with
Thomas Grenville, the representative of Charles Fox, the British Secretary of State for the Northern Department, in charge of foreign
affairs. In his diary of the peace negotiations Franklin records a visit of
Grenville's in May, 1782. Grenville, as was very natural, came to speak
of the different objectives which France pursued in the war—objectives which would transcend the aims for which the Franco-American
alliance had been concluded. He, of course, was alluding to the fact that

France, through her alliance with Spain, had accepted obligations which were incompatible with the terms of the Franco-American alliance. Whereas France and the United States had obliged themselves to continue the war until American independence would have been acknowledged by the British, the Franco-Spanish treaty made the end of the war dependent upon the conquest of Gibraltar. Grenville then asked Franklin whether the United States would actually feel itself bound to continue the war for goals which were foreign to American intentions. This question raised Franklin's moral indignation to the highest pitch. He immediately produced two letters which he had written on the subject to Hartley. Grenville, grasping the hopelessness of the situation, wanted to turn the conversation to another subject, but he had not taken into account Franklin's assiduity. Franklin could not possibly abandon an opportunity for lecturing on political ethics:

I gave him a little more of my Sentiments on the general Subject of Benefits, Obligations, and Gratitude. I said I thought People had often imperfect Notions of their Duty on those Points, and that a State of Obligation, was to many so uneasy a State, that they became ingenious in finding out Reasons and Arguments to prove that they had been laid under no Obligation at all, or that they had discharg'd it, and that they too easily satisfied themselves with such Arguments.[8]

Franklin now used an example. A man would lend a stranger money in order to save him from imprisonment for debts; the stranger after some time might repay the money; but, Poor Richard wondered,

has he then discharg'd the Obligation? No. He has discharg'd the Money Debt, but the Obligation remains, and he is a Debtor for the Kindness of A, in lending him the sum so seasonably. If B should afterwards find A in the same Circumstances, that he, B, had been in when A lent him the Money, he may then discharge this Obligation or Debt of Kindness *in part*, by lending him an equal Sum. *In part*, I said, and not *wholly*, because, when A lent B the Money, there had been no prior Benefit received to induce him to it. And therefore if A should a second time need the same Assistance, I thought B, if in his Power, was in duty bound to afford it to him.

Mr. Grenville conceiv'd that it was carrying Gratitude very far, to apply this Doctrine to our Situation in respect to France, who was really the Party serv'd and oblig'd by our Separation from England, as it lessened the Power of her Rival and relatively increas'd her own.[9]

Grenville, in other words, stated the whole affair in terms of the balance of power. Our philosopher, however, did not give Grenville the satisfaction of seeing the alliance from the same angle. Franklin replied simply that he was so strongly impress'd with the kind Assistance afforded us by France in our Distress, and the generous and noble manner in which it was granted, without exacting or stipulating for a single Privilege, or particular Advantage to herself in our Commerce, or otherwise, that I could never suffer myself to think of such Reasonings for lessening the Obligation; and I hoped, and, indeed, did not doubt, but my Countrymen were all of the same Sentiments.[10]

With one single sentence Franklin brings this moral disquisition down to earth: "Thus he gain'd nothing of the point he came to push."[11] In other words, Franklin knew only too well that a show of unity was an essential device in the political struggle. The English, naturally, sought to destroy Franco-American understanding and co-operation. Franklin knew how to counter the Briton's policy of *divide et impera.* Only thus, he thought, could he exact favorable peace terms from the harassed British.

AMERICAN ATTACKS UPON FRANKLIN'S DIPLOMACY

Franklin's purpose in praising the French alliance to Englishmen is obvious. Upon further investigation, however, we shall find that his expressions of gratitude to and confidence in France are not limited to his correspondence or conversations with Englishmen. Even among some of his countrymen, Franklin gained the reputation of neglecting America's essential interests.

In order to understand this second aspect of Franklin's outwardly (and possibly also inwardly) pro-French attitude, it is necessary to touch briefly upon the background of his position as America's chief diplomatic representative in France—from the fall of 1776 onward as joint commissioner to France; as minister plenipotentiary in Paris from September 14, 1778, when Congress revoked the joint commission; and, finally, in his capacity as member of the commission of five ministers which Congress appointed in June, 1781, to negotiate a peace treaty with England.[12]

Why were Franklin's diplomatic activities the object of so much criticism? How did some people come to hold the opinion that "Dr. Franklin's knowledge in electricity does not prove him to be acquainted with the politics of the courts of Europe; nor does his leading the lightening with a thread prove that he had lead us into any secrets of the British court."[13] How did it come about that Samuel Adams, for instance, thought it so difficult to persuade some people who had long been "habituated to admire the Wisdom of the Philosopher . . . to believe that in the different Character of a Politician he may be lyable to human Frailties at the age of more than three Score and ten."[14] Why did some people think that "the political salvation of America depends upon the recalling of Dr. Franklin"?[15] Certainly, Franklin's position in relation to his fellow-commissioners in Europe and in relation to Congress was much more precarious than his Olympian position in the heaven of the European Enlightenment.

The controversy on Franklin's role in France started in Paris. Much of it is a question of personal antipathy rather than differences of policies. Unrest was brought into the American representation in Paris by Arthur Lee and by Ralph Izard (the latter having been appointed in May, 1777, by Congress to the court of Tuscany, which court, however, he was never allowed to reach and therefore remained at Paris). Apart from the terribly suspicious temperament of Arthur Lee and the no less passionate one of Izard, there were other more particular causes of the bitter dissensions which tore the American group in Paris and jeopardized the reputation and efficiency of American diplomacy in these critical years.

First of all, the mutual antipathy between Arthur Lee and Franklin can be traced back to the 1760's, when both Lee and Franklin resided in London and worked for two rival land companies, Lee for the unsuccessful Mississippi Company, founded in 1763, and Franklin for the more successful Illinois and Indiana companies. The latter's claims conflicted with the claim of Virginia for the whole of the unsettled western territory.[16] The exasperation and suspicion of Lee, the Virginian, toward Franklin were transplanted to Paris when the two men found themselves in the commission to treat with France at the end of 1776.

The second reason was the Lee-Deane controversy on the payment for the French secret aid furnished through the fictitious firm of Hortalez and Company, set up and run by Beaumarchais. It was Deane who dealt with these matters in Paris, and Lee accused him of attempting to enrich himself with government money. Franklin and Deane got along with each other very well, and Franklin did not hesitate to write a warm recommendation for Deane,[17] in whose honesty he firmly—and rightly—believed.

A third cause was the quarrel between Deane and Franklin, on the one hand, and Arthur Lee and Ralph Izard, on the other, about the question of the "molasses article" in the Treaty of Amity and Commerce. At this time molasses was the chief export from the French West Indies to New England, where it was turned into rum. Consequently, it seemed important to Deane, who came from Connecticut, to insert an article into the treaty to prevent the French from laying export duties on molasses. The French demanded an equivalent benefit, and so Franklin formulated an article by which the United States promised not to put any export duties on merchandise going to the French West Indies. This article aroused the deepest suspicions of Arthur Lee and Ralph Izard, who thought that it gave more than reciprocal advantage to France and betrayed American interests. The two articles were included in the treaty, but after ratifying it Congress requested the deletion of these two articles, and France agreed.[18]

Franklin's sympathy for Deane was sufficient to arouse the wrath of Arthur Lee, but a fourth reason must be added. Lee accused Franklin of neglecting the work of the legation and of having more of a good time than would appear appropriate for the diplomatic representative of a country in distress and fighting a life-and-death struggle. "Dissipation" was Lee's war cry in his anti-Franklin campaign. It is quite possible that Lee was exasperated at Franklin's dining out six times every week; on the other hand, it is certainly true that Franklin's extensive social life also fulfilled a diplomatic function. So much has been written about the popularity of Franklin and its propagandistic significance for the cause of the American struggle that this point needs no elaboration.[19] Two other points might also have furnished some ground for Lee's exaggerations. Franklin himself confessed in his *Autobiography* that orderliness was not among his greatest virtues.[20] When John Adams arrived in Paris as successor to Deane, he consequently had to set about bringing some order into the legation at Passy.[21] Franklin's routine work for several years also comprised consular duties; he frequently complained of these administrative details and also of the innumerable visitors who bothered him with all sorts of applications. In the midst of all these activities, Franklin (who, after all, had passed his seventieth year when he came to France) was somewhat overwhelmed by all the work which was supposed to be done by him.

More valid than the impassioned accusations of Arthur Lee and Ralph Izard[22] are the remarks which Vergennes himself addressed to the French minister in Philadelphia. Vergennes, who, as we shall see presently, constantly defended Franklin against the charges of Lee and his friends, nevertheless had cause to note that,

although I have a high esteem and consideration for M. Franklin, I am nevertheless obliged to concede that his age and his love of tranquillity produce an apathy incompatible with the affairs in his charge, which is all the more painful to me as there are important matters about which this minister keeps silent, while his office would require him to transmit his opinion about these matters to Congress.[23]

It is indeed remarkable that Franklin reported to Congress only on rare occasions. Compared with the reports of Deane, John Jay, or John Adams, Franklin's diplomatic correspondence is neither numerous nor rich in comments or speculations on the political situation in Europe. Franklin thus got out of touch with Congress, which naturally did him more harm than good. Gérard reported from Philadelphia that, "as to Doctor Franklin, he never writes."[24] A little later Gérard again had to report that "none of the two parties puts that confidence in Doctor Franklin which his enlightenment and his sincerity would merit."[25] This was written in 1779, but at the end of 1780 the situation was still the same. Massachusetts and South Carolina, instigated by Messrs. Lee and Izard, were the only states to advocate the recall of Franklin, but the new French minister, La Luzerne, wrote to Vergennes that Franklin had no support in Congress; and, whereas few people believed the exaggerations of Lee and Izard that Franklin "lost in France the cause of America," "nevertheless the silence which this minister [Franklin] observes towards his constituents persuades them that he occupies himself very little with public affairs."[26] All this led to the appointment by Congress of Colonel John Laurens as special envoy to the court of France to negotiate a new loan. This lack of confidence hurt Franklin exceedingly and was most probably the chief reason for his offer of resignation, the refusal of which he accepted with gratification.[27]

A fifth reason for the dissensions among the American diplomats in Paris and a hostile attitude toward Franklin in America was Franklin's tremendous prestige in France, both in government circles and in public opinion. This unique popularity overshadowed the role of people like Arthur Lee and John Adams, whose jealous and suspicious temperaments could not bear to be slighted in such a way. "On Dr. Franklin the eyes of all Europe are fixed, . . . neither Lee nor myself are

looked upon of much consequence."[28] Before the conclusion of the
treaties in February, 1778, Lee could hardly—and he never did—reproach Franklin's attendance at the French court. However, when
after the alliance Franklin's attitude ostensibly changed—when, moreover, after the recall of Deane, Franklin became the unquestioned
favorite of the French government for the transaction of business concerning America—John Adams and Lee could not help but clash with
Franklin on matters of principle. The latter's endeavors to create good
will seemed to them incompatible with national honor and dignity.
Franklin himself told his son-in-law that "my too great reputation,
and the general good will this people have for me, and the respect
they show me, all grieve those unhappy gentlemen."[29] He was determined, however, not to reverse his conduct "for the alleviation of
their torments."[30]

Adams versus Franklin

With regard to policy, John Adams became the most serious and
most important opponent of Franklin's diplomacy. The differences
of these two men are all the more interesting in view of the fact that
in 1776 the opinions of both of them about the proposed course of
American foreign policy were in perfect agreement. Did only Franklin,
as Adams charged, change his concept? Or did Adams change? Or
did both men somewhat modify their systems, but in different ways?
These are the questions which we now must attempt to answer.

It may be stated at the outset that, after the conclusion of the two
treaties with France, both Franklin and Adams basically agreed about
two fundamental things: first of all, that the French alliance was a
good thing and, second, that it was likely to be lasting. Adams explicitly founded his belief in the value of the French alliance on the
principles of power politics. He thought that this alliance was truly
natural, for "as long as Great Britain shall have Canada, Nova Scotia,
and the Floridas, or any of them, so long will Great Britain be the
enemy of the United States, let her disguise it as much as she will."[31]
It was not much to the honor of human nature, Adams regretfully
noted, "but the fact is certain that neighbouring nations are never
friends in reality. In the times of the most perfect peace between them
their hearts and their passions are hostile, and this will certainly be
the case forever between the thirteen United States and the English
colonies. . . . The hatred and jealousy between the nations are eternal

and irradicable."[32] Adams held that France, the most powerful nation on the European continent, "enjoying the benefit of our trade"—which, it should be noted, does not mean a monopoly—and the United States together would be "a sufficient curb upon the naval power of Great Britain."[33]

Franklin, as we have seen, disliked those pessimists who "affect to discover self-interested views everywhere at the bottom of the fairest, the most generous conduct."[34] Accordingly, his language is less outspoken, more peaceful, and more hopeful; but, with regard to policy, there exists no fundamental cleavage between him and Adams. "Our states have now a solid support for their liberty and independence in their alliance with France," Franklin, Deane, and Lee wrote in a letter to Congress which shows the traces of Franklin's pen. France would continue to support, and other powers were likely to join, the alliance, because all were interested "in the freedom of commerce and in keeping down the power of Britain."[35] "The universal Wish to see the English Pride humiliated, and their Power curtailed," Franklin wrote in a private letter to America, was "encouraging" and gave "hopes of a happy Issue."[36]

Adams as well as Franklin attempted to combat the idea of the perfidy and inconstancy of France, deeply rooted in Americans as part of the British heritage. Both referred repeatedly to the fact that France had kept faith with Switzerland for more than one hundred and fifty years.[37]

The disagreement between Franklin and Adams was a matter of diplomatic tactics rather than of basic policy. Franklin, we have seen, extolled the magnanimity and generosity of France in terms which at times touch slightly on the ridiculous. Franklin maintained this language also vis-à-vis his own countrymen. "The king has treated with us Generously and Magnanimously,"[38] Franklin reported to his old correspondent in Massachusetts, Thomas Cushing, and he exhorted the Americans to use every means "to remove ancient prejudices, and cultivate a friendship that must be so useful to both nations."[39] He certainly tried to give a good example when, in the summer of 1780, he openly disavowed John Adams' self-righteous conduct at the French court (which will be discussed presently) in a letter to Vergennes, assuring the French minister that America's sentiments differed widely from those of John Adams and that Americans were "filled with the strongest expressions of the friendship of France, of the generous manner in which his majesty was pleased to enter in an equal treaty with us, and of the great obligations our country is under for the important aids he has since afforded us."[40]

In what way had Adams given occasion for this rebuff? Adams, moving about rather awkwardly in the world of European diplomacy, felt that American simplicity and inexperience were not equal to the refinements and secret ways of Old World diplomacy. Ever distrustful of human motives, he reported a few months after his first arrival in Europe that, although the French on the whole seemed to be "well convinced of the utility to their interests of the American alliance," they seemed to expect too much subservience from the people of America;[41] Adams felt that the French alliance was a necessary but nevertheless "a delicate and dangerous connection."[42] He feared that "your ministers here may have too much diffidence of themselves and too much complaisance for the court."[43] Fourteen months later, being back in Paris for the second time, Adams' suspicions had taken on a more definite shape. He had experienced the exertions of the French minister in Philadelphia to slow down America's expansionist desires and to sacrifice them to an understanding with Spain. Adams now had many reasons to think that no European power wished "to see America rise very fast to power. We ought, therefore, to be cautious how we magnify our ideas and exaggerate our expressions of the generosity and magnanimity of any of those powers. Let us treat them with gratitude, but with dignity. Let us remember what is due to ourselves and to our posterity, as well as to them."[44] Franklin reported to Congress Adams' complaint to him that "America has been too free in expressions of gratitude to France, for that she is more obliged to us than we to her, and that we should show spirit in our applications."[45] Adams, so Franklin told Congress, held that "a little apparent stoutness and a greater air of independence and boldness in our demands will procure us more ample assistance."[46]

Adams did not fail to display his notions of independence and boldness in his contact with Vergennes some time after his arrival in Paris early in 1780 as minister plenipotentiary of Congress to negotiate a peace settlement. Now the time of Adams' "shirt-sleeves" diplomacy had come. First of all, he spent several weeks in Paris without paying a call on Vergennes; then he took to lecturing Vergennes about problems of naval strategy, which the latter quite naturally resented; furthermore, Adams insisted on notifying the British of his powers to negotiate peace and a commercial treaty and of his willingness to go to London as soon as possible. Vergennes was staggered when he heard of Adams' intentions; this amounted to telling the English that all injuries and sufferings were forgotten. Vergennes in a stormy scene told Adams to keep his powers secret and, furthermore, not to meddle in matters of Franco-American relations. A further cause of irritation was Adams' objection to a projected French protest in Philadelphia about the injuries French merchants had suffered from Congress' devaluation of its paper money at a rate of 40:1. This clash between Adams and Vergennes reached its highest pitch when Vergennes remitted to Franklin his correspondence with Adams and asked Franklin to report to Congress about Adams' misbehavior.

This gave Franklin an opportunity to spell out and to interpret the difference between his own and Adams' approach to diplomacy and, in particular, to the French alliance. Franklin said that Adams mistook his ground and that "this court is to be treated with decency and delicacy."[47] Franklin continued:

The king, a young and virtuous prince, has, I am persuaded, a pleasure in reflecting on the generous benevolence of the action in assisting an oppressed people, and proposes it as a part of the glory of his reign. I think it right to increase this pleasure by our thankful acknowledgments. . . .

. . . It is my intention, while I stay here, to procure what advantages I can for our country by endeavouring to please this court; and I wish I could prevent anything being said by any of our countrymen here that may have a contrary effect and increase an opinion lately showing itself in Paris, that we seek a difference, and with a view of reconciling ourselves to England.[48]

This was written in 1780. About two years later Franklin was even more explicit about the underlying motives of his diplomatic approach. In a lesser-known passage he said:

This is really a generous nation, fond of glory, and particularly that of protecting the oppressed. Trade is not the admiration of their noblesse, who always govern here. Telling them their *commerce* will be advantaged by our success, and that it is their *interest* to help us, seems as much as to say, help us, and we shall not be obliged to you. Such indiscreet and improper language has been sometimes held here by some of our people, and produced no good effects.[49]

Franklin, in other words, laid all the stress on the psychological factor of creating an atmosphere of mutual understanding and good will; ostensibly he almost obliterated the assets which America could contribute to her connection with France. Adams always emphasized his conviction that the alliance, "notwithstanding all that has been justly said of the advantages to us, is no less advantageous to our allies,"[50] and he was keen to make this point understood by Vergennes.

Franklin's belief in the efficacy of subtle suasion and Adams' reliance on a more direct kind of pressure represent two methods of diplomacy. The difference between Franklin's and Adams' outlook is nowhere more strikingly revealed than in the different ways in which Franklin and Adams pleaded to Congress for one and the same thing. Both were agreed that a single minister plenipotentiary would be far preferable to the group of three or four commissioners, whose rivalries and hatred jeopardized America's prestige. But how different are their respective arguments for the same objective! Adams, ever true to his firm belief in the theory of balancing powers, thought that

an opposition in parliament, in a house of assembly, in a council, in congress, is highly useful and necessary to balance individuals and bodies and interests one against another, and bring the truth to light and justice to prevail. But an opposition in a foreign embassy, in the circumstances of this country and of Europe, is ruin. There can be no secrecy, no confidence, when such an opposition takes place, much less where there are such infernal quarrels as were between my colleagues.[51]

In other words, the theory of checks and balances, transplanted to the scene of international affairs, categorically must be replaced by national unity. A united front abroad was the first prerequisite of security. Franklin certainly did subscribe to the second part of Adams' thesis, but he did it in a much subtler way: unity and a show of force are not enough; in fact, the latter may even be highly detrimental to national interests. Adams remained in the sphere of the tangible balance of power. Franklin was at home there, too, but he also moved in the realm of imponderables. As for the three ministers instead of one, Franklin told Congress that

all the advantages in negotiation that result from secrecy of sentiment, and uniformity in expressing it and in common business from dispatch are lost. In a court, too, where every word is watched and weighed, if a number of commissioners do not every one hold the same language, in giving their opinion on any public transaction, this lessens their weight; and when it may be prudent to put on, or avoid certain appearances of concern, for example, or indifference, satisfaction, or dislike, where the utmost sincerity or candor should be used, and would gain credit if no semblance of art showed itself in the inadvertent discourse perhaps of only one of them, the hazard is in proportion to the number.[52]

These words, written in July, 1778, certainly show that America, at the very beginning of her stormy course through world politics, had at least one man who should have allayed Adams' fears that American simplicity and inexperience could not match the subtleties of Old World diplomacy. But it was Franklin whom Adams reproached as exhibiting an undue degree of servility and subservience to the French court.

Adams made Franklin's letter to Congress of August 9, 1780, the subject of an extremely bitter and lengthy attack in an article for the *Boston Patriot* of May 15, 1811.[53] A main point of his charge against Franklin—a charge which Franklin had reported in his letter to Congress—was that America, through the intermediary of Franklin, had been too free in expressions of gratitude to France. Interestingly enough, Adams passes by Franklin's subsequent justification for his conduct, namely, that it was his intention "to procure what advantages I can for our country by endeavouring to please this court." He also passes by another point in the same letter in which Franklin explicitly puts his diplomacy of gratefulness on the basis of political expediency as well as morality. Franklin expressly said that "such an expression of gratitude is not only our duty, but our interest. A different conduct seems to me what is not only improper and unbecoming, but what may be hurtful to us."[54] These words go far to show that his ostensible "change of system," of which he was accused in Adams' *Autobiography*,[55] and the change from a terminology of "isolationism" in 1776 and 1777 to one of fervent international friendship after the conclusion of the French alliance are not so profound as Adams supposed or as a reader of Franklin's writings would at first suspect.

Discussing Franklin's exaggerated appearance of gratitude, Adams makes a very strange remark. He quotes (or misquotes) a statement by Franklin with the intent of proving Franklin's servility to France, which, seen in its proper context, indicates just the contrary, namely, that Franklin changed only very little or not at all from his earlier "system" of policy, which had been highly approved of by Adams. Adams writes in this article:

I will give one example very much to the present purpose, because it explains the system of his conduct. He has said to me, not only once or twice, but many times, that Congress were out in their policy in sending so many ministers to several courts in Europe; that all their affairs in Europe ought to be under one direction, and that the French court ought to be the centre; that one minister was quite sufficient for all American affairs in Europe! It is not at all unlikely to me that he had expressed the same opinion to the Count and to many of his friends. I do not know, however, that he did. This sentiment, however, appears as extravagantly complaisant to the French and to himself, as mine can be thought extravagantly complaisant to America.[56]

What Adams depicts here as a telling example of Franklin's subservience to France has generally—and we think correctly—been interpreted as an indication of what has been called signs of "isolationism" in Franklin. The reader may recall that Franklin early in 1777 said that "I have never yet changed the opinion I gave in Congress, that a virgin state should preserve the virgin character, and not go about suitoring for alliances, but wait with decent dignity for the application of others."[57] It is true Franklin added that he was overruled and "perhaps for the best." That comment must be seen in the context of the time it was made. In March, 1777, as we have seen, the commissioners in Paris had reached a low ebb of despair and had been strengthened by Congress in their decision to offer much more than their original instructions—and the opinion of people like Franklin or Adams—had warranted.

The successful conclusion of the French alliance, contrary to all appearances, did not change Franklin's basic opinion. He remained in opposition to the system of "militia diplomacy."[58] One of the actions of "militia diplomacy" was the designation of Francis Dana as minister plenipotentiary to St. Petersburg without first receiving the agreement of the Russian court; Dana's mission ended in complete frustration. On his way from America to Russia, Dana stopped in Paris and consulted Franklin, who now (April, 1781) spelled out in greater detail than ever before the reasons which induced him to oppose the policy of Congress to "send so many ministers to several courts in Europe," an opposition interpreted by Adams as a sign of subservience to France. Franklin wrote to Dana:

I have long imagined that we let ourselves down in our offering our alliance before it is desired, and that it would have been better if we had never issued commissions for ministers to the courts of Spain, Vienna, Prussia, Tuscany, or Holland till we had first privately learnt whether they would be received, since a refusal from one is an actual slight that lessens our reputation and makes others less willing to form a connexion with us.[59]

The importance which Franklin attached to this point is stressed by the fact that he included it in the most significant diplomatic document he wrote, his *Journal of the Negotiation for Peace with Great Britain*

(1782): "It seems to me that we have in most Instances, hurt our Credit and Importance, by sending all over Europe, begging Alliances, and soliciting Declarations of our Independence. The Nations perhaps from thence seem to think that our independence is something they have to sell, and that we don't offer enough for it."[60]

This shows conclusively that Franklin after 1778, as well as before, adhered to a policy of prudent detachment with regard to European entanglements. His remark to Adams that the French court ought to be the center of American activities in Europe does not necessarily imply subservience to France. It meant that America had to concentrate her efforts in Paris, because France, as a matter of fact, had been the power most inclined to aid the Americans, and she had been the first and only power to take active steps on her own initiative to implement this aid. How little Franklin's thoughts in this respect were motivated by exaggerated reliance on and subservience to European powers, including France, emerges even more strikingly from a letter to John Adams in the fall of 1780:

> Our credit and weight in Europe depend more on what we do than on what we say; and I have long been humiliated with the idea of our running about from court to court begging for money and friendship, which are the more withheld, the more eagerly they are solicited, and would perhaps have been offered if they had not been asked. The supposed necessity is our only excuse. *The proverb says, God helps them that help themselves.* And the world, too, in this sense, is very godly.[61]

This opens another interesting aspect of our problem. Besides adding further evidence that Franklin after 1778 did not deviate from his fundamental policy of "reserve," it indicates that his concern with financial matters also had something to do with the attitude criticized by Adams. Adams did not understand Franklin's reasoning. "I have felt the mortification of soliciting money as well as you," he replied to this letter, "but it has been because the solicitations have not succeeded. I see no reason at all why we should be ashamed of asking to borrow money, after maintaining a war against Great Britain and her allies for about six years without borrowing money abroad."[62]

Franklin, on the other hand, on whose shoulders fell all the burden of the financial demands of Congress and of America's envoys in Europe, never ceased to exhort Congress and his colleagues to reduce their demands for financial help. He particularly pointed out that the business of raising money for the new country was a political rather than a financial task. Moneyed men, he told Robert Morris, would rather risk to lend to their own governments or to neighbors than "hazard it over the Atlantic with a new state which to them hardly appears to be yet firmly established." This explained the failure of procuring private loans for America; the "only chance of pecuniary aids" was to be expected from the governments of France or Spain, "who, being at war with our enemy, are somewhat interested in assisting us."[63] He warned Congress that "the best friends may be overburthened; . . . by too frequent, too large, and too importunate demands upon it the most cordial friendship may be wearied."[64] A statement of Robert Morris in a letter to Franklin that "no country is truly independent until with her own credit and resources she is able to defend herself and correct her enemies" appeared to Franklin "perfectly just."[65] To Morris, Poor Richard complained that "it is absurd the pretending to be lovers of liberty while they grudge paying for the defense of it."[66] Punctuality and modesty in financial matters assumed a definite political significance for Franklin. Importunity, Franklin had said, might destroy even the most cordial friendship.[67] The lack of reliability, he added on another occasion, would disgrace Congress "in a political as well as a pecuniary light through all the courts of Europe."[68]

Franklin's reluctance to apply for financial help, which Adams stigmatized as another sign of Franklin's unwillingness to support vigorously the interests of America, and which finally contributed to the decision of Congress to send a special envoy to France to procure a substantial loan,[69] appears as another phase of his constant efforts to strengthen America's prestige in Europe.

Adams, much more than Franklin, believed in the efficacy of constant direct pressure, in the policy of the big stick, even if it had not yet grown big. Franklin knew that, owing to the precarious situation of his country, a reputation for determination and firmness had to take the place of the material aspects of power. This kind of reputation could be built only upon the foundations of trust and confidence. To create this atmosphere of confidence was Franklin's task in Paris. He knew that Europe's faith in the stability and permanency of the American Revolution was the first prerequisite of effective help. The French suspected wrongly, but from their point of view not altogether implausibly, that those Americans opposing close connection with France desired reconciliation with England.[70] Franklin knew that the appearance of reconciliation with England was a double-edged sword. America's independence and power by 1780 or 1781 were far from having reached a sufficient degree as to be able to play off France against England or, in other words, to assume the role of a balancer.[71]

Franklin never revealed his innermost thoughts on this subject more clearly than in January, 1782, when he, as he had already done so frequently, declined another suggestion for a separate deal with England. He wrote to David Hartley:

> We should have so covered ourselves with infamy by treachery to our first friend as that no other nation can ever after be disposed to assist us, however cruelly you might think fit to treat us. Believe me, my dear friend, America has too much understanding, and it is too sensible of the value of the world's good opinion, to forfeit it all by such perfidy. . . .
> The supposition of our being disposed to make a separate peace I could not be silent upon, as it materially affected our reputation and its essential interests.[72]

One would indeed misunderstand Franklin greatly if one saw in his diplomacy of gratitude nothing but the reflection of a grateful mind, deluded by the appearance of altruistic generosity on the part of France. Franklin, in reality, was too good a diplomat not to anticipate the hour when mutual confidence and good will would be put to test. He knew that the hour might come when it would be his greatest asset to point proudly to the fact that "it is not possible for any one to be more sensible than I am of what I and every American owe to the King for the many and great benefits and favors he has bestowed upon us. All my letters to America are proofs of this; all tending to make the same impressions on the minds of my countrymen that I felt in my own."[73]

It was on this solid basis of his spotless record of confidence and gratitude, Franklin felt, that the complementary method of pressure and threats could effectually be used, once necessity compelled him to employ it. This emergency arose for the first time in the winter of 1780–81, when financial disaster brought America to the verge of collapse. Money from France or peace with England: these were the alternatives which Washington himself put before Franklin. In this hour of greatest need, Franklin, with the comforting assurance that he had always done his best to lighten the French commitment to America, put aside his usual reserve and threw the whole weight of his personal reputation, as well as the potential power of America, into his message to Vergennes:

I am grown old. I feel myself much enfeebled by my late long illness, and it is probable I shall not long have any more concern in these affairs. I therefore take this occasion to express my opinion to your excellency that the present conjuncture is critical; that there is some danger lest the Congress should lose its influence over the people if it is found unable to procure the aids that are wanted, and that the whole system of the new government in America may thereby be shaken. That if the English are suffered once to recover that country, such an opportunity of effectual separation as the present may not occur again in the course of ages; and that the possession of those fertile and extensive regions and that vast seacoast will afford them so broad a basis for future greatness, by the rapid growth of their commerce and breed of seamen and soldiers, as will enable them to become the *terror of Europe,* and to exercise with impunity that insolence which is so natural to their nation, and which will increase enormously with the increase of their power.[74]

With one stroke all moralizing about generosity is gone. This is the language of a man who knew that great political commitments were too important and too serious a matter to be talked about lightly and constantly. Franklin realized that the value of certain arguments increased with the scarcity of their use and that one should not paint the devil on the wall except in rare cases. This was such a case, and Franklin carried his point: a free gift of six million livres was the immediate result.[75]

THE MOTIVATION FOR FRANKLIN'S DIPLOMACY OF GRATITUDE

To summarize this analysis of Adams' charge that Franklin had been too free in expressions of gratitude to France, there emerge six main motives which may be assumed to have been the cause of Franklin's constant stress on French generosity after the alliance of 1778.

In the first place, Franklin, for reasons of pure expediency, opposed British attempts to drive a wedge into the Franco-American bloc with a constant affirmation of unity forged by ties stronger than mere treaties. On these occasions, at least partly for reasons of policy, he refused to accept even the language of national interests.

Second, Franklin took into account his experience of the psychology of the French people. As has often been told, he played the role which the enthusiasm of the French Enlightenment required of him to perfection. The appeal to the French predilection for noble causes rather than to material interests belonged to his stock in trade in

France. It must remain open to doubt whether Franklin, when he extolled the virtues of Louis XVI and his pleasure in helping an oppressed people, was aware of the king's original reluctance to come to the succor of rebels against monarchical principles.[76] Furthermore, it might not be amiss to ask what Franklin—who never ceased to praise the honesty and sincerity of Vergennes and always averred America's gratitude to him—would have said, had he seen Vergennes's memoir to the Spanish court, proposing common assistance to America which ought to be "sufficient to assure a total separation from England and to compel the Americans to gratitude."[77]

Third, the paramount importance which financial support assumed for the success of the American cause and the necessity to establish America's credit in Europe also prompted Franklin to speak in terms of good will, modesty, and obligations rather than to utter wild threats.

Fourth, closely tied with the third point but going beyond it, was Franklin's continuous concern for the political prestige of America. "The essential interests of our reputation" were fostered by him with particular care as a substitute for material power.

Fifth, one encounters a peculiar and characteristic element of Franklin's political ideas. This element stands out clearly when one contrasts it with an opposite approach to the same problem. After the conclusion of the French alliance, the then president of Congress, Henry Laurens, told Washington about the approaching reception of the first French minister in Philadelphia and could not "forbear disclosing to you, Sir, that there is a reluctance in my mind to acknowledgements of obligations or generosity where benefits have been, to say the least, reciprocal."[78] This reluctance, it must be said, was utterly absent in Franklin's mind. He never was stingy with the acknowledgment of "generosity" when, in fact, only mutual interests were satisfied. His own political career in England had been shipwrecked by the narrow and deluded notions of self-interest he had encountered there. France, on the other hand, had given up "the jealousy of commerce"; she had grasped her golden opportunity. France, in contrast to England, had wisely contrived to establish a harmony of interests with America, and this enlightened concept of her interests had bestowed tremendous, indispensable benefits upon America. This course of action, Franklin may have sincerely thought, might well be termed generous.

Finally, one may say that it was the greatest wisdom of Franklin's diplomacy to distinguish between normal and extreme situations. In contrast to Adams, he knew how to produce the right admixture of suasion and coercion. Constant threats in the Adams manner were bluffs, and the French did call these bluffs more than once. Franklin never lost sight of the permanent interests of America, which called for the continuing good will of France. In order to protect and encourage this good will, extraordinary pressures or departures had to be limited to extraordinary cases and not be made the daily bread of diplomacy. In other words, tests of mutual reliability were fraught with potential danger and had to be kept to an absolute minimum.

Two important problems still remain unanswered. The first problem is this: Even granted that Franklin was motivated by the interests of America rather than anything else, did his estimate of French policy and his belief that it was actually founded upon reciprocal advantages correspond to reality, or did he misjudge it? We shall attempt to throw some light on this question by discussing briefly Franklin's election as a commissioner to negotiate peace with England and by inquiring into his attitude during the peace negotiations of 1782. The second problem to be examined is the question as to whether Franklin's reliance on "generous France" was conditioned by the peculiar needs of the War of Independence or whether he conceived Franco-American friendship under the larger perspective of the permanent post-Revolutionary relationships of America with the Old World.

FRANKLIN'S ELECTION TO THE PEACE COMMISSION

The discrepancy of American and French interests kept increasing as the war went on. One disturbing development took its rise from the great quarrel between Vergennes and Adams in the summer of 1780. Vergennes, influenced by false reports from Gérard in Philadelphia that the Lee-Adams faction was pro-English, was now thoroughly alarmed about Adams' behaving like a "bull in a china shop" and about the prospect of having Adams as sole American minister at the peace negotiations. These negotiations, because of mediation efforts of Austria and Russia, and also because of the desperate financial situation in France, seemed nearer than ever before in 1781. Following instructions from Vergennes,[79] the French minister in Philadelphia requested Congress to issue instructions to the American peace commissioner enjoining him to "manifest a perfect and open confidence in the French ministers" and "to take no step without the approbation of his Majesty."[80] Obviously this request was prompted by Vergennes's expectation of seeing Adams alone at the peace conference. Congress accepted this suggestion without much debate and on June 15, 1781, proceeded to instruct its commissioner or commissioners

to make the most candid and confidential communications upon all subjects to the ministers of our generous ally, the King of France; to undertake nothing in the negotiations for peace or truce without their knowledge and concurrence; and ultimately to govern yourselves by their advice and opinion, endeavouring in your whole conduct to make them sensible how much we rely on His Majesty's influence for effectual support in every thing that may be necessary to the present security, or future prosperity of the United States of America.[81]

These instructions actually meant the surrender of diplomatic freedom of action on the part of the United States; they were caused by the French desire to curb John Adams. However, before they were finally adopted, Congress surrounded Adams with four other ministers to treat for peace: John Jay, Thomas Jefferson, Benjamin Franklin, and Henry Laurens. Franklin, it ought to be noted, was elected only against considerable opposition; the argument was advanced that Franklin's interest in lands at the left bank of the Ohio, granted by the British Crown, would predispose him, at best, to a lukewarm defense of the United States claim to western territory.[82] Finally, however, the conviction prevailed that "his abilities, character and influence are what will be of most use to us in Europe."[83]

This conviction had been materially encouraged by the French minister in Philadelphia. Vergennes wanted La Luzerne to tell Congress without hesitation that Franklin's conduct "is as zealous and patriotic as it is wise and circumspect, and you may affirm with assurance, on all occasions where you think it proper, that the method he pursues is much more efficacious than it would be if he were to assume a tone of importunity in multiplying his demands, and above all supporting them by menaces, to which we should neither give credence nor value."[84] La Luzerne, realizing the difficulties connected with the recall of Adams, suggested that two men be added to the commission and had, of course, Franklin in mind. General Sullivan, who was delegate to Congress from New Hampshire and who actually was bribed by La Luzerne to inform him of proceedings in Congress and to make French influence felt in Congress, nominated Franklin. Franklin's appointment succeeded only after Jefferson and Henry Laurens had been added to the commission.[85] The ostensible reason for multiplying the number of the plenipotentiaries was the removal of "every suspicion or fear that the interests of one part would be sacrificed to secure that of another."[86]

Jefferson declined his appointment. Henry Laurens, on a mission to Holland, was captured by the British and thrown into the Tower. John Adams, John Jay, and Benjamin Franklin remained. Congress sent them the truly subservient instructions cited above. The instructions called forth rather divergent reactions. John Adams thought them shameful.[87] Adams' indignation is not surprising. More strange is the violently hostile reaction of John Jay from Spain. Jay had been sent to Spain as representative of the pro-French party of the East Coast. However, the unwillingness of Spain to conclude an alliance or to grant a loan to the United States during his residence in Spain of more than two years had been a deep mortification to Jay, and this bitter experience had turned him from a friend of European connections to an ardent foe of "entanglements." Jay summed up his feelings about the instructions by saying that

this instruction, besides breathing a degree of complacency not quite republican, puts it out of the power of your ministers to improve those chances and opportunities which in the course of human affairs happens more or less frequently to all men. Nor is it clear that America, thus casting herself into the arms of the King of France, will advance either her interest or reputation with that or other nations.

Jay was so embittered that he asked Congress to relieve him early from a commission which obliged him to receive directions "of those on whom I really think no American minister ought to be dependent."[88]

What a tremendous contrast to this outbreak of wounded pride is Franklin's complaisant acknowledgment of these instructions. He had no more to say than that "I have had so much experience of his majesty's goodness to us, in the aids afforded us from time to time, and of the sincerity of this upright and able minister, who never promised me anything which he did not punctually perform, that I can not but think the confidence well and judiciously placed, and that it will have happy effects."[89]

Franklin had given material proof of his confidence in Vergennes. As early as the fall of 1778, Franklin had resorted to Vergennes's help to prevent his mischievous colleagues from sending him to Holland; there he would have been "put on ice," whereas Adams in Paris and Lee in Madrid would have dominated the places of political interest.[90] Franklin, moreover, never failed to turn over to Vergennes his correspondence with British peace emissaries, for instance, with David Hartley.[91]

FRANKLIN AND FRANCE DURING THE PEACE NEGOTIATIONS OF 1782

A critical and decisive stage of Franklin's cordial relationship with the French ministry was reached when the surrender of Cornwallis at Yorktown (October 19, 1781) was followed by the eclipse of Lord North's ministry in England (March 20, 1782) and the accession to power of the Whigs, under Rockingham's leadership. England had now decided for peace. Franklin had attentively watched the changing mood of British opinion, and from March, 1782, we find him engaged in a correspondence with Lord Shelburne, an old acquaintance of his from his London days and Secretary of State for the Southern Department in charge of colonies in the new ministry. Presently Shelburne's representative, Oswald, appeared in Paris to talk things over informally with Franklin. From April until John Jay's arrival in Paris at the end of June, Franklin alone handled the informal peace talks in Paris. We shall not go into the details of the negotiations,[92] which developed slowly and were complicated by the fact that the two rivals in the British cabinet, Shelburne and Charles Fox, both sent representatives to Paris, Shelburne in his capacity as Colonial Secretary and Fox as Foreign Secretary.

Reduced to its bare essentials, the situation presented itself simply enough: England was anxious to cut America loose from the French alliance and to come to a separate settlement with the states, if possible, on the basis of some kind of "federal alliance"; on the basis of total independence, if necessary.[93] In any case, America had again to be drawn into the orbit of English influence.

France, on the other hand, was interested in retaining her influence over the United States for a twofold reason. First of all, France, in the secret convention of Aranjuez with Spain (1779), had bought Spain's entrance into the war with the promise to continue it until the acquisition of Gibraltar by Spain. From this moment, France had been torn between the conflicting objectives of her obligations to Spain and to the United States. The Franco-American alliance had stipulated the obligation to conclude no separate peace. At that time American independence had been the only goal, but now Gibraltar had inserted itself as a mighty stumbling block in Franco-American relations. This stumbling block had made itself felt in the French attempts to move Congress to a moderate and conciliatory attitude toward Spanish claims in North America, conflicting with the American desire for free navigation on the Mississippi and for the lands between the Appalachian range and the Mississippi.

Second, France herself, although having no territorial ambitions on the American continent, wanted to keep the young republic within reasonable bounds—that is to say, American security should never be so perfect as to render reliance on France dispensable. It is true that, before embarking on aid to the revolting colonies, Vergennes had in 1775 uttered the opinion—rather commonplace among the political concepts of the eighteenth century—that republics were rarely possessed by the spirit of conquest[94] and that consequently French intervention in favor of the United States would not produce great dangers for the Spanish colonial empire. However, by 1782, or, more correctly, from 1778 onward, the territorial aspirations of the United States had appeared rather exaggerated to the French minister; Canada, for instance, he thought ought to remain in British hands as a check against America's desires to emancipate herself from French advice and influence.[95] Spanish claims to Florida and to the lands east of the Mississippi and south of the Ohio did not appear unreasonable to the French. Besides, the French had a particular interest in receiving a share in the Newfoundland fisheries held by the English; it being very unlikely that the British would concede to the French as well as to the Americans a share in the fisheries, France wanted to get the privileges for herself. The United States, of course, although it soon gave up the hope of getting Florida, never renounced the desire for Canada, and it was most determined to insist on the Mississippi boundaries and the fishing rights in Newfoundland.

In this sketchy survey Franklin's dilemma appears clearly. America's territorial ambitions—and we shall see in the next chapter more fully that Franklin never gave up his early ardent expansionism—just did not square with France's wishes for restraint and moderation. In spite of these divergences, the evidence for Franklin's continued pro-French attitude during the peace negotiations seems impressive. In his very first interview with Oswald, the British negotiator, Franklin let him know that "America would not treat but in Concert with France."[96] He affirmed his faith in the indissoluble bonds of gratitude and obligation to France to Grenville in May, 1782, in the strong words already cited.[97] The English again and again tempted Franklin in the direction of a separate settlement, pointing to the unreasonableness of America's continuing a war for the sake of Spanish ambition: "If Spain and Holland, and even if France should insist on unreasonable Terms of Advantage to themselves, after you have obtain'd all you want, and are satisfied, can it be right that America should be dragg'd on in a War for their Interests only?"[98] Grenville asked Franklin in a later interview. Franklin stuck to his customary tactics: "I resolv'd from various Reasons, to evade the Discussion and therefore answer'd, that the intended Treaty not being yet begun, it appear'd unnecessary to enter at present into Considerations of that kind."[99]

Franklin's empirical and diplomatic mind always prevented him from trying to cross a bridge before he came to it. For the moment, he drew even closer to France than ever before. On April 12 the great naval victory of the British Admiral Rodney over the French fleet under De Grasse had reinforced Britain's strength. Franklin was fearful that this success would give the British new hopes and would cause them to delay a settlement;[100] in this belief he was strengthened by the extreme reluctance of the British government to issue powers to its representatives in Paris which would unequivocally, and previous to the treaty proposals, acknowledge the American commissioners as representatives of the United States of America.

On June 11 Franklin talked to Vergennes about the desire of the British to separate the allies

by large Offers to each particular Power, plainly in the View of dealing more advantageously with the rest; . . . it was possible, that after making a Peace with all, they [the British] might pick out one of us to make War with separately. Against which Project I thought it would not be amiss, if, before the Treaties of Peace were signed, we who were at War against England should enter into another Treaty, engaging ourselves, that in such Case we should again make it a common Cause, and renew the general War.[101]

About two weeks later Franklin defended in the strongest terms his concept of faith in the French alliance and gave expression to his deep-seated distrust of British measures. But a new cause had been added to his apprehensions: he had heard from the French Foreign Ministry that General Carleton had made proposals in America tending to retain the king's sovereignty over America under terms similar to those being made to Ireland.

> The firm, united resolution of France, Spain, and Holland, joined with ours, not to treat of a particular, but a general peace, notwithstanding the separate tempting offers to each, will in the end give us the command of that peace. Every one of the other powers sees clearly its interest in this, and persists in that resolution. The Congress, I am persuaded, are as clear-sighted as any of them, and will not depart from the system, which has been attended with so much success, and promises to make America soon both great and happy.[102]

This was addressed to the Foreign Secretary in Philadelphia. A private letter to America makes clear how conscious Franklin was of America's potential weight in the European balance of power and the precious advantages to be derived from this fact. "We have no safety but in our independence; with that we shall be respected, and soon become great and happy. Without it, we shall be despised, lose all our friends, and then either be cruelly oppressed by the King, who hates, and is incapable of forgiving us, or, having all that nation's enemies for ours, shall sink with it."[103]

Franklin, who stuck to his principle that *"appearances* should . . . be attended to . . . as well as *realities,"*[104] did not fail to remit copies of both these letters to Gérard de Rayneval, private secretary of Vergennes, with the request to show them to Vergennes "to convince him that we held no underhand dealings here."[105]

So far, so good. The spirit of Franklin's utterances seemed in perfect agreement with the famous instructions of Congress. However, this was only a part of the story. Franklin's widely reputed taciturnity—which drove people like John Adams to despair and exasperation[106]—could work both ways. On the one hand, Franklin had seemed to acquiesce in Vergennes's statement to Grenville in a common interview that American independence had been declared long before the United States had received the slightest encouragement from France: "There sits Mr. Franklin, who knows the Fact, and can contradict me if I do not speak the Truth."[107] Franklin knew the truth—he had himself negotiated with the French secret agent Bonvouloir in Philadelphia as early as December, 1775—but he did not contradict Vergennes, not even in his diary, where he reported this episode. On the other hand, Franklin's silence worked against France also. Franklin had already in April, 1782, confidentially suggested to Oswald the cession of Canada.[108] This was never revealed to Vergennes. In the second week of May, Franklin is even reported to have told Thomas Grenville, the envoy of Charles Fox, that *if the Colonies had their Independence, their Treaty with France was at an end.*[109] This alleged statement certainly did not correspond to the terms of the Treaty of Alliance, which provided that no side should make peace without the consent of the other. Furthermore, it is contradicted by Franklin's account of an interview he had with Grenville on May 14, in the course of which Franklin indignantly rejected Grenville's allusions about following the interests of America rather than feelings of friendship for France.[110] The most satisfactory interpretation of this somewhat mystifying episode is given by V. T. Harlow, who thinks that "it seems possible that Franklin had, in fact, dropped one or two guarded hints about the future by way of encouraging Britain to make peace proposals and that Grenville had sharpened them in his mind into a declaration of readiness in certain contingencies to desert an ally."[111] However, much more significant was the fact that on July 10, 1782, Franklin presented his first detailed peace proposals which actually were to form the basis of negotiation without having consulted or even informed Vergennes. These proposals—divided in "necessary" and "advisable" articles—did include the demand for Canada among the "advisable" articles.[112] In other words, Franklin, whose first reaction to the instructions of Congress "to proceed only under the full confidence and advice of the French Minister"[113] had been most complaisant, was the first among the American plenipotentiaries to disobey the orders of Congress when these orders seemed to conflict with what he deemed to be the essential interests of the United States.

At the end of June, 1782, John Jay arrived in Paris. In August, Franklin fell ill, and Jay became the moving force on the American side of the negotiations. Jay had come to Paris full of bitterness about Spain, full of suspicions about France, and full of indignation about the subservient instructions of Congress. From then onward the Americans traveled a faster road toward a separate settlement with the British. It is difficult to form a coherent picture of Franklin's attitude toward France during those months from July to December, 1782; his *Journal* stops abruptly on July 1, and he wrote few letters during this period. Therefore, we shall first sketch Jay's impressions of French policy and then compare them with Franklin's reactions.

Jay had made up his mind not only as to Spain but also as to France, and several events during the summer contributed to his decided opinion that

so far, and in such matters as this court may think it their interest to support us, they certainly will, but no further, in my opinion.

They are interested in separating us from Great Britain, and on that point we may, I believe, depend upon them; but it is not their interest that we should become a great and formidable people, and therefore they will not help us to become so.[114]

This is certainly different from—and, as a great deal of evidence indicates, more correct than—Franklin's statement that loyalty to the French alliance alone would make America great and happy, if we supposed, as well we may, that greatness for Franklin meant territorial expansion. Four particular factors had a cumulative effect on Jay's mind.

First of all, there was Vergennes's insistence that the Americans ought to be satisfied with the commission of the English plenipotentiary which arrived in Paris in the second week of August. The tortuous wording of this commission carefully avoided recognition of the United States and simply spoke of the "said colonies and plantations." Jay, legalistic by nature and suspicious of European diplomacy by experience, thought that Vergennes's counsel was motivated by the desire to postpone American independence until French and Spanish wishes had been satisfied by a peace. Vergennes's confidential correspondence of that time shows that Jay's suspicions were not wholly unfounded.[115]

Second, there was the question of the western boundary. Jay was profoundly upset by a memoir remitted to him by Vergennes's confidential secretary, Gérard de Rayneval, purporting to present his own suggestions but, in fact, being the result of discussions between Rayneval and the Spanish ambassador, Aranda. This proposal would have deprived the United States of the Mississippi boundary, leaving the country north of the Ohio to England and the southwestern part of the western lands as a Spanish Indian protectorate.[116]

This memoir, sent to Jay on September 6, was followed by the news that Rayneval had suddenly gone to London on September 7.

Finally, on September 10, Jay received a copy of an intercepted letter of the French chargé d'affaires in Philadelphia, Barbé-Marbois, to Vergennes, speaking against American participation in the New-foundland fisheries.

These four events, taken together, convinced Jay that the French envoy had gone to London to notify Shelburne of France's willing-ness to renounce her demand for English recognition of American independence previous to a treaty, to acquiesce in the partition of the western lands between Spain and England to the detriment of America, and to share the fisheries with England to the exclusion of all other powers. Consequently, Jay took the unprecedented step of sending Benjamin Vaughan, confidant of Shelburne and Franklin's friend, to London to tell Shelburne that, by immediately acknowledging Ameri-can independence, granting America a share in the fisheries, and allowing America access to the Mississippi, England was now in a position "immediately to cut the cords which tied us to France, for that, though we were determined faithfully to fulfill our treaty and engagements with this court, *yet it was a different thing to be guided by their or our construction of it.*"[117]

The way not only for separate negotiations but even for separate preliminary articles was open, and it was chosen by Shelburne as well as by the Americans. Articles were signed, granting to America the Mississippi boundaries as well as the fisheries, without the knowl-edge of the French, on November 30, 1782, whereupon Franklin duly notified Vergennes of what had happened.

How did Franklin react to all this? In regard to Vergennes's rec-ommendation to accept the rather doubtful British commission for the peace negotiations, Franklin was quite willing to approve the French minister's ideas. "The Doctor said," so Jay reported to Con-gress, "he believed the commission would do."[118] Franklin's mind was decidedly not legalistic, and Vergennes's argument that "names signified little; that the King of Great Britain's styling himself the King of France was no obstacle to the King of France's treating with him,"[119] seemed to satisfy him. Now, in 1782, Franklin knew that American independence in substance was assured; that France had waged war because of this independence and in this respect would not let the

United States down. Franklin expressed these ideas on the way home from the interview with Vergennes. Franklin, according to Jay, "imputed this conduct to the moderation of the minister, and to his desire of removing every obstacle to speedy negotiations for peace. He observed that this court had hitherto treated us very fairly and that suspicions to their disadvantage should not be readily entertained. He also mentioned our instructions as further reasons for our acquiescence in the advice and opinion of the minister."[120] Jay, on the other hand, stuck to his opinion that Vergennes "did not wish to see our independence acknowledged by Britain until they had made all their uses of us,"[121] that is, until the great coalition would have forced Britain to yield with regard to Spain. It definitely seems that Jay evaluated French policy more correctly than Franklin.

With regard to French desires for the fisheries, although he himself always took a firm stand on American rights in this question, Franklin felt obliged to exculpate the French court from dark designs when he wrote to Samuel Cooper about the controversial Barbé-Marbois letter that, even "supposing it all genuine, the forward, mistaken zeal of a secretary of legation should not be imputed to the King, who has in so many ways proved himself our faithful and firm friend and ally."[122] However, Franklin signed the joint letter of the American commissioners after the signing of the preliminaries and so assented to the statement that "we had reason to imagine that the articles respecting the boundaries, the refugees, and fisheries did not correspond with the policy of this court."[123]

In the question of the western boundary, Franklin's attitude was less ambiguous, although, it must be added, he showed in this matter, too, with the exception of the preceding assertion, extreme reluctance to place any responsibility on the French government. Jay has recorded a conference with Vergennes on the western boundary at which they discussed the exorbitant demands of Spain. "Dr. Franklin joined with me," Jay reported, "in pointing out the extravagance of this line; and I must do him the justice to say, that in all his letters to me, and in all his conversations with me respecting our western extent, he has invariably declared it to be his opinion that we should insist upon the Mississippi as our western boundary, and that we ought not, by any means, to part with our right to the free navigation of it."[124]

Rayneval, at this occasion, thought that the Americans claimed more than they had a right, but Vergennes gave Franklin the great pleasure of being "very cautious and reserved,"[125] possibly purposely avoiding putting Franklin into the painful dilemma of choosing between his confidence in Vergennes and his patriotic duties. Franklin, in fact, had the good chance to prove his attachment to the Mississippi boundary without insulting Vergennes. He was in the happy situation of throwing all his indignation on the Spanish government, with whom no treaty and little gratitude united the American minister in Paris. In this case, he felt no compulsion to hide that "he was a little out of humour with that court," and he had written to John Jay in Madrid (April 26, 1782) that "Spain has taken four years to consider whether she should treat with us or not. Give her forty, and let us in the meantime mind our own business."[126] Two days after the aforementioned conference with Vergennes, Franklin found an outlet for his concern over the Mississippi boundary and reported to Foreign Secretary Livingston that "my conjecture of that court's [Spain's] design to coop us up within the Allegany Mountains is now manifested. I hope Congress will insist on the Mississippi as the boundary, and the free navigation of the river, from which they could entirely exclude us."[127]

Franklin continued to manifest confidence in Vergennes's intentions. He did not share Jay's apprehensions about Rayneval's trip to London, and Jay saw that "he did not concur with me in sentiment respecting the objects of it, but appeared to have a great degree of confidence in this court, and to be much embarrassed and constrained by our instructions."[128] Consequently, Jay sent Vaughan to London without the knowledge of Franklin! However, in the last week of October, in the memorable words of John Adams, who had arrived in Paris on October 26, "Franklin turned to Mr. Jay and said, I am of your opinion, and will go on with these gentlemen in the business without consulting this Court. He has, accordingly, met us in most of our conferences, and has gone on with us in entire harmony and unanimity throughout, and has been able and useful, both by his sagacity and his reputation, in the whole negotiation."[129]

As we have indicated before, this decision was not so new or so startling as it appears in Adams' diary and as it has traditionally been presented.[130] Franklin, as a matter of fact, had been the first of the three commissioners to leave the path of full confidence with the

French ministry, but he had somehow retained a middle way. He had certainly not gone so far as Jay in either his suspicions of France or his implementation of those suspicions.

Naturally it fell to Franklin's lot to justify the commissioners' course of action before Vergennes. Franklin did this in a famous letter which has often been called a diplomatic masterpiece. He pointed to the fact that the terms of the Treaty of Alliance had not been violated, since the preliminaries signed with the British were to take effect only in the case of a general peace. Technically, the commissioners had committed an entirely "domestic" offense—they had violated the instructions of Congress to proceed only in constant consultation with the French government. Politically, they had certainly abandoned the path of close collaboration which the French had expected. American interests had taken precedence over French interests. "Nothing has been agreed in the preliminaries contrary to the interests of France,"[131] Franklin told Vergennes, omitting mention of the Anglo-American deal on the fisheries. Franklin distinguished sharply between the obligations of the Treaty of Alliance and the instructions from Congress: "No peace is to take place between us and England till you have concluded yours. Your observation is, however, apparently just, that in not consulting you before they were signed, we have been guilty in neglecting a point of *bienséance.*" Franklin was perfectly honest when he justified his action with an indirect reference to America's national interest: "But as this was not from a want of respect to the king, whom we all love and honor, we hope it will be excused." Again, as he always did when the gravity of the situation warranted it, he dropped the language of mere gratitude and spoke the more decisive language of political interests. He hoped, so Franklin continued, that

the great work, which has hitherto been so happily conducted, is so nearly brought to perfection, and is so glorious to his reign, will not be ruined by a single indiscretion of ours. And certainly the whole edifice sinks into the ground immediately if you refuse on that account to give us any further assistance.

... *The English, I just now learn, flatter themselves they have already divided us.* I hope this little misunderstanding will therefore be kept a secret, and that they will find themselves totally mistaken.[132]

In fact, the British were not totally mistaken. It is true that Franklin's conciliatory letter was followed, on January 20, 1783, by a formal declaration, signed by Franklin and Adams, to the effect that the preliminary articles were not designed to "alter the relation of the

United States toward England"[133] as long as peace should not be concluded between France and England. For all practical purposes, however, the first entangling alliance of America's history, "the indispensable instrument of our deliverance as a nation," had come to an
end.[134] Long before Washington issued his neutrality declaration and
repudiated entangling alliances, the French Foreign Office itself had
declared that France had "never pretended to make America a useful
ally"; that she had had "no other end in view than to deprive Great
Britain of that vast continent."[135]

THE PERMANENCE OF FRANKLIN'S PRO-FRENCH ATTITUDE

The story of Franklin's attitude toward the French alliance, however, is not yet quite finished. His hope that the English would find
themselves "totally mistaken" in having divided America and France
meant more than the soothing formula of a clever diplomat who
wants to calm the apprehensions of his partner. Franklin continued to strive for a close understanding between France and America
even after having transacted business without consulting the French
court. Shortly after the conclusion of the provisional articles, Franklin
wrote a letter to his American friend, Samuel Cooper, which provides
an excellent clue to his political concept. He alluded to the anti-French
attitude of John Adams and the Lee-Adams group in America and
insisted that

it is our firm connexion with France that gives us weight with England and respect throughout Europe. If we were to break our faith with this nation, on
whatever pretense, England would again trample on us and every other nation
despise us. . . .
In my opinion, the true political interest of America consists in observing and
fulfilling, with the greatest exactitude, the engagements of our alliance with
France, and behaving at the same time towards England so as not entirely to
extinguish her hopes of a reconciliation.[136]

Our suspicions might be aroused when we hear that Franklin remitted a copy of this private letter to the French Foreign Office.[137] No
doubt he was extremely interested in convincing the French of his
unchanged sentiments; for Franklin, while negotiating the preliminaries with England, was at the same time charged with procuring a
new loan from France. He contrived to tell Vergennes of the conclusion of the preliminaries and at the same time to apply for more

financial help. Only five days after Franklin had taken part in the secret signing of the preliminary articles with England, he felt obliged to defend France again: "It is vain for me to repeat again what I have so often written, and what I find taken so little notice of, that there are bounds to everything, and that the faculties of this nation are limited like those of all other nations."[138]

The French, in spite of the American commissioners' breach of confidence, did grant a loan of six million livres. To Franklin this was new proof of the French good will toward America which he had never ceased to extol. He seems to have been well aware of the desperate state of the French finances, and he appreciated French "generosity" all the more highly. In April, 1783, Franklin wrote to the American Foreign Secretary:

> The finances here are embarrassed, and a new loan is proposed by way of lottery. . . . I mention this to furnish you with a fresh convincing proof against cavillers of the King's generosity toward us, in lending us his millions this year at five per cent., and of his concern for our credit. . . . You have been told that France might help us more liberally if she would. This last transaction is a demonstration of the contrary.[139]

This reason for Franklin's attempt to erase ill feeling between America and France became even more apparent when he complained about John Adams' undisguised hostility toward France. "The violent and extravagant language held here by a public person, in public company . . . distressed me much at the time, being then, at your earnest insistence, soliciting for more aids of money, the success of which solicitation such ungrateful and provoking language might, I feared, have had a tendency to prevent."[140]

Critics of Franklin's pro-French attitude have in the main attacked his faulty judgment of French motives, and there seems to be little doubt that in the fateful summer of 1782, for instance, he did not distinguish sharply enough between France's unswerving devotion to the goal of American independence as such and the French intention to surround the new republic by certain checks in order to prevent it from becoming too independent. Franklin reaffirmed most emphatically his faith in French policy several months after the conclusion of the provisional articles.

He wrote to Secretary Livingston:

With respect to myself, neither the letter from M. Marbois, handed us through the British negociators (a suspicious channel), nor the conversations respecting the fishery, the boundaries, royalists, &c., recommending moderation in our demands, are of weight sufficient in my mind to fix an opinion that this court wished to restrain us in obtaining any degree of advantage we could prevail on our enemies to accord, since those discourses are fairly resolvable by supposing a very natural apprehension that we, relying too much on the ability of France to continue the war in our favor and supply us constantly with money, might insist on more advantages than the English would be willing to grant, and thereby lose the opportunity of making peace, so necessary to all our friends.[141]

To all appearances, Franklin saw neither the fact that France had tried to add the weight of America to her own scale in the balance of power nor that she also attempted to prevent the United States from becoming the balancer itself and to keep it permanently tied to French interests. However, he may have applied his maxim, "Let all men know thee, but let no man know thee thoroughly," in this instance as on so many other occasions. Franklin's professed interpretation of French conduct did furnish new fuel to the charges which had been made against him since the conclusion of the French alliance. Upon receiving news from Samuel Cooper that there were people in America who believed that Franklin "favored, or did not oppose"[142] the design of France to deprive the United States of the fisheries and the western territory, Franklin felt that he "ought not to suffer an accusation, which falls little short of treason to my country, to pass without notice, when the means of effectual vindication are at hand."[143] He asked Jay and Adams to give testimony of his good conduct. Adams replied politely but coldly; Jay, however, in a very cordial manner.[144]

Absorbed in the question of Franklin's assessment of French motives and the charge of "subservience" to France, critics of his diplomacy have infrequently stressed the significance of the financial motive in his approach to France, and they have rarely pointed out with adequate emphasis that his reliance on France might have been to a large extent prompted by a continuing distrust of England.

The British naval victory over the French Admiral De Grasse in April, 1782, pushed Franklin so far into the arms of the French as to let him suggest an explicit renewal of the military alliance for future wars.[145] But even after he had understood that the British meant business in proposing peace negotiations, and after he had gone far in separate negotiations with the British representative, Oswald, in July, 1782, Franklin's apprehensions of Britain emerged again and again. Jay's firm refusal to treat with the English envoy except on the basis of an explicit acknowledgment of the "United States of America" was held by Franklin "rather too positive, and therefore rather imprudent." In case "Britain should remain firm, and future circumstances should compel us to submit to their mode of treating, we should do it with an ill grace after such a decided and peremptory refusal."[146] As a matter of fact, Franklin's apparently all too timid reasoning was not unjustified. Jay and Franklin were finally forced to desert that ground which Jay in particular had defended with great éclat. They eventually accepted a commission of Oswald, issued according to the resolution of the cabinet, "to treat with the Commissioners appointed by the Colonys, under the title of Thirteen United States, inasmuch as the Commissioners have offered under that condition to accept the Independence of America as the First Article of the Treaty."[147] On October 14, 1782, when the final negotiations were already under way, Franklin reported to the American Foreign Secretary that "the court and people of England are very changeable. A little turn of fortune in their favour sometimes turns their heads; and I shall not think a speedy peace to be depended on, till I see the treaties signed."[148] Even shortly after the successful conclusion of the preliminaries, Franklin continued to speak pessimistically about the British: "We should not, however, imagine ourselves already in peace. The other powers are not yet agreed, and war may still continue longer than we expect. . . . A little more success in the West Indies this winter may totally turn the heads of that giddy nation."[149]

Now we may be in a better position to trust in the sincerity of Franklin's assertion, only three days later, that *"it is our firm connection with France, that gives us weight with England, and respect throughout Europe."*[150] The favorable terms of the preliminary peace articles had not suppressed his suspicions. They had not destroyed his deeply ingrained conviction of England's pride, corruption, and insolence, and this conviction remained after the conclusion of the peace. In December, 1783, Franklin exhorted Congress to be on its guard against England. He thought that the English court, although having made peace with America, was not in truth reconciled "to its loss of us, but still flatters itself with hopes that some change in the affairs of Europe or some disunion among ourselves may afford them an opportunity of recovering their dominion."[151] As late as May, 1784, Franklin stuck to a principle which now appears as the truly fundamental idea behind his "diplomacy of gratitude." France, he wrote to Samuel Mather in America, continued her friendship for the United States.

> It is a friendship of the utmost importance to our security, and should be carefully cultivated. Britain has not yet well digested the loss of its dominion over us, and has still at times some flattering hopes of recovering it. Accidents may increase those hopes, and encourage dangerous attempts. A breach between us and France would infallibly bring the English again upon our backs; and yet we have some wild heads among our countrymen, who are endeavouring to weaken that connexion! Let us preserve our reputation by performing our engagements; our credit by fulfilling our contracts; and friends by gratitude and kindness; for we know not how soon we may again have occasion for all of them.[152]

It was his concern for the security of his country which prompted Franklin again and again to urge a policy of building up or preserving a reserve of friends, credit, and reputation.[153]

It has been said that Franklin's insistence on America's "firm connection with France" was "looking at the situation too exclusively from the interest of the United States at the end of 1782."[154] It is true that John Jay had already at that time given a rather different prospect of America's future foreign policy: "It is our policy to be independent in the most independent sense, and to observe a proper distance towards all nations, minding our own business, and not interfering with, or being influenced by, the views of any, further than may respect us."[155] We agree with the statement that "it was John Jay rather than Benjamin Franklin who forecast the American foreign policy of the future."[156]

However, there are two considerations which tend to minimize the difference between Franklin's and Jay's ideas. First of all, Franklin's apprehensions of British policy even after the peace were founded on the failure of the United States to acquire Canada. We have seen in our discussion of Franklin's Canada pamphlet, and we shall see again in the next chapter, how Franklin argued that security on the North American continent, so long as two great powers dominated it, was more than fragile. And we should remember that even a man who, much more than John Jay, laid down the principles of American isolationism, John Adams, proclaimed after the end of the War of

Independence, quite in agreement with Franklin's misgivings, that friendship with France was essential to America's safety as long as England remained in possession of Canada.[157] Neither Jay nor Adams nor Franklin at that time could foresee the eventual development of American-Canadian relations.

To the apprehensions about Britain's continuing power position on the North American continent there was added, in Franklin's mind, the satisfaction and joy over France's policy of moderation. Franklin wrote in 1783 that

the character of this court and nation seems, of late years to be considerably changed. The ideas of aggrandizement by conquest are out of fashion, and those of commerce are more enlightened and more generous than heretofore. . . . The wise here think France great enough; and its ambition at present seems to be only that of justice and magnanimity towards other nations, fidelity and utility to its allies.[158]

Three reflections suggest themselves. First of all, there is a similarity between this conception and Vergennes's program of a "policy of prestige" for France and his argument that territorial conquest or commercial monopolies would weaken rather than strengthen France's badly damaged reputation. Second, the change from territorial ambitions to a more moderate policy must have been particularly striking to Franklin, who had given so much thought to the menace of French power on the North American continent; moreover, Vergennes's renunciation of a commercial monopoly in America and, more important, his advocacy of the armed neutrality for the protection of neutral shipping and the rule "free ships, free goods,"[159] definitely did make a great impression upon Franklin. Third, there is an unmistakable flavor of "Enlightenment" in Franklin's praise of French policy. Vergennes, of course, employed his disinterestedness in territorial or commercial privileges as an ideological factor in his effort to redress the balance of the Old World by calling into existence the New.[160] We cannot conclusively prove whether Franklin really did not see this aspect of Vergennes's policy or whether he merely did not want to see it.

This much, however, seems to be established: Franklin did not approach France in 1776, 1777, and 1778 with utopian optimism, with great expectations, or with exaggerated confidence and trust; on the contrary, it was dire necessity, as he said himself repeatedly, that caused him to apply for French help. Even then, his approach was

made reluctantly, and Franklin never gave up this reluctance in apply-
ing to other European nations.[161] "God helps them that help themselves," remained his motto in international affairs. His unfailing expressions of gratitude to France and the strongly moralistic touch of
his diplomacy at times obscured, but never succeeded in obliterating,
his fundamental conviction that mutual interests were the only firm
basis of political connections. The great common interest of the United
States and France was the common enmity to England, and, in Franklin's thought, this enmity would not disappear on the part of America
as long as the presence of England on the North American continent
constituted a potential threat to America's security. There is no reason
to suppose that a change of French policy from moderation to ambition—which the Napoleonic Wars were to produce—accompanied by
a prudent policy in England, would have found Franklin putting
reasons of gratitude above those of security.

A French diplomat has said the following about Franklin's successor
as American minister to the court of France:

Mr. Jefferson loves us because he detests England; he seeks an understanding
with us because he dreads us less than Great Britain; but tomorrow perhaps he
would change this sentiment in our regard if tomorrow Britain ceased to inspire
his fear. Jefferson, though a lover of liberty and science, though an admirer of
the efforts that we have made to break our fetters and scatter the cloud of ignorance that weighs upon mankind, Jefferson, I say, is an American, and on that
account is unable to be sincerely our friend. An American is the born enemy of
every European nation.[162]

This, it seems to us, also describes the attitude of Jefferson's predecessor
in Paris to perfection.[163]

CHAPTER VI

RECONCILIATION

FRANKLIN'S "PACIFISM"

BENEVOLENCE in diplomacy may well rebound with a vengeance, or so it may have appeared to Benjamin Franklin in 1780 when he suggested to his English friend, David Hartley, that Congress had probably intrusted the negotiation of peace with England to John Adams rather than to himself because "they may have heard of a very singular Opinion of mine, that there hardly ever existed such a thing as a bad Peace, or a good War, and that I might therefore easily be induc'd to make improper Concessions."[1] In fact, the dictum that "there has never been, nor ever will be, any such thing as a *good* War, or a *bad* Peace,"[2] was a favorite with Franklin during and after the War of Independence. He desired urgently prevention of "further carnage"[3] and desperately wished for "some happy invention to stop the spreading of the flames, and put an end to so horrid a conflagration."[4] Franklin's profoundly peace-loving and antimilitary nature was shocked beyond description by the atrocities of war, and his utilitarian mind was appalled by the waste of resources, money, and energy inevitably involved in war. "Abstracted from the inhumanity of it," he said in the last years of his life, "I think it wrong in point of human prudence."[5] An army Franklin described as a "devouring monster," and the acquisition of territory, the free passage of rivers, or the establishment of free trade with another nation, so he suggested, might much more profitably be made by purchase than by war.[6]

During his stay in England, Franklin had hailed the new and enlightened notions of international intercourse propagated by David Hume and by the physiocrats, and he had bitterly complained about the narrowness of the views prevailing in Great Britain, where the "interest of humanity" had fallen into oblivion and only particular interests were looked after.[7]

During the War of Independence, Edmund Burke addressed a letter,

186

"not to the Ambassador of America, but to Doctor Franklin the Philosopher; my friend; & the lover of his species."[8] It was indeed the benevolent philosopher rather than the ambassador of a hostile nation who replied to Burke that "since the foolish part of mankind will make wars from time to time with each other, not having sense enough otherwise to settle their differences, it certainly becomes the wiser part, who cannot prevent those wars, to alleviate as much as possible the calamities attending them."[9] That these loyalties and sympathies for the whole of mankind might spell hope for England was the wish of Lord Shelburne, who initiated peace talks with Franklin (upon the latter's suggestion) with the following words: "I find myself returned nearly to the same Situation, which you remember me to have occupied nineteen years ago; and I should be very glad to talk to you as I did then, and afterwards, in 1767, upon the means of promoting the Happiness of Mankind, a Subject much more agreeable to my nature, than the best concerted Plans for spreading Misery and Devastation."[10]

Shelburne must have been happy to hear from the representative, Oswald, whom he had intrusted with conveying this letter and with discussing the conditions of peace with Franklin, that his expectations had not been disappointed. "On these occasions," Oswald reported after the first month of conversations, "the Doctor spoke the language more of a Philosopher than as fettered by the ties of a particular Commission."[11] Oswald thought Franklin to be "happy in the enjoyment of the most liberal Sentiments of benevolence & humanity."[12] Some weeks later Benjamin Vaughan happily reported to Shelburne that "Mr. Jay I find very much tastes the idea of a philosophic peace. Dr Franklin does so of course."[13]

Franklin's constant assurances of his good will and his wishes for peace not only colored the approach to and opinion about Franklin by his own contemporaries but also influenced the judgment of posterity. Later students of Franklin have, in words apparently inspired by Lord Shelburne, marveled at Franklin's pacifism and commented on his attitude in 1782. "For the sake of humanity Franklin was now urging haste to put an end to what he called 'this abominable war.' He was interested in promoting the happiness of mankind rather than in spreading misery and devastation. He talked and acted a good deal like a pacifist."[14]

THE WAR-GUILT QUESTION

The point has less often been made that Franklin's laments about the War of Independence not only concerned the distress and ultimate uselessness of war as such but that they also pointed to very particular aspects of the War of Independence: its injustice and wickedness. "I abominate . . . all Murder, and I may add, that the Slaughter of Men in an unjust Cause is nothing less than Murder."[15] It is this sentiment perhaps even more than condemnation of war in general that fills the pages of Franklin's correspondence with expressions of moral indignation. In other words, his reaction to the war with England was colored by expressions of American righteousness as well as by general humanitarian reflections. "Of all the Wars in my time, this on the part of England appears to me the wickedest; having no Cause but Malice against Liberty, and the Jealousy of Commerce."[16]

This reminds us of Franklin's solemn statement in the decisive days of the summer of 1776, when he had interpreted the struggle between mother-country and colonies as a war for gainful monopoly. Once the responsibility for the war had been firmly placed on Great Britain, his denunciations of the war frequently shifted from considerations of its inhumanity to those of its injustice. Consequently—and this makes all the difference—peace as such ceased to be the ultimate goal of Franklin's action. His interlocutor in England, the indefatigable David Hartley, kept reminding him that "Peace is a *Bonum in se.* Whereas the most favourable events of War are but relatively lesser evils: But certainly they are evils. *Mala in se,* not *Bona in se.*"[17] Whereupon Franklin clearly separated cosmopolitan from national, or rather humanitarian from political, considerations:

I should not be against a Truce, but this is merely on Motives of *general Humanity,* to obviate the Evils Men devilishly inflict on Men in Time of War, and to lessen as much as possible the similarity of Earth and Hell. For with regard to particular Advantages, respecting the States I am connected with, I am persuaded it is theirs to continue the War, till England shall be reduced to that perfect impotence of Mischief, which alone can prevail with her to let other Nations enjoy "*Peace, Liberty, and Safety.*"[18]

In the midst of his perfectly sincere lamentations about the evils of war, Franklin rarely neglected the opportunity of dealing a blow at the British. When things were not going too well for the Americans, he characteristically wrote to an English friend: "When will Men be convinc'd that even successful Wars at length become *Misfortunes to those who unjustly commenced them,* & who triumph'd blindly in their Success, not seeing all its Consequences."[19] Many people of good will who spend innumerable hours in propagating the cause of peace would be as stunned as an eighteenth-century pacifist, the chief of the English and American Moravians, James Hutton, must have been, when Franklin with one stroke wiped out any ideas of pacifism for its own sake: "Assure yourself, that nobody more sincerely wishes perpetual Peace among Men than I do; but there is a prior Wish, that they would be equitable and just, otherwise such Peace is not possible, and indeed wicked Men have no right to expect it."[20]

Equity and justice, then, are more highly valued than peace. Justice in international relations, indeed, may require the subordination of peace to its demands. Franklin's friend, Benjamin Rush, at almost the same time wrote that "individuals may forgive each other, because there is a power in magistrates to prevent a repetition of injuries, but states being amenable to no laws can do themselves justice only by revenge and retaliating injuries."[21]

Franklin knew this, too (witness his letter to Hartley cited above); but Franklin, attempting to prevent the repetition of mischief and violence, went one step further than advocating that power be checked by greater power. He set out to search for the conditions of an equitable and lasting peace, instead of a mere cease-fire, and he did so with the tremendous moral support of his firm conviction that to his cause belonged all righteousness, whereas he burdened the British nation with the appalling responsibility of exclusive war guilt. Justice must get its due, Franklin proclaimed; but, entirely true to his moral and political concepts, he did not so much value justice as an abstract idea; rather he saw in justice—or, one should say, in "equity"—the only sound basis of a harmonious social life in general. Justice, then, becomes a precondition of "reconciliation"; and this is indeed the central concept of Franklin's efforts to solve the Anglo-American struggle.

THE CONCEPT OF "RECONCILIATION"

Franklin was greatly pleased, so he wrote to David Hartley, to see the word "reconciliation" frequently used in newspapers and in parliamentary speeches. Reconciliation, Franklin pointed out,

certainly means more than a mere peace. It is a sweet expression. Revolve in your mind, my dear friend, the means of bringing about this *reconciliation*. When you consider the injustice of your war with us, and the barbarous manner in which it has been carried on, the many suffering families among us from your burning of towns, scalping by savages, &c., &c., will it not appear to you that though a cessation of war may be a peace, it may not be a reconciliation? Will not some voluntary acts of justice, and even of kindness on your part, have excellent effects towards producing such a *reconciliation?*[22]

It has become apparent that Franklin's use of "reconciliation" does not imply any transigence or concession on his part. Those Americans and Englishmen who were suspicious of his soft approach and conciliatory language as meaning possible abandonment of American claims were indeed mistaken. Peace and reconciliation take on their true meaning for Franklin only in the context of righteousness and equity. He himself, as we have seen, was concerned at the misinterpretation which had been given to his humanitarian feelings. He was concerned to find, as he complained to Hartley, that "one cannot give Vent to a simple Wish for Peace, a mere Sentiment of Humanity, without having it interpreted as *a Disposition to submit to any base Conditions* that may be offered us, rather than continue the War."[23]

Franklin's peculiar gift of backing his appeal to generosity by the threat of ultimate violence came to the fore when he was about to sign the French alliance. The triumphant style of a letter to an Englishman betrays the feeling of satisfaction and victory he experienced at this time:

You have lost by this mad War, and the Barbarity with which it has been carried on, not only the Government and Commerce of America, and the public Revenues and private Wealth arising from that Commerce, but what is more, you have lost the Esteem, Respect, Friendship, and Affection of all that great and growing People, who consider you at present, and whose Posterity will consider you, as the worst and wickedest Nation upon Earth. A Peace you may undoubtedly obtain by dropping all your Pretensions to govern us; . . . but, if you do not, with the Peace, recover the Affections of that People, it will not be a lasting nor a profitable one, nor will it afford you any part of that Strength, which you once had by your Union with them, and might (if you had been wise enough to take Advice) have still retained.[24]

Franklin's appeal for a policy of generosity on the part of the British, then, turns out to be a hint that the British had better follow the counsels of their own enlightened self-interest in appeasing the wrath of the Americans, or else they will run into the acute danger of provoking the eternal resentment and enmity of the rising country beyond the seas.

We may distinguish three issues in which Franklin employed his doctrine of "reconciliation": first, matters dealing with an exchange of prisoners of war; second, the thorny question of the American Loyalists and their indemnification; and, third, the most important issue of them all, the territorial settlement on the North American continent.

THE EXCHANGE OF PRISONERS OF WAR

We have no reason to doubt the sincerity and depth of Franklin's feelings as they are movingly expressed in his pleas to Englishmen to do something about American prisoners of war. "For the sake of Humanity it is to be wish'd that Men would endeavour to alleviate as much as possible the unavoidable Miseries attending a State of War," so ran his first approach to Lord Stormont, British ambassador in Paris, in the spring of 1777.[25] The ambassador returned the letter, seemingly unopened, accompanied by the proud message that "the King's Ambassador receives no Letters from Rebels but when they come to implore His Majesty's Mercy."[26] Franklin was to be somewhat more successful in his next approach, this time to David Hartley, who kept imploring Franklin during the whole war to bring about a reconciliation between the two countries short of complete independence. In October, 1777, Franklin took great pains to point out to Hartley that

our captains have set at liberty above 200 of your people, made prisoners by our armed vessels and brought into France, besides a great number dismissed at sea on your coasts, to whom vessels were given to carry them in: But you have not returned us a man in exchange. If we had sold your people to the Moors at Sallee, as you have many of ours to the African and East India Companies, could you have complained?[27]

At this point one ought to note, however, that Franklin did have second thoughts behind his undoubtedly sincere indignation about the unequal treatment of prisoners of war in the two camps. Before the entrance of France into the war in 1778 the Americans had much more interest in the exchange of captured seamen than the British. Ships under the American flag fighting in European waters had only the alternatives of either keeping captured seamen in their own limited accommodations or of releasing them on French soil, where they were no longer prisoners of war.[28] Franklin's appeal to Hartley, then, was not wholly disinterested or as disinterested as depicted by the humanitarian philosopher. Delicately Franklin hinted at the results to be expected from kind and obliging treatment of prisoners. "Some considerable act of kindness towards our people would take off the reproach of inhumanity in that respect from the nation,"[29] so he told Hartley, and he did not fail to touch Hartley's soft spot when he mentioned that "between nations long exasperated against each other in war, some act of generosity and kindness towards prisoners on one side has softened resentment, and abated animosity on the other, so as to bring on an accommodation."[30]

Four years later, when the fortunes of the war had definitely turned in favor of the Americans, Franklin's language had become firmer; he was now giving good advice rather than begging a favor. It was on this occasion that he threatened that "though a cessation of war may be a peace, it may not be a reconciliation,"[31] and invited the British to produce some voluntary acts of justice and even of kindness. Franklin suggested that England might begin her "measures of *reconciliation*"[32] by setting at liberty the twelve hundred American prisoners held in England and Ireland; this would produce, he assured his English correspondent, the liberty of an equal number of English prisoners, "even without a previous stipulation; and the confidence in our equity, with the apparent good will in the action, would give very good impressions of your change of disposition towards us."[33]

Franklin's insistence on equity, on good will, and on appearances allows us an insight into the very essence of his political philosophy and of his approach to political action. Generosity and good will alone (without the firm basis of equity) may at worst be detrimental, and at best useless, unless appearance comes to the support of reality.[34] Franklin, we may add in parentheses, would not have agreed with Wordsworth's thought on

> That best portion of a good man's life,
> His little, nameless, unremembered acts
> Of kindness and of love.[35]

Franklin's political morality—and this point is at times obscured by his constant invitations to "voluntary acts of kindness"—was too much governed by prudence to neglect the significance of a long memory.

REPARATIONS AND THE LOYALISTS

This aspect of his political thought appears much more strikingly when we analyze Franklin's suggestions as to the "advisable" articles of peace, designed to bring about that kind of reconciliation which the necessary articles, intended to produce the cessation of hostilities, could not possibly obtain. In fact, he reveals himself as a predecessor of more recent peacemakers with strong feelings on moral principles when he suggested, as Oswald reported to Lord Shelburne, "some sort of acknowledgment, in some public Act of Parliament, or otherwise, of our [the British's] error in distressing those countries so much as we had done. A few words of that kind, the Doctor said, would do more good than people could imagine."[36] The question of an explicit acknowledgment of war guilt was never taken seriously by the English and was not discussed further.

Another closely related question, however, raised by Franklin at the very beginning of his informal peace talks with Oswald in April, 1782, was again to play a decisive role at the end of the negotiations, namely, the threat of demands for reparation. Franklin's theory of reconciliation fitted this request beautifully, and he himself has given a perfect account of his arguments.

I then remarked, that his Nation seem'd to desire Reconciliation with America; that I heartily wish'd the same thing, that a mere Peace would not produce half its Advantages if not attended with a sincere Reconciliation; that to obtain this the Party which had been the Aggressor and had cruelly treated the other, should show some Mark of Concern for what was past, and some Disposition to make Reparation; that perhaps there were things, which America might demand by way of Reparation, and which England might yield, and that the Effect would be vastly greater, if they appeared to be voluntary, and to spring from returning Good Will; that I therefore wish'd England would think of offering something to re-lieve those who had suffer'd by its Scalping and Burning Parties. Lives indeed could not be restor'd nor compensated, but the Villages and Houses wantonly de-stroy'd might be rebuilt, &c.[37]

Lord Shelburne rejected Franklin's rather tentative suggestion in very outspoken terms, as appears from Oswald's new instructions.[38] No reparation was to be thought of; English money spent in America was more than sufficient indemnification for all particular losses; on the contrary, Oswald was to endeavor to get acknowledgment of "all debts whatever due to British subjects" and even "to restore the loyalists to a full enjoyment of their rights and privileges." Lord Shelburne, this paper said, "will never give up the loyalists."[39]

Franklin himself at the beginning of the peace talks had suggested, somewhat rashly, that money raised by the selling of vacant land in Canada would present a "Sum sufficient to pay for the Houses burnt by the British Troops and their Indians; and also to indemnify the Royalists for the Confiscation of their Estates."[40] However, hardly had he made this suggestion and given the note in which it was contained to Oswald, than he regretted his rashness and noted in his *Journal* that he "was not pleas'd with my having hinted a Reparation to the Tories for their forfeited Estates."[41] When the subject came up again several weeks later, Franklin adopted the line which he and the other American commissioners were to observe until the end of the negotiations. He countered English claims for indemnification of the Loyalists by referring to the fact that the confiscation of their estates had been carried out under the jurisdiction of the several states and that Congress or the envoys of Congress could do nothing about it.[42] There was no progress one way or the other on these questions. Franklin repeated his suggestion for voluntary reparations when he proposed the "necessary" and "advisable" articles on July 10.[43]

Franklin, we have already had occasion to note, played a less prominent role toward the end of the negotiations than at the initiation of the peace talks, but it was precisely on this question of indemnification and reparations, an eminently "moral" issue, that he made his most personal contribution to the last phase of the negotiations. This problem had now come up again as a consequence of the enhancement of Britain's power position. A new and tougher envoy was sent to Paris to strengthen the position of the all too philosophically minded Oswald. New instructions were issued by Lord Shelburne, claiming all the lands between the Alleghenies and the Mississippi and north of the Ohio for Canada, the province of Maine for Nova Scotia, and some smaller territorial concessions.[44] These claims were not made for their own sake but in order to gain some compensation for the Loyalists, "either by direct cession of territory in their favor or by half or some portion of the proceeds from the sale of the backlands, or at least by a favorable boundary for Nova Scotia."[45] The British negotiators were instructed not to regard these claims as an ultimatum but to give way, however, only after the most strenuous efforts should have been made to obtain some guarantee for the Loyalists. It was British obstinacy on the matter of the Loyalists which called forth a powerful indictment on the part of Franklin. In fact, he proved to be the most intransigent of all the American commissioners. John Adams himself, who never had ceased to denounce Franklin's weakness and servility to France, had to admit that "Dr. Franklin is very stanch against the tories; more decided a great deal on this point than Mr. Jay or myself."[46]

Franklin's arguments and ideas on true reconciliation as opposed to mere peace, on the absolute righteousness of the American cause, and on the profound wickedness and injustice of the war broke forth like a torrent. He wrote a letter to Oswald and recalled the conversations they had had in the spring, before the arrival of all the other commissioners. He then turned to a curious but very striking argument. He took all advantage he could of the fact that members of the Shelburne ministry actually had been in opposition most of the time during the war and had combated it as unreasonable and unjust. It must have been a secret pleasure for Franklin to produce his reasoning. He wrote somewhat patronizingly:

> The present British ministers, when they reflect a little, will certainly be too equitable to suppose that their nation has a right to make an *unjust* War (which they have always allowed this against us to be), and do all sorts of unnecessary mischief, unjustifiable by the practice of any civilized people, while those they make war with are to suffer without claiming any satisfaction. . . . The British Troops can never excuse their barbarities. They were unprovoked. The Loyalists may say, in excuse of theirs, that they were exasperated by the loss of their estates, and it was revenge. They have, then, had their revenge. *Is it right that they should have both?*[47]

Franklin now painted before the eyes of the British commissioners a most horrible picture of retaliation. All right, he conceded, let us draw up an article providing for the listing of all losses suffered by the Loyalists; but at the same time let us provide for the accounts of all the damages done by the Loyalists to the republican Americans, and let the balance decide![48] Whereupon, on the suggestion of Oswald, a compromise article was composed, according to which Congress ought to "earnestly recommend" to the several states the restitution of confiscated Loyalist estates.[49] This wish was platonic enough.

There was one more hurdle to master. The English commissioners at the very end of the negotiations declared that they were bound by their instructions with regard to the problem of the fisheries, whereas the Americans, in this question under the obvious leadership of John Adams, insisted on the grant of fishery privileges for Americans as they had possessed them before the war.[50] But even Adams was willing to grant a little more time to allow the English commissioners to get new instructions from London, when Franklin again intervened and remarked that "if another messenger was to be sent to London, he ought to carry something more respecting a compensation to the sufferers in America."[51] Franklin, so Adams recorded in his *Diary,* "produced a paper from his pocket, in which he had drawn up a claim; and he said, the first principle of the treaty was equality and reciprocity. Now, they demanded of us payment of debts, and restitution or compensation to the refugees."[52] Franklin read his carefully prepared facts, that is, he "stated the carrying off of goods from Boston, Philadelphia, and the Carolinas, Georgia, Virginia, &c. and the burning of towns, &c. and desired that this might be sent with the rest."[53] Adams and Jay joined in Franklin's terrible indictment, whereupon the English commissioners retired and finally accepted the American terms respecting the Loyalists and the fisheries.[54]

Even the happy conclusion of the preliminaries, which brought such a tremendous increase of territory to the United States, did not quite calm Franklin's concern over the reparations issue. The fact that the preliminary peace articles were not, as originally desired by the Americans, accompanied by commercial articles stipulating free trade between the two countries gave Franklin the idea that the postponed negotiation of a commercial treaty might be used to "obtain some compensation for the injuries done us, as a condition of opening again our trade."[55] His failure to get reparations obviously annoyed him, and the question of war guilt still bothered him considerably. In a characteristic passage of his letter to Foreign Secretary Livingston after the conclusion of the preliminaries—a passage which has no equivalent in Jay's or Adams' correspondence—Franklin consoled himself about this point: "Every one of the present British ministry has, while in the minority, declared the war against us unjust; and nothing is clearer in reason, than that those, who injure others by an unjust war, should make full reparation. They have stipulated, too, in these preliminaries, that, in evacuating our towns, they shall carry off no plunder, which is a kind of acknowledgement that they ought not to have done it before."[56] This was not yet the end of Franklin's exasperation. Three months later he sent American newspapers with news on British "barbarities" in America to Benjamin Vaughan in London and suggested publication, considering that in view of "such Provocations, some Value may be set upon our Moderation in not demanding Reparations for the wanton Devastations made of our fine Towns and Plantations."[57]

Carl Van Doren, his perceptive biographer, has thought that "about the loyalists Franklin was, for a moralist, strangely implacable."[58] This only shows how successful Franklin's ambiguous diction was in obscuring the difference which does exist between a morality of forgiveness and a morality of righteousness. He often spoke of generosity, when he meant equity; he spoke of magnanimity, when he meant the enlightened comprehension of mutual interests; he suggested "voluntary acts of kindness," when he had in mind appeasement dictated by prudence; he extolled reconciliation, when in fact he was demanding atonement. And his benevolence, real as it was, should not lead us astray as it has many of Franklin's contemporaries and biographers. His profound conviction that England's war against the colonies was unjust, a conviction which he stated with fervor after independence had been declared, never left him during the years of tribulation and of success. This conviction of the righteousness of his own cause, grown and hardened in many years of unrewarded striving for equity and enlightened self-interest, got the better of his much-exalted benevolence. Righteousness rather than forgiveness was the keynote of Franklin's political morality.

THE TERRITORIAL SETTLEMENT IN NORTH AMERICA

The ambiguity—or, one should rather say, the paradox—of Franklin's theory of reconciliation is nowhere more strikingly revealed than in his program for the territorial settlement on the North American continent. In the winter of 1778, with the French alliance not yet signed but already secured, he had this to suggest to an old English acquaintance of his, James Hutton, the head of the English and American Moravians:

In proposing terms, you should not only grant such as the Necessity of your Affairs may evidently oblige you to grant, but such additional ones as may show your Generosity, and thereby demonstrate your good Will. For instance, perhaps you might, by your Treaty, retain all Canada, Nova Scotia, and the Floridas. But if you would have a real friendly as well as able Ally in America, and avoid all occasions of future Discord, which will otherwise be continually arising on your American Frontiers, you should throw in those Countries.[59]

This extraordinary and truly breath-taking theory of "reconciliation" recalls to our mind the bold Franklin of the fifties, the great propagator of westward expansion, the man who earlier than all other Americans conceived the "Manifest Destiny" of his country. Concentrating on his "diplomacy of gratitude" to France, discussing the charges of treason and subservience to foreign powers, attempting to interpret his seemingly all-to-timid and complaisant reliance on France, finally, analyzing his "pacifism," we might well have lost sight of this different and ostensibly incompatible aspect of his thought on international relations. This grandiose concept confirms our contention that Franklin's delicate concern for moral principles at times veiled, but never destroyed, his grasp of political issues.

A. FRANKLIN'S EXPANSIONISM BETWEEN 1763 AND 1776

We left the discussion of Franklin's expansionism in the hour of its greatest triumph, namely, after the conclusion of the Great War for the Empire in 1763. Canada, Louisiana east of the Mississippi, and Florida had come into the hands of the British Empire; the pressure which farseeing Colonials had feared would suffocate the old colonies had been loosened; and Spanish Louisiana, beyond the Mississippi, was still very far away indeed. Franklin's quest for security had been abundantly satisfied by the Treaty of Paris, and he had not hesitated to express his joy and his pride at the time. In this context it is interesting to note that as late as 1782 Franklin, in a general reflection on the sorry fate of peacemakers who never can fulfil the exaggerated claims of their constituents, alluded to the Treaty of Paris as "the most advantageous and glorious . . . England . . . ever made."[60]

However, although the danger spots for British America's security after 1763 had been removed in the main, they had not been wholly eradicated, and this fact did not escape Franklin's attention. In September, 1766, he expressly confirmed that he had "long been of Opinion that a well-conducted western Colony, if it could be settled with the Approbation of the Indians, would be of great National Advantage with respect to the Trade, and particularly useful to the old Colonies as a Security to their Frontiers."[61] Almost a year later Franklin revealed his bold strategic vision even more explicitly. He reported to his son, the governor of New Jersey, a talk he had had with Lord Shelburne, then, as fifteen years later, in charge of Colonial business. In this conversation, Franklin told his son, he had advocated the settlement of the Illinois country and expatiated "on the various advantages, viz. furnishing provisions cheaper to the garrisons, securing the country, retaining the trade, raising a strength there which on occasion of a future war, might easily be poured down the Mississippi upon the lower country, and into the Bay of Mexico, to be used against Cuba or Mexico itself."[62]

The Quebec Act of 1774, incorporating all the country between the Ohio and the Mississippi—the Old Northwest—into Canada, presented a decisive deterioration of the security situation of the thirteen colonies. The country which had attracted the attention of people like Thomas Pownall and Benjamin Franklin as far back as 1754, the very region in which the French danger before and during the Seven Years' War had loomed largest, the areas which had been desired by the Illinois Land Company of 1766, of which Benjamin Franklin had been a member—all this had now been added to British Canada. The situation for the thirteen colonies was not altogether dissimilar from the one they had experienced before and during the Seven Years' War: again an absolute government, hostile to the desires of the colonies, had been established in their hinterland.[63] New France seemed to have come back from the oblivion of history. In the last phase of his London mission, Franklin repeatedly urged the repeal of the Quebec Act and a "free Government granted to Canada."[64] He argued that "the Establishing an arbitrary Government on the back of our Settlement might be dangerous to us all; and that loving Liberty ourselves, we wish'd it to be extended among all Mankind, and to have no Foundation for future Slavery laid in America."[65] To move the Canadians to make common cause with the thirteen colonies, consequently, was one of the most-cherished wishes of Congress early in 1776, and Benjamin Franklin himself joined a mission appointed by Congress to convince the Canadians of the virtues of a union with the thirteen colonies, but in vain.[66]

B. FRANKLIN'S PEACE PROPOSALS OF 1776

After the failure of the Canada mission in the spring of 1776, then, the United Colonies found themselves in a predicament distinguished from the one they had faced eighteen years before chiefly by the fact that at that time English aid had naturally been more easily available than French help now. One thing, however, had not changed at all: the grandeur of Franklin's vision. Already in 1775 he had included a provision for the acceptance of the British colonies of Quebec, St. John's, Nova Scotia, East and West Florida, the Bermudas, the West Indies, and even of Ireland in his plan for the confederation of the United Colonies.[67] One year later, ready to sail for France, Franklin drew up a "Sketch of Propositions for a Peace," including reasons for proposing a peace at this time. This sketch consisted of only three points, but in these three points the essentials of Franklin's political program were contained: first of all, acknowledgment of American independence by Great Britain; second, free trade for British merchants in America; and, third,

to prevent those occasions of misunderstanding, which are apt to arise when the territories of different powers border on each other, through the bad conduct of frontier inhabitants on both sides, Britain shall cede to the United States the provinces or colonies of Quebec, St. John's, Nova Scotia, Bermuda, East and West Florida, and the Bahama Islands, with all their adjoining and intermediate territories now claimed by her.[68]

The United States, in turn, would pay a sum of money, the amount not specified, for a certain number of years. The argument for this purchase of a whole continent was thoroughly Franklinian.

It is worth our while to offer such a sum for the countries to be ceded, since the vacant lands will in time sell for a great part of what we shall give, if not more; and, if we are to obtain them by conquest, after perhaps a long war, they will probably cost us more than that sum. It is absolutely necessary for us to have them for our own security; and though the sum may seem large to the present generation, in less than half the term it will be to the whole United States a mere trifle.[69]

We shall now follow briefly Franklin's program of continental expansion through the war years to the peace negotiations of 1782. We shall deal, first, with the western lands between the Appalachian range and the Mississippi; second, with Florida; and, third, with Canada.

C. THE WESTERN LANDS

Neither in the sketch of peace proposals nor in his plan of confederation does Franklin mention the western lands. The explanation, of course, is that he considered the claim of the United States to these lands as a matter of course and beyond the range of dispute.[70] The silence of the instructions of September, 1776, for Franklin and his fellow-commissioners to France, as well as of the Treaty of Alliance of 1778 with regard to the West, seems to confirm this opinion. The conquest or acquisition of countries like Canada, Florida, or the Bermudas is discussed in both cases, but the silence about the land between the Appalachians and the Mississippi suggests that at that time the French as well as the Americans held it as belonging already without any doubt to the domain of the United States.[71] The French efforts to bring Spain into the war—Spain whose policy it was to keep the new republic away from her own possessions and who wanted to obtain the monopoly of the commerce of the Gulf of Mexico—as well as French intentions to limit American growth, contributed to a shift in French policy,[72] and the possibility of peace negotiations with England combined to call forth vigorous debates in Congress on the extent and the legal foundations of America's claims to the West.

Upon the approach of peace negotiations, Foreign Secretary Livingston wrote a letter to Franklin which represents one of the most interesting documents of the ideology of American expansionism during the American Revolution. The rights of the United States to the western country were founded upon two claims. In the first place, there were the grants made by the British Crown to certain colonies, above all, to Virginia.[73] Apart from the charter rights of the several colonies or states, and in legal conflict with them, Livingston, in the second place, proclaimed that the western lands had come under the sovereignty of the king of Great Britain only by virtue of his being the king of the people of America; ceasing to be king of the people of America at the moment of the Declaration of Independence, the king's rights to these backlands had also ceased.[74]

Franklin acknowledged this letter with great warmth and took care to point out that the sentiments of Congress gave him great pleasure, "and the more, as they agree so perfectly with my own opinions, and furnish me with additional arguments in their support."[75] He promised more detailed comments on the ideas and arguments of Congress, but, we note regretfully, on second thought he decided to omit his comments, fearing the letter might be intercepted. Franklin contented himself with some enigmatic hints, revealing that he meant to give Livingston some additions to the arguments of Congress; and indicated his hope that, "unless the campaign should afford our enemies some considerable advantage," the United States might obtain more than had been expected.[76]

Apart from this acknowledgment of the arguments for the United

States rights to the West, Franklin was reticent about this question in the years up to 1782. Vergennes did not choose to negotiate with him on this subject,[77] and Vergennes's opinion or his wishes with respect to the Mississippi boundary were conveyed to Congress through the French envoy in Philadelphia. We have already noted that Franklin during the negotiations of the summer and fall of 1782, although, of course, familiar with the divergence of his own and the French court's opinion on the western lands, did not utter one hostile word against Vergennes or France and directed his indignation to the address of the Spanish government. "Mr. Franklin," the British negotiator, Oswald, gladly reported to Lord Shelburne, "although he has frequently talkt of their Obligations to France, has never . . . mentioned Spain in that or any such way, when I had occasion to be with him."[78] Franklin was assured that France herself had no territorial ambitions on the North American continent, and, bent on the preservation of a cordial relationship with France as he was, he could certainly see no reason for provoking discussions which would bring differences into the open prematurely.

With regard to Spain, Franklin did not mince words in his only utterance with regard to the Mississippi and the western lands before the final peace negotiations. This passage, however, completely reveals his way of thinking on western expansion and compensates us richly for the lack of legal arguments. "Poor as we are," Franklin replied to Jay, who had written with disgust about his frustrating experiences in Madrid, "yet as I know we shall be rich, I would rather agree with them to buy at a great price the whole of their right on the Mississippi than sell a drop of its waters. A neighbour might as well ask me to sell my street door."[79]

After peace negotiations had actually started in the spring of 1782, Franklin included the accession to America's "street door" among the "necessary" articles which he presented to Oswald in July. The claim to the western lands, indeed, appeared so vital and self-evident to Franklin that he hardly ever mentioned it in his preliminary talks with Oswald, where he discussed much more ambitious and far-reaching projects. On July 10, 1782, Oswald reported to Lord Shelburne Franklin's first detailed proposals. No boundary settlement between the United States and the British possessions would be acceptable to Franklin which did not push back the boundary of Canada at least to where it had been before the Quebec Act of 1774,[80] which had driven a wedge between the thirteen colonies and the Mississippi by incorporating the land between the Great Lakes, the Ohio, and the Mississippi into Canada. Shelburne, a devoted follower of the great Chatham, was an imperialist, and he did not share the views propagated by the Whigs and held by his rival and colleague in the cabinet from March to June, 1782, Charles James Fox, that colonies were inevitably destined to separate themselves from the mother-country like ripe fruits falling from the tree. It was necessity rather than theory that convinced Shelburne to acquiesce in the unalterable fact of an independent United States. Shelburne's hesitation during the summer of 1782 to acknowledge independence as unconditionally and as unequivocally as Fox had advised it may be explained by tactical rather than fundamental considerations.[81] Shelburne spoke the truth when he replied to Oswald upon his information of Franklin's proposals:

I have never made a secret of the deep concern I feel in the separation of countries united by blood, by principles, habits, and every tie short of territorial proximity. But you very well know that I have long since given it up, decidedly though reluctantly, and the same motives which made me perhaps the last to give up all hope of reunion, make me most anxious if it is given up, that it shall be done decidedly, so as to avoid all future risks of enmity, and lay the foundation of a new connection better adapted to the present temper and interests of both countries.[82]

Accordingly, Shelburne in the same letter notified Oswald of his willingness to accept Franklin's necessary articles as the basis of the discussions, that is, he accepted Franklin's request for the cession of the western lands, and he took Franklin's hint to Oswald not to force America "into the hands of other people."[83] Shelburne's decision to strengthen the independence of the new republic by the cession of the western lands was, of course, part and parcel of his policy of detaching the United States from its French connection and eradicating or at least lessening greatly the sources of future discord in America as well as in Europe. "England & generosity on the one side, or France & consistant [sic] politics on the other"[84]—these were the alternatives of the American issue, and Shelburne acted accordingly. The foundations of the western settlement were laid, then, before Franklin passed the leading role in the negotiations to John Jay.[85]

A long struggle was still ahead to secure these foundations laid by Franklin and Shelburne, threatened, oddly enough, not by America's enemies, but by her ally, Spain, which enjoyed to a considerable extent the support of France.[86] A few weeks after Shelburne had voiced his basic agreement with Franklin's "necessary" articles, Franklin saw his suspicions confirmed: Spain's design to "coop us up within the Allegheny Mountains" had now become manifest.[87] Spain's desire to secure the whole land east of the Mississippi, modified only by the French compromise (but anti-American) proposal to leave the country north of the Ohio to the British and to divide the Old Southwest into a western Indian protectorate under Spanish control and an eastern part under American control, drove John Jay into the arms of the British. The knowledge of the deepening dissensions in the Franco-Hispanico-American camp, conveyed to Shelburne by the French as well as by Jay, and also the considerable enhancement of Britain's strength after the definitive breakdown of Spain's assaults on Gibraltar,[88] led Shelburne to assert the British claims on the western lands as a bargaining point in order to obtain some compensation for the Loyalists.[89] However, the Americans were intransigent. And so the preliminary peace treaty confirmed the Mississippi as the western boundary of the United States and provided for its free navigation by the new republic. With regard to the last threat to the backlands after the British victory at Gibraltar, Franklin noted laconically: "They wanted to bring their boundary down to the Ohio and to settle their loyalists in the Illinois country. We did not choose such neighbors."[90]

One may conclude that the scarcity of Franklin's utterances about the western lands does not by any means imply an indifferent or luke-warm attitude, as some of his hostile contemporaries believed. His reticence in speaking about them may be traced to four causes. First of all, he considered at the beginning of the war the claims of the United States to the West to be self-evident and—apart from the British—uncontested. Second, when Spain entered the stage, Franklin found himself removed from the centers of discussion; Vergennes conducted his negotiations with Congress by the intermediary of his envoy in Philadelphia. Third, America's diplomatic dealings with Spain (with one exception—the short interlude at the beginning of 1777) never lay in the hands of Franklin. As has been noted frequently, Franklin rarely deemed it useful or appropriate to speak about things which did not belong to his immediate concern. Finally, his frequent reluctance to mention western problems is probably connected with his discreet handling of the French government—witness the marked difference of his comments on the attitude of Spain and France with regard to the Mississippi question. John Jay was right when he assured Franklin that "your letters to me, when in Spain, considered our territory as extending to the Mississippi, and expressed your opinion against ceding the navigation of that river in very strong and pointed terms," and Jay added that during the negotiations in Paris he "did not perceive the least disposition in either of us to recede from our claims, or be satisfied with less than we obtained."[91]

D. FLORIDA

We may be very brief in respect to Franklin's concern for Florida. Florida had been ceded to Britain by Spain as late as 1763,[92] and the United States could not assert the sort of rights which it—rightly or wrongly—had claimed over the western lands. Nevertheless, in the "Plan of Treaties" of 1776 Congress had explicitly included Florida as being one of the British possessions on the "Continent of North America," and it had been "the true Intent and meaning of this Treaty, that the said United States, shall have the sole, exclusive, undivided and perpetual Possessions of the Countries, Cities, and Towns, on the said Continent . . . which now are, or lately were under the Jurisdiction of or Subject to the King or Crown of Great Britain."[93] However, the need for a Spanish alliance soon caused Congress to reduce its desires and to offer assistance "in reducing to the possession of Spain the town and harbor of Pensacola."[94]

The ninth article of the congressional "Plan of Treaties" re-emerged in a somewhat reduced form in Articles V and VI of the Treaty of Alliance with France. There was no enumeration of all British possessions on the "Continent of North America"; it was simply stated that "if the united States Should think fit to attempt the Reduction of the British Power remaining in *the Northern Parts of America*,"[95] those countries should be confederated with or dependent upon the United States. Two months after the conclusion of the alliance a controversy sprang up which has been given scant attention by the historians of the French alliance or by Franklin's biographers. The ever watchful and suspicious Ralph Izard suspected some dark design behind the substitution of the vague formulation of "the northern parts of America" for the explicit terms of the congressional plan; that is, he thought that this was intended to exclude the United States from the possession of Florida. Izard submitted his apprehensions to the other commissioners on May 3, and he reported that "Dr. Franklin did not think they were well founded, nor that any such construction could possibly be put upon the article. North America, he said, strictly speaking, comprised all parts of the continent north of the equator, and the Floridas, being in the latitude of 30 degrees north, would be comprehended within the meaning of the words 'northern parts of America.' "[96]

Izard suggested getting some more detailed information on this from the French Foreign Office, but Franklin, characteristically, objected. First of all, he referred to the instructions of Congress concerning the cession of part of Florida to Spain, and, second, he thought that an application to the French ministry might be taken ill, and if Izard's "apprehensions were ever so just, it was too late for any remedy in France, but that the commissioner for the court of Madrid might guard against any bad consequences in the treaty which he had to conclude with that court."[97] Arthur Lee confirmed that "Dr. Franklin's answer was that Congress had receded from those claims since by the concessions directed to be made to Spain."[98] Franklin, of course, referred to the offer of Congress to cede the town and harbor of Pensacola to Spain.

Izard was probably not so wrong when he, "with all due deference to Dr. Franklin," declared that he was firmly persuaded that "the court of France would not have substituted the eighth article in the place of the above if they had not had some designs contrary to the intentions of Congress, so clearly expressed in their ninth article."[99] Modern scholarship has noted that "the Floridas, in significant distinction to 'the northern parts of America,' were not specifically mentioned" in the Treaty of Alliance[100] and consequently agrees with Izard's rather than with Franklin's interpretation. In fact, although Vergennes at that time acknowledged that the Floridas entered "into the plan of conquest of the Americans," he immediately added, foreseeing the interests of Spain, that the French minister in Philadelphia ought to prepare the Americans for an eventual withdrawal from their claims.[101] By 1779 Congress, anxious to conclude a treaty with Spain, had receded from its claims to the Floridas in exchange for privileges of navigation, more particularly free navigation, on the Mississippi.[102]

This phase, however, was beyond Franklin's diplomatic tasks.

It seems, then, from the point of view of American interests, that Franklin's estimation of French policy gave more credit to it than it actually deserved. It betrays, furthermore, his characteristic concern to do nothing which could endanger cordial relations with the new ally. Another point, however, we may reasonably conjecture, might have been Franklin's expectation that an alliance with Spain would have to be bought at least with the price of the Floridas and that insistence on America's rights to the West and to free navigation on the Mississippi was by far more essential to America's interest than the Floridas.

The problem of Florida reappears in Franklin's diplomacy only on the occasion of the peace negotiations in 1782. Then, as we have seen, the menace of Spain's ambition to the exclusive possession of the Mississippi Valley required extraordinary measures to assure the United States' access to the Mississippi. We know that this threat drove John Jay, who was now conducting negotiations together with Franklin in Paris, into the camp of the British. Jay supposed that England would be more willing to grant the western lands if it was assured of a continuing western trade. By retaining Canada *and* West Florida, England would have two well-placed "side-door entries" to the western trade, and, in Professor Bemis's words, "by luring the British into West Florida as an easy entrance to the trade of the American West, Jay hoped to keep the Spanish away from the east bank of the Mississippi above West Florida."[103] According to Benjamin Vaughan, Franklin also preferred the British rather than the Spaniards as neighbors in the South. He suggested that the British exchange Gibraltar against Puerto Rico or Florida.[104] A British memoir advising the recovery of West Florida—which was actually in Spanish hands—stated among other reasons for such action "that of gratifying the Americans it being what has been most earnestly recommended by their Commissioners, and for reasons that have appeared sufficiently interesting to them and us in the view of future Connections arising out of the Trade of the said Western Country, as well as a sign of their confidence in wishing that the Key of that Trade should remain in our hands rather than in those of a different Nation."[105] Franklin's and Jay's apprehensions about Spain were embodied in the only secret article of the preliminaries, which guaranteed American recognition

of Britain's right in West Florida in case Britain should put herself
into the possession of West Florida in the time which was to elapse
between the preliminary and the definitive treaty. England did not
do so, and the secret article came to naught. With regard to the future
development of American expansion, it appears that Franklin's agita-
tion about Spain's ambition and insolence led him to overestimate the
Spanish danger and blinded him to the future conflict with Great
Britain which would be occasioned by a British trading belt supported
by territorial possessions to the south as well as to the north of the
United States.[106]

E. CANADA

Canada may well be called Franklin's diplomatic hobbyhorse. As
we have seen, Canada was included in the sketch of peace proposals
which Franklin drafted when he was about to cross the Atlantic in
1776. His concern for Canada has rarely been viewed in its proper
context. It has even been suggested that in 1782 Franklin "jocosely suggested that Canada might be voluntarily ceded to America";[107] other
historians, while taking the matter more seriously, have thought that
the mission of Franklin to Canada in the spring of 1776 "had the
result of fixing Canada as a quest in Franklin's subtle mind."[108] However, it seems to us that one need not stress particularly his trip to
Canada in 1776. We need only remember that Franklin, sixteen years
before the outbreak of the Revolution, had laid down his thoughts on
the paramount importance of Canada in the thirteen colonies' system
of foreign policy. What he did during the years of his diplomatic
mission in France was nothing else than to apply the insights of his
Canada pamphlet to the new circumstances.[109]

During the preliminary peace talks with Oswald in the spring of
1782, the question of Canada looms large in Franklin's account of his
conversations.[110] He repeated the arguments which he had presented
in 1778 to James Hutton.[111] "A mere Peace would not produce half its
Advantages if not attended with a sincere Reconciliation," Franklin
told Oswald, and presently let him read and even take to London
a paper on this subject. "The Territory of the United States and that
of Canada, by long extended Frontiers, touch each other," so Franklin stated, and he pointed out that "the Settlers on the Frontiers of
the American Provinces are generally the most disorderly of the Peo-

ple, who, being far removed from the Eye and Controll of their respective Governments, are more bold in committing Offences against Neighbours, and are for ever occasioning Complaints and furnishing Matter for fresh Differences between their States." Franklin then suggested how humiliating it might be for England to cede Canada on the express demand of America. He even brought up an argument which he had read more than thirty years before in the memoir of his old friend, James Logan, on the international situation of the American colonies. Some of America's political rulers, Franklin thought, might possibly "consider the fear of such a Neighbour, as a means of keeping 13 states more united among themselves, and more attentive to Military Discipline."[112] But on the minds of the people in general, he continued, the voluntary cession of Canada would have an excellent effect; it would smooth the people's resentments, and England would not be the loser, because the right of free trade could be stipulated and, furthermore, so much of the vacant land could be sold as would be necessary to indemnify the Loyalists for the confiscation of their estates in the United States.[113] This latter consideration, however, Franklin regretted as soon as he had handed the paper over,[114] and on later occasions he tried to retract this particular suggestion.[115]

Franklin never forgot to add another, more threatening, argument. At the same time, he recorded in his *Journal,* he was "hinting . . . but not expressing too plainly that *such a Situation* [in which England would retain Canada], *to us so dangerous, would necessarily oblige us to cultivate and strengthen our Union with France."*[116] Franklin kept repeating these ideas for four months, and still in August, 1782, we find Oswald describing in his journal one of his frequent meetings with Franklin: "The Doctor at last touched upon Canada, as he generally does upon the like occasions, and said there could be no dependence on peace and good neighbourhood, while that country continued under a different government, as it touched their States in so great a stretch of frontier."[117] Franklin also included the cession of Canada among the "advisable articles" in his peace proposals of July 10.

How were Franklin's suggestions of "reconciliation" instead of an unstable peace and his appeal to British generosity received by the English? Oswald was all for England's giving up Canada. He did not think that England, in view of her dejected situation, could possibly refuse this request. On one occasion he told Franklin that he had in London "given it as his Opinion, that Canada should be given up to the United States, as it would prevent the Occasions of future Difference, and as the Government of such a Country was worth nothing, and of no Importance, if they could have there a free Commerce."[118] Oswald also assured Franklin that Shelburne and Rockingham, "tho' they spoke reservedly, did not seem very averse to it"; only Charles Fox appeared to be startled at the proposition.[119] Oswald's account of Shelburne's and Rockingham's opinion seems to be an understatement. The only comment we have on the reception of Franklin's paper on Canada by Shelburne is negative, as is shown by the "Remarks on the Private Papers" which Oswald retained from his consultation with Shelburne after having submitted Franklin's paper:

> The private paper desires Canada for three reasons.
>   1st. By way of reparation. Answer. No reparation can be heard of.
>   2nd. To prevent future wars. Answer. It is to be hoped some more friendly method will be found.
>   3rd. Loyalists, as a fund of Indemnification to them. Answer. No independence to be acknowledged without their being taken care of.[120]

Oswald, however, communicated to Franklin only that he hoped a solution of the Canadian problem satisfactory for the United States could be found and that the discussion of the problem ought to be postponed until the end of the negotiations.[121] When the end of the negotiations approached, the Americans were faced with an enhanced British bargaining power, on the one side, and with the exorbitant demands of Spain, on the other. The struggle for the western lands had priority over the concern for Canada.

It seems that Oswald and Jay were still discussing Canada in the last days of September, 1782,[122] but there was no mention of Canada in Jay's proposals of October 5, which were to form the basis of the definitive peace negotiations. During these days Franklin was ill, and the neglect and ultimate loss of Canada has been charged to John Jay's legalistic scruples about the ambiguities of the British commissions, which delayed the peace settlement until the assault on Gibraltar had failed. There is no evidence, however, that Franklin would have succeeded in securing Canada even unhampered by Jay's apprehensions. Whereas at times the British cabinet discussed the eventuality of buying the peace by surrendering Gibraltar, there is no indication that the abandonment of Canada was ever contemplated.[123] On the contrary,

Shelburne, as we have seen, rejected Franklin's first proposal concerning the surrender of Canada, and his instructions to General Carleton in June, 1782, "were as explicit about the retention and defence of Canada as about the intention to cede the 'Back Lands' to the Thirteen States."[124] It has also been pointed out that even at the end of August, 1782, when British willingness for compromise reached the highest point, the maximum concession to be offered was a contraction of the enlarged Canada of 1774 to the limits of 1763.[125]

The last two months of the peace negotiations, dominated on the American side by John Jay and later on by John Adams, were occupied (so far as territorial problems were concerned) with determining the boundary between Canada and the United States. We need not deal with the details of these negotiations, which have been treated competently elsewhere and in which Franklin played no decisive role.[126]

Franklin, John Jay, and John Adams themselves justified their not insisting on Canada in unequivocal terms when they reported and explained to Congress their course of action during the peace negotiations: "We knew this court [France] and Spain to be against our claims to the western country, and having no reason to think that lines more favorable could ever have been obtained, we finally agreed to those described in this article; indeed they appear to leave us little to complain of and not much to desire."[127] In view of the paramount importance of the Mississippi boundary for the expanding republic, the regions north and south of the main road of America's "Manifest Destiny" indeed take on but secondary roles. The advance of the United States to the Mississippi did present a concession on the part of England which stunned America's allies. Vergennes was of the opinion that Britain's "concessions, in fact, as much as to the boundaries as to the fisheries and the loyalists, exceed all that I should have thought possible."[128] He thought that "the English buy the peace more than they make it."[129]

PACIFISM AND EXPANSIONISM RECONCILED

The English, indeed, had not gone so far as Franklin would have wished them to go, but they did go a long way in order to conclude what Benjamin Vaughan called a real peace "instead of the sort of truce for ten or twenty years, which we conclude with other nations."[130]

Shelburne, let us repeat, once he had given up the hope of reunion, had done so decidedly, "so as to avoid all future risks of enmity, and lay the foundation of a new connection better adapted to the present temper and interests of both countries."[131] "In this view," Shelburne had added, "I go further with Dr. Franklin than he is aware of."[132] Shelburne's objects were, Vaughan told James Monroe, "to leave no ground either for *fears* or *hopes*, which could disturb the tranquillity of the two countries."[133]

This, in fact, emerges as the most fundamental object of Benjamin Franklin's diplomacy of "reconciliation" with England. There are several elements in his line of policy which seem to be incompatible with one another or at least strangely disjointed. There is his love of peace and horror of war, ostensibly suspended, however, by his insistence on a "just" peace and the threat of continuing hostility in case of nonfulfilment of his terms. There is his program of "reconciliation," which, on further investigation, turns out to be boundless expansionism, bolstered by exorbitant claims. Franklin's love of peace and his love for his country seem to clash. It would be wrong, however, to gather the impression from the preceding analysis of his concept of foreign affairs that wishes for eternal peace or for generosity and reconciliation were mere "ideological disguises" of his expansionism. The very magnitude of Franklin's territorial demands was motivated by his belief that it was bad policy to heal differences by removing only part of their causes, *"as it is bad surgery to leave splinters in a wound, which must prevent its healing, or in time occasion it to open afresh."*[134] He had had nothing but contempt for the English policy in America in the years preceding the Revolution. "Instead of *preventing* complaints by removing the causes, it has been thought best that Soldiers should be sent to *silence* them."[135] Franklin, in other words, proposed a more radical cure. The roots of the evil had to be eradicated. He found a unique combination of expansionism and pacifism when he introduced his paper on the cession of Canada to the United States by the remark that *"to make a Peace durable, what may give Occasion for future Wars should if practicable be removed."*[136] Here we see the common denominator of Franklin's patriotism and his pacifism, and it has never been more pointedly described than in an account Benjamin Vaughan gave to Lord Shelburne of a conversation he had with Franklin:

Yesterday Dr. Franklin told me that it would entirely depend upon the approaching treaty, whether the attachments of America were to be renewed & increased, or were to be extirpated; that if it was meant (for instance) to keep America in *danger* (as by retaining garrisoned places, making treaties with the Indians, & the like) persons would be found in America very well disposed to excite an aversion to England, & an union with France; & that as they would certainly succeed, the consequence would be wars, & hatred, in various ways; that for his part, he was for reconciliation, which he thought practicable, even under the circumstances of England as she stands; but that nothing lasting could be done, if America were to be kept *in danger*. . . . Besides I am convinced that the chief reason why Dr. Franklin wishes for reconciliation, is that America may be kept out of all wars. For if England disarms herself America need not fear England, & not fearing England she need not cultivate France; &, as a lover of mankind, the Dr. may be happy in thinking that when England & France lose this motive for war, *their* wars also may be less frequent.[137]

Happy indeed the man who, like Franklin, contrives to unite his loyalty to mankind with allegiance to his country! To inquire into the causes and alternatives of this reconciliation of all-too-often sadly conflicting values will be the task of the following chapter.

CHAPTER VII

FRANKLIN AND THE NEW DIPLOMACY

The Quest for the Harmony of Interests and the Problem of Ideology

THE perennial revolt of man's conscience and of man's hopes against the dark powers of violence and coercion, of ambition and pride, against what has come to be disapprovingly and ambiguously called "power politics," has manifested itself in different ways. It has appealed to man's moral as well as to his intellectual qualities. It has opposed unselfishness to selfishness, devotion to egotism, as well as reason to passion, or enlightenment to obscurantism. To the age-old experience of clashes of interest and of ambition, the "progressives" of all ages have opposed the fervent belief that a more perfect—and perhaps ultimately perfect—concord of wants and interests may be achieved. In their efforts to replace wicked and foolish policies by good and wise ones, men of good will have operated in three dimensions which, though closely interrelated and indeed inseparable in practice, ought to be kept distinct for the sake of analysis: the dimensions of morals, of law, and of science. Since time immemorial men have attempted to restrain the rule of the stronger by the obligations of religion and natural law on the moral plane and by the provision of legitimate and supposedly impartial means of coercion on the legal plane. The attempt not only to restrain but even to eliminate the sources of friction and conflict in social relationships by the devices of science has been, however, the distinct mark of modern times.

Earlier ages, content with trying to reduce and check the divergence of interests, thought a perfect harmony in this world impossible or at least unlikely. In modern times the harmony of interests has been thought to be attainable by different means. Different schools of thought, animated by different views of human nature, have laid unequal stress on the three vehicles of reform: morals, laws, and science. In the eighteenth century, for instance, which was truly haunted by the quest for the harmony of interests, three basic trends of thought may be discerned. First, there were those who believed in the intrinsic goodness of human nature, in an innate "moral sense" which would teach man that he could reach his highest fulfilment only by devoting himself in the first place to the good of his fellow-men. This theory of the "fusion of interests" is different from the second school of thought, which held that men normally are too selfish to work voluntarily for the common good but that evil effects of selfishness may be overcome by the right sort of legislation, inspired by the insights of enlightened reason. In other words, this second idea states that human nature is not intrinsically evil; it may be tamed and molded by the progressive development of man's intellectual powers. This has been called "the artificial identification of interests." Third, we have the view that particular and general interests somehow coincide naturally and that it is the great task of science, more particularly of the science of economics, to discover and explain those natural rules and principles which foster "the natural identity of interests."[1]

The quest for the harmony of interests obviously takes on particular significance in a domain where chaos, anarchy, and violence more than anywhere else have maintained their cruel regime: the realm of international relations. The outstanding factor in international relations is the moral ambivalence of the state: the very existence of a far-reaching harmony of interests on the national level means frequently increased self-assertion and clashes of interests on the international level. What appears "good" from the angle of national affairs seems "bad" from the point of view of humanity at large.

Civilized man desires to adhere and usually does adhere to values claiming absolute and universal validity, and he does aspire to universal harmony, if for no other reason than that "confidence in the meaningfulness of human existence" is one of the primary sources of human vitality[2] and that the eternal strife between nations deprives man of this confidence. Reinhold Niebuhr has poignantly observed that there is a moral paradox involved in the existence of every nation:

Every nation must come to terms with the fact that, though the force of collective self-interest is so great, that national policy must be based upon it; yet also the sensitive conscience recognizes that the moral obligation of the individual transcends his particular community. Loyalty to the community is therefore morally tolerable only if it includes values wider than those of the community.[3]

This goes far to show that the moral—or, as it is frequently but some-what loosely called, the "ideological"—factor in politics is indeed a fundamental and ineradicable element of political life, not limited to a particular country or to a particular period of recent history.[4] On the other hand, it is undoubtedly true that beginning with the American Revolution there has been a considerable increase of the importance of the ideological factor in international politics which has tended to obscure and, in the minds of some people, even to obliterate the phenomenon of political power. Three chief causes seem to account for this development. First of all, the rise of urban agglomeration and urban civilization has fostered the spread of nonterritorial ideologies among the urban population,[5] always intellectually more alert and eager for innovations than the conservative peasantry. Second, professional armies that did not care in whose service they fought were superseded by militias or popular armies, which produced naturally the need for thorough propaganda and indoctrination. Third, and most important, the rise of liberalism and of democracy brought with it a new vision of human nature and presented a tremendous challenge to custom and tradition in politics by stimulating the search for new principles of legitimacy.[6]

The "New Diplomacy" of the Eighteenth Century

"I should desire you particularly to distinguish between the love of our country and that spirit of rivalship and ambition which has been common among nations," Franklin's friend, Richard Price, preached in a famous discourse in 1789.

What has the love of their country hitherto been among mankind? What has it been but a love of domination, a desire of conquest, and a thirst for grandeur and glory, by extending territory and enslaving surrounding countries?[7]

The noblest principle in our nature is the regard to general justice and that good-will which embraces all the world. . . . Though our immediate attention must be employed in promoting our own interest and that of our nearest connexions; yet we must remember, that a narrower interest ought always to give way to a more extensive interest. In pursuing particularly the interest of our country, we ought to carry our views beyond it. We should love it ardently, but not exclusively. We ought to seek its good, by all the means that our different circumstances and abilities will allow; but at the same time we ought to consider ourselves as citizens of the world, and take care to maintain a just regard to the rights of other countries.[8]

This breathes the spirit of what as early as 1793 was called the "New Diplomacy." This term was usually connected with a kind of diplomacy opposed to the traditional politics of the balance of power, to a kind of politics where gain to one nation meant loss to another and where the whims and passions of the rulers reigned supreme. The "New Diplomacy," on the other hand, would remove the obstacles to free commercial intercourse among nations and would replace conquest and expansion by friendship and co-operation[9] as well as double-dealing by sincerity. The initial distinctive feature of the "New Diplomacy" was its emphasis on free trade as opposed to mercantilism, on a commercial instead of a political diplomacy. It was in this context that the term was coined. The twentieth century, confronted with the failure of free trade as a panacea for world conflict, placed much greater stress on the rule of law,[10] and since World War I the "New Diplomacy" has opposed "the new juridical method" to the "old diplomatic method" in international relations.

It has been said that the independence of America inaugurated a new era in diplomacy.[11] Indeed, if we recall the mutual assurances of concern for the "happiness of mankind" which Franklin and Shelburne exchanged at the beginning of the peace negotiations in Paris in 1783, if we recall Franklin's repeated condemnations of war and ambition, if we find that his partner in Great Britain, Lord Shelburne, once was of the opinion that "I have long thought that the people have but one cause throughout the world. It is sovereigns who have different interests. . . . If the people of different countries could once understand each other, and be brought to adopt half-a-dozen general principles, their servants would not venture to play such tricks"[12]—if we see all this, we might indeed be inclined to regard Franklin's diplomatic mission in France as the beginning of the era of "New Diplomacy."[13] Finally, Franklin's own words seem to confirm this contention. No diplomatic document could better express the new enlightened spirit permeating international relations than the passport which he issued for the protection of the Englisher explorer and navigator, Captain Cook. During the War of Independence, Franklin described Cook's enterprise as "an Undertaking truly laudable in itself, as the Increase of Geographical Knowledge facilitates the Communication between distant Nations"; the "Exchange of useful Products and Manufactures" as well as "the Extension of Arts," thus encouraged and furthered, would augment the "Enjoyments of human Life," and increase "Science of other kinds . . . to the benefit of Mankind in general." Therefore Franklin "most earnestly" recommended to all captains of American ships to afford Captain Cook, and his people, "as common Friends to Mankind, all the Assistance in your Power, which they may happen to stand in need of."[14] In a similar vein of benevolent enlightenment is Franklin's well-known proposal to David Hartley after the War of Independence "of a family compact between England, France, and America. America w^d be as happy as the Sabine girls, if she c^d be the means of uniting in perpetual peace her father and her husband."[15]

We have indicated the nature of those principles with the help of which the enlightened spirits planned to tame the evil of power and ambition, and we specified three categories: the legal, the moral, and the scientific. To be sure, there were shifts of emphasis, according to different schools of thought or different historical circumstances; but if we reflect for a moment on the peculiar characteristics of those devices and methods of the "New Diplomacy" associated with the names of famous liberals like Gladstone and Wilson, with the movements for arbitration and a League of Nations, we find that "power politics" was to be superseded by the rule of law, by the adjustment of the morality of nations to the standards of individual morality (which in turn were supposed to accord with the teachings of Christianity), and by the application of the insights of economic and social science to the conduct of international affairs.

Accordingly, Franklin's concept of international affairs will be analyzed under these three heads. Inevitably, some repetition of problems discussed in earlier chapters will occur, in which cases we shall content ourselves with summarizing what has been said in another context.

FRANKLIN AND THE LEGAL APPROACH TO INTERNATIONAL POLITICS

The attempt to restrain or control the clash of national interests or ambitions by "the rule of law" may manifest itself in several ways. First of all, actual or desired changes in the international power situation may be represented in legal terms, that is, the claims of a country are explained by reference to the provisions of treaties, in the eighteenth century very frequently by reference to the rules of dynastic claims to hereditary succession; often more general principles of international or natural law are invoked, for instance, the "natural law of self-preservation," which played a prominent role in the history of early American expansionism.[16] Legal arguments of this kind are, of course, all too often mere disguises of national ambition. In view of the ineffectiveness of this approach, efforts have been made to create a machinery of international organization, eventually leading up to a world federation or a world state, and thus to enforce effectively the rule of law among the members of the international or supranational community. Finally, short of these rather ambitious efforts, endeavors have been made to improve the intercourse between sovereign nations by developing rules of international law voluntarily adhered to by all or by a majority of nations.

A. LEGAL CLAIMS FOR TERRITORIES

Benjamin Franklin never did care much for legal arguments in international relations. An important indication of this is his remark to Oswald in the summer of 1782 when they were dealing with the subtle question of the acknowledgment of American independence in the commission of the English plenipotentiary: "Mr. Jay was a lawyer, and might think of things that did not occur to those who were not lawyers."[17] Franklin's carelessness about the letter of the law, as long as its spirit was observed, reveals itself in the somewhat casual manner in which he treated the formal recognition of American rights and wants by England. We may recall that early in 1769 Franklin was inclined not to insist on England's renouncing the right of legislation for the colonies: "If continuing the Claim pleases you, continue it as long as you please, provided you never execute it: We shall consider it in the same Light with the Claim of the Spanish Monarch to the Title of King of Jerusalem."[18] This characteristic attitude also prevailed during Franklin's mission to France. Details of England's formal and explicit acknowledgment of America's independence, so long as it was recognized substantially, did not matter much to him. Soon after the conclusion of the French alliance, Franklin told David Hartley that a treaty between America, France, and England might be concluded, "in which England *expressly* Renouncing the Dependence of

America seems no more necessary, than her renouncing the Title of King of France, which has always been claimed for her Kings."[19] About two months later Franklin had no objection to Vergennes's inquiry whether "the United States would accept a peace in which independence would be tacitly assured by a truce, instead of positively by a definite treaty."[20] The turn of the fortunes of the war naturally increased Franklin's intransigence; however, his attitude during the peace talks of 1782, when he insisted firmly on all guarantees which would effectively secure American independence,[21] while he did not bother too much about John Jay's violent apprehensions of French and English double-dealing with American independence, reveals the same point of view. It was on the occasion of Jay's and Franklin's interview with Vergennes early in August, 1782, that Vergennes, in order to dispel Jay's fears, used exactly the argument which Franklin had employed only three years before, namely, "that names signified little; that the King of Great Britain's styling himself the King of France was no obstacle to the King of France's treating with him."[22] As we already know, Franklin, in contrast to Jay, agreed to Vergennes's assurances.

Firmness with regard to substance and more carelessness than might possibly be warranted with regard to legally confirmed rights thus distinguishes Franklin's demeanor.

Even more striking is the complete absence of legal arguments in Franklin's pleas for the grant or cession of new territory to the thirteen colonies, later the United States. If we recall Franklin's writings against the French danger on the North American continent before and during the Great War for the Empire in the 1750's and 1760's, we look in vain for any indication of legal rights to the territories in question.

We know that the Continental Congress and Secretary Livingston took great pains to justify their ambitions for the western lands by legal titles: by the charter claims of certain provinces from Colonial times as well as by the right, contradictory to the charter claims, of the American people to the American land (arguing that the king of England had ruled over the land only by virtue of his sovereignty over the American people).[23] With respect to areas where these kinds of claims could not possibly be maintained, namely, with respect to the Floridas or to Canada, the Americans resorted to another notion, at the same time more realistic and nevertheless still vaguer than the preceding arguments: the notion of security. The desire for security alone, it has been argued, "does not in itself account for the sense of right with which expansionists asserted or implied a rather extraordinary pretension, that the complete assurance of their future security was paramount to another nation's legal possessions. To explain this it is also necessary to bring into view the idea of natural rights."[24]

Here we are concerned with security not as a term of power politics but rather as an expression surrounded by the halo of a natural right. Eighteenth-century jurists of the natural law school held that conquest in a just war was also just.[25] The article on conquest in the French *Encyclopédie* based just conquest on *"la loi de la nature, qui fait que tout tend à la conservation des espèces."*[26] The invasion of Canada in 1776 was explained by the Continental Congress by "the great law of self-preservation."[27] Samuel Adams, expressing the hope that America would acquire Canada, Nova Scotia, and Florida, thought that "we shall never be upon a solid Footing till Britain cedes to us what Nature designs we should have, or till we wrest it from her."[28]

Franklin was as ardent an expansionist as any of the Founding Fathers, and he was as conscious of the security motive as any of his fellow-Americans. However, he never endeavored to introduce the laws of "nature or nature's God" into his pleas for territorial aggrandizement. For Franklin, security remained a political term, measured by the criteria of future peace and stability. His only reference to a "right for security" is too deeply connected with purely political considerations to be taken as reference to natural law:

> In short, security and quiet of princes and states have ever been deemed sufficient reasons, when supported by power, for disposing of rights; and such disposition has never been looked on as want of moderation. . . . There can be no cession that is not supposed at least to increase the power of the party to whom it is made. It is enough that he has a right to ask it, and that he does it not merely to serve the purposes of a dangerous ambition.[29]

It was this pragmatic test of moderation and stability which Franklin deemed sufficient to support his claims for Canada in 1760 as well as in 1776 or 1782. The significant fact remains that Franklin, while indorsing the legal justifications for expansion put forward by other men, never based his own arguments on this sort of reasoning.

B. INTERNATIONAL ORGANIZATION

The absence of legalistic thinking appears even more strikingly when we investigate Franklin's attitude to the problem of international organization. Plans for international organization were not unknown to the eighteenth century. Earlier projects by Sully, by Éméric Crucé, by Franklin's countryman, William Penn, and by the French Abbé de St. Pierre had attempted to solve the problem of international anarchy by setting up machinery for federation and the settling of international disputes.[30] Unfortunately we do not know of any comments by Franklin on these projects, but there are some revealing remarks in connection with a lesser known *Project of Universal and Perpetual Peace,* written by Pierre-André Gargaz and printed by Franklin during his mission in France—in fact, at the time of the peace negotiations in 1782.

This M. Gargaz was a schoolteacher of the little village of Thèze in the Dauphiné in southeastern France who had been sentenced in 1761 to the galleys for twenty years. Toward the end of his imprisonment he sent a letter to Franklin, dated from Toulon, attaching two manuscripts dealing with the problem of establishing perpetual peace and asking Franklin for the favor of printing, publishing, and distributing his project.[31] Franklin indorsed this letter in these words, "Project of Universal Peace by a Galley Slave."[32] Soon after having been released from the galleys, Gargaz walked to Paris and presented his project personally to Franklin. Franklin, on July 10, 1782, wrote to David Hartley that "an honest peasant, from the mountains of Provence," brought a manuscript for which he could procure no permission for printing. Franklin thought that there was "much good sense in it," and he therefore let some copies be printed on his own printing press. He told Hartley that Gargaz could not afford "the expence of riding to Paris, so he came on foot; such was his zeal for peace, and the hope of forwarding and securing it, by communicating his ideas to great men here. His rustic and poor appearance has prevented his access to them, or his attaining their attention; but he does not seem to be discouraged. I honour much the character of this *véritable philosophe.*"[33]

We may conjecture that Franklin was particularly pleased with Gargaz's emphasis on justice as an essential prerequisite to peace, as well as with his argument that wars did not pay. Also, Gargaz's point that wars rarely produce definite solutions, because violence breeds again violence, may have appealed to Franklin, who wanted to substitute purchase of territory for conquest. The main problem, of course, was the procedure of bringing about the new peaceful world. Gargaz grasped the fact that a union of nations under the presidency of the most powerful sovereign would give a kind of superiority to this nation "which would not be pleasing to all of the Sovereigns, and which would prevent many of them from joining the union, as they would not be willing to recognize a sort of Superior."[34] He therefore suggested that a perpetual "Congress" be established, composed of one "Mediator" for every sovereign power. These mediators were to "pass judgement, by a plurality of votes, upon all the differences of their masters."[35] The president would have the power to break a tie, and, in order to eliminate all jealousies and prejudices, he would be the representative of the oldest hereditary sovereign member of this union."[36]

We have no comment of Franklin on this seniority rule, but we know his general opinion about plans for a perpetual peace. In a conversation with a young Englishman to whom we owe the record of his words, Franklin

observed that nothing could be more disgraceful than the scandalous inattention to treaties, which appeared in almost every manifesto; and that he thought the world would grow wiser, and wars become less frequent. But *he observed that the plans which he had seen for this purpose were in general impracticable in this respect, viz., that they supposed a general agreement among the sovereigns of Europe to send delegates to a particular place.* Now, though perhaps two or three of them might be willing to come into this measure, it is improbable and next to impossible that all, or even a majority of them, would do it. "But," said he, *"if they would have patience, I think they might accomplish it, agree upon an alliance against all aggressors,* and agree to refer all disputes between each other to some third person, or set of men, or power. Other nations, seeing the advantage of this, would gradually accede; and perhaps in one hundred and fifty or two hundred years, all Europe would be included."[37]

The strongly realistic strain in Franklin's thought is strikingly revealed in his remark that no sudden and simultaneous meeting of all the enlightened spirits would produce this union; rather, the experience of almost two hundred years might be needed to convince the sovereigns of Europe of the expediency of such a scheme. Even more significant is his thought that union would be brought about by fear of a common enemy rather than by any spontaneous agreement of *véritables philosophes*. An alliance against all aggressors would be the primary motive of closer union. Thus Franklin appears as a forerunner of modern advocates of collective security.

Franklin's skepticism about disinterested mediation or arbitration in international relations became apparent when he was himself confronted with the alternatives of either direct negotiations with England during the War of Independence or the mediation of third powers (at this time Russia and Austria). He appeared to be extremely hesitant, to say the least, as to the virtues of this kind of mediation. In a conversation with Oswald about the prospects of mediation, Franklin, if we may believe Oswald's words,

indeed repeatedly declared his opinion against the expediency of such Interpretation—Saying, that in References on the Subject of private affairs, the Arbitrators, having no particular Concerns of their own in question, were supposed to decide according to the merits of the Case depending singly between the submitting Parties. Whereas, in a matter of this kind, when foreign & neighboring States are joined in the process of discussion, it would be difficult to prevent their mixing some things relative to their particular views, which might tend to disturb the main purpose of the submission.[38]

This was said only a few weeks before M. Gargaz appeared in Paris and submitted his plan for union and mediation to the sage of Passy. It goes a long way toward explaining Franklin's skeptical view on the possibilities of setting up international organizations for the settling of political disputes.

Five years later the successful close of the Federal Convention in Philadelphia inspired Franklin to write more hopefully to a friend in France. The new constitution, he told his correspondent, was now being sent to the several states for their confirmation. "If it succeeds," Franklin hoped, "I do not see why you might not in Europe carry the Project of good Henry the 4th into Execution, by forming a Federal Union and One Grand Republick of all its different States and Kingdoms, by means of a like Convention, *for we had many Interests to reconcile.*"[39] To conceive of the fundamental law of the republic as the expression of a compromise of interests rather than as the embodiment of rules of "reason" and science—certainly the political rather than legalistic nature of Franklin's thought emerges here most clearly.

C. INTERNATIONAL LAW

One more question remains to be answered. What was Franklin's attitude to the international law of his day? At the very beginning of his diplomatic activity in behalf of the revolting colonies, in December, 1775, Franklin wrote to that devoted friend of America, Charles W. F. Dumas, in Holland, as follows:

> I am much obliged by the kind present you have made us of your edition of Vattel. It came to us in good season, when the circumstances of a rising state make it necessary frequently to consult the law of nations. Accordingly, that copy which I kept . . . has been continually in the hands of the members of our Congress, now sitting, who are much pleased with your notes and preface, and have entertained a high and just esteem for their author.[40]

Vattel's *Law of Nations or the Principles of Natural Law* was first published in 1758.[41] Vattel was not so much an original thinker as an interpreter and popularizer of the philosophies of Leibnitz and Wolff, with particular emphasis on international law. His liberalism was well advanced beyond Grotius and reflected many characteristics of the Age of Enlightenment. The book was a great success in Europe, and it arrived in America just in time to provide considerable technical and ideological support to the revolting colonists.[42] Vattel's reassurance that the natural equality of men found an analogy in the status of nations and that "strength or weakness, in this case, counts for nothing"[43] must have evoked the profound agreement of the revolting colonists in general and Franklin in particular. Indeed, who could be more satisfied than the Americans in reading that "a dwarf is as much a man as a giant is; a small Republic is no less a sovereign State than the most powerful Kingdom."[44]

Franklin was certainly one of those for whom Vattel's treatise was written. It was Vattel's purpose to be of service "to those in power who have a love for mankind and a respect for justice; if it furnish them with a weapon for the defence of a just cause, and a means of compelling unjust rulers to observe at least some limits and to keep within the bounds of propriety."[45]

In spite of this far-reaching coincidence of views, there is only one passage in Franklin's diplomatic correspondence alluding to Vattel. This was occasioned by the forced liberation by Denmark of two English prizes which had been brought to the harbor of Bergen by an American privateer (Denmark by 1779 had not yet recognized the United States). Franklin's protest to the Danish foreign minister is drafted in political and psychological terms rather than in terms of international law. He quoted Vattel as saying that, whereas the ancients "did not conceive themselves bound under any obligation towards a people with whom they were not connected by a treaty of friendship," civilized nations at length "acknowledged all mankind as brothers."[46] Franklin drew the conclusion that there existed obligations of justice also to those nations with whom no treaty had yet been made. However, he did not dwell too long on this topic. He rather stressed the fact that the United States, being at war only with England, "have never done any Injury to other Nations, particularly none to the Danish Nation; on the contrary, they are in some degree its Benefactors, as they have opened a Trade of which England made a Monopoly, and of which the Danes may now have their Share, and, by dividing the British Empire, have made it less dangerous to its Neighbours."[47]

This is another piece of evidence that Franklin full well grasped the political significance of America's foreign policy of "commercial, not political, connections" with Europe. He added another argument, entirely characteristic of his method of compensating present weakness with the expectation of future strength: "The United States, oppressed by, and in War with, one of the most powerful nations of Europe, may well be suppos'd incapable in their present Infant State of exacting Justice from other Nations not disposed to grant it; but it is in human Nature, that Injuries as well as Benefits receiv'd in Times of Weakness and Distress, national as well as personal, make deep and lasting Impressions."[48]

Franklin's appeal to enlightened self-interest and to prudence rather than to any abstract principles did not weaken at all his warm and unfeigned efforts to ease the hardships and the evils of war. Had he not written to Edmund Burke that "since the foolish part of mankind will make wars from time to time with each other . . . it certainly becomes the wiser part, who cannot prevent those wars, to alleviate as much as possible the calamities attending them"?[49]

It is in this connection that Franklin endeavored to introduce a new principle of international law, a principle, let us state at the outset, which was to be embodied in only one international treaty. He devoted much personal effort to the task of gaining recognition of a principle which would limit warlike actions strictly to military bodies and would protect the husbandmen and merchants not only of neutral but even of warring nations from the injuries of war.

D. FRANKLIN'S "REFORM OF THE LAW OF NATIONS"

Franklin's idea to "reform the law of nations," as he himself indicated the nature of his task, apparently first occurred to him on the occasion of a phase of the War of Independence upon which we have not touched so far, a phase which has rendered the history of this war important for the development of international law. It was the attempt of the neutral powers to enforce the rule that "free ships make free goods" by an Armed Neutrality. The fundamental issue involved was the question whether or not neutral ships were entitled to carry property of warring countries without fear of confiscation or not; contraband, of course, was always subject to confiscation. From the thirteenth century to the Age of Discovery, the law applied in the Mediterranean world had been the *consolato del mare*: "neutral property (contraband always excepted) was safe from capture on enemy ships, but that enemy property was subject to capture on neutral ships." This distinction recognized the advantage which a larger navy gave to the stronger sea power. States with small navies

naturally desired to have recourse to neutral shipping to carry on their commerce and bring in their military supplies, because they could not protect their own ships with their own naval forces. The policy of the big-navy states impelled the small-navy powers, who were generally neutral carriers in time of war, to negotiate treaties, wherever and whenever possible, by which enemy property in neutral ships passed free; as a concession to the big-navy powers they agreed that neutral property on enemy ships should be subject to confiscation. Thus evolved the maxim of free ships free goods, unfree ships unfree goods.[50]

At the time of the War of Independence, French interests coincided with those of the neutral powers, because the *consolato del mare* granted to England all the advantage of the greatest naval power.[51]

We need not concern ourselves with the complicated and tedious negotiations which produced a "system of Armed Neutrality" under the inspiration and leadership of Russia, soon followed by Denmark and Sweden, later by Holland, and finally adhered to even by the Holy Roman Empire and the Kingdom of the Two Sicilies. Although Russia was stirred to action by a Spanish capture of Russian goods on a Dutch vessel, the Armed Neutrality was to turn against England, particularly since Vergennes eagerly grasped the opportunity offered by the opposition of Russia, Sweden, and Denmark against the old maritime practice of utilizing it for the purposes of French interests.

This position of America's European ally coincided with the interests of the United States, since the United States at that time was indeed a small naval power. We mentioned already that the American "Plan of Treaties" of 1776 included the provision for "free ships, free goods," and it was included in the Treaty of Amity and Commerce with France of February, 1778.

However, mention of the principle "free ships, free goods" appears in Franklin's correspondence only after the Declaration of the Empress of Russia of February 28, 1780, "regarding the Principles of Armed Neutrality."[52] Two months after that declaration Franklin justified the seizure of a Dutch vessel with cargo for England by an American privateer by "there being yet no treaty between Holland and America to that purpose, I apprehend that, the goods being declared by the captain to be English, a neutral ship will not protect them; the law of nations governing in this case."[53] Shortly afterward, Franklin shifted his attitude in spite of the fact that no treaty between Holland and the United States had been concluded. In a letter to an agent of American privateers, he now gave notice that no more English goods found in Dutch vessels, except contraband, should be captured and gave the following reason:

All the neutral states of Europe seem at present disposed to change what had never before been deemed the law of nations, to wit, that an enemy's property may be taken wherever found, and to establish a rule that free ships shall make free goods. The rule is in itself so reasonable, and of nature so beneficial to mankind, that I can not but wish it may become general; and I make no doubt that the Congress will agree to it in as full an extent as France and Spain.[54]

In his reports to Congress, Franklin stressed more the political than the "benevolent" side of the question. He justified his order to American captains to stop the seizure of neutral ships by informing Congress that "it is a critical time with respect to such cases, for whatever may formerly have been the law of nations, all the neutral powers, at the instance of Russia, seem at present disposed to change it, and to enforce the rule that free ships shall make free goods, except in the case of contraband. . . . I have therefore instructed our privateers to bring in no more neutral ships, as such prizes occasion much litigation and create ill blood."[55]

The prudential strain in Franklin's reasoning is undeniable. On the other hand, we ought not to place undue emphasis on the political motivation in this case. Franklin's concern for the common good of humanity, his "love of mankind," was genuine enough, as appears from the following letter, in which he informed Robert Morris of the Armed Neutrality: "I wish they would extend it still further, and ordain that unarmed trading ships, as well as fishermen and tanners, should be respected as working for the common benefit of mankind, and never to be interrupted in their operations even by national enemies; but let those only fight with one another whose trade it is, and who are armed and paid for the purpose."[56]

Franklin did not leave the matter at that; he took the initiative toward realization of this principle. On July 10, 1782, the very day on which he asked Oswald for Canada, reparations, and a recognition of war guilt, he addressed a letter to Benjamin Vaughan, outlining his conception of the development of the law of nations. The death of prisoners had been replaced by slavery; slavery had been superseded by the exchange of prisoners. Franklin went on:

Why should not this Law of Nations go on improving? Ages have interven'd between its several Steps; but as Knowledge of late increases rapidly, why should not those Steps be quicken'd? Why should it not be agreed to as the future Law of Nations that in any War hereafter the following Descriptions of Men should be undisturbed, have the Protections of both Sides, and be permitted to follow their Employments in Surety, viz

1. Cultivators of the Earth, because they Labour for the subsistence of Mankind.

2. Fishermen, for the same Reason.

3. Merchants and Traders, in unarm'd Ships, who accommodate different Nations by communicating and exchanging the Necessaries and Conveniences of Life.

4. Artists and Mechanics, inhabiting and working in open towns.

It is hardly necessary to add that the Hospitals of Enemies should be unmolested; they ought to be assisted.

In short, It would have nobody fought but those who are paid for Fighting. . . .

This once Established, that Encouragement to War which arises from a Spirit of Rapine, would be taken away, and Peace therefore more likely to continue and be lasting.[57]

Shortly after the conclusion of the preliminaries with England on November 30, 1782, Oswald reported to his master in London, Lord Shelburne, that Franklin had submitted to him a paper concerning a subject "he had spoke of to me six months ago."[58] Franklin's paper[59] contained the arguments which he had submitted to Benjamin Vaughan several months before. To this Franklin now had added the draft of an article to the effect of limiting warlike action to military forces and to abolish privateering. This article he wanted to have included in the definitive treaty of peace between England and America:

> If war should hereafter arise between Great Britain and the United States, which God forbid, the merchants of either country then residing in the other shall be allowed to remain nine months to collect their debts, and settle their affairs, and may depart freely, carrying off all their effects without molestation or hindrance. And all fishermen, all cultivators of the earth, and all artisans or manufacturers unarmed, and inhabiting unfortified towns, villages, or places, who labour for the common subsistence and benefit of mankind, and peaceably follow their respective employments, shall be allowed to continue the same, and shall not be molested by the armed force of the enemy in whose power by the events of the war they may happen to fall; but, if any thing is necessary to be taken from them, for the use of such armed force, the same shall be paid for at a reasonable price. And all merchants or traders with their unarmed vessels, employed in commerce, exchanging the products of different places, and thereby rendering the necessaries, conveniences, and comforts of human life more easy to obtain, and more general, shall be allowed to pass freely, unmolested. And neither of the powers, parties to this treaty, shall grant or issue any commission to any private armed vessels, empowering them to take or destroy such trading ships, or interrupt such commerce.[60]

Oswald, as he told Shelburne, was rather "reserved on that Occasion," "deplored the Depravity & avidity of Mankind," and declined to accept Franklin's papers.[61] Franklin was not so easily discouraged and gave proof of the greatest tenacity. One month later he addressed a letter to Oswald inclosing the two papers which he had read to him before. Franklin told Oswald that these papers had not yet been considered by his colleagues; that he thought Amercia might offer these innovations with a better grace, as she was a country "that is likely to suffer least and gain most by continuing the ancient Practice; which is our Case, as the American Ships, laden only with the gross Productions of the Earth, cannot be so valuable as yours, filled with Sugars or with Manufactures."[62]

Franklin's idealism and love of peace appear in every word he had written for that purpose; but it would not have been Franklin had not a drop of pessimism and experience of human nature injected itself in this undertaking. "I rather wish than expect, that it will be adopted."[63]

Nothing came of Franklin's intervention with Oswald, and the days of Shelburne's ministry were numbered. Charles James Fox came again to power, and he sent Franklin's old friend, David Hartley, to Paris to succeed Shelburne's confidant, Oswald. On May 8, 1783, Franklin sent the same papers to Hartley which he had in vain conveyed to Oswald, again arguing that the abolishment of privateering would actually hurt America more than England, as America could easily control the whole West India trade and that America's own commerce consisted of much less precious articles. Franklin hoped therefore that "this proposition, if made by us, will appear in its true light, as having humanity only for its motive."[64]

Hartley transmitted Franklin's proposals without comment to London, where they were filed and never again heard of.

Franklin, though, did have the satisfaction of concluding his diplomatic career in Europe by putting his name on a document which embodied his cherished proposals. The Treaty of Amity and Commerce between Prussia and the United States, signed by Franklin on July 9, 1785,[65] reproduced in its Article 23 almost literally Franklin's draft article cited above.[66] John Adams, who also participated in this treaty, was charmed to find Frederick the Great "do us the honor to agree to the platonic philosophy of some of our articles, which are at least a good lesson to mankind, and will derive more influence from a treaty ratified by the King of Prussia, than from the writings of Plato or Sir Thomas More."[67] Franklin's merits in suggesting and struggling for this piece of "platonic philosophy" in international relations were duly recognized. Almost thirty years later, when circumstances had greatly changed, James Madison declared that the United States could have no special interest in the rule of "free ships, free goods," unless combined with another principle, of which an example is found in our Treaty with Prussia, and probably in no other; namely, that unarmed merchant vessels, like wagons or ploughs, the property of one belligerent, should be unmolested by the other. This principle has, I believe, an undisputed American father in Doctor Franklin."[68]

Legal arguments and considerations in international relations, we may conclude, did not have great force with Franklin. To harmonize the interests of different countries by pressing them into a legal framework might be possible under the stimulation of outside threats. When Franklin turned to his concern for the good of mankind, psychological, political, and economic rather than legal considerations provided the moving power of his efforts.

FRANKLIN AND THE MORAL APPROACH TO INTERNATIONAL POLITICS

A. POLITICAL VERSUS INDIVIDUAL MORALITY AND THE PROBLEM OF IDEOLOGY

However, to oppose the rule of law to the regime of power politics is not the only, perhaps not even the main, device of the "New Diplomacy." The moral basis of international politics may be even more decisive than the legal basis. The great efforts of all idealists since the time when Machiavelli threw his great challenge into the arena of political discussion have been directed toward re-establishing some reconciliation between the spheres of politics, emancipated from traditional morality, and morality, loosely but generally identified with the doctrines of Christianity. In other words, to destroy the tragic divorce of political and individual morality has been the great occupation of the protagonists of a new diplomacy.

Within the framework of this discussion, the stage for an interesting contrast is set. On the one hand, we find that the most convinced French protagonists of support for the new republic, Beaumarchais and Vergennes, stuck to the time-honored belief of so many practitioners of politics that "the national policy which preserves states differs in every respect almost entirely from the civil morality which governs individuals."[69] These are the words of the author of *The Marriage of Figaro*. Count Vergennes expressed himself hardly less unequivocally, when he told Louis XVI that "kings are perhaps not subject, when the safety of their people is in question, to the rules of such strict morality as are ordinary individuals in their private actions."[70] On the other hand, we find the categorical statement of Franklin's close friend and fervent admirer, the French physiocrat Barbeu-Dubourg, who proclaimed in a book dedicated to Franklin and professedly inspired by Franklin's ideas,[71] that "the reciprocal duties and rights of nations to each other are essentially the same as between families or between individuals. . . . Nations no less than individuals are subject to the laws of eternal justice."[72] With much greater authority, of course, speaks the voice of the master himself. After having spent eight years as American minister to Paris, and having been as much entangled as any American diplomat in "European power politics," Franklin still clung to the same doctrine: "Justice is as strictly due between neighbour Nations as between neighbour Citizens. A Highwayman is as much a Robber when he plunders in a Gang, as when single; and a Nation that makes an unjust War, is only a *great Gang*. . . . A War . . . can hardly be just on both sides."[73]

The contrast seems striking and complete. Before passing a definite judgment, however, we ought to pause for a moment to ask ourselves what those moralists mean who confront individual morality with political morality. This contrast implies altruism or at least disinterestedness on the side of individual morality. To make this point clear, we may be permitted to leap for a moment into the nineteenth and twentieth centuries and to compare the thought of two great liberals, John Stuart Mill and Woodrow Wilson, with the thought of that true eighteenth-century liberal, Benjamin Franklin.

Mill, discussing the principle of nonintervention, was scornful of the British politicians' (particularly Palmerston's) "shabby refrain— 'We did not interfere, because no English interest was involved'; 'We ought not to interfere where no English interest is concerned.' " "England is thus exhibited as a country whose most distinguished men are not ashamed to profess, as politicians, a rule of action which no one, not utterly base, could endure to be accused of as the maxim by which he guides his private life; not to move a finger for others unless he sees his private advantage in it."[74]

Woodrow Wilson proclaimed in his famous Mobile speech in 1913:

It is a very perilous thing to determine the foreign policy of a nation in the terms of material interest. It not only is unfair to those with whom you are dealing, but it is degrading as regards your own actions. . . . We dare not turn from the principle that morality and not expediency is the thing that must guide us, and that we will never condone iniquity because it is most convenient to do so.[75]

Interest is a very base thing indeed for Mill and Wilson. There must be some higher cause than "interest," which is definitely banished into the evil sphere of "power politics."

Let us return to Franklin. Did he have a higher cause for which to fight? There are some weighty indications that he did. In fact, it was nothing less than "the cause of all mankind" which demanded Franklin's service. After all, he was the envoy of a country which, particularly since Thomas Paine's passionate appeal and since the Declaration of Independence, had become much more than a confedera-

234 BENJAMIN FRANKLIN AND AMERICAN FOREIGN POLICY

tion of rebellious colonies. "Freedom hath been hunted round the globe. Asia and Africa have long expelled her. Europe regards her like a stranger, and England hath given her warning to depart. O! receive the fugitive, and prepare in time an asylum for mankind."[76] Paine's enthusiastic and powerful appeal was echoed by Franklin, when he proudly and happily wrote that "the Almighty has favoured the just Cause"; and he was thankful and prayed that God might "perfect his Work, and establish Freedom in the new World, as an Asylum for those of the Old, who deserve it."[77] Franklin, in fact, was not impervious at all to the ideology of the American Revolution.[78] Obviously, he never forgot in his appeals to the public to mention "the Satisfaction generous Minds must have in reflecting, that by Loans to America they are opposing Tyranny, and aiding the Cause of Liberty, which is the Cause of all Mankind."[79] In private letters to old friends Franklin is no less excited about the greatness of his cause:

All Europe is on our Side of the Question, as far as Applause and good Wishes can carry them. Those who live under arbitrary Power do nevertheless approve of Liberty, and wish for it; they almost despair of recovering it in Europe; they read the Translations of our separate Colony Constitutions with Rapture; and there are such Numbers everywhere, who talk of Removing to America, with their Families and Fortunes, as soon as Peace and our Independence shall be established, that 'tis generally believed we shall have a prodigious Addition of Strength, Wealth, and Arts, from the Emigrations of Europe; and 'tis thought, that, to lessen or prevent such Emigrations, the Tyrannies established there must relax, and allow more Liberty to their People. Hence 'tis a Common Observation here, that our Cause is *the Cause of all Mankind,* and that we are fighting for their Liberty in defending our own. 'Tis a glorious task assign'd us by Providence; which has, I trust, given us Spirit and Virtue equal to it, and will at last crown it with Success.[80]

There is a revealing phrase in the midst of all Franklin's joy about Europe's enthusiasm and the glory of his country's cause: "we are fighting for their Liberty in defending our own." In other words, the War of Independence was a crusade because of a fortunate co-incidence of America's interests and the interests of mankind, but not for any other reason.

The age of Franklin had not yet arrived at the sweeping condemna-tion of the pursuit of "self-interest" which characterized the age of John Stuart Mill, Gladstone, or Woodrow Wilson. In Franklin's age self-interest was recognized by many as a legitimate and important spring of human action; on the whole, the problem was one of narrow versus enlightened self-interest rather than of self-interest versus disinterestedness.

Franklin, we have had ample opportunity to observe, knew full well that political connections were durable only when founded on mutual interests, although, as we have also noticed, he was convinced of the "duty to do good" regardless of immediate consequences, at least in private life.[81] In the last analysis, he was not so far removed from those who assert that, when the safety and the essential interests of the political community are at stake, political and individual morality may go different ways. During the War of Independence, Franklin, in a sentence which seems to have escaped the notice of most students of his political thought, observed that "moral and political rights sometimes differ, and sometimes are both subdu'd by Might."[82]

Franklin, it now appears, did recognize the autonomy of the political sphere in some cases; this by no means implies that he would have denied the legitimacy of moral judgment in the domain of politics. With much dexterity and finesse Franklin made a second distinction, between "political rights" and "might" pure and simple. His insistence on the "injustice" of England's war against the colonies, for instance, would otherwise become incomprehensible.

Two significant traits of the "New Diplomacy," then, cannot be applied to Franklin. There is no attempt in his thought to base his diplomacy upon some general ideological principle, like "liberty," instead of upon the interests of America, although he did derive satisfaction and joy from the feeling that he was promoting the "cause of all mankind" by defending his own country. But there are no indications that he desired to carry the struggle against the principles of tyranny and oppression farther than the interests of the new republic would warrant it. Furthermore, the wish and belief of the disciples of a new diplomacy to abolish the moral autonomy which the state enjoyed in the eyes of most statesmen and diplomatists was repudiated by Franklin's distinction of moral and political rights.

B. THE CREATION OF CONFIDENCE AND THE REPUDIATION OF OPEN DIPLOMACY

The moralistic element of Franklin's diplomacy rather seems to consist in his attempt to create the psychological atmosphere most appropriate for a far-reaching and lasting adjustment of conflicting interests. The overwhelming problem of adjusting and reconciling interests, indeed, always stood foremost in his mind. Nothing is more revealing of Franklin's approach to international affairs than his remark to an American friend after the conclusion of the preliminaries between England and America but before the conclusion of a general peace between the other powers and England: "There are so many interests to be considered between five nations, and so many claims to adjust, that I can hardly flatter myself to see the peace soon concluded, though I wish and pray for it, and use my best endeavours to promote it."[83]

Neither "the cause of all mankind" nor "the commands of individual morality," then, lay at the roots of Franklin's "moralistic" approach to diplomatic negotiations, but the attempt to create mutual confidence and mutual good will, the fundamental premises of every lasting settlement. Of Franklin's much-debated attitude toward the French court, Jefferson has given the following well-known testimony: "He possessed the confidence of that government in the highest degree, insomuch, that it may truly be said, that they were more under his influence, than he was under theirs. . . . *Mutual confidence produces, of course, mutual influence,* and this was all which subsisted between Dr. Franklin and the government of France."[84]

Franklin himself was very pleased with the success of his method of confidence, as appears from his so far not widely known conversation with Benjamin Vaughan, which has been recorded in the latter's report to Lord Shelburne: Talking about the character of the first British ambassador who ought to be sent to Paris after the conclusion of the peace, Franklin voiced his opinion that

he thought from what he knew of this court that a plain, downright, honest man, was best likely to succeed here; that *finesse* might serve to gain a point at first but it afterwards would be found the longest & most difficult way of doing business; whereas confidence would be found to shorten things & also to facilitate them. . . . Indeed (he added) the character he had described was, he believed, the fittest for all courts, taking things in the long run.[85]

This great stress on the psychological factor has an interesting result if it is applied to another favorite object of the reform plans of the "New Diplomacy," namely, the problem of "open diplomacy." From the eighteenth century down to the days of the League of Nations and the United Nations, secrecy has been denounced as one of the very basic evils of power politics and as proof that the princes and politicians negotiating in secrecy try to hide their personal ambitions and prejudices from the eyes of the public, who feel cheated and betrayed in their true interests. Indeed, if international relations are nothing else but the attempt to find certain general rules of conduct and principles with the help of which strife and violence can be abolished, there is every reason for publicity. If, on the other hand, international relations consist in hard bargaining for advantages, compromises, and adjustments, secrecy becomes essential.

Franklin, whose reticence and taciturnity about important matters were two of his best-known qualities during his mission in France, had no contempt for secret diplomacy. He unequivocally extolled the "advantages in negotiation that result from secrecy of sentiment."[86] More than that, he repeatedly spoke very scornfully about the evils of the influence of party politics and domestic propaganda on diplomatic negotiations. Franklin wrote to his fellow-commissioner, Henry Laurens:

I have never yet known of a Peace made, that did not occasion a great deal of popular Discontent, Clamour, and Censure on both sides. This is, perhaps, owing to the usual Management of the Ministers and Leaders of the contending Nations, who to keep up the spirits of their People for continuing the War, generally represent the State of their own Affairs in a better Light, and that of the Enemy in a Worse, than is consistent with the Truth; hence the Populace on each Side expect better Terms than really can be obtained, and are apt to ascribe their Disappointment to Treachery.[87]

On this topic Franklin was even more outspoken in a conversation with Benjamin Vaughan, as described to Lord Shelburne:

War, he said, was made according to the mistaken imaginations of the people, & peace according to their real necessities, as seen by the peace-makers; and hence comes the chief abuse upon peace-makers. . . . He said that being obliged to provide for a party, prevented great persons agreeing . . . it seemed to him . . . that there were those who wished the ministers just now to make a bad peace in order to abuse him for it when he had done it.[88]

Franklin, indeed, has a lesson to teach about the conduct of foreign affairs in a democracy. There are no signs that he clung to the belief, so characteristic of the "New Diplomacy," that the people are necessarily more peaceful than rulers; right and wrong, reason and passion, could be pretty equally divided among the rulers and the ruled.

Franklin and the Economic Approach to International Politics

An analysis of the moralistic element in Franklin's approach to foreign affairs seems to show that there are several remarkable and significant points of difference which establish his disagreement with some of the most fundamental tenets of the "New Diplomacy." However, we have not yet exhausted the manifold possibilities in which the human mind has attempted to subdue the evils of power and ambition. There was one important school of thought, for instance, which despised legal institutions and attempts at international organization[89] and which still believed in the achievement of international harmony; these people were the physiocrats. The physiocrats, with many of whom Franklin was closely associated during his stay in France, believed that "all political problems would be solved if the right economic principles were followed, the right economic measures adopted."[90]

Franklin, we recall, had greeted with great enthusiasm works like Hume's essay on the *Jealousy of Trade* or Dupont de Nemours's book on *Physiocratie*.[91] Well before the outbreak of the American Revolution, Franklin had come to accept the doctrines of free trade, subject, however, to the requirements of imperial defense as laid down in the essentials of the Navigation Acts. By the Declaration of Independence, America had liberated herself from these fetters, and Franklin now could extol the virtues of free trade without any restraint. The interests of the new republic and the doctrines of the new science of economics happily coincided to a very large degree. After 1776 his occasional comments on the virtues of free trade occur mostly in the context of his diplomatic correspondence. The opposition of his colleagues, Arthur Lee and Ralph Izard, to the molasses article of the commercial treaty with France gave one opportunity for Franklin to formulate his views anew:

Commerce among nations, as well as between private persons, should be fair and equitable, by equivalent exchanges and mutual supplies. The taking unfair advantages of a neighbour's necessities, though attended with temporary success, always breeds bad blood. To lay duty on a commodity exported, which our neighbours want, is a knavish attempt to get something for nothing. . . . As we produce no commodity that is peculiar to our country, and which may not be obtained elsewhere, the discouraging the consumption of ours by duties on exportation, and thereby encouraging a rivalship from other nations in the ports we trade to, is absolute folly, which indeed is mixed more or less with all knavery.[92]

Much more important was the futile effort of Franklin and his colleagues to establish free trade with Great Britain during the peace negotiations in 1782 and 1783. One of his "advisable" articles of July 10, 1782, proposed, in fact, that "Colony ships and trade to be received, and have the same privileges in Great Britain and Ireland, as British ships and trade. . . . British and Irish ships in the Colonies to be, in like manner, on the same footing with their own ships."[93] Upon British insistence, the negotiation of the commercial provisions was separated from the preliminary articles, and a separate treaty of commerce was subsequently to be concluded. It was for this purpose that Franklin's friend, David Hartley, the envoy of the Fox-North ministry in Paris, negotiated with the American commissioners during the spring and summer of 1783. Hartley himself shared the liberal and enlightened views of the Americans, but he had not the backing of his government. A British order-in-council of July 2, 1783, cut off all American participation in the trade of the British West Indies. The negotiations came to naught, and Franklin could only remark sadly that "restraints on the freedom of Commerce and intercourse between us, can afford no advantage equivalent to the Mischief they will do by keeping up ill humour, and promoting a total alienation."[94]

Franklin summed up his philosophy of free trade in a letter to Vergennes in 1783:

In general, I would only observe that commerce, consisting in a mutual exchange of the necessaries and conveniences of life, the more free and unrestrained it is, the more it flourishes; and the happier are all the nations concerned in it. Most of the restraints put upon it in different countries have seemed to have been the projects of particulars for their private interest, under pretence of public good.[95]

Franklin wholeheartedly shared the physiocrats' doctrine of the folly of wars for trade in the old mercantilist fashion, and in 1787 he congratulated an English friend on Great Britain's treaty of commerce with France, which, he said, "seems to show a growing Improvement in the Sentiments of both Nations in the Oeconomical Science," and he added that "all Europe might be a great deal happier with a little more Understanding."[96]

Franklin's desire to see wars for commercial monopoly abolished found its expression in his efforts—which met, however, with no response—to neutralize the West Indian sugar islands. It has been pointed out before how large the West Indies loomed on the horizon of world politics in the age of mercantilism. At an early stage of his negotiations with the British in 1782, Franklin suggested making "all Sugar Islands neutral so as to be under the dominion of no particular Nation."[97] Almost three months later, Benjamin Vaughan reported to Shelburne in words vividly reflecting the "New Diplomacy" that "to prevent future wars (from the hope of getting or the fear of losing them) Dr. Franklin & Mr. Turgot have proposed to make the islands in the West Indies into free states; by which they think nothing would be lost, but the appointment to a few offices, & many expenses saved."[98] After the conclusion of the preliminary articles, Franklin again took up his suggestion, this time linked with his proposal for the improvement of the law of nations. He now argued that "the cost of sugar to the consumer in those nations consists not merely in the price he pays for it by the pound, but in the accumulated charge of all the taxes he pays in every war, to fit out fleets and maintain troops for the defence of the islands that raise the sugar, and the ships that bring it home." He thought that "it would be better for the nations now possessing sugar colonies to give up their claim to them, let them govern themselves, and put them under the protection of all the powers of Europe as neutral countries, open to the commerce of all, the profits of the present monopolies being by no means equivalent to the expense of maintaining them."[99]

Franklin went even further than that; not only wars for commercial monopoly but even wars for territory were futile and a waste of manpower and money. We remember that in 1776 he had suggested that Canada be bought by the United States, and in the last years of his life he advocated in many letters the same procedure for other countries. There is some evidence that Franklin's conviction of the futility of territorial acquisition by conquest rather than by purchase was influenced by the failure of the United States expedition to Canada in the spring of 1776. His bitter disappointment about this event and its causes becomes apparent in a letter to John Jay in 1779, in which he explained the postponement of a new expedition to Canada:

Besides the Reasons given in it for deferring the Expedition to Canada, there is one that would weigh much with me, and that is our Want of Sufficient Quantity of hard Money. The Canadians are afraid of Paper, and would never take the Congress Money. To enter a Country which you mean to make a friend of, with an army that must have occasion every Day for fresh Provision, Horses, Carriage labour of every kind, having no acceptable Money to pay to those that serve you, and to be obliged, therefore, from the Necessity of the Case, to take that Service by Force, is the sure way to disgust, offend, and by Degrees make Enemies of the whole People, after which all your operations will be more difficult, all your Motions discover'd, and every endeavour used to have you driven back out of their Country.[100]

Franklin's scheme of rational politics seems perfect—as perfect as the system of the physiocrats, whose faith in human reason convinced them that their program of transforming politics into a purely economic procedure could be carried out. He, however, had one great reservation, and this reservation undermined a structure of rational "economic" politics badly indeed: "A war, to acquire that territory and to retain it, will cost both parties much more, perhaps ten times more, than such sum of purchase money. *But the hope of glory, and the ambition of princes, are not subject to arithmetical calculation.*"[101] "To make & accept such an Offer, these Potentates should be both of them reasonable Creatures, and free from the Ambition of Glory, which perhaps is too much to be supposed,"[102] Franklin sadly concluded. He hoped indeed that, "as by degrees men are convinced of the folly of wars for religion, for dominion, or for commerce, they will be happier and happier,"[103] only to retract his all-too-cheerful statement a few months later and to content himself with the more modest hope that "if glory cannot be valued, and therefore the wars for it cannot be subject to arithmetical calculation so as to show their advantage or disadvantage, at least wars for trade, which have gain for their object, may be proper subjects for such computation."[104]

In other words, Franklin's grasp of the lust for dominion, of the will-to-power, his conception of human nature, prevented him from acknowledging the new science of economics as the panacea which the physiocrats hoped to have discovered and which many a nineteenth-century liberal hoped to see realized in his own days.

America's Independence and Social Structure as Factors of Peace

Franklin, indeed, had no blueprints to offer for world peace; neither legal, nor moral, nor scientific devices to bring about the millennium were invented or adopted by him, and most of his French enlightened friends surpassed him greatly in their unbroken optimism. However, Franklin did feel in his later days that a great deal had been accomplished and that wars would be less frequent. Two facts seem to account for his cautious optimism. First of all, wars for trade and for religion seemed indeed on the way to oblivion. Religious tolerance and the new science of economics could achieve something, even if they could not completely change human nature. The second factor was the independence of America. This event, independent of all theorizing about the rule of law, the new morality, or the new science of economics, perhaps contributed more than anything else to bring about Franklin's feeling of cautious—and at times not so cautious—optimism that world politics had taken a turn for the better.

The Peace of Versailles of 1783, which confirmed American independence, must be seen against the background of the Peace of Paris of 1763. In 1763 what may well be called the first world war of modern times had been concluded. Pitt's famous dictum that he conquered Canada in Germany is truly symbolic and indicates how aware the leading protagonists were of the universality of their struggle. We have already mentioned that the European balance of power, by 1750, and down to the War of Independence, was held to hinge upon the colonial balance of power, above all, upon the balance of power in North America. The independence of America and the opening-up of the North American continent for the free trade of the whole world— the breakdown of England's mercantile system—meant a revolution with regard to concepts of international relations[105] which, it seems, in its effect on the thought of the times, goes well beyond the problems of legal, moral, or scientific innovations. The tremendous change in world politics and in the outlook on world politics brought about by the American Revolution is nowhere better described than in a memoir of Franklin's fellow-commissioner in France, Silas Deane:

The Colonies, therefore, in offering their Commerce to France, do really offer her that from which the Wealth of Great Britain has been principally derived, and which will afford every benefit that could result even from the Sovereignty of those Colonies, without any of the Burthens necessarily attending Sovereignty. . . . In Conjunction with Great Britain they [the colonies] would enable her to conquer the possessions of other States in America, but separated from her, both interest and Inclination will lead them to observe a just and peaceable conduct toward the rest of the World for many, very many ages to come; happy in having been able to secure and enjoy their own Rights, they will not think of invading those of other People, and from their Local situation, the Circumstances by which they are surrounded, their habits, Interests, & Dispositions, & above all from the immense extent of uncultivated Territory which they possess, their attention must for a Multitude of Years necessarily be fixed upon Agriculture, the most natural, beneficial, and inoffensive of all human Employments. By this they will constantly produce abundant Quantities of those productions & Materials which are suited for European Consumption and European Manufactures. And to obtain suitable markets for these articles, as well as suitable supplies of European Manufactures & Commodities for their own Wants, it must ever be their Interest to pursue an inviolable Peace with the States of Europe, more especially with France; they can therefore never resolve, even were they to become sufficiently powerful, to embroil themselves with those European States who have possessions in America, by attempting the Conquest of such possessions. They are indeed strongly prejudiced against all Tropical Establishments.[106]

This is a document of great significance. It explains better than any economic theory the replacement of the competition of interests by the hope for a future harmony of interests. Franklin's friend, Thomas Pownall, wrote in 1780 a book in which he attempted to analyze the meaning of the change which had occurred. He extolled the new system of commercial liberty: "The Commercial System of Europe is changing in fact, and in wisdom and policy should be changed; . . . the great Commerce of North America, emancipated from its provincial state, *not only coincides with, but is a concurring cause of, this change.*"[107]

It explains a second important factor: The world would become more peaceful, not only because the contest for the balance of power between England and France had been eliminated from North America and had accordingly been reduced to smaller proportions, but also because no new war-loving nation would take the place of the two expelled powers. The Americans, in John Adams' magnificent words, addressed to Franklin, for a long time to come would be too much occupied with conquering land "from the trees and rocks and wild beasts," and during that time "we shall never go abroad to trouble other nations."[108] The agricultural structure of the new republic was taken as the surest guarantor of peace for many ages to come. Not only would its inhabitants be too busy to wage wars of conquest; but the country, fortunately, was not rich enough. As Thomas Paine put it, "Her trade will always be a protection, and her barrenness of gold and silver secure her from invaders."[109]

The structure of American society rather than any legal or scientific theory or an all-too-optimistic view of human nature prompted Franklin to prophesy the coming of a more peaceful era:

The Americans are Cultivators of Land; those engag'd in Fishery and Commerce are a small Number, compar'd with the Body of the People. They have ever conducted their several Governments with Wisdom, avoiding **Wars and** vain, expensive Projects, delighting only in their peaceable Occupations, which must, considering the Extent of their yet uncultivated Territory, find them Employment still for Ages. Whereas England, ever unquiet, ambitious, avaricious, imprudent, and quarrelsome, is half her Time engag'd in some War or other, always at an expence infinitely greater than the advantages proposed if it could be obtained.[110]

In other words, the question of peace and war is not exclusively a question of one's view of human nature. Employment in agriculture and lack of population pressure opened up for America a long period of peace. "The body of our people are not merchants, but humble husbandmen, who delight in the cultivation of their lands . . . and we have too much land to have the least temptation to extend our territory by conquest from peaceable neighbours, as well as too much justice to think of it."[111] These two statements were written for the eye of the public or of the enemy during the War of Independence; however, we know how sincerely Franklin had praised the agricultural structure of American society long before the war, and in his old age he reaffirmed that agriculture was esteemed by him as "the most independent, the most useful & therefore the most honourable of all our Employments."[112] Franklin cherished America's agricultural society for two reasons: first of all, the growth of overpopulation and manufactures would bring about extremes of poverty and riches—manufactures are founded in poverty, so Franklin had proclaimed in 1760!—and thus would put into jeopardy Franklin's ideal of independence and equality for all; second, peaceful development and expansion might also be destroyed. He wanted to secure expansion by peaceful means. After his retirement from his diplomatic service, Franklin again took up the idea of buying countries instead of conquering them. In 1786 he suggested that he would rather be for buying the Spaniards out of North America "entirely by a fair Purchase for some valuable Consideration, than to think of driving them out by Force, being almost sure it would be cheaper as well as honester. Perhaps it might not be amiss to set on foot such a Treaty immediately. A Guarantee of their other Possessions in America might have Weight in it."[113] However, in the case of a very rich America, the danger of armed conflict would increase enormously. Not only that America in that case would offer a new temptation for aggression from abroad; Franklin also had once formulated a theory of wars for commerce which might well have contributed to his aversion against great concentrations of wealth. In a letter written in the time of postwar prosperity after the Great War for the Empire and which has been published only recently, Franklin, back in Philadelphia, wrote to his friend and substitute, Jackson, in London "an Observation, that your Commerce is now become so profitable, and naturally brings so much Gold and Silver into your Island, that if you had not now and then some expensive foreign War, to draw it off, your country would, like ours, have a Plethora in its Veins, productive of the same Sloth, and the same feverish Extravagance."[114]

As early as 1763, then, Franklin anticipated the Jeffersonian argument of the intimate connection of human peacefulness and "goodness" with the peculiar and fortunate structure of American society in the eighteenth century. Americans would remain virtuous and peaceful, Jefferson held, "as long as agriculture is our principal object, which will be the case while there remain vacant lands in any part of America. When we get piled up upon one another in large cities, as in Europe, we shall become corrupt as in Europe, and go on eating one another as they do there."[115]

Old Diplomacy and New

The change for the better, through the breakdown of the British mercantile system and through American independence and more enlightened notions of international commerce, was great enough; but it was by no means great enough to bring about that state of perfect harmony which was so ardently desired by the enlightened spirits of the Age of Reason. It is interesting to note that the protagonists of a new era in human history, the would-be "new diplomats," rarely were utopian enough to fail to adapt themselves to the political exigencies of the present. Lord Shelburne, whose faith in the community of the peoples' interest we have cited at the beginning of this chapter, at another time presented a much gloomier picture:

No man can be trusted with power over another. The heads of the most sensible men turn with it, and lose both their sense and memory; while fools, who form the great majority of mankind, have neither of these at any time. No gratitude can withstand power. Every man from the monarch down to the peasant is sure to abuse it. A man therefore must be ever upon his guard against any weakness, accident, momentary necessity, or effusion of heart, which can lead him to put himself in the power of another.[116]

Shelburne was a convinced follower of the new gospel of free trade; the science of economics, however, provided no complete cure. Another man in the group of enlightened diplomats who moved between Paris and London in the eighties was David Hartley. With more naïveté and greater optimism than any of his more illustrious colleagues or superiors, he expressed in a letter to Franklin the hope that

> simply the adoption of *reason* among nations, and the mere rectification of obsolete and gothic absurdities, which carry no gratification, would afford a fund of remuneration to all parties for renouncing those objects of mutual contention, which, *in the eye of reason,* are no better than creatures of passion, jealousy, and false pride. Until the principles of *reason* and equity shall be adopted in national transactions, peace will not be durable amongst men.[117]

But even Hartley, sadly but wisely, recognized that "until a confirmed millennium, founded upon wiser principles, shall be generally established, the *reputation* of nations is not merely a *bubble*. It forms their real security."[118]

Nobody knew this better than Benjamin Franklin. The American people, to be sure, were engaged in the conquest of a virgin continent, and their concern with agriculture would keep them away from many dangerous sources of conflict. However, Franklin did not trust the peace so long as other powers, that is, England and Spain, still retained a foothold on the North American continent. Love of peace never meant for him neglect of all precautions which a world of power politics required. The various elements of his concept of foreign affairs are well summed up in a letter he wrote the very day after the exchange of the ratifications of the peace treaty with England:

> A few years of Peace, will improve, will restore and encrease our strength; but our future safety will depend on our union and our virtue. Britain will long be watching for advantages, to recover what she has lost. If we do not convince the world, that we are a Nation to be depended on for fidelity in Treaties, if we appear negligent in paying our Debts, and ungrateful to those who have served and befriended us; our reputation and all the strength it is capable of procuring, will be lost, and fresh attacks upon us will be encouraged and promoted by better prospects of success. Let us therefore beware of being lulled into a dangerous security; and of being both enervated and impoverished by luxury; of being weakened by internal contentions and divisions; . . . of neglect in military exercises and discipline, and in providing stores of arms and munitions of war, to be ready on occasion; for all these are circumstances that give confidence to enemies and diffidence to friends; and the expenses required to prevent a war are much lighter than those that will, if not prevented, be absolutely necessary to maintain it.[119]

CHAPTER VIII

CONCLUSION

FRANKLIN'S century recognized the pursuit of national interests as a legitimate—indeed, as the chief legitimate—goal of international politics; ideological considerations played a smaller role than in the preceding or the succeeding centuries. We found that Franklin himself used the term the "national interest" and even began his career as a political writer with the statement that the knowledge of the true interests of one's country was the most useful and most commendable of all sciences.[1] However, this statement presented us with two difficulties, one of a more general nature and the other more peculiarly related to Franklin's position.

The notion of the national interest always demands more specific explanation in terms of the structure of a given society and of the needs and desires of the individuals who compose this society. The concrete formulation of the "national interest," furthermore, will depend always upon the greater or lesser degree of diffusion of power within a society. In the English-speaking world of the eighteenth century, for instance, power was more widely shared than in most countries of the European continent. Moreover, in the eyes of the radical Whig, Franklin, the nation assumed a less monolithic stature than it had in the past age of royal absolutism and succeeding ages of state idolatry. Franklin proclaimed the principle of the accountability of the rulers, and for him the state was an association in which equals ought to share with equals for common purposes. It was the freedom and well-being of the individual which emerged as his highest political ideal. Franklin probably never expressed his social credo more movingly than in his account of his journey to Ireland, when he was exceedingly shocked by the extreme contrast of abundance and wretchedness which he found there; he compared this with "the Happiness of New England, where every Man is a Freeholder, has a Vote in publick Affairs, lives in a tidy, warm House, has plenty of good Food and Fewel, with whole cloaths from Head

247

to Foot, the Manufacture perhaps of his own Family. Long may they continue in this Situation!"[2]

A second factor which weakened the compactness of the "sovereign nation" in favor of its individual components was, of course, the fact that Franklin learned to look upon politics not from the capital of a sovereign state, like London, but from provincial or colonial centers, like Philadelphia or Albany. When he first spoke of "his country's true interest," he did not mean England or the British Empire, but Pennsylvania; and his first statement on political economy, his essay on the paper currency of 1723, was called forth precisely by a clash of interests between Pennsylvania and the mother-country. After the Albany Congress in 1754 Franklin thought—and regretted—that the North American colonies and England belonged to different communities with different interests, and during the sixties and seventies Franklin repeatedly referred to the colonies and England as two countries. In or shortly after 1766 Franklin called "fallacious and unsatisfactory" the arguments holding the interest of Britain and the colonies to be the same and pointed out that, like partners in trade, the two countries had a common interest in the flourishing of the partnership business, "but they may moreover have each a *separate* Interest; and in pursuit of that *separate* Interest, one of them may endeavour to impose on the other."[3] In other words, Franklin, in defense of Colonial interests, contested the prevailing mercantilistic theory that the mother-country alone had a right to determine the political course of the empire and thus contributed to blurring the solid simplicity of the "national interest" which distinguished the age of mercantilism.

This opens up a most interesting problem: the growth of a loyalty to America as one nation or political unit. It is, of course, true that before the Revolution the colonists' loyalties were divided between their respective colonies and the mother-country and that no room was left for a loyalty to America pure and simple. And after 1776 many people looked upon Congress as a diplomatic assembly rather than anything else. It is well worth remembering that before the adoption of the Constitution "the only men who had constantly to think of the United States as one nation were the American ministers abroad."[4] It has been pointed out with regard to Jefferson that his diplomatic mission in Paris from 1784 onward "brought home to him the fact that the United States could not hope to face successfully external dangers or even survive unless they gave up some of their liberty for more security, while reserving some of their inalienable rights."[5] Franklin, of course, was exposed to this experience eight years before Jefferson. But this is not the whole story. Significantly it is Franklin who is credited with the famous saying at the outbreak of the Revolution that "we all must hang together or we will hang separately." At that time, it is true, he had behind him two protracted stays in England as agent not only for Pennsylvania but finally for a considerable number of American colonies, and already in 1760 he thought that his stay in London might "be of some Service to the general Interest of America."[6] However, it seems the unique and distinctive sign of Franklin's statesmanship that he, at least, did not need to wait for an ambassadorship in Paris or even for the agency in London to have the vision of the essential unity of America and of the manifest destiny of a whole continent. "Join or Die"—this motto, which might well be put over the whole of Franklin's political concepts, was his battle cry as early as 1754 before he embarked upon his first mission to London. And even three years earlier, in his *Observations concerning the Increase of Mankind,* he had developed in the quiet of his study his fundamental views about the characteristic features of the sociological development of the North American continent.

Franklin distinguished himself at the Federal Convention of 1787 by his rather unique combination of radical democratic views with the advocacy of a strong central government. His support, in 1776 as well as 1787, for the idea of the proportional representation of the states in Congress and his arguments about the inefficiency of the bicameral system also point in the same direction. The quest for unity runs like a red thread through Franklin's political life; this central theme of his political efforts was called forth above all by his quest for security and by his keen appreciation of the factor of foreign danger—an appreciation which was perhaps more highly developed in him than in the mind of any of his American contemporaries. It was Franklin's grasp of the issues of international politics and of the threats which they presented to the colonies that caused him to transcend the provincial and intercolonial quarrels and jealousies which loomed so large during all his lifetime.

It was the threat of French power which prompted Franklin to write *Plain Truth* in 1747, his first systematic statement on foreign policy; it was again the French menace which led him to call for intercolonial unity in 1751, and it was the failure to achieve this unity which produced his resort to the legislative intervention of the British Parliament in his schemes for defense and co-operation submitted to the Albany Congress in 1754. Again it was the quest for security which played such a prominent part in Franklin's thinking on imperial relations down to 1775, for instance, in his indorsement of the Navigation Acts and his pleas for compromise and at times even compliance in the matter of legal rights for the sake of imperial defense and of the preservation of imperial prestige vis-à-vis foreign powers. He assigned to England the role of providing sufficient protection for the colonies "so that we can without Interruption go on with our Improvements, and increase our Numbers," and, when England finally failed to provide this, his efforts as America's first ambassador abroad were directed to secure by new combinations of international politics the unmolested "improvement" of the new republic.

The goals of the freedom and well-being of the individual, expressed in terms of the ideal of honest subsistence with independence, on the one hand, and of common security from foreign danger through co-operation and unity, on the other, are the double roots for the third fundamental factor in Franklin's concept of America's interests, namely, continental expansion. His expansionism and the problems it poses have been frequently neglected by students of his political thought who were much impressed with his ardent desire for peace and what commonly is called his "internationalism,"[7] and even a scholar like Charles A. Beard does less than justice to Franklin when he calls Jefferson "America's first great expansionist,"[8] a title which decidedly belongs to Franklin. Franklin's expansionism was called forth in the first place by the quest for greater security. The desire of preventing French encroachments upon the "security belt" between the Appalachian range, on the one hand, and the Great Lakes and the Mississippi, on the other, provides an essential motive for Franklin's program of western settlement as outlined in the Albany Plan and in the *Plan for Settling Two Western Colonies* soon thereafter.

To cut off the roots of future conflict was the radical cure which Franklin pursued in his policies with regard to Canada. They were crowned with success in 1763, and they failed in 1782. In this context it has rarely been pointed out that the democratic principle of national self-determination had to give way to the overriding urgency of the quest for security. Franklin, in proposing the purchase of Canada in 1776 and again in 1782, seems to have paid no more heed than anyone else to the wishes of the populations whose fate was at stake, in particular the French Canadians.[9] Gilbert Chinard puts well the case for Franklin's expansionism: "To limit oneself voluntarily and deliberately is one thing; to feel that one's future development may be determined and hampered by the presence and threats of a none too friendly nation is quite another matter, which cannot be easily dismissed."[10]

The second motive for Franklin's expansionism, going beyond the mere quest for security, was his fervor for the "increase of mankind." The rapid growth of America's population was indeed an everlasting source of profound concern for him, and his moral indignation was never more deeply aroused than when obstacles to that growth appeared on the horizon. To check this increase, in fact, seemed to Franklin a terrible crime, comparable to mass murder. Expansion, of course, was particularly essential if the kind of society which he cherished most, a society based on agriculture, should be preserved. Too great density of population would create an industrial society, and manufactures, in his eyes, were founded upon the poverty of a considerable part of the population. With poverty, vice and corruption would also find their way into America, which could retain her virtue only as long as land was abundant, where no man "continues long a Labourer for others, . . . but goes among those new Settlers, and sets up for himself."[11] The preservation of agriculture, that most honest of all human employments, depended, then, upon continuous territorial expansion. Franklin never worried about the time when the continent would be densely populated; he never foresaw the speed of the expansion of the generations which were to come after him.

Franklin attempted to reconcile expansionism and his love for peace in proposing, in 1776 as well as in 1782, the purchase of Canada instead of armed conquest, and he envisaged the same procedure for the Spanish possessions in the South. His plans, then, foreshadow the Louisiana Purchase, as, in general, Franklin initiated the distinctive features of Jeffersonian foreign policy. The apt name of "protective imperialism"[12] which has been coined for Jefferson's foreign policy may be applied with equal justification to Benjamin Franklin. This kind of imperialism, motivated by security considerations rather than by other political or economic motives, presents an interesting precedent if we accept a recent interpretation of American foreign policy which lays particular stress on the persistent and paramount importance of a rather extensive security concept in American diplomatic history.[13]

An agricultural democracy whose lasting security was guaranteed by the greatest possible unity within the nation and by continuous expansion and elimination of foreign threats on the continent of North America—in this formula we may sum up Franklin's concept of the national interest of the United States. The question of "isolationism" or "internationalism," in fact, assumes merely secondary importance. Naturally, the Founding Fathers frowned upon entanglements in the affairs of Europe, if they could avoid them, and Franklin at least did not need Tom Paine's *Common Sense* to acquire this insight. On the other hand, Franklin was too wise and too noncommittal a diplomat to indulge in abstract formulas. Isolationism, for him no less than for the other Founding Fathers, essentially meant a policy of freedom of action,[14] a policy of avoiding the subordination of American to foreign interests; whether the American interests were promoted or threatened by "entanglements" was a question which was to be decided in every case upon its merits. Franklin, for instance, thought that the chance of acquiring Canada was worth an alliance with France, which he otherwise approached only with the greatest reluctance. He knew that, as long as European powers retained the control of a part of the North American continent, just so long would the United States remain involved in the fortunes of the European state system. And Franklin was convinced of the commercial no less than of the political interdependence of the Old and of the New World.

It is this very fact of the impossibility of posing the "national interest" in a vacuum which presents the most baffling problems to the student as well as to the practitioner of international politics. The statesmen of the American Revolution were not unaware of this, as appears strikingly from the following words of Robert Morris, written in 1776:

It appears clear to me that we may very soon involve all Europe in a War by managing properly the apparent forwardness of the Court of France; it's a horrid consideration that our own Safety should call on us to involve other nations in the Calamities of War. Can this be morally right or have Morality and Policy nothing to do with each other? Perhaps it may not be good Policy to investigate the Question at this time.[15]

As has been well said, "the one thing which saves the idea of the national interest from itself is its essential reciprocity."[16] Or, as Edmund Burke put it: "Nothing is so fatal to a nation as an extreme of self partiality, and the total want of consideration of what others will naturally hope or fear."[17]

There is no other statesman in the early period of American national history who was more convinced of the wisdom of this insight than Benjamin Franklin. That mutuality and reciprocity of interests form the only firm bases for every "fair connection" of social life, he preached incessantly. To redress the balance of the relationship between colonies and mother-country in terms of true mutuality was Franklin's steady purpose from 1729 until 1775. His joy over the French alliance, which was explicitly built upon the basis of equality and reciprocity, and his remark to a British agent at the time of the conclusion of the French alliance that any settlement with England ought to be based on "the broad bottom of mutual interests" furnish further indications of this attitude. The most decisive evidence of it, however, is provided by the great and unfeigned reluctance with which Franklin approached France for help, in the knowledge that a far-reaching identity of interests existed, but also that neither the United States nor France would be served by bleeding France to death. His never ceasing exhortations to his fellow-countrymen not to overplay the instrument of French help and rather to rely on themselves, in contrast to John Adams' pretentious diplomacy of the big stick, present the most outstanding example of Franklin's delicate regard for the needs and interests of other countries—a regard which enabled him to speak with the voice of authority in the hour of greatest need, as, for instance, in 1778, early in 1781, or late in 1782. We do not suggest that without Benjamin Franklin there would have been no French alliance. On the contrary, the history of the French alliance seems to indicate rather clearly that interests and not personalities decided the issue. The Battle of Saratoga, and not Franklin, brought the decision. On the other hand, it is equally obvious that his social and intellectual prestige was a factor of great significance in rallying public opinion behind the policies embarked upon by Vergennes, and, moreover, Franklin's modesty and his marked contrast to John Adams' self-righteous demeanor were invaluable for a smooth and efficient cooperation between the two allies.

As a third dimension in the hierarchy of the values of international politics, above the concern for the national interest and the mutuality of interests, there appear certain general principles like the "general good of mankind," a favorite expression of Franklin's. To be sure, the statement that his "ultimate political ideal included nothing short of the welfare and the commercial federation of the world,"[18] must be taken with the qualification that he never lost sight of the special interests of his country. Franklin wished ardently for universal peace, but it had to be a just peace; that is, the fundamental interests of America had to be satisfied. By a fortunate coincidence, of which he was well aware, the War of Independence also happened to promote more general values, like political liberty and the freedom of trade. However, Franklin's efforts to improve the law of nations, or his circular to American vessels during the War of Independence to exempt the ship of Captain Cook from hostile actions, because Cook's voyage would benefit mankind in general, would seem to show sufficiently that the concern for human welfare in general, even in the midst of a war of life and death, never left Franklin's philanthropic mind.

If we turn to the means of political action, we find that Franklin did not, like his cordially detested colleague, John Adams, use the word "power" on every occasion. But there seems to remain little doubt of his grasp of the phenomenon of power. Franklin was explicit about its psychological aspect. His remark in the *Autobiography,* summing up the experiences of a long life, that there is "perhaps no one of our natural passions so hard to subdue as *pride,*"[19] and his efforts in the Federal Convention to provide for a system of mutual checks to the passions of ambition and avarice are cases in point. More baffling is Franklin's attitude toward the concept of the balance of power. He was decidedly out of tune with his century, which was, after all, the classic century of the balance of power, when he spoke— in what seems to be his only direct reference to that term—of "Whims about the Ballance of Power."[20] On the other hand, an analysis of Franklin's diplomacy reveals that he thought in terms of power, even if he, particularly after the conclusion of the French alliance, expressed himself much more frequently in terms of morality. He took care to point out that the mutual "protection" which political partners—in this case, Great Britain and the American colonies—could give each other was "mutual and equal in Proportion to Numbers & Wealth."[21] We have dwelt in some detail on the connection of Franklin's political thought with the basic tenets of mercantilism, in which power takes on such a prominent role. In fact, Franklin himself could not help speaking at times in terms of checks and balances; thus he discussed the possibility that America's "growing Weight might in time be thrown into" the scale of Ireland in support of Irish grievances against England;[22] we also recall his word that "where the Beam *is moveable,* it is only by equal Weights in opposite Scales that it can possibly be kept even."[23]

Three reasons may be suggested which perhaps explain Franklin's dislike of the concept of the balance of power. First of all, he might have agreed with critics of the mechanistic balance-of-power concept like his friend Thomas Pownall. Two years before making the acquaintance of Franklin, Pownall published a book, *Principles of Polity, Being the Grounds and Reasons of Civil Empire,* in which he pointed out that much of the current talk on balanced government missed the point: "We hear of Governments mixed and compounded of the three pure Forms as of three actual distinct things. . . . We distract that Communion, by which alone these could have any Subsistence at all."[24] Without agreement on the fundamental principles of social life, anarchy rather than a smooth equilibrium would be the result of checks and balances.[25] Consequently, the theory of the balance of power on the domestic scene in many cases had degenerated to a mere disguise for factious schemes. Franklin's overriding concern for unity and efficiency as well as his desire for equality and his dislike of class rule very likely led him to similar conclusions about the complicated and at times hypocritical conception of checks and balances. It was not difficult to transplant these arguments to the international scene. In fact, Pownall himself had linked the two spheres together: "Now as betwixt Nation and Nation the preserving and guarantying such foreign Balance has linked all the Powers of

Europe in a perpetual Series of War and Bloodshed, so the supporting and restoring this domestic Balance amidst the Powers of Government, has been the Pretence and Occasion of all the Factions, Rebellions, and Civil Wars that this Kingdom hath been torn and distracted with."[26] If we add to this Franklin's aversion against "romantick European Continental Connections," the context of his derogatory comment of "Whims about the Ballance of Power"—expressed together with his distaste for these "Continental Connections"—seems to be established. In other words, his opposition to a British policy of involvement in Europe, a policy which always went under the banner of maintaining the balance of power, his "isolationism" in England, emerges as a second reason for his rejection of this concept.[27] Finally, it may be pointed out, the notion of checks and balances always suggests the coercive aspects of power, and it was the distinctive mark of Franklin's approach to politics and diplomacy to rely on persuasion rather than on compulsion.[28]

Franklin really believed in diplomacy as a substitute to naked force. Authority or power, he had said repeatedly, must rest either on love and good will or on fear and force. If the first alternative does not work, rule by coercion becomes imperative, Franklin had added. But with good will, he held, greater and more lasting things could be achieved. Franklin's whole diplomacy in Europe rests firmly upon the conviction that the creation of an atmosphere of good will and confidence, supported only in rare cases by the threat of force and in extreme cases by the actual use of force, would lead to enduring results. To be sure, his concept of good will, as applied in his diplomacy, does not mean the introduction of altruism and self-denying generosity into the realm of international politics. Its basis is self-reliance—God helps those that help themselves, Franklin used to exhort—and the conviction that effective support from foreign countries may be realized only under two conditions. First of all, the partner must be persuaded of the seriousness of one's intentions as well as one's actual efforts. Secondly, effective international co-operation is possible only on the basis of mutual interests.

The concept of good will has two further implications. It conveys the belief that in an atmosphere of mutual good will one may more easily separate essential and nonessential factors of the national interests and that an accommodation and adjustment of conflicting interests may be more profitably undertaken. This does not mean that there are no real conflicts of interests. Franklin never professed belief in a complete harmony of interests, although toward the end of his life the revolution in international relations brought about by the independence of America and the new doctrine of free trade did make his outlook more optimistic. The second implication of Franklin's concept of good will is the paramount significance attributed by him to what he called "appearances" in support of "realities," in other words, the importance of "prestige" and "reputation." It seems indeed that his endeavor to establish firmly the reputation of the new republic in Europe offers a significant clue for his language, at times so deferential, during his diplomatic assignment in Paris.

Many epithets have been applied to Franklin, some flattering and some derogatory. He has been called an opportunist, in spite of the truly astounding steadiness of purpose which runs through his political life. He has been called an internationalist, in spite of the fact that he ignored the principle of self-determination when it came to the protection of America's security. He has been called a pacifist, although he made active war propaganda at the end of the Great War for the Empire and wrote the purely power-political Canada pamphlet. He has been called a moralist, although he once remarked that moral and political rights did not aways coincide. He has been called the embodiment of the Age of Reason, although his opinion of human reason was not too high, and he relied much more on habit and experience. It is not easy to grasp the essential quality of Franklin's political concepts in terms of present-day debates on the nature of politics. So many contemporary controversies of the issue of moral politics versus power politics have somewhat shifted the focus of what "moral politics" is supposed to be. These discussions, while all agreeing on the evils of power, ambition, aggressiveness, pride, imperialism, etc., reveal much muddled thinking as soon as they attempt to elucidate the question of what the moral alternative to the condemned policies ought to be. Frequently the profound differences between a prudential morality of give-and-take and the officially, at least, highly revered Christian values of brotherly love, of altruism, and of forgiveness is hopelessly blurred. The proneness of the human mind to think in contrasts of black and white all too often obscures the significance of intermediate hues.

As far as this investigation is concerned, Franklin's ways of expression greatly contribute to this kind of confusion. We have encountered strangely inverted meanings of terms like "the good of the whole," "generosity and magnanimity," and "reconciliation," when, in fact, "enlightened self-interest" would easily have provided a common denominator. It is true that Franklin himself laid great stress on the generous and benevolent appearance of those expressions, which evoke in the first place altruistic rather than prudential associations. Frequently, he fell prey to the contradiction of one of his admired guides in the realm of philosophy, Shaftesbury, who wanted to make the best of both worlds in retaining the language of benevolent altruism and, in effect, preaching a program of long-term utilitarianism and hedonism.

The awareness of the discrepancy between a prudential morality and the nonprudential teachings of Christianity, although not unknown to the eighteenth century, is almost completely lacking in Benjamin Franklin. The idea that "in every fair connection each party ought to find its interest" remains the outstanding feature of his concept of politics. No antagonism between immoral and moral policies, between selfishness and altruism, between interest and disinterestedness, can ever provide a pattern helpful to the understanding of Franklin's approach to politics. Instead, a pattern of three dimensions suggests itself for the solution of this question. True disinterestedness and generosity, expecting no returns for services rendered, would appear to him too lofty and utopian a phenomenon to warrant more than suspicious consideration. On the other hand, narrow self-interest deluded by the passions of avarice and pride is even more detrimental. As the third dimension there remains the notion of enlightened self-interest, based upon the principle of mutuality and equity.

Neither unselfish crusading for abstract principles nor power politics, run wild in overestimation of its own strength, present workable alternatives of foreign policy, so we may interpret the legacy of Benjamin Franklin's concept of international relations. Power politics, to be sure, could hardly be abolished. There was only scant hope of eradicating the pride of man. He never gave up his belief that the best way to secure peace is to be prepared for war. When everything else failed, Franklin faced the necessity of the use of force calmly and with complete determination. However, all this was no cause for total despair. He ever refused to become the prisoner of extreme alternatives. Sometimes it might be possible to prevent conflict by removing the causes. By the efforts of good will it might be possible to subdue at least one of the evils of international politics: fear. What Franklin said on the occasion of a plea for the abolition of slavery is as valid for the behavior of states: "Reason and conscience have but little influence over his conduct, because he is chiefly governed by the passion of fear."[29] To somebody who held that disputes between states could be decided only by the sword, Franklin retorted characteristically: "Why not by Mediation, by Arbitration, or by considerate & prudent Argument?"[30] It is the belief in the essential reciprocity of enlightened self-interest which is the core of his political theory and practice. Nobody put it more eloquently than Thomas Jefferson:

The fact is, that his temper was so amiable and conciliatory, his conduct so rational, never urging impossibilities, or even things unreasonably inconvenient to them [the French], in short, so moderate and attentive to their difficulties, as well as our own, that what his enemies called subserviency, I saw was only that reasonable disposition, which, sensible that advantages are not all to be on one side, yielding what is just and liberal, is the more certain of obtaining liberality and justice.[31]

NOTES

BIBLIOGRAPHICAL NOTE

Bibliographical references to special topics and to works cited are included in the Notes. The most important Franklin bibliographies are: Paul Leicester Ford, *Franklin Bibliography: A List of Books Written by, or Relating to, Benjamin Franklin* (Brooklyn, N.Y., 1889); F. L. Mott and Chester E. Jorgenson (eds.), *Benjamin Franklin: Representative Selections, with Introduction, Bibliography, and Notes* (New York: American Book Co., 1936), pp. cli–clxxxviii; and Robert E. Spiller *et al., Literary History of the United States* (3 vols.; New York: Macmillan Co., 1948), III, 507–15. Volume III of the French edition of Bernard Faÿ, *Benjamin Franklin: Bourgeois d'Amérique* (Paris: Calmann-Levy, 1931), consists of extensive but unreliable bibliographical notes. For the relationship of Great Britain and North America in the eighteenth century see Stanley Pargellis and D. J. Medley (eds.), *Bibliography of British History: The Eighteenth Century* (Oxford: Clarendon Press, 1951). For the diplomacy of the United States see Samuel Flagg Bemis and Grace Gardner Griffin, *Guide to the Diplomatic History of the United States, 1775–1921* (Washington, D.C.: Government Printing Office, 1935). Since 1959, the publication of *The Papers of Benjamin Franklin*, ed. Leonard W. Labaree *et al.* (New Haven and London: Yale University Press, 1959——) has been in progress. This edition is referred to hereinafter as *Papers*.

NOTES TO CHAPTER I

1. Thomas Paine, *Common Sense* (*The Complete Writings of Thomas Paine*, ed. Philip S. Foner [2 vols.; New York: Citadel Press, 1945], I, 4–5).

2. Georg Schwarzenberger, *Power Politics: A Study of International Society* (2d rev. ed.; New York: F. A. Praeger, 1951), p. 14.

3. Cf. Herbert Schneider's statement: "Never in America were philosophical thinking and social action more closely joined. . . . It will not do to dismiss the thought of the Enlightenment as mere rationalization" (*A History of American Philosophy* [New York: Columbia University Press, 1946], p. 35).

4. John Adams, *Works*, ed. C. F. Adams (10 vols.; Boston: Little, Brown & Co., 1850–56), I, 660.

5. Benjamin Franklin, *The Writings of Benjamin Franklin*, ed. Albert Henry Smyth (10 vols.; New York: Macmillan Co., 1905–7), VI, 370. (Hereafter cited as "*Writings.*")

6. Marquis de Condorcet, *Œuvres du Marquis de Condorcet*, publiées par A. Condorcet O'Connor et M. F. Arago (2d ed.; Paris: Firmin Didot Frères, 1847–49), III, 420. (My translation.)

7. Georg Forster, "Erinnerungen aus dem Jahre 1790," in "Kleine Schriften," *Georg Forster's saemmtliche Schriften,* herausgegeben von dessen Tochter (9 vols.; Leipzig: F. A. Brockhaus, 1843), VI, 207. (My translation.)

8. Bernard Fay, *The Revolutionary Spirit in France and America*, trans. Ramon Guthrie (New York: Harcourt, Brace & Co., 1927), p. 292.

9. Ralph Barton Perry, *Puritanism and Democracy* (New York: Vanguard Press, 1944), p. 177.

10. J. B. Bury, *The Idea of Progress* (New York: Macmillan Co., 1932), p. xxxvii.

11. Henry Steele Commager, "Franklin, the American," review of Carl Van Doren's *Benjamin Franklin*, in *New York Times Book Review*, October 9, 1938, p. 1.

12. Carl Becker, review of the Franklin Institute's *Meet Dr. Franklin*, in *American Historical Review*, L (October, 1944), 142.

13. This is Turgot's famous epigram on Franklin. For an interesting account of the history and the identification of this epigram see the essay, "Benjamin Franklin and John Slidell at Paris," in Charles Sumner, *The Works of Charles Sumner* (15 vols.; Boston: Lee & Shepard, 1870-82), VIII, 1-38.

14. John Adams to Benjamin Rush, April 4, 1790, in Benjamin Rush, *Letters of Benjamin Rush,* ed. L. H. Butterfield (2 vols.; Princeton: Princeton University Press, 1951), II, 1207.

15. To Mary Stephenson, June 11, 1760 (*Writings,* IV, 22).

16. *Autobiography* (*Writings,* I, 298 ff.).

17. James Parton, *Life and Times of Benjamin Franklin* (2 vols.; 2d ed.; Boston and New York: Houghton, Mifflin & Co., 1897), I, 160; see also *Writings,* II, 89.

18. The authors who so far have most closely scrutinized Franklin's political thought do not see the relevance of many of the younger Franklin's remarks on human nature, arbitrary government, or the nature of political disputes to his conception of politics in theory and practice. Cf. R. D. Miles, "The Political Philosophy of Benjamin Franklin" (doctoral dissertation, University of Michigan, 1949), p. 36; F. L. Mott and Chester E. Jorgenson (eds.), *Benjamin Franklin: Representative Selections* (New York: American Book Co., 1936), p. lxxxii; M. R. Eiselen, *Franklin's Political Theories* (Garden City, N.Y.: Doubleday, Doran & Co., 1928), p. 13.

The most recent work in this field, Clinton Rossiter's article on "The Political Theory of Benjamin Franklin" (*Pennsylvania Magazine of History and Biography,* LXXVI [1952], 259-93), pays no attention to Franklin's conception of human nature and his attitude to the problem of power and to the ends of political life. Rossiter's contention (p. 268) is that Franklin "was not a political philosopher; he was not a philosopher at all. He was a man prepared to investigate and discuss every principle and institution known to the human race, but only in the most practical and unspeculative terms. He limited his own thought process to the one devastating question: *Does it work?* or more exactly, *Does it work well?*" However, to classify a man as a "pragmatist" does not solve anything. Franklin, like everybody else, had certain ends and goals in view, and the question of "Does it work?" is meaningless without the context of certain basic desiderata.

19. This little work has been omitted in the Smyth edition of Franklin's works. It is, however, reprinted as an appendix to Parton, *op. cit.,* and has since been republished independently with a bibliographical note by Lawrence C. Wroth (New York: Facsimile Text Society, 1930).

20. Cf. Herbert Schneider, "The Significance of Benjamin Franklin's Moral Philosophy," *Studies in the History of Ideas,* ed. the Department of Philosophy, Columbia University, II (1918), 298.

21. In his *Autobiography* Franklin acknowledges his debt to Shaftesbury and Collins for becoming "a real doubter in many points of our religious doctrine" (*Writings,* I, 244). The question of Franklin's attitude to the great moral philosophers and of their influence upon him is considerably more difficult to determine than the same question with regard to, for instance, John Adams or Thomas Jefferson. With the exception of the authors mentioned in the *Autobiography,* comments on books Franklin read are extremely rare. His library has not been preserved, although there exists a list of books known to have been in Franklin's library at the time of his death (compiled by Dr. George Simpson Eddy in Princeton University; photostat in the library of the American Philosophical Society in Philadelphia). See also the article by George Simpson Eddy, "Dr. Benjamin Franklin's Library," in *Proceedings of the American Antiquarian Society,* XXXIV (new. ser.; 1924), 206–26. Except for notes in some English pamphlets, there exists nothing like the voluminous marginal notes of John Adams in his books or a commonplace book like Jefferson's. Also he was not able to keep a correspondence like Adams' or Jefferson's, discussing great problems from the perspective of a long life in retirement after the great events of their lives had taken place. Immersed in public business almost until his death, Franklin does not seem to have had much time left over for reading. Benjamin Rush told John Adams that "Dr. Franklin thought a great deal, wrote occasionally, but read during the middle and later years of his life very little" (October 31, 1807 [Rush, *op. cit.,* II, 953]). For a compilation of the authors with whom Franklin was acquainted see chap. i of Lois Margaret MacLaurin, *Franklin's Vocabulary* (Garden City, N.Y.: Doubleday, Doran & Co., 1928), and Mott and Jorgenson (eds.), *op. cit.,* p. lv.

22. Basil Willey, *The Eighteenth Century Background* (London: Chatto & Windus, 1940), chap. iii, *passim.*

23. Pope's epitaph intended for Newton's tomb.

24. A. O. Lovejoy, *The Great Chain of Being* (Cambridge: Harvard University Press, 1936), p. 189. This brilliant analysis of that complex of ideas has been applied to Franklin only once, although it offers very important clues for an understanding of Franklin's conception of human nature. Arthur Stuart Pitt in "The Sources, Significance, and Date of Franklin's 'An Arabian Tale,'" *Publications of the Modern Language Association,* LVII (1942), 155–68, applies Lovejoy's analysis to one small piece of Franklin's and does not refer to relevant writings of Franklin's youth in which these ideas may also be found. Pitt's article is valuable in pointing out the sources from which Franklin could have accepted this idea directly, namely, Locke, Milton, Addison, and Pope.

25. Willey, *op. cit.,* p. 47.

26. *Ibid.,* pp. 47–48.

27. Parton, *op. cit.,* p. 605.

28. Lovejoy, *op. cit.,* p. 199.

29. *Ibid.,* p. 200.

30. Alexander Pope, "An Essay on Man," Epistle 1, in *Selected Works* (New York: "Modern Library" [Random House], 1948), p. 101.

31. The term "Augustan Age," as applied to literature, denotes primarily the period 31 B.C.–A.D. 14. It is also applied to the period of the late Stuarts and the early Hanoverians in England, because this period exhibited similar characteristics (external splendor, internal decadence) as the earlier. Cf. F. J. C. Hearn-

shaw (ed.), *The Social and Political Ideas of Some English Thinkers of the Augustan Age* (London: George G. Harrap & Co., Ltd., 1928), p. 5.

32. Pope, *op. cit.,* Epistle 4, p. 127.

33. Willey, *op. cit.,* p. 56.

34. *Autobiography (Writings,* I, 226).

35. *Writings,* I, 247, n. 1.

36. Parton, *op. cit.,* I, 617.

37. *Ibid.*

38. Carl Becker, *The Heavenly City of the Eighteenth Century Philosophers* (New Haven: Yale University Press, 1932), pp. 69–70.

39. Leonard W. Labaree *et al.,* eds. *The Autobiography of Benjamin Franklin,* (New Haven and London: Yale University Press, 1964), pp. 114–15. Cf. also letter to Benjamin Vaughan, November 9, 1779 (*Writings,* VII, 412).

40. Cf. *Writings,* I, 341; II, 215; III, 145; X, 83. In 1784 Franklin acknowledged his indebtedness to Cotton Mather's *Bonifacius* or *Essays To Do Good,* published in 1710 (*Writings,* IX, 208). On Mather's *Essays* see chap. xxiv of Perry Miller's *The New England Mind: From Colony to Province* (Cambridge: Harvard University Press, 1953), pp. 395–416.

41. This distinction is Roland Bainton's, in "The Appeal to Reason and the American Revolution," in Conyers Read (ed.), *The Constitution Reconsidered* (New York: Columbia University Press, 1938), p. 121.

42. "The authors who were perhaps the most influential and the most representative in the early and mid-eighteenth century, made a great point of reducing man's claims to 'reason' to a minimum" (A. O. Lovejoy, " 'Pride' in Eighteenth Century Thought," *Essays in the History of Ideas* [Baltimore: Johns Hopkins Press, 1948], p. 68).

43. Bernard Mandeville, *The Fable of the Bees,* edited and with an Introduction by F. B. Kaye (2 vols.; Oxford: Clarendon Press, 1924), I, 48–49. Franklin met Mandeville during his first stay in London in 1725–26 (*Autobiography* [*Writings,* I, 278]). According to a list in the Mason-Franklin Collection of Yale University Library, Franklin owned a copy of the *Fable of the Bees.*

44. Quoted by Alfred O. Aldridge, "Franklin's 'Shaftesburian' Dialogues Not Franklin's: A Revision of the Franklin Canon," *American Literature,* XXI (1949–50), 156 and 157. Until Aldridge's discovery, the evidence of Franklin's adherence to Shaftesburian ideas rested chiefly upon two dialogues "between Philocles and Horatio, . . . concerning Virtue and Pleasure," published by Franklin in the *Pennsylvania Gazette* in 1730 and included in all editions of his collected writings. Carl Van Doren, in what remains so far the most authoritative and all-inclusive Franklin biography, devotes five pages to interpreting the dialogues as an attempt to resolve the inner conflict "between his instinct toward pleasure and his faith in reasonable virtue" (*Benjamin Franklin* [New York: Viking Press, 1938], p. 83). Also, Chester E. Jorgenson's article, "The Source of Benjamin Franklin's Dialogues between Philocles and Horatio (1730)," *American Literature,* VI (1934–35), 337–39, must now be replaced by Aldridge's article. Aldridge shows that the two dialogues "concerning Virtue and Pleasure" were copied from the *London Journal* of 1729. A reference in Franklin's *Autobiography* (*Writings,* I, 343) to "a Socratic dialogue" and "a discourse on self-denial," traditionally having been interpreted as concerning the two dialogues between Philocles and Horatio, is now shown to concern a dialogue between Crito and Socrates from No. 346 of the

Pennsylvania Gazette (July 17, 1735), never before correctly attributed to Franklin, and a discourse from No. 347 of the *Pennsylvania Gazette* proving that self-denial is not the essence of virtue, reprinted in the Sparks and the Bigelow editions of Franklin's *Works* (*The Works of Benjamin Franklin,* ed. Jared Sparks [10 vols.; Boston: Tappan & Willmore, 1836–40]; *The Complete Works of Benjamin Franklin,* ed. John Bigelow [10 vols.; New York and London: G. P. Putnam's Sons, 1887–88], I, 414–17). Aldridge points out that his discovery "does not necessitate a radical reappraisal of Franklin's thought. . . . By reprinting them, Franklin registered himself as a Shaftesburian, and he confirmed this intellectual affiliation by later composing and printing the two essays which are described in his autobiography" (Aldridge, *op. cit.,* pp. 154–55). "Be in general virtuous, and you will be happy"—in this way Franklin tried to have his cake and eat it too (letter to John Alleyne, August 9, 1768 [*Writings,* V, 159]).

45. *Writings,* II, 92; see also X, 124. Cf. n. 24 above.

46. *Papers,* I, 261–2.

47. Franklin's marginal notes in [Matthew Wheelock], *Reflections Moral and Political on Great Britain and Her Colonies* (London, 1770), p. 48. Franklin's copy is in the Jefferson Collection of the Library of Congress (see E. Millicent Sowerby [comp.], *Catalogue of the Library of Thomas Jefferson* [5 vols.; Washington, D.C.: Library of Congress, 1952——], III, 248–49).

48. See *Writings,* IX, 489 and 530.

49. In 1771, at the house of Bishop Shipley, Franklin began his *Autobiography.* There he noted that he had "gone so far through life with a considerable share of felicity" (*Writings,* I, 226).

50. To Rev. John Lathrop, Philadelphia, May 31, 1788 (*Writings,* IX, 651).

51. *Ibid.*

52. Quoted by Bury, *op. cit.,* pp. 221–22.

53. To Joseph Priestley, June 7, 1782 (*Writings,* VIII, 451–52).

54. *Writings,* VIII, 452.

55. *Writings,* II, 203.

56. To unknown addressee, Philadelphia, July 3, 1786 (*Writings,* IX, 521–22). See also II, 393, and IX, 600–601.

57. *Writings,* I, 267. See also V, 225, and IX, 512.

58. To William Franklin, August 16, 1784 (*Writings,* IX, 252).

59. To Jane Mecom, September 29, 1769, in Carl Van Doren (ed.), *The Letters of Benjamin Franklin & Jane Mecom* (Princeton: Princeton University Press, 1950), p. 112.

60. To J. Shipley, February 24, 1786 (*Writings,* IX, 489). See also III, 16–17, and IV, 120.

61. To William Strahan, June 25, 1764 (*Writings,* IV, 250). See also VI, 424.

62. To John Whitehurst, New York, June 27, 1763 (*Papers,* IX, 303).

63. To Hugh Roberts, September 16, 1758 (*Papers,* VIII, 160).

64. To William Hunter, November 24, 1786 (*Writings,* IX, 548).

65. Rev. L. Tyerman, *Life of the Rev. George Whitefield* (London, 1876), II, 540–41, quoted by Mott and Jorgenson (eds.), *op. cit.,* p. cxxxvi.

66. To Jane Mecom, December 30, 1770, in Van Doren (ed.), *The Letters of Benjamin Franklin & Jane Mecom,* p. 124.

67. To Jane Mecom, July 17, 1771, *ibid.,* pp. 125–26. See also *Writings,* II, 61, IV, 388, and IX, 247.

68. *Papers,* I, 108.

69. To Thomas Cushing, June 10, 1771 (*Writings,* V, 325).

70. To Jane Mecom, December 30, 1770, in Van Doren (ed.), *The Letters of Benjamin Franklin & Jane Mecom,* p. 123.

71. April 12, 1750 (*Writings,* III, 5).

72. June 2, 1750 (*Writings,* III, 6). Cf. Benjamin Rush to John Adams, August 19, 1811, in Rush, *op. cit.,* II, 1093: "The doctor was a rigid economist, but he was in every stage of his life charitable, hospitable and generous."

73. *Dogood Papers,* No. VI, June, 1722 (Papers, I, 21). Cf. also No. XIV (*Writings,* II, 47).

74. *Dogood Papers,* No. IX, July, 1722 (*Writings,* II, 29–30).

75. Lovejoy, " 'Pride' in Eighteenth Century Thought," *op. cit.,* pp. 62–68.

76. Pope, *op. cit.,* Epistle 1, p. 103.

77. *The Busy-Body* (*Writings,* II, 108).

78. To Jared Eliot, September 12, 1751 (*Writings,* III, 54–55).

79. *Autobiography* (*Writings,* I, 337).

80. Labaree *et al., Autobiography,* 197. Franklin is less than candid when he speaks about his getting offices "entirely unsolicited." He was, for instance, very anxious to obtain the post of deputy postmaster for the American colonies, although he made a point never to ask for and never to resign from an office. For Franklin's acknowledgment of his own political ambition see also *Writings,* V, 148 (July 2, 1768); V, 357 (January 13, 1772); V, 206 (April 27, 1769); IX, 488 (February 24, 1786); and IX, 621 (November 4, 1787).

81. *Ibid.* (end of the part written in Passy, 1784), 160.

82. To John Wright, November 4, 1789 (*Writings,* X, 62).

83. *Writings,* IX, 591. Madison reports that after Franklin's speech "no debate ensued. . . . It was treated with great respect, but rather for the author of it, than for any apparent conviction of its expediency or practicability" (quoted by Max Farrand, *The Framing of the Constitution of the United States* [New Haven: Yale University Press, 1913], pp. 199–200).

84. To Jonathan Shipley, May 17, 1783 (*Writings,* IX, 23).

85. To Henry Laurens, February 12, 1784 (*Writings,* IX, 170).

86. To William Strahan, February 16, 1784 (*Writings,* IX, 172).

87. To William Strahan, August 19, 1784 (*Writings,* IX, 260).

88. *A Modest Enquiry into the Nature and Necessity of a Paper Currency* (*Writings,* II, 139).

89. Labaree *et. al., Autobiography,* 161. For similar "realistic" statements see also II, 196, or IV, 322.

90. June 9, 1788 (*Writings,* IX, 659).

91. To Benjamin Vaughan, July 26, 1784 (*Writings,* IX, 241).

92. *Writings,* X, 120–21. See also IV, 35.

93. *Morals of Chess* (1779) (*Writings,* VII, 358).

94. To Alexander Small, September 28, 1787 (*Writings,* IX, 614–15).

95. March 20, 1751 (*Papers,* IV, 118).

96. March 5, 1780 (*Writings,* VIII, 28). Cf. the expression of the same idea thirty-six years earlier in a letter to W. Strahan (*Writings,* II, 242).

97. *Good Humour, or, A Way with the Colonists* (London, 1766), pp. 26–27. Franklin's copy with marginal notes is in the library of the Historical Society of Pennsylvania, Philadelphia. Franklin's comments are reprinted in Jared Sparks

(ed.), *A Collection of Familiar Letters and Miscellaneous Papers of Benjamin Franklin* (Boston: C. Bowen, 1833), p. 229.

98. Jefferson to Thomas Law, June 13, 1814, quoted in Adrienne Koch, *The Philosophy of Thomas Jefferson* (New York: Columbia University Press, 1943), p. 19.

99. Jefferson to Judge William Johnson, June 12, 1823, *ibid.,* p. 139.

100. V. L. Parrington, *Main Currents in American Thought* (3 vols.; New York: Harcourt, Brace & Co., 1930), I, 176–77.

101. Charles A. Beard, *An Economic Interpretation of the Constitution* (New York: Macmillan Co., 1913), p. 197.

102. July 2, 1756 (*Papers,* VI, 469).

103. December 19, 1763 (*Papers,* X, 407–8). "Ad exemplum Regis" is a favorite phrase with Franklin. Cf. *Papers,* III, 383, and IX, 347.

104. To Samuel Cooper, April 27, 1769 (*Writings,* V, 204).

105. To Samuel Cooper, June 8, 1770 (*Writings,* V, 261).

106. *Writings,* V, 133; see also V, 121, 134, and 150, and Carl Van Doren (ed.), *Letters and Papers of Benjamin Franklin and Richard Jackson, 1753–1785* (Philadelphia: American Philosophical Society, 1947), p. 139.

107. Van Doren (ed.), *Letters and Papers of Benjamin Franklin and Richard Jackson, 1753–1785,* p. 35 (May 9, 1753).

108. *Ibid.,* p. 34.

109. To Alexander Small, November 5, 1789 (*Writings,* X, 64). This argument is spelled out in greater detail in Franklin's *On the Labouring Poor* (1768) (*Writings,* V, 122–27) and *On the Price of Corn, and Management of the Poor* (undated) (*Writings,* V, 534–39).

110. The paradox of Franklin's position is thrown into relief if one considers that even Jefferson, in his *Notes on Virginia,* raised his voice against the dangers of an "elective despotism," and exalted "those benefits" which a "proper complication of principles" would produce (Thomas Jefferson, *The Works of Thomas Jefferson,* ed. Paul Leicester Ford [12 vols.; New York and London: G. P. Putnam's Sons, 1904–5], IV, 19).

111. Condorcet, *op. cit.,* III, 401–2. (My translation.)

112. See J. Paul Selsam, *The Pennsylvania Constitution of 1776* (Philadelphia: University of Pennsylvania Press, 1926), *passim,* and Charles M. Andrews, *The Colonial Period of American History* (4 vols.; New Haven: Yale University Press, 1934–38), III, 320.

113. Quoted in Zoltán Haraszti, *John Adams and the Prophets of Progress* (Cambridge: Harvard University Press, 1952), p. 167. Cf. also *ibid.,* pp. 186, 203, 204, 214, 254, 256.

114. *A Serious Address to the People of Pennsylvania on the Present Situation of Their Affairs* (December, 1778), in *The Complete Writings of Thomas Paine* (Foner ed.), II, 284.

115. *Constitutional Reform* (1805), *ibid.,* pp. 998–99.

116. *A Dialogue between X, Y, & Z concerning the Present State of Affairs in Pennsylvania* (*Writings,* III, 309).

117. *Writings,* III, 231. Date December 3, 1754, according to *Papers,* V, 443.

118. To the Duke de la Rochefoucauld, April 15, 1787 (*Writings,* IX, 564).

119. *Writings,* IX, 638. The same feeling is expressed in *Writings,* X, 7, and in an unpublished letter to Charles Vaughan of February 12, 1788 (MS in the library of the American Philosophical Society, Philadelphia).

120. "To the Editor of the Federal Gazette" (*Writings*, IX, 702).

121. Speech of June 2, 1787 (*Writings*, IX, 593).

122. Franklin's account of his negotiations in London, written in 1775 (*Writings*, VI, 370–71). For other attacks on the principle of hereditary honors and privileges see *Writings*, IX, 162 and 336.

123. Quoted by Haraszti, *op. cit.*, p. 36, from John Adams, *op. cit.*, VI, 65.

124. *Queries and Remarks* . . . (*Writings*, X, 58–61). Franklin voices his disagreement with the bicameral system of the United States Constitution in two letters to Le Veillard of April and October, 1788 (*Writings*, IX, 645 and 674).

125. To Joseph Galloway, April 14, 1767 (MS in the William L. Clements Library, Ann Arbor, Michigan).

126. B. F. Wright, "The *Federalist* on the Nature of Political Man," *Ethics*, LIX, No. 2, Part II (1948/49), 11.

127. Louis Hartz, "American Political Thought and the American Revolution," *American Political Science Review*, XLVI (1952), 324.

128. Quoted by G. H. Guttridge, *English Whiggism and the American Revolution* ("University of California Publications in History," Vol. XXVIII [Berkeley, 1942], p. 62).

129. This piece is undated but was certainly written before 1775 (*Writings*, X, 130).

130. *Ibid.* For more details see the author's "Reason and Power in Benjamin Franklin's Political Thought," *American Political Science Review*, XLVII (December, 1953), 1112.

131. *Writings*, IX, 593.

132. *Ibid.*

133. *Autobiography* (*Writings*, I, 226 and 374).

134. R. M. MacIver, "European Doctrine and the Constitution," in Read (ed.), *op. cit.*, p. 55.

135. Van Doren (ed.), *Letters and Papers of Benjamin Franklin and Richard Jackson*, p. 145 (March 14, 1764).

136. *Writings*, II, 56.

137. Verner W. Crane (ed.), *Benjamin Franklin's Letters to the Press* (Chapel Hill: University of North Carolina Press, 1950), p. 193.

138. *Writings*, II, 56. See also VI, 129.

139. To C. Colden, August 30, 1754 (*Writings*, III, 228).

140. *Papers*, V, 443.

141. Speech of September 17, 1787 (*Writings*, IX, 607).

142. Pope, "Essay on Man," Epistle 3, *op. cit.*, p. 124.

143. [Allen Ramsay], *Thoughts on the Origin and Nature of Government* (written 1766, printed London, 1769). Franklin's copy is in the Jefferson Collection of the Library of Congress (see Sowerby [comp.], *op. cit.*, III, 248–49).

144. *Ibid.*, p. 10.

145. *Dogood Papers*, No. VIII (*Writings*, II, 26). Cf. Crane (ed.), *op. cit.*, p. 140.

146. Marginal notes to Ramsay, *op. cit.*, pp. 33–34.

147. *Ibid.*, p. 12. Franklin underlined the words "equality" and "independence."

148. *Ibid.*

149. *Ibid.*, p. 13.

150. *Ibid.*

151. To Joseph Galloway, January 9, 1769, in Carl Van Doren (ed.), *Benjamin Franklin's Autobiographical Writings* (New York: Viking Press, 1945), pp. 184–85. Cf also *Writings,* IV, 269, and VII, 390.

152. To Samuel Mather, July 8, 1773 (*Writings,* VI, 87).

NOTES TO CHAPTER II

1. Samuel Flagg Bemis (ed.), *The American Secretaries of State and Their Diplomacy* (10 vols.; New York: Alfred A. Knopf, 1927–29), historical introduction by James Brown Scott, I, 3; quoted by Max Savelle, "Colonial Origins of American Diplomatic Principles," *Pacific Historical Review,* III (1934), 334.

2. Lawrence Henry Gipson, "The American Revolution as an Aftermath of the Great War for the Empire, 1754–1763," *Political Science Quarterly,* LXV (1950), 87.

3. *Ibid.,* and in the same author's work, *The British Empire before the American Revolution,* Vols. I–III (Caldwell, Idaho: Caxton Printers, 1936), Vols. IV ff. (New York: Alfred A. Knopf, 1939———).

4. Theodore H. von Laue, *Leopold Ranke: The Formative Years* (Princeton: Princeton University Press, 1950), p. 167. (The whole "Dialogue on Politics," translated by Laue, is appended to his book.) The paramount importance of the law of self-preservation leads us back to Hobbes's teachings. It has been stated that "the primacy of foreign policy is taught not only by Hobbes but in all specifically modern political philosophy, whether implicitly or explicitly" (Leo Strauss, *The Political Philosophy of Hobbes* [Chicago: University of Chicago Press, 1952], p. 163). Detailed discussions of this problem may be found in Max von Szczepansky, "Rankes Anschauungen über den Zusammenhang zwischen der auswärtigen und inneren Politik der Staaten," *Zeitschrift für Politik,* VII (1914), 489 ff.; Rudolf Goldscheid, *Das Verhältnis der äusseren Politik zur inneren* (Vienna and Leipzig, 1915); Hermann Oncken, "Über die Zusammenhänge zwischen äusserer und innerer Politik," *Vorträge der Gehe-Stiftung in Dresden,* IX (1918), 113–52; Hans Rothfels, "Vom Primat der Aussenpolitik," *Aussenpolitik,* I (1950), 274 ff., and *Gesellschaftsform und auswärtige Politik* (Laupheim: U. Steiner, 1951). Cf. also Heinrich Heffter, "Vom Primat der Aussenpolitik," *Historische Zeitschrift,* CLXXI (1951), 1 ff.; and Ferdinand Schevill, "Ranke: Rise, Decline, and Persistence of a Reputation," *Journal of Modern History,* XXIV (1952), 224.

The idea of the primacy of foreign policy has explicitly been applied to the analysis of the history of the United States by Hermann Oncken, "Amerika und die grossen Mächte: Eine Studie über die Epochen des amerikanischen Imperialismus," *Historisch-politische Aufsätze und Reden* (2 vols.; München and Berlin: R. Oldenbourg, 1914), I, 39 ff. American scholars, influenced by traditions either of isolationism or of democracy or both, have vigorously asserted the primacy of domestic policy. Charles A. Beard often made the point that "the foreign policies of nations are aspects of domestic policies and configurations" (*The Open Door at Home* [New York: Macmillan Co., 1934], p. 130). Cf. also Beard's statements in *The Idea of National Interest* (New York: Macmillan Co., 1934), pp. 128 and 311, and in *A Foreign Policy for America* (New York: Alfred A. Knopf, 1940), pp. 3 and 9.

5. F. J. Turner, "The Significance of the Mississippi Valley in American History," in *The Frontier in American History* (New York: Henry Holt & Co., 1920), pp. 187–88.

6. Mentioned by Richard W. Van Alstyne, "The Significance of the Mississippi

Valley in American Diplomatic History, 1686–1890," *Mississippi Valley Historical Review,* XXXVI (1949), 216.

7. *Ibid.,* p. 222.

8. "The American Revolution as an Aftermath of the Great War for the Empire, 1754–1763," *op. cit.,* pp. 86–87 and 102.

9. Jacob Viner, "Power versus Plenty as Objectives of Foreign Policy in the Seventeenth and Eighteenth Centuries," *World Politics,* I (1947), 9. Cf. also Philipp W. Buck, *The Politics of Mercantilism* (New York: Henry Holt & Co., 1942), p. 113.

10. *Leviathan,* chap. xvii, quoted by Strauss, *op. cit.,* p. 163.

11. "Some Considerations of the Consequences of the Lowering of Interest, Etc.," in *Several Papers Relating to Money, Interest, Trade, Etc.,* quoted by Eli Heckscher, *Mercantilism* (London: George Allen & Unwin, 1935), II, 23.

12. Cf. Lawrence A. Harper, *The English Navigation Laws* (New York: Columbia University Press, 1939), pp. 9 ff.

13. Georg Schwarzenberger, *Power Politics: A Study of International Society* (2d rev. ed.; New York: F. A. Praeger, 1951), p. 14.

14. C. K., *Some Seasonable and Modest Thoughts Partly Occasioned by, and Partly concerning the Scots East-India Company* (Edinburgh, 1696), quoted by Harper, *op. cit.,* p. 233.

15. Cf. Hans J. Morgenthau, *Politics among Nations* (New York: Alfred A. Knopf, 1948), p. 32.

16. Harper, *op. cit.,* p. 15.

17. *Reasons for Keeping Guadaloupe at a Peace, Preferable to Canada, Explained in Five Letters from a Gentleman in Guadaloupe to His Friend in London* (London: Printed for M. Cooper, 1761), pp. 37–39.

18. "D'autres nations ont fait céder des intérêts du commerce à des intérêts politiques: celle-ci a toujours fait céder ses intérêts politiques aux intérêts de son commerce" (Montesquieu, *De l'Esprit des lois* [1748], Book XX, chap. vii, quoted by Jacob Viner, "English Theories of Foreign Trade before Adam Smith," *Journal of Political Economy,* XXXVIII [August, 1930], 451, n. 154). Historians of succeeding generations, Albert Sorel being one of the most famous among them, have often concurred. A more detailed exposition of this view may be found in Jacques Bardoux, *Angleterre et France, leurs politiques étrangères: Essai d'une définition psychologique* (Oxford: Clarendon Press, 1937), pp. 5 ff.

19. This is the thesis of Heckscher, *op. cit.,* II, 17.

20. Charles M. Andrews, *The Colonial Period of American History,* Vol. IV: *England's Commercial and Colonial Policy* (New Haven: Yale University Press, 1938), p. 319. See also *ibid.,* p. 321.

21. Viner, "English Theories of Foreign Trade before Adam Smith," *op. cit.,* p. 449.

22. *Ibid.,* p. 450.

23. *Ibid.*

24. *Ibid.,* p. 449.

25. *Ibid.,* p. 451.

26. Sir Alfred Zimmern, *Quo Vadimus?* p. 11, quoted by E. H. Carr, *The Twenty Years Crisis* (London: Macmillan & Co., 1946), p. 119.

27. F. L. Schuman, *International Politics,* p. 356, quoted by Carr, *op. cit.,* p. 119.

28. Cf. the excellent remarks on this by Carr, *op. cit.,* p. 120.

29. *Wealth of Nations* (Cannan ed.; New York: "Modern Library" [Random House], 1937), p. 431.

30. Klaus E. Knorr, *British Colonial Theories, 1570–1850* (Toronto: University of Toronto Press, 1944), p. 10. Cf. also *ibid.*, pp. 162 ff.

31. Lawrence H. Gipson, "The Art of Preserving an Empire," review article of R. L. Schuyler's *The Fall of the Old Colonial System,* in *William and Mary Quarterly,* II (3d ser., 1945), 407.

32. Cf. Stanley Pargellis, *Lord Loudon in North America* (New Haven: Yale University Press, 1933), p. 4; cf. also *ibid.*, p. 17.

33. Clarence Walworth Alvord, *The Mississippi Valley in British Politics* (Cleveland: Arthur H. Clark Co., 1917), I, 85.

34. Max Savelle, *The Diplomatic History of the Canadian Boundary, 1749–1763* (New Haven: Yale University Press, 1940), p. xii. Cf. also *ibid.*, pp. 149–53.

35. Gerald S. Graham, "The Maritime Foundations of Imperial History," *Canadian Historical Review,* XXXI (1950), 120.

36. For this see the fundamental work of Gipson, *The British Empire before the American Revolution,* Vols. IV, V, and VI, *passim.*

37. Gipson, "The Art of Preserving an Empire," *op. cit.,* p. 407.

38. On the origins of this feeling see William T. Morgan, "English Fear of 'Encirclement' in the Seventeenth Century," *Canadian Historical Review,* X (1929), 4–22.

39. James Logan, *Of the States of the British Plantations in America,* printed in Joseph E. J. Johnson, "A Quaker Imperialist's View of the British Colonies in America: 1732," *Pennsylvania Magazine of History and Biography,* LX (1936), 117. (My italics.) This memoir Logan sent to a member of Parliament who submitted it to Sir Robert Walpole. The copy in Franklin's handwriting in the Franklin Collection of the University of Pennsylvania is the only existing copy.

40. *Ibid.*, p. 118.

41. Archibald Kennedy, *Considerations on the Present State of the Affairs of the Northern Colonies* (New York and London, 1754), p. 4. On political tracts at mid-century in general and Kennedy's writings in particular see the suggestive study of Lawrence C. Wroth, *An American Bookshelf 1755* (Philadelphia: University of Pennsylvania Press, 1934), esp. pp. 10 ff. and 118–26.

42. Lewis Evans, *Geographical, Political, Philosophical and Mechanical Essays: The First, Containing an Analysis of a General Map of the Middle British Colonies in America* . . . (Philadelphia: Printed by B. Franklin and D. Hall, 1755), p. 15. A facsimile of this essay is to be found in Lawrence Henry Gipson, *Lewis Evans* (Philadelphia: Historical Society of Pennsylvania, 1939); the above quotation occurs on p. 159. On the friendship of Evans with Franklin and Thomas Pownall see *ibid.*, pp. 9 and 78.

43. Shirley to James Hamilton, February 20, 1748, in Charles Henry Lincoln (ed.), *The Correspondence of William Shirley* (New York: Macmillan Co., 1912), I, 469.

44. *Observations on the Late and Present Conduct of the French, with Regard to Their Encroachments upon the British Colonies in North America.* It was published together with Franklin's *Observations concerning the Increase of Mankind, Peopling of Countries, Etc.,* for which see below, pp. 54–61. Clarke's pamphlet is reprinted in the *Magazine of History with Notes and Queries,* Extra Number, No. 62, 1917; the quoted passage is on p. 20.

45. "Memoir by M. de la Galissonnière on the French Colonies in North

America, December, 1750," in E. B. O'Callaghan (ed.), *Documents Relative to the Colonial History of the State of New York* (Albany: Weed, Parsons & Co., 1858), X, 220. See also Claude de Bonnault, "M. de la Galissonnière, gouverneur général du Canada, 1747–1749," *Franco-American Review*, II (1937–38), 27–36.

46. "Memoir by M. de la Galissonnière on the French Colonies in North America, December, 1750," in O'Callaghan (ed.), *op. cit.*, X, 223.

47. *Ibid.*

48. *Autobiography* (Benjamin Franklin, *The Writings of Benjamin Franklin*, ed. Albert Henry Smyth [10 vols.; New York: Macmillan Co., 1905–7], I, 360). (Hereafter cited as "*Writings*.")

49. *Ibid.* Cf. also Carl Van Doren, *Benjamin Franklin* (New York: Viking Press, 1938), pp. 183 ff.

50. Except for *A Modest Enquiry into the Nature and Necessity of a Paper Currency* (1729), which belongs to the domain of political economy rather than politics.

51. *Writings*, II, 351. See also a letter to Cadwallader Colden, two weeks after the publication of *Plain Truth* (*Writings*, II, 354).

52. *Writings*, II, 338.

53. *Papers*, III, 196.

54. *Writings*, II, 349.

55. *Writings*, II, 349–50.

56. *Writings*, I, 367.

57. Franklin seemed to be very fond of a story which he included in his *Autobiography* and also told John Jay during their stay in Paris. In 1745 the Pennsylvania Assembly was requested by Governor Thomas to grant money for the support of the garrison at Louisbourg. The Assembly finally resolved to appropriate £4,000 for "Bread, Pork, Flour, Wheat or other Grain," the latter article, of course, implying gunpowder. In his *Autobiography* Franklin speaks of £3,000. The correct references for this story and several similar solutions of the Quaker's dilemma may be found in the short but excellent discussion of the controversies on defense in J. Paul Selsam, *The Pennsylvania Constitution of 1776* (Philadelphia: University of Pennsylvania Press, 1936), pp. 18–30. See *Writings*, I, 367–68, and Frank Monaghan, *Some Conversations of Dr. Franklin and Mr. Jay* (New Haven: Three Monks Press, 1936), pp. 14–15. Jay records the conversation in March, 1784, and the relevant part of the *Autobiography* was written in Passy in 1784.

58. *Writings*, I, 364. Cf. also Franklin's letter to Peter Collinson, August 27, 1755 (*Writings*, III, 277–78). See also *A Dialogue between X, Y, & Z concerning the Present State of Affairs in Pennsylvania* (*Writings*, III, 316).

59. *Papers*, III, 199.

60. Selsam, *op. cit.*, pp. 29–30. See also Theodore Thayer, *Israel Pemberton, King of the Quakers* (Philadelphia: Historical Society of Pennsylvania, 1943), pp. 119–20.

61. *Writings*, II, 348.

62. *Ibid.* (My italics.)

63. *Writings*, II, 341–42, 352.

64. "Observe the *Mean*, the *Motive*, and the *End*," Poor Richard had exhorted his readers in the preceding year (*Writings*, II, 295).

65. *Papers*, III, 194.

66. Gipson, *The British Empire before the American Revolution*, IV, 3 and 4.

67. John Carl Parish, *The Emergence of the Idea of Manifest Destiny* (Los Angeles: University of California Press, 1932), pp. 5–6.

68. Merrill Jensen, "The Cession of the Old Northwest," *Mississippi Valley Historical Review*, XXIII (1936–37), 28.

69. *Ibid.*

70. See W. Neil Franklin, "Pennsylvania-Virginia Rivalry for the Indian Trade of the Ohio Valley," *Mississippi Valley Historical Review*, XX (1933–34), 463–80; Alvord, *op. cit.*, I, 90.

71. *Writings*, III, 218.

72. Jensen, *op. cit.*, p. 28.

73. After the end of the Great War for the Empire, Franklin participated in several important enterprises in land speculation (see below, chap. vi, n. 62). For the scant evidence of his projects up to the end of the war see Carl Van Doren (ed.), *Letters and Papers of Benjamin Franklin and Richard Jackson, 1753–1785* (Philadelphia: American Philosophical Society, 1947), pp. 90–97, and below, p. 62. In general, see Thomas P. Abernethy, *Western Lands and the American Revolution* (New York and London: D. Appleton–Century Co., 1937).

74. Logan, *Of the States of the British Plantations in America*, printed in Johnson, "A Quaker Imperialist's View of the British Colonies in America: 1732," *op. cit.*, pp. 120–21. Logan died in 1751. It is not unlikely that Franklin read and copied Logan's memoir when both were closely associated in providing for the defense of Pennsylvania in 1747. Cf. *ibid.*, pp. 101–2.

75. *Writings*, III, 40.

76. *Papers*, IV, 119.

77. *Ibid.*

78. See above, p. 9.

79. *Papers*, IV, 118.

80. *Writings*, III, 42.

81. *Writings*, III, 42–43.

82. See above, p. 28.

83. Gipson, *The British Empire before the American Revolution*, V, 124–25. See now the important discussion in *Papers*, V, 374–87.

84. We refer the reader to the brilliant and exhaustive treatment of the Albany Congress in chaps. iv and v of Vol. V of Gipson's *The British Empire before the American Revolution*.

85. *Ibid.*, V, 139–40.

86. *Writings*, III, 203–4.

87. *Writings*, III, 199.

88. *Writings*, III, 198.

89. *Papers*, V, 401.

90. *Writings*, III, 219.

91. Cf. above, p. 41, and Johnson, "A Quaker Imperialist's View of the British Colonies in America: 1732," *op. cit.*, p. 117.

92. The best short account of Franklin's expansionism is to be found in Gilbert Chinard, "Looking Westward," in *Meet Dr. Franklin* (Philadelphia: Franklin Institute, 1943), pp. 135–50.

93. Carl Van Doren (ed.), *Benjamin Franklin's Autobiographical Writings* (New York: Viking Press, 1945), p. 158.

94. Van Doren, *Benjamin Franklin*, p. 216.

95. Andrews, *op. cit.*, IV, 337.

96. Cf. Knorr, *op. cit.,* p. 93.

97. George Louis Beer, *British Colonial Policy, 1754–1765* (New York: Macmillan Co., 1907), pp. 134–35.

98. Andrews, *op. cit.,* IV, 339.

99. Wood, *A Survey of Trade,* quoted by Andrews, *op. cit.,* IV, 342.

100. *Writings,* III, 64; cf. also IV, 49.

101. Lewis J. Carey, *Franklin's Economic Views* (Garden City, N.Y.: Doubleday, Doran & Co., 1928), p. 48.

102. *Writings,* III, 65–66.

103. For a detailed discussion of Franklin's population doctrines and their relationship with earlier and later demographic thought see Alfred O. Aldridge, "Franklin as Demographer," *Journal of Economic History,* IX (1949), 25–44. Good discussions of mercantilist population doctrines will be found in Buck, *op. cit.,* pp. 43–48; and, with particular reference to the Colonial problems, Knorr, *op. cit.,* pp. 68–81.

104. Sir William Petty, *A Treatise of Taxes & Contributions* (1662), quoted by Knorr, *op. cit.,* p. 69.

105. Cf. Knorr, *op. cit.,* p. 73.

106. See *Writings,* III, 67–68.

107. *Papers,* IV, 232.

108. *Writings,* III, 67.

109. *Writings,* III, 68–69.

110. *Writings,* III, 71–72.

111. *Papers,* IV, 233.

112. *Ibid.*

113. For the mercantilist attitude on agriculture see Buck, *op. cit.,* pp. 48–52.

114. *Writings,* III, 68–69. (My italics.)

115. To Peter Collinson, June 26, 1755 (*Writings,* III, 265–66). The date of the writing of the *Plan* is not exactly known, but it seems unlikely that Franklin's reference in this letter to Collinson to "a Paper of mine on the Means of settling a new Colony westward of Pensilvania" (*Writings,* III, 265), seen, according to Franklin, in the fall of 1754 by the Philadelphia merchant Samuel Hazard, could concern anything but the *Plan.* For a discusssion of Hazard's western land schemes see Wroth, *op. cit.,* pp. 172–75. Wroth says that the paper seen by Hazard and the *Plan* are identical. The evidence of Franklin's letter to Collinson is overlooked by T. P. Abernethy, who, without producing any contrary evidence, says that "when two years had passed and nothing had been done putting the Albany Plan into operation Franklin came forward with another proposition," namely, the *Plan* (Abernethy, *op. cit.,* p. 15). The letter to Collinson is also overlooked by John A. Schutz in his *Thomas Pownall: British Defender of American Liberty* (Glendale, Calif.: Arthur H. Clark Co., 1951), who says that the *Plan* was written in 1756 (p. 48) and bases this statement on a comparison of the *Plan* with a plan for western settlement drawn up by Pownall apparently in 1755 (p. 49). Schutz mistakenly ascribes a lengthy note on the origin of the *Plan* to John Bigelow, who in fact acknowledged that he took it over from Jared Sparks (Schutz, *op. cit.,* p. 49; Benjamin Franklin, *The Complete Works of Benjamin Franklin,* ed. John Bigelow [10 vols.; New York and London: G. P. Putnam's Sons, 1887–88], II, 474–75; *The Works of Benjamin Franklin,* ed. Jared Sparks [10 vols.; Boston: Tappan & Wilmore, 1836–40], III, 69–70). See now *Papers,* V, 456–57.

116. *Writings,* III, 359.
117. *Papers,* V, 462.
118. Ibid., V, 457.
119. *Writings,* III, 359.
120. *Ibid.*
121. *Papers,* V, 458.
122. *Writings,* III, 365. (My italics.)
123. *Writings,* III, 364.
124. *Papers,* V, 462.
125. *Autobiography* (*Writings,* I, 389).
126. In 1756 Franklin's *Plan* was presented to the Duke of Cumberland in a memorial by Thomas Pownall. Pownall, subsequently governor of Massachusetts, was one of the most enlightened English thinkers on Colonial affairs. Pownall attended the Albany Congress and formed a friendship with Franklin which continued later in England. Pownall as well as Franklin was actively interested in western expansion. For Pownall's plans see Schutz, *op. cit.,* esp. pp. 45 ff. Unfortunately we have no evidence of the exact character of Franklin's relationship with Pownall in the years following the Albany Congress. For an indication that it must have been very close see Gipson, *Lewis Evans,* p. 76, n. 6.
127. Franklin to Richard Jackson, October 7, 1755, in Van Doren (ed.), *Letters and Papers of Benjamin Franklin and Richard Jackson, 1753–1785,* p. 57.
128. Cf. above, p. 42, and n. 44 to this chapter. The quotation is on p. 3. Clarke's pamphlet is one of the most systematic and thorough statements of the attitude of farseeing Americans toward the British-French conflict.
129. July 2, 1756 (*Writings,* III, 339). This letter is a good example to show that Franklin was not so strictly "utilitarian" and so devoid of feelings of another sort as is usually believed. "Life, like a dramatic peace, should not only be conducted with Regularity, but methinks it should finish handsomely. Being now in the last Act, I begin to cast about for something fit to end with. . . . In such an Enterprise, I could spend the Remainder of Life with Pleasure . . ." (*ibid.*). In his *Autobiography* Franklin devotes several unusually enthusiastic pages to his admiration and friendship for Whitefield (*Writings,* I, 354–59).

Franklin reprinted in 1756 his friend's *A Short Address to Persons of All Denominations, Occasioned by the Alarm of an Intended Invasion.* Whitefield's "ideological warfare" against the French can astonish only those who have exaggerated notions of the coolness and rationality of eighteenth-century politics. Whitefield draws an amazing picture of Britain as self-appointed judge over the misdeeds of France: "For if God himself is pleased to stile himself a Man of War, surely in a just & righteous Cause (such as the British War at present is) we may as lawfully draw our Swords, in order to defend ourselves against our common & public Enemy, as a civil Magistrate may sit on a Bench, & condemn a public Robber to Death" (p. 7). He then went on to charge explicitly the Quakers with inconsistency in "grasping at every degree of worldly Power" while refusing to assume the responsibilities of defense. Whitefield argued not unjustly that "we may soon be convinced, that *Civil Magistracy & Defensive War must stand or fall together.* . . . Both are built upon the same Basis; & there cannot be so much as one single Argument urged to establish the one, *which doth not at the same time corroborate & confirm the other*" (p. 8). But, finally, Whitefield went so far as to call the French "Catholic Butchers."

130. *Writings,* III, 235. Date December 4, 1754, according to *Papers,* V, 443. This phrase recurs in almost the same words in the Canada pamphlet of 1760 (*Writings,* IV, 50).

131. *Papers,* V, 447. See also his *Dialogue between X, Y, & Z concerning the Present State of Affairs in Pennsylvania* (*Writings,* III, 310).

132. (My italics.)

133. *Writings,* III, 320.

134. This was the high time of a common American-British patriotism in general. Max Savelle has investigated this in his suggestive article on "The Appearance of an American Attitude toward External Affairs, 1750–1775," *American Historical Review,* LII (1946/47), 655–66.

135. These are to be found in Beer, *op. cit.,* pp. 156–59; Alvord, *op. cit.,* I, 45–75; W. L. Grant, "Canada versus Guadeloupe, an Episode of the Seven Years' War," *American Historical Review,* XVII (1911–12), 735–43; and L. B. Namier, *England in the Age of the American Revolution* (London: Macmillan & Co., 1930), pp. 317–27.

136. Cf. above, **p. 55.**

137. Alvord, *op. cit.,* I, 53.

138. R. A. Humphreys, "Lord Shelburne and the Proclamation of 1763," *English Historical Review,* XLIX (1934), 245. The same author opposes Beer's theory in "British Colonial Policy and the American Revolution, 1763–1776," *History,* XIX (1934–35), 44.

139. Richard Pares, *War and Trade in the West Indies, 1739–1763* (Oxford: Clarendon Press, 1936), p. 179.

140. *Ibid.,* p. 219. See also Namier, *op. cit.,* p. 321.

141. *Writings,* Introduction by Smyth, I, 145.

142. [John Douglas], *A Letter Addressed to Two Great Men, on the Prospects of Peace; and on the Terms Necessary To Be Insisted Upon in the Negotiation* (1st ed.; London, December, 1759; 2d ed.; London and Boston, 1760). I used a copy printed in Dublin in 1760 in the University of Chicago Library. The quotation is on p. 24.

143. *Ibid.,* p. 26.

144. The characteristic arguments of the pro-Guadeloupe writers are all dealt with now, even if some of the pamphlets quoted were published only after Franklin's Canada pamphlet.

145. *An Examination of the Commercial Principles of the Late Negotiation between Great Britain and France in MDCCLXI* (London, 1762), pp. 3–4. (My italics.)

146. *Ibid.,* p. 11.

147. *Ibid.,* p. 61.

148. (London: Printed for M. Cooper, 1761), p. 25. This is certainly the ablest contribution to the whole controversy.

149. *Ibid.,* p. 63.

150. *Ibid.,* p. 6.

151. *Ibid.,* p. 54.

152. [William Burke], *Remarks on the Letter Address'd to Two Great Men* (London, 1760), p. 6.

153. *Ibid.,* pp. 21–22.

154. *Ibid.,* pp. 24–25.

155. *Ibid.*, p. 17.

156. *Ibid.*

157. *Ibid.*

158. Franklin refers in his *Autobiography* to this work as "my Canada Pamphlet." It was, however, written with the assistance of Richard Jackson. Jackson, of the Inner Temple in London, of whom Dr. Johnson spoke as "the all-knowing," was closely associated with Franklin during the latter's activities as Colonial agent in London. Jackson was Colonial agent for Connecticut in 1760 and in 1763 agent for Pennsylvania. After Franklin's return to England in 1765, Jackson was appointed joint agent until 1769. He was also a member of Parliament. For details see the Introduction by Van Doren in his edition of the *Letters and Papers of Benjamin Franklin and Richard Jackson, 1753–1785*, pp. 1–30.

There has long been great uncertainty about the degree to which Franklin and Jackson, respectively, contributed to the authorship, and Smyth, editor of the *Writings*, refers to the Canada pamphlet as the joint production of both. In the Historical Society of Pennsylvania there exists a copy of the work dedicated to the Reverend Dr. Mayhew "by the Author" in Franklin's own hand. His son also spoke in a letter to Joseph Galloway of June 16, 1760, of "a Pamphlet wrote by my father." Franklin's nephew, Benjamin Mecom, felt entitled to reprint the Canada pamphlet with the initials "B . . . n F . . . LL.D." On the other hand, there exists a letter by Francis Maseres (cursitor baron of the exchequer), who presumably knew Richard Jackson, to Benjamin Vaughan, first editor of Franklin's political works. In this letter Maseres indicates the passages written by Franklin, which amount only to half of the part supposedly written by Jackson. However, Verner W. Crane ("Certain Writings of Benjamin Franklin on the British Empire and the American Colonies," *Papers of the Bibliographical Society of America*, XXVIII [1934], 5–12) and Van Doren (*Letters and Papers of Benjamin Franklin and Richard Jackson, 1753–1785*) have elaborately shown that external and internal evidence strongly suggests that Maseres must have been mistaken. Van Doren comes to the conclusion that the Canada pamphlet is "in style and composition and movement and temper . . . thoroughly like him [Franklin] and is like nothing else known to be by Jackson. There is no proof that Jackson knew what was claimed for him by Maseres, or knew that Maseres had made any such claim; while Franklin, on all other occasions uniformly careful to give full credit to his fellow-workers, here claimed the whole of the pamphlet for his own, though with 'considerable assistance' from his 'learned friend' " (*ibid.*, pp. 15–16). In the Historical Society of Pennsylvania there exists a copy of Burke's *Remarks on the Letter Address'd to Two Great Men* with annotations by Franklin, evidently proposed replies. These notes refer to passages uncontestedly written by Jackson according to Maseres. For the internal evidence produced from a careful investigation of scattered manuscript pages in Franklin's hand in the American Philosophical Society and of the marginal notes in Burke's work in the Historical Society of Pennsylvania see Crane, *op. cit.* See now the discussion in *Papers*, IX, 47–59.

159. *Writings*, IV, 35.

160. Cf. chap. i, p. 20.

161. *Writings*, IV, 35.

162. [Burke], *op. cit.*, pp. 18, 27.

163. *Ibid.*, p. 29.

164. *Ibid.*, p. 28.

165. *Ibid.*, p. 19.

166. *Writings,* IV, 36.

167. Walter Lippmann, *U.S. Foreign Policy, Shield of the Republic* (New York: Pocket Books, Inc., 1943), p. 3.

168. [Burke], *op. cit.,* p. 25.

169. *Writings,* IV, 38.

170. *Writings,* IV, 39.

171. *Ibid.*

172. *Papers,* IX, 65.

173. [Burke], *op. cit.,* p. 22.

174. *Ibid.,* pp. 22–23.

175. *Writings,* IV, 36.

176. *Papers,* IX, 62.

177. *Reasons for Keeping Guadaloupe* . . . , p. 49.

178. *Writings,* IV, 40–41.

179. *Writings,* IV, 46.

180. *Writings,* IV, 41.

181. *Writings,* IV, 46.

182. *Ibid.*

183. *Writings,* IV, 49.

184. *Ibid.*

185. *Writings,* IV, 48.

186. *Papers,* IX, 73.

187. *Writings,* IV, 55.

188. *Writings,* IV, 57. (My italics.) For the political importance of an increasing population see *Writings,* IV, 56.

189. *Papers,* IX, 78.

190. Johnson, "A Quaker Imperialist's View of the British Colonies in America: 1732," *op. cit.,* p. 128.

191. *Writings,* IV, 73.

192. Johnson, "A Quaker Imperialist's View of the British Colonies in America: 1732," *op. cit.,* p. 127.

193. *Papers,* IX, 90.

194. *Ibid.*

195. *Writings,* IV, 74.

196. *Writings,* IV, 75.

197. *Writings,* IV, 76–77.

198. *Writings,* IV, 78.

199. *Writings,* IV, 73.

200. *Writings,* IV, 81.

201. Verner W. Crane (ed.), *Benjamin Franklin's Letters to the Press, 1758–1775* (Chapel Hill: University of North Carolina Press, 1950), p. xxxiv.

202. *Ibid.,* p. 8.

203. *Ibid.,* pp. 11–13.

204. *Ibid.,* pp. 13–16.

205. *Ibid.,* p. 18. Smyth, editor of the *Writings,* carries the draft of this work, which does not mention Campanella's name. Franklin invented the edition as well as the chapter. Franklin said that the work appeared in 1629 in England; the earliest traceable edition is from 1654.

206. *Writings,* IV, 92. During the spring of 1759 Franklin had been rather

pessimistic about the outcome of the Canadian campaign. He feared a return of the French to the Ohio "if the present Expedition against Canada, should, as most Expeditions do, fail of Success." He hoped that Pittsburgh at least would be retained by Great Britain in any case (letter to Joseph Galloway, April 7, 1759, in the Mason-Franklin Collection of Yale University Library).

207. *Papers,* IX, 345–46.

208. January 3, 1760 (*Papers,* IX, 7).

209. February 23, 1763 (*Writings,* IV, 191).

210. *Papers,* X, 236. (from a letter also to Strahan, March 28, 1763). Cf. also his letter to Mary Stephenson, March 25, 1763 (*Writings,* IV, 194), and to Dr. John Pringle and Strahan, February 22, 1763, in I. Minis Hays (ed.), *Calendar of the Papers of Benjamin Franklin in the Library of the American Philosophical Society* (Philadelphia: American Philosophical Society, 1908), III, 454. On Franklin's pride about his own contributions in the press campaign for the retention of Canada see also the unpublished letters in the library of the American Philosophical Society: to an unknown correspondent, *ca.* 1760, in Hays (ed.), *op. cit.,* III, 451, and to Mr. Ringold, November 26, 1761, *ibid.,* p. 453.

NOTES TO CHAPTER III

1. *A Modest Enquiry into the Nature and Necessity of a Paper Currency* (Benjamin Franklin, *The Writings of Benjamin Franklin,* ed. Albert Henry Smyth [10 vols.; New York: Macmillan Co., 1905–7], II, 134). (Hereafter cited as "*Writings.*") Cf. also *Dogood Papers,* No. III (*Writings,* II, 8).

2. Charles A. Beard, *The Idea of National Interest* (New York: Macmillan Co., 1934), p. 4.

3. To Governor Shirley, December 22, 1754 (*Writings,* III, 239).

4. Cf. chap. i, p. 31.

5. To Thomas Cushing, July 7, 1773 (*Writings,* VI, 77).

6. This topic has authoritatively been dealt with in the writings of Verner W. Crane: *Benjamin Franklin, Englishman and American* (Baltimore: Williams & Wilkins Co., 1936), pp. 72–139; "Benjamin Franklin and the Stamp Act," *Colonial Society of Massachusetts, Transactions,* XXXII (1934–37), 56–77; and his Introduction to his edition of *Benjamin Franklin's Letters to the Press, 1758–1775* (Chapel Hill: University of North Carolina Press, 1950). See also the doctoral dissertation of D. R. Miles, "The Political Philosophy of Benjamin Franklin" (University of Michigan, 1949). Cf. also R. G. Adams, *Political Ideas of the American Revolution* (Durham, N.C.: Trinity College Press, 1922).

7. *Exporting of Felons to the Colonies* (*Writings,* III, 47). Franklin has reported his method of arriving at "rational decisions" by "Moral or Prudential Algebra" in a letter to Joseph Priestley of September 19, 1772 (*Writings,* V, 437–38).

8. To James Parker (*Writings,* III, 41–42).

9. *A Modest Enquiry* . . . (*Writings,* II, 140). Cf. John Adams, who told the Continental Congress that France might help the colonies because "interest could not lie" (John Adams, *Works,* ed. C. F. Adams [10 vols.; Boston: Little, Brown & Co., 1850–56], II, 505).

10. *Writings,* II, 139.

11. *Writings,* II, 142.

12. "The Colonists Advocate," No. VIII (1770), in Crane (ed.), *Benjamin Franklin's Letters to the Press,* p. 197.

13. *Observations concerning the Increase of Mankind* (*Writings*, III, 66).

14. *Papers*, V, 450.

15. *Exporting of Felons to the Colonies* (*Writings*, III, 47).

16. E.g., *Writings*, IV, 336; V, 15; VI, 50, 173, 250; etc.

17. This is meant when Franklin says that "a good Understanding between the Parts of a great Empire is the Strength of the Whole" (1773), in Crane (ed.), *Benjamin Franklin's Letters to the Press*, p. 228. Cf. also *Writings*, III, 236–37, and VI, 128.

18. *Queries by Mr. Strahan, respecting American Affairs, and Dr. Franklin's Answers* (*Writings*, V, 243).

19. *The Results of England's Persistance in Her Policy towards the Colonies Illustrated* (*Writings*, VI, 290–91). Cf. also the same argument in *Writings*, V, 86.

20. To Thomas Cushing, July 7, 1773 (*Writings*, VI, 77–78).

21. See chap. ii above, p. 51. Quotation from *Writings*, III, 41–42.

22. *Papers*, V, 400.

23. A recent instance is Vincent T. Harlow, *The Founding of the Second British Empire, 1763–1793*, Vol. I: *Discovery and Revolution* (London, New York, and Toronto: Longmans, Green & Co., 1952), pp. 164–65. Cf. also Gilbert Chinard, "Looking Westward," in *Meet Dr. Franklin* (Philadelphia: Franklin Institute, 1943), p. 145.

24. Franklin's letter to Jackson, December 19, 1763, in Carl Van Doren (ed.), *Letters and Papers of Benjamin Franklin and Richard Jackson, 1753–1785* (Philadelphia: American Philosophical Society, 1947), p. 118.

25. *Autobiography* (*Writings*, I, 388). For similar reflections with regard to Pennsylvania affairs see the letter to P. Collinson, June 26, 1755 (*Writings*, III, 265).

26. *Tract Relative to the Affair of Hutchinson's Letters* (*Writings*, VI, 259–60). Cf. also *Writings*, V, 181–82. Cf. also the comment on Franklin in the *Memoirs of the Rev. Dr. Joseph Priestley . . . Written by Himself, with a Continuation to the Time of His Decease by His Son, Joseph Priestley* (London, 1809), p. 79.

27. *Papers*, IX, 75. (The last sentence is in my italics.)

28. *Writings*, IV, 47. (The last four words are in my italics.)

29. See particularly his letter to John Hughes, January 7, 1760, where he discusses his publicist activities for securing Canada and insuring a glorious peace. "And on the whole," he added, "I flatter myself that my being here at this time may be of some Service *to the general Interest of America*" (*Writings*, IV, 8). (My italics.) In a similar vein Franklin, after his return to Philadelphia, wrote (March 8, 1763) to Richard Jackson that the preliminaries of the Peace of Paris "are universally approved of in these Parts [America]" (Van Doren [ed.], *op. cit.*, p. 91).

30. *Writings*, IV, 438–39.

31. *Writings*, IV, 439.

32. Crane (ed.), *Benjamin Franklin's Letters to the Press*, p. 89.

33. *Ibid.*, p. 96. (My italics.) Franklin here addresses an English public; "our interest" therefore means English interest. Cf. also Crane's footnotes on p. 89 (n. 1) and on p. 96 (n. 5). See also *Writings*, V, 167.

34. [Matthew C. Wheelock], *Reflections Moral and Political on Great Britain and her Colonies* (London, 1770), p. 40.

35. Franklin's marginal note (*ibid.*); Franklin's copy in the Jefferson Collection of the Library of Congress. See also Franklin's marginal notes in *An Inquiry into*

the Nature and Causes of the Disputes between the British Colonies in America and Their Mother Country (London, 1769), which are printed in Benjamin Franklin, *The Complete Works of Benjamin Franklin,* ed. John Bigelow (10 vols.; New York and London: G. P. Putnam's Sons, 1887–88), IV, 319–23.

36. [Wheelock], *op. cit.,* p. 26.

37. Franklin's marginal note (*ibid.*).

38. *Writings,* IV, 51.

39. L. H. Gipson, "The American Revolution as an Aftermath of the Great War for the Empire, 1754–1763," *Political Science Quarterly,* LXV (1950), 91.

40. To David Hall, February 14, 1765 (*Writings,* IV, 363).

41. *Vindication and Offer from Congress to Parliament* (*Writings,* VI, 416).

42. "The Colonists Advocate," No. VI, in Crane (ed.), *Benjamin Franklin's Letters to the Press,* p. 183.

43. To Joseph Galloway, January 9, 1769, in Carl Van Doren (ed.), *Benjamin Franklin's Autobiographical Writings* (New York: Viking Press, 1938), p. 184.

44. *Ibid.*

45. *Letter concerning the Gratitude of America* (*Writings,* IV, 404).

46. Crane (ed.), *Benjamin Franklin's Letters to the Press,* p. 140. See also n. 2. Cf. also *ibid.,* p. 142.

47. To Joseph Galloway, January 11, 1770 (unpublished), in the William L. Clements Library, Ann Arbor, Michigan. Cf. also Franklin's letter to Samuel Cooper, December 30, 1770 (*Writings,* V, 285).

48. For this topic see Crane's *Benjamin Franklin, Englishman and American,* p. 36 and *passim,* and particularly the article by Conyers Read, "The English Elements in Benjamin Franklin," *Pennsylvania Magazine of History and Biography,* LXIV (1940), 314–30. See also *Writings,* IV, 182, 217; V, 144, 382.

49. To Lord Kames, April 11, 1767 (*Writings,* V, 17).

50. To an unknown correspondent, November 28, 1768 (*Writings,* V, 181). Cf. also Crane (ed.), *Benjamin Franklin's Letters to the Press,* p. 141, and *Writings,* V, 74, 133.

51. Franklin's indignation about the corrupt practices of English party life is very striking. Franklin's maxim that honesty is the best policy and his belief in "industry and frugality" were deeply shocked by the lavish expenditure of election campaigns. See, e.g., *Writings,* V, 100, 112, 117 ("This whole venal nation is now at the market, will be sold for about two millions, and might be bought out of the hands of the present bidders [if he would offer half a million more] by the very Devil himself" [written 1767/68]), and 133; cf. also Crane (ed.), *Benjamin Franklin's Letters to the Press,* pp. 59, 164, 232.

52. August 8, 1767 (*Writings,* V, 40–41).

53. To William Franklin, February 14, 1773 (*Writings,* VI, 13).

54. To Joseph Galloway, February 5, 1775, in Van Doren (ed.), *Benjamin Franklin's Autobiographical Writings,* p. 345.

55. *Writings,* VI, 119.

56. *Writings,* VI, 128.

57. *Ibid.*

58. *Writings,* VI, 136.

59. In Antonio Pace's article, "Franklin and Machiavelli," *Symposion,* I (1947), 36–42, parallels between Machiavelli's *Prince* and Franklin's *Rules* are drawn

which strongly suggest that Franklin was well acquainted with Machiavelli's work. Pace also refers to Franklin's mention of Machiavelli in the Canada pamphlet (see above, chap. ii, p. 79) as the only appearance of Machiavelli in Franklin's collected writings. Pace could not know that Franklin also mentions Machiavelli in an anonymous newspaper letter, published in 1950 for the first time by Crane (ed.), in *Benjamin Franklin's Letters to the Press*, pp. 45–46. ("*To the Printer of the* London Chronicle," signed "N. N.," January 9, 1766): "I send you also an extract from Machiavell's discourses on Livy." Franklin's letter was followed by an extract from chap. xxiii of the second book of the *Discourses*, "the title of which chapter is, *How the* Romans, *upon any accident which necessitated them to give judgement upon their subjects, avoided always the middle way . . .*" (*ibid.*, p. 46, n. 3). This is the first time we hear of Franklin's acquaintance with the *Discourses*. Pace had only confirmed Franklin's knowledge of the *Prince*.

60. To Joseph Galloway, February 25, 1775 (*Writings*, VI, 311–12).

61. To Lord Kames, April 11, 1767 (*Writings*, V, 21). Cf. Franklin's remarkable letter to the Committee of Correspondence in Massachusetts of May 15, 1771 (*Writings*, V, 318). A similar argument is presented in a newspaper article of 1770 in Crane (ed.), *Benjamin Franklin's Letters to the Press*, p. 220.

62. *Writings*, V, 21–22.

63. "To the Printer of *The London Public Advertiser*," August 25, 1768 (*Writings*, V, 162–63).

64. To Thomas Cushing, June 4, 1773 (*Writings*, VI, 57).

65. To Thomas Cushing, January 13, 1772 (*Writings*, V, 367).

66. To Thomas Cushing, January 5, 1773 (*Writings*, VI, 3–4). See also VI, 22 and 213.

67. *Writings*, IV, 73.

68. Marginal note in Franklin's copy of Josiah Tucker's *A Letter from a Merchant in London to His Nephew in America* (1766). The pamphlet with Franklin's notes is reprinted in *Pennsylvania Magazine of History and Biography*, XXV (1901), 307 ff., 516 ff., and XXVI (1902), 81 ff., 255 ff. This quotation is on p. 85 of Vol. XXVI. See also Franklin's marginal comments in *An Inquiry into Nature and Causes of the Disputes . . .* , in *The Complete Works of Benjamin Franklin*, ed. Bigelow, IV, 323.

69. *Writings*, II, 155.

70. To Governor Shirley, December 22, 1754 (*Writings*, III, 239).

71. To Peter Collinson, April 30, 1764 (*Writings*, IV, 243).

72. Franklin's examination before the House of Commons (*Writings*, IV, 444).

73. Franklin's marginal note, Preface page of Wheelock, *op. cit.*

74. Franklin's marginal note, pp. 29–30 of Wheelock, *op. cit.* It might be added that in two instances where Franklin explicitly speaks of the "national interest," the first one, written in 1760, does not clarify the issue (*Writings*, IV, 90), whereas the second instance (*Writings*, X, 6), dating from 1789, obviously refers to the United States of America.

75. To Peter Collinson, May 28, 1754 (*Papers*, V, 332).

76. To Lord Kames, April 11, 1767 (*Writings*, V, 19).

77. Crane, *Benjamin Franklin, Englishman and American*, p. 138.

78. *Writings*, VI, 77.

79. To William Franklin, March 13, 1768 (*Writings*, V, 115). (The last nineteen words are in my italics.)

80. To the Committee of Correspondence in Massachusetts, May 15, 1771 (*Writings*, V, 319).

81. To Thomas Cushing, June 10, 1771 (*Writings*, V, 323–24).

82. To Joseph Galloway, January 9, 1769, in Van Doren (ed.), *Benjamin Franklin's Autobiographical Writings*, p. 188. Cf. also *ibid.*, p. 184 (same letter).

83. Cf. Oliver M. Dickerson, *The Navigation Acts and the American Revolution* (Philadelphia: University of Pennsylvania Press, 1951), pp. 52 ff.

84. Cf. also the suggestive article by Curtis P. Nettels, "British Mercantilism and the Economic Development of the Thirteen Colonies," *Journal of Economic History*, XII (1952), 107.

85. *Writings*, V, 446–47. Franklin considered economic independence as very important for political integrity. This attitude is particularly well expressed in his letter to Peter Timothy of November 3, 1772: "I am sorry you talk of leaving off your Business with a View of getting some Post. . . . The Proverb says; *He who has a Trade has an Office of Profit and Honour;* because he does not hold it during any other Man's Pleasure, and it affords him honest Subsistence with Independence" (*ibid.*).

86. To Joshua Babcock, January 13, 1772 (*Writings*, V, 362); cf. also letter to Thomas Cushing on the same day (*Writings*, V, 368).

87. *Writings*, IV, 49.

88. Lewis J. Carey, *Franklin's Economic Views* (Garden City, N.Y.: Doubleday, Doran & Co., 1928), pp. 140–41.

89. To Cadwallader Colden, February 20, 1768 (*Writings*, V, 102).

90. *Writings*, V, 202.

91. *Ibid.*

92. *Ibid.*

93. *On the Labouring Poor* (*Writings*, V, 126).

94. To Thomas Cushing, June 10, 1771 (*Writings*, V, 327). Cf. also II, 338, and *The Complete Works of Benjamin Franklin*, ed. Bigelow, IV, 319. See also above, p. 44, and below, p. 243.

95. To David Hume, September 27, 1760 (*Papers*, IX, 229).

96. *Ibid.*

97. To Dupont de Nemours, July 28, 1768 (*Writings*, V, 155–56).

98. To Peter Collinson, April 30, 1764 (*Writings*, IV, 243–44). Cf. the almost identical words in a letter to Jean B. Le Roy, January 31, 1769 (*Writings*, V, 193).

99. *Remarks on the Plan for Regulating the Indian Affairs* (*Writings*, IV, 469).

100. Crane (ed.), *Benjamin Franklin's Letters to the Press*, p. 195.

101. *Writings*, VI, 323. Cf. also *Vindication and Offer from Congress to Parliament* (*Writings*, VI, 418).

102. Carey, *op. cit.*, p. 140.

103. F. L. Mott and Chester E. Jorgenson (eds.), *Benjamin Franklin: Representative Selections with Introduction, Bibliography, and Notes* (New York: American Book Co., 1936), p. lxix.

104. Miles, *op. cit.*, p. 234.

105. Cf. Eli Heckscher, *Mercantilism* (London: George Allen & Unwin, 1935), II, 14.

106. T. H. Green and T. H. Grose (eds.), *The Philosophical Works of David Hume* (new ed.; London: Longmans, Green & Co., 1889), III, 345.

107. *Writings*, VI, 323 and 418. See also Dickerson, *op. cit.*, pp. 111–14.

108. *Writings*, II, 142. Cf. also Franklin's *Note respecting Trade and Manu-*

factures, dated July 7, 1769, which argues that prohibition on free imports diminishes the "enjoyments and conveniences of life" (Benjamin Franklin, *The Works of Benjamin Franklin,* ed. Jared Sparks [10 vols.; Boston: Tappan & Willmore, 1836–40], II, 366). For Franklin's connection with and not very considerable influence on Adam Smith cf. Thomas D. Eliot, "The Relations between Adam Smith and Benjamin Franklin before 1776," *Political Science Quarterly,* XXIX (1924), 67–96.

109. Green and Grose (eds.), *op. cit.,* III, 346.

110. See above, p. 107.

111. Cf. Dickerson, *op. cit., passim.*

112. *An Account of Negotiations in London for Effecting a Reconciliation between Great Britain and the American Colonies* (*Writings,* VI, 331–32). (My italics.) Consequently, the statement that "to Franklin Laissez-Faire was born of the Navigation Acts" (Read, *op. cit.,* p. 329) is valid only under certain qualifications.

113. *Writings,* IV, 40.

114. *Writings,* VI, 460–61.

115. *Ibid.*

NOTES TO CHAPTER IV

1. [William Burke], *Remarks on the Letter Address'd to Two Great Men* (London, 1760), p. 52.

2. Max Savelle, "The American Balance of Power and European Diplomacy, 1713–78," in Richard B. Morris (ed.), *The Era of the American Revolution* (New York: Columbia University Press, 1939), p. 158. This is a brilliant and suggestive work of research.

3. "Memoir by M. de la Galissonnière on the French Colonies in North America" (December, 1750), in E. B. O'Callaghan (ed.), *Documents Relative to the Colonial History of the State of New York* (Albany, N.Y.: Weed, Parsons & Co., 1858), X, 224. Cf. also *ibid.,* p. 232.

4. Savelle, *op. cit.,* pp. 160–61, quoting from a dispatch of Choiseuil to the French ambassador in Madrid of September 7, 1759, printed in France, Commission des Archives Diplomatiques, *Recueil des instructions données aux ambassadeurs et ministres de la France depuis les Traités de Westphalie jusqu'à la Révolution française* (Paris: F. Alcan, 1884——); Vols. XI–XIIbis, *Espagne,* ed. A. Morel-Fatio and H. Léonardon; XIIbis (3), 349. Similarly, Choiseuil wrote in a dispatch to the French ambassador in Sweden on March 21, 1759: "We must not deceive ourselves. *The true balance of power really resides in commerce and in America.*" Quoted by Edward S. Corwin, *French Policy and the American Alliance of 1778* (Princeton: Princeton University Press, 1916, p. 33), from M. de Flassan, *Histoire générale et raisonnée de la diplomatie française depuis la fondation de la Monarchie jusqu'à la fin du Règne de Louis XVI* (2d ed.; Paris, 1811), VI, 160.

5. *Observations on the Late and Present Conduct of the French, with Regard to Their Encroachments upon the British Colonies in North America,* reprinted in the *Magazine of History with Notes and Queries,* Extra Number 12, 1917.

6. *Ibid.,* p. 31. Cf. also Max Savelle, "The Appearance of an American Attitude toward External Affairs, 1750–1775," *American Historical Review,* LII (1946/47), 663.

7. Corwin, *op. cit.,* p. 40, quoting Choiseuil's *Mémoire* of 1765.

8. For details see Josephine F. Pacheco, "French Secret Agents in America" (doctoral dissertation, University of Chicago, 1950).

9. Corwin, *op. cit.,* p. 43, citing F. Kapp, *Life of Kalb* (New York, 1870), pp. 45–51.

10. To William Franklin, August 28, 1767 (Benjamin Franklin, *The Writings of Benjamin Franklin,* ed. Albert Henry Smyth [10 vols.; New York: Macmillan Co., 1905–7], V, 47). (Hereafter cited as *"Writings."*) Cf. also the letter to his son of August 19, 1772 (*Writings,* V, 414). Durand relied on Franklin's replies in his interrogation in the House of Commons in a letter to Choiseuil of August 11, 1767, printed in Cornelis de Witt, *Thomas Jefferson: Étude historique sur la démocratie américaine* (3d ed.; Paris: Didier & Co., 1861), pp. 420 ff.

11. To Samuel Cooper, September 30, 1769 (*Writings,* V, 231). The evidence of this letter and of the following quotations speaks against the statement of Marcel Trudel, *Louis XVI, le congrès américain et le Canada, 1774–1789* (Quebec: Publications de l'Université Laval, Éditions du Quartier Latin, 1949), pp. 9–10, that "ce que les diplomates n'avaient pu faire, un voyage à Paris l'accomplira: Franklin reviendra ébloui de tout ce qu'il aura vu, il sera fâché de se retrouver à Londres." Franklin's enthusiasm about French "civility," about the comforts and pleasures of life in Paris, and about the French "esprit" has nothing to do with his political loyalties.

12. April 14, 1770 (*Writings,* V, 254).

13. Josiah Tucker, *A Letter from a Merchant in London to His Nephew in America* (1766); this passage with Franklin's marginal comment printed in *Pennsylvania Magazine of History and Biography,* XXVI (1902), 261.

14. *Ibid.,* marginal note.

15. *Writings,* IV, 444.

16. To Thomas Cushing, June 10, 1771 (*Writings,* V, 327). Cf. also *Writings,* VI, 3.

17. *Vindication and Offer from Congress to Parliament* (*Writings,* VI, 416).

18. "The Colonists' Advocate," No. VI (January, 1770), in Verner W. Crane (ed.), *Benjamin Franklin's Letters to the Press, 1758–1775* (Chapel Hill: University of North Carolina Press, 1950), p. 185. See also *ibid.,* p. 233.

19. Peter Orlando Hutchinson (comp.), *The Diary and Letters of . . . Thomas Hutchinson* (2 vols.; London: Sampson Low, Marston, Searle & Rivington, 1883–86), II, 237–38. Cf. Carl Van Doren (ed.), *Benjamin Franklin's Autobiographical Writings* (New York: Viking Press, 1945), p. 407.

20. July 7, 1775 (*Writings,* VI, 409), and Van Doren (ed.), *op. cit.,* p. 409.

21. John Penn from North Carolina to Thomas Person, in Samuel Flagg Bemis, *The Diplomacy of the American Revolution* (New York and London: D. Appleton–Century Co., 1935), p. 30, quoting from Edmund C. Burnett (ed.), *Letters of Members of the Continental Congress* (8 vols.; Washington: Carnegie Institution of Washington, 1921–36), I, 349.

22. Bemis, *op. cit.,* p. 30.

23. Franklin's grandson, William Temple Franklin, editor of *The Memoirs of the Life of Benjamin Franklin* (*The Works of Dr. Benjamin Franklin* [6 vols.; Philadelphia, 1808–18], I, 360), says that "Dr. Franklin had no inconsiderable share, at least in furnishing materials for that work." Paine himself has publicly recognized this (*Crisis,* III [published April 19, 1777] [Thomas Paine, *The Com-*

plete Writings of Thomas Paine, ed. Philip S. Foner (2 vols.; New York: Citadel Press, 1945), I, 88–89 n.]). See the very detailed account of Arnold Kimsey King, "Thomas Paine in America, 1774–1787" (doctoral dissertation, University of Chicago, 1951), p. 65. We may add that, according to Benjamin Rush, Franklin did see the draft of *Common Sense* (*The Autobiography of Benjamin Rush: His "Travels through Life" Together with the Commonplace Book for 1789–1813,* edited with Introduction and Notes by George W. Corner [Princeton: Princeton University Press, 1948], p. 114). On another occasion Rush said that Franklin made no addition to *Common Sense;* he also once said that he believed that Franklin's "head and hand were equally distant from the author while he wrote it" (Benjamin Rush, *The Letters of Benjamin Rush,* ed. Lyman H. Butterfield [Princeton: Princeton University Press, 1951], II, 1008 and 1014 [letters to J. Cheetham, July 17, 1809, and to John Adams, August 14, 1809]).

24. Paine, *op. cit.,* I, 20 and 21.

25. Bemis, *op. cit.,* p. 12.

26. *Ibid.*

27. Felix Gilbert, "The English Background of American Isolationism in the Eighteenth Century," *William and Mary Quarterly,* I (3d ser., 1944), 159.

28. Felix Gilbert, "The 'New Diplomacy' of the Eighteenth Century," *World Politics,* IV (1951/52), 23.

29. John Adams, *Works,* ed. C. F. Adams (10 vols.; Boston: Little, Brown & Co., 1850–56), II, 488–89.

30. Lee's motion (*Journals of the Continental Congress, 1774–1789* [34 vols.; Library of Congress ed.; Washington: Government Printing Office, 1904–37], V, 425).

31. To John M. Jackson, December 30, 1817, in John Adams, *op. cit.,* X, 269.

32. Franklin has left very little record of this decisive time in America. The connections with England were more or less interrupted; besides, Franklin was too busy to write many letters: he was the first postmaster-general of the Confederation, member of the Committee of Safety in Philadelphia, member of Congress and many congressional committees, member of the unsuccessful mission of Congress to Canada in the spring of 1776, and president of the Constitutional Convention of Pennsylvania in the summer of 1776. Franklin's main activities were devoted to his service for Congress. Moreover, as a member of Congress, Franklin, who was never a good speaker, kept to his widely known taciturnity more than ever. Jefferson said that Franklin in Congress, like Washington in the legislature of Virginia, never "speaks ten minutes at a time, nor to any but the main point which was to decide the question" (quoted by Carl Van Doren, *Benjamin Franklin* [New York: Viking Press, 1938], p. 529). John Adams remarked that Franklin was "commonly as silent on committees as in Congress" (*Autobiography* [*op. cit.,* II, 516]).

33. Gilbert, "The 'New Diplomacy' . . . ," *op. cit.,* pp. 19–22.

34. *Ibid.,* p. 21, n. 64.

35. Franklin to Dumas, under the date of December 19, 1775, in Francis Wharton, *The Revolutionary Diplomatic Correspondence of the United States* (6 vols.; Washington: Government Printing Office, 1889), II, 64. According to *Writings,* VI, 433, letter dated December 9, 1775.

36. Franklin *et al.* to Silas Deane, March 3, 1776, in Wharton, *op. cit.,* II, 79.

37. Committee of Secret Correspondence to Deane, October 2, 1776, *ibid.,* p. 162.

38. Quoted from John Adams, *Autobiography* (*op. cit.,* II, 509). He made a statement to the same effect in a letter to Benjamin Rush, September 30, 1805 (*ibid.,* I, 200).

39. S. F. Bemis thinks that it is "quite possible and likely that Adams independently developed a reasoning against involvement in European wars and politics, even before Paine" (*op. cit.,* p. 13, n. 12). On the other hand, Chinard thinks that "it is very doubtful that this principle appeared so clearly at the time in the mind of Adams" (Gilbert Chinard, *Honest John Adams* [Boston: Little, Brown & Co., 1933], p. 88). Felix Gilbert argues that "this would have made Adams an advocate of a complete system of isolationist foreign policy as early as 1775," and he observes that "Adams' views hardened into rigid isolationism only during his stay in Europe" ("The 'New Diplomacy' . . . ," *op. cit.,* p. 23, n. 69). However, we fail to see that the cited passages necessarily imply "rigid isolationism." There is no essential difference of content between Adams' remark of 1805 about his early refusal to conclude "treaties of alliance with any European power," supposed to express "rigid isolationism," and a letter he wrote in June, 1776, in which he urged the conclusion of "commercial treaties of friendship and alliance" with European powers (to William Cushing, June 9, 1776 [Burnett (ed.), *op. cit.,* I, 478]), which latter type treaties he is held to have believed compatible with his early hopes for "a complete change of the foreign policy of all powers, to be achieved by a 'reformation' of the commercial system" (Gilbert, "The 'New Diplomacy' . . . ," *op. cit.,* p. 23, n. 69). One might well argue that Adams' view of America's position and tasks in world politics did not change. It was his view of Europe which was transformed, and this change is reflected in sharper terminology.

40. Discussed by Gilbert, "The English Background . . . ," *op. cit.,* p. 147. Cf. the special bibliography of the Canada-Guadeloupe controversy in Clarence Walworth Alvord, *The Mississippi Valley in British Politics* (Cleveland: Arthur H. Clark Co., 1917), II, 258.

41. James Burgh, *Political Disquisitions* (Philadelphia, 1775), III, 288, quoted by Gilbert, "The English Background. . . ," *op. cit.,* p. 152. For his acquaintance with Franklin see Burgh, *op. cit.,* II, 276, mentioned by Gilbert, "The English Background . . . ," *op. cit.,* p. 152. See also Crane (ed.), *op. cit.,* p. 286.

42. "The Colonists Advocate," No. VI, in Crane (ed.), *op. cit.,* p. 184.

43. Marginal comment in *An Inquiry into the Nature and Causes of the Present Disputes* (London, 1769), quoted by Verner W. Crane, "Certain Writings of Benjamin Franklin on the British Empire and the American Colonies," in *Papers of the Bibliographical Society of America,* XXVIII, Part I (1934), 23, n. 51. Franklin's comments are also printed in John Bigelow (ed.), *The Complete Works of Benjamin Franklin* (10 vols.; New York and London: G. P. Putnam's Sons, 1887–88), IV, 308–26. (My italics.) The original copy is in the New York Public Library.

44. To Joseph Galloway, February 25, 1775 (*Writings,* VI, 312).

45. This reassessment of the *Dialogue* has been made by George S. Wykoff, "Problems concerning Franklin's 'A Dialogue between Britain, France, Spain, Holland, Saxony, and America,'" *American Literature,* XI (1939/40), 439–48.

46. *Writings,* VII, 85.

47. July 7, 1775 (*Writings,* VI, 409).

48. Gilbert, "The 'New Diplomacy' . . . ," *op. cit.,* p. 21.

49. It is true that at times (e.g., in December, 1775) Colonial leaders apparently did contemplate the possibility of offering a commercial monopoly to France for a limited time (see below, p. 122). On the other hand, as Felix Gilbert observes, in the fall of 1775 the opinion was expressed in Congress that "with the separation of the American colonies from Britain's imperial system, the possibility of trading with the colonies would be enough attraction to the French to undertake the protection of the trade with America" ("The 'New Diplomacy' . . . ," *op. cit.,* p. 20; see also John Adams' notes on the debates in Congress, in *Journals of the Continental Congress, 1774–1789,* III, 471 ff., esp. p. 479). It seems to us that the wording of Franklin's letter to Priestley does not warrant Gilbert's interpretation. After all, very similar language was used at a time when the plan of the Treaty of Amity and Commerce with France already had been accepted by Congress and the offer of a commercial monopoly was out of the question. On December 21, 1776, Robert Morris wrote to Franklin, Deane, and Arthur Lee in Paris: "If the court of France open their eyes to their own interest, and think the commerce of North America will compensate them for the expence and evil of a war with Britain, they may readily create a diversion, and afford us succors that will change the fate of affairs" (Wharton, *op. cit.,* II, 235).

50. *Journals of the Continental Congress, 1774–1789,* III, 502 (Chase's speech on October 21, 1775).

51. *Ibid.*

52. On November 29, 1775, Congress appointed a committee "for the sole purpose of corresponding with our friends in Great Britain, Ireland, and other parts of the world." The original members, besides Franklin, were John Dickinson, John Jay, Thomas Jefferson, and Benjamin Harrison. After April 17, 1777, the committee was called "Committee of Foreign Affairs," and only in 1781 was it replaced by one Secretary of Foreign Affairs (Bemis, *op. cit.,* pp. 32–33). The committee was the final modest result of Chase's motion, seconded by John Adams, to send ambassadors to France (cf. John Adams, *op. cit.,* I, 200–201, and IX, 421).

53. For Dumas see Wharton, *op. cit.,* I, 603–4.

54. *Ibid.,* II, 65, under the date of December 19, 1775; according to *Writings,* VI, 433, letter dated December 9, 1775. On Dumas's account of how he conveyed these two questions to the French ambassador see his answer to Franklin, April 30, 1776, in Wharton, *op. cit.,* II, 86.

55. Wharton, *op. cit.,* II, 86.

56. December 12, 1775 (*Writings,* VI, 437).

57. Fred Rippy and Angie Debo, *The Historical Background of the American Policy of Isolation* ("Smith College Studies in History," Vol. IX [Northampton, 1924]), p. 82.

58. The French original is printed in Henri Doniol, *Histoire de la participation de la France à l'établissement des États-Unis d'Amérique* (5 vols.; Paris: Imprimerie Nationale, 1886–92), I, 290 (report to the French ambassador in London). The translation is taken from John Durand (ed.), *New Materials for the History of the American Revolution* (New York: Henry Holt & Co., 1889), p. 10.

59. Wharton, *op. cit.,* II, 79 (instructions of March 3, 1776). They are signed by all members of the committee but written by Franklin. Cf. Doniol, *op. cit.,* I, 486–87, and B. F. Stevens (comp.), *Facsimiles of Manuscripts from European Archives Relating to America, 1773–1783* (24 vols.; London, 1889–93) (hereafter

cited as "Stevens' *Facsimiles*"), Vol. IX, No. 890 (Dr. Bancroft's information on the mission of Silas Deane, August 14, 1776). Still, Deane felt entitled to offer a tobacco monopoly to France (cf. Gilbert, "The 'New Diplomacy' . . . ," *op. cit.*, p. 21, n. 63).

60. Wharton, *op. cit.*, II, 79.

61. Gilbert, "The 'New Diplomacy' . . . ," *op. cit.*, p. 23.

62. *Autobiography* (John Adams, *op. cit.*, II, 516). (My italics.)

63. To Arthur Lee, March 21, 1777 (*Writings*, VII, 35).

64. John Adams, *op. cit.*, II, 516.

65. Our short discussion of the treaty is much indebted to the article by Felix Gilbert on "The 'New Diplomacy' of the Eighteenth Century" (*op. cit.*). Cf. also the discussion in Arthur Burr Darling, *Our Rising Empire, 1763–1803* (New Haven: Yale University Press, 1940), pp. 7–12; James Brown Scott's Introduction to Gilbert Chinard (ed.), *The Treaties of 1778 and Allied Documents* (Baltimore: Johns Hopkins Press, 1928); and Edmund C. Burnett, "Note on the American Negotiations for Commercial Treaties, 1776–1786," *American Historical Review*, XVI (1910/11), 579–87.

66. *Journals of the Continental Congress, 1774–1789*, V, 769. The first draft of the treaty is *ibid.*, pp. 576–87; the adopted form, *ibid.*, pp. 768–78; the instructions accompanying the treaty, *ibid.*, pp. 813–17.

67. Gilbert, "The 'New Diplomacy' . . . ," *op. cit.*, p. 26.

68. *Journals of the Continental Congress, 1774–1789*, V, 770.

69. *Ibid.*, p. 814.

70. *Ibid.*, p. 817.

71. Both issues, of course, have been recognized and dealt with. But either one has been dealt with at the expense of the other, or the difference between the two problems has not been pointed out. Gilbert, in his article on "The 'New Diplomacy' . . ." (*op. cit.*), deals exclusively with the issue of economics versus politics. Burnett discusses not at all the problem of "economic versus political connections" and does not see clearly the ambiguities of the word "alliance," but he has some interesting remarks and quotes on the militia diplomacy of going "a-begging and a-offering amongst the minor courts of Europe" (*The Continental Congress*, p. 211; cf. also *ibid.*, pp. 212 and 378). George C. Wood, "Congressional Control of Foreign Relations during the American Revolution, 1774–1789" (doctoral dissertation, New York University, 1919), has much on this second issue but nothing on the question of economic versus political connections. John C. Meng, in his Introduction to the *Despatches and Instructions of Conrad Alexandre Gérard, 1778–1780* (Baltimore: Johns Hopkins Press, 1939), deals with the problem of economic versus political connections, but he attributes to the early use of the term "alliance" a definitely political meaning (pp. 68 and 86). However, discussing the foreign policies of the congressional factions from 1778 to 1780, he implies that the radicals, who were from the beginning for unconditional independence and who gathered under the leadership of Richard Henry Lee from Virginia and Samuel Adams from Massachusetts (what came to be called the "Lee-Adams Junto"), never advocated a political connection with France: "It will be recalled that the desire of Congress in opening relations with France was to secure recognition and commercial assistance. Alliance did not enter into the proposals first advanced. . . . Although the alliance with France proved the salvation of the cause of independence that New England had been the first to espouse, the New Eng-

landers never wanted a political connection with France" (*ibid.,* pp. 92–93). This view is not correct. It describes John Adams' attitude, but it omits his testimony, given above on p. 118, that he differed in this respect from his own friends, Richard Henry Lee and Samuel Adams, and it omits the numerous passages where Richard Henry Lee urged a close political connection with France. For the early proalliance attitude of Lee and Samuel Adams (although there is only incomplete evidence for the latter), see Rippy and Debo, *op. cit.,* pp. 83–86.

72. Edmund C. Burnett, *The Continental Congress* (New York: Macmillan Co., 1941), p. 209.

73. See above, p. 124, and Wharton, *op. cit.,* II, 298: "I was overruled—perhaps for the best."

74. Burnett, *The Continental Congress,* p. 210.

75. This and the following quotations are from Gilbert, "The 'New Diplomacy' . . . ," *op. cit.,* p. 28.

76. *Ibid.,* n. 81.

77. Rippy and Debo, *op. cit.*

78. Cf. Beaumarchais's flattering utterances about this "masculine republican," in Stevens' *Facsimiles,* Vol. XIV, No. 1447 (Beaumarchais to Vergennes, March 8, 1777).

79. June 7, 1777, in Wharton, *op. cit.,* II, 333.

80. Cf. Gilbert, "The 'New Diplomacy' . . . ," *op. cit.,* pp. 10–11.

81. *Ibid.,* pp. 11–12.

82. Wharton, *op. cit.,* II, 332.

83. *Ibid.* (My italics.)

84. Gilbert, "The 'New Diplomacy' . . . ," *op. cit.,* p. 28, n. 81.

85. Wharton, *op. cit.,* II, 332.

86. *Ibid.*

87. *Journals of the Continental Congress, 1774–1789,* V, 815.

88. December 21, 1776, in Wharton, *op. cit.,* II, 235.

89. Franklin, Deane, and Lee to Vergennes, January 5, 1777, *ibid.,* p. 246. A somewhat blunter expression of this idea may be found in some of Deane's memoirs; e.g., his memoir for the French Foreign Ministry of September 24, 1776 (Stevens' *Facsimiles,* Vol. VI, No. 585).

90. Franklin, Deane, and Lee to Vergennes, February 1, 1777, in Wharton, *op. cit.,* II, 258. (My italics.)

91. To Jan Ingenhousz, April 26, 1777 (*Writings,* VII, 48).

92. To John Winthrop, May 1, 1777 (*Writings,* VII, 57; Wharton, *op. cit.,* II, 311). Cf. the almost identical wording in a joint letter of Franklin, Deane, and Lee to the Committee of Foreign Affairs of September 8, 1777, in Wharton, *op. cit.,* II, 389. See also the joint letter of Franklin and Deane to Congress, May 26, 1777, *ibid.,* p. 327.

93. Franklin, Deane, and Lee to Committee of Foreign Affairs, September 8, 1777, *ibid.,* p. 389. A comparison of this letter with Franklin's private letter to John Winthrop of May 1, 1777, and its style suggest strongly Franklin's pen.

94. Stevens' *Facsimiles,* Vol. III, No. 277.

95. Journal of Arthur Lee, November 27, 1777, in Richard Henry Lee, *Life of Arthur Lee* (Boston: Wells & Lilly, 1829), I, 354.

96. *Ibid.*

97. Comte de Lauraguais to Vergennes, September 20, 1777, in Stevens' *Facsimiles,* Vol. XVIII, No. 1691. (Stevens' translation.)

98. W. Carmichael to Mr. Tourville, November 1, 1777, *ibid.,* Vol. III, No. 288. Cf. Van Doren (ed.), *Benjamin Franklin's Autobiographical Writings,* p. 411 (to Bishop Shipley, September 13, 1775).

99. R. H. Lee, *op. cit.,* I, 354.

100. *Ibid.,* p. 353; cf. Wharton, *op. cit.,* II, 436. Cf. also one of the rare political interviews given by Franklin in France. The Duc de Croÿ records Franklin's friendly invitation: "Parlez, je répondrai!" and he adds "Et c'est ce qu'il ne faisait à personne." The duke mentioned that everybody would help the Americans secretly but nobody overtly. Franklin replied characteristically: "L'Europe fera comme cela et verra venir, c'est à nous de faire effort" (conversation of February 17, 1777, in *Journal inédit du Duc de Croÿ,* publié d'après le manuscrit autographe conservé à la Bibliothèque de l'Institut par le Vicomte de Grouchy et Paul Cottin [4 vols.; Paris, 1906–7], III, 301–2). It is indeed remarkable, and for our purposes regrettable, that the most frequently mentioned quality of Franklin during his stay in France is his taciturnity. One of the very few references to Franklin in the famous literary correspondence of Grimm and Diderot notes in July, 1778: "M. le docteur Franklin parle peu; et au commencement de son séjour à Paris, lorsque la France refusait encore de se déclarer ouvertement en faveur des colonies, il parlait encore moins" (Maurice Tourneaux [ed.], *Correspondance littéraire, philosophique et critique,* par Grimm, Diderot, Raynal, Meister, etc. [Paris: Garnier Frères, 1877–82], XII, 133). See also the numerous references to Franklin's taciturnity in many documents of Stevens' *Facsimiles,* e.g., Nos. 200, 277, 694, 702, 769, and 1763. Adams had this to say: "His rigorous taciturnity was very favourable to this singular felicity [of being considered a friend to all men and an enemy to none]. He conversed only with individuals, and freely only with confidential friends. In company he was totally silent" (John Adams, *op. cit.,* I, 661).

101. Stevens' *Facsimiles,* Vol. III, No. 288.

102. Vergennes, paper submitted to the king, January 7, 1778, *ibid.,* Vol. XXI, No. 1824. (Translation.)

103. Vergennes to Ossun, January 7, 1777, in Doniol, *op. cit.,* II, 114–15. (My translation.)

104. A great deal has been written about French motives for the help for and eventual alliance with the Americans. Basically, five different theories have been upheld: First, that France wanted to recover the territorial losses of the Seven Years' War, that is, Canada from the British and Louisiana from Spain. Second, that her intervention could be explained by her concern for the security of her West Indian possessions, by fear of a combined Anglo-American assault on the isles which would be conceivable in the case of either an American or an English victory. Third, that the passion of the French Enlightenment for the cause of liberty and progress was the basic motive of French participation in this struggle for the "cause of all mankind." Fourth, that France wanted to get hold of the commercial privileges and monopolies formerly held by Great Britain. Fifth, that the objective of French policy appeared to be something less tangible than either territorial or commercial gain: prestige and a change in the balance of power. An excellent brief summary of those theories is to be found in Darling, *op. cit.,*

pp. 22–26. A critical discussion of the first theory is given by Corwin, *op. cit.,* pp. 9–11. The second theory is advanced in Claude H. Van Tyne, "Influences Which Determined the French Government To Make the Treaty with America, 1778," *American Historical Review,* XXI (1915–16), 528–41. Cf. the critical discussion of it in Corwin, *op. cit.,* pp. 3–9, 146–48. The third point of view, which might be called the "theory of moral affinity," has found its best-known advocate in Bancroft, who said that "many causes combined to procure the alliance of France and the American Republic; but the force which brought all influences harmoniously together, . . . was the movement of intellectual freedom" (George Bancroft, *History of the United States of America* [author's last revision; New York: D. Appleton & Co., 1884], V, 256). A more recent and even more extreme interpretation of this kind has been presented by the French scholar and Franklin specialist, Bernard Faÿ, in his *The Revolutionary Spirit in France and America* (New York: Harcourt, Brace & Co., 1927), esp. pp. 50, 101 ff., and 253. This approach does not take into account, however, the opposition of such famous personalities of the French Enlightenment as D'Alembert, Turgot, and Mably against French entanglements in the British-American quarrel. For a critical discussion of this approach of "moral affinity" see particularly Louis Gottschalk, *The Place of the American Revolution in the Causal Pattern of the French Revolution* (Easton, Pa.: American Friends of Lafayette, 1948), pp. 1–5. The fourth approach has been dismissed by Vergennes himself (see below, p. 138). The most cogent exposition of the fifth theory is Corwin's work on *French Policy and the American Alliance of 1778,* to which this study is much indebted.

105. "Exposé succinct sur la situation politique de la France rélativement à différentes puissances" (Doniol, *op. cit.,* I, 20). (My translation.)

106. June 21, 1779, to Baron de Breteuil, French ambassador in Vienna, quoted by Paul del Perugia, "Le Comte de Vergennes au Ministère," *Revue d'histoire diplomatique,* LVI (1942), 94. (My translation.) Cf. the almost identical mémoire to the king of April 12, 1777, in Doniol, *op. cit.,* II, 430.

107. "Reflexions" (end of 1775) (Doniol, *op. cit.,* I, 244). (My translation.)

108. *Ibid.,* p. 243.

109. Vergennes to the French ambassador in Madrid, Montmorin, June 20, 1778, *ibid.,* III, 140. (This translation is by Corwin, *op. cit.,* p. 14.)

110. Vergennes to Montmorin, December 13, 1777, in Stevens' *Facsimiles,* Vol. XX, No. 1775.

111. Gérard's narrative of a conference with the American commissioners, *ibid.,* Vol. XXI, No. 1831. (Stevens' translation.) A good chronological account of the genesis of the Franco-American negotiations and the decisions of the French court from the arrival of the news of Saratoga on December 4 to the conclusion of the alliance is to be found in the Introduction by John C. Meng to his edition of the *Despatches and Instructions of Conrad Alexandre Gérard, 1778–1780,* pp. 76–90. Another interesting account of these proceedings is given in chap. viii of Weldon A. Brown, *Empire or Independence: A Study in the Failure of Reconciliation, 1774–1783* (Baton Rouge: Louisiana State University Press, 1941), pp. 169–204. However, there is no awareness of the ambiguity of the term "alliance" (cf. *ibid.,* p. 193).

112. Stevens' *Facsimiles,* Vol. XXI, No. 1831. (Underlined by Gérard.)

113. *Ibid.*

114. *Ibid.*

115. *Ibid.*
116. *Ibid.*
117. Chinard (ed.), *The Treaties of 1778*, p. 52.
118. *Journals of the Continental Congress, 1774–1789*, V, 770.
119. Chinard (ed.), *The Treaties of 1778*, p. 53.
120. *Ibid.*, p. 54.
121. "Personal Pledge of Commissioners," Paris, February 2, 1777, in Wharton, *op. cit.*, II, 260.
122. Committee of Secret Correspondence to the Commissioners at Paris, Baltimore, December 30, 1776, *ibid.*, p. 240.
123. Franklin to D'Aranda, Spanish ambassador in Paris, April 7, 1777, *ibid.*, p. 304.
124. Corwin, *op. cit.*, pp. 96–97.
125. Deane to Vergennes, March 18, 1777, in *The Deane Papers* ("Collections of the New York Historical Society," Vols. XIX–XXIII [5 vols.; New York, 1886–90]), II, 25–26; Doniol, *op. cit.*, II, 321–22.
126. Stevens' *Facsimiles*, Vol. XXI, No. 1831. Strangely enough, Trudel in his book on *Canada, the American Congress, and France* does not mention this highly interesting remark. Nor do other writers on the French alliance sufficiently stress Franklin's particular reasons for the alliance.
127. Chinard (ed.), *The Treaties of 1778*, p. 55.
128. Garnier to Vergennes, August 16, 1776, in Stevens' *Facsimiles*, Vol. IX, No. 891.
129. Instead of reciprocity, as provided in the American "Plan of Treaties," or unconditional most-favored-nation treatment, as provided for in the instructions of Congress for the commissioners, the conditional most-favored-nation clause was, apparently upon French suggestion, inserted into the treaty. Cf. Vernon G. Setser, "Did Americans Originate the Conditional Most-Favored-Nation Clause?" *Journal of Modern History*, V (1933), 319–23.
130. Translated text in Wharton, *op. cit.*, II, 526. The French original of the instructions is printed by Doniol, *op. cit.*, III, 153–57, and Meng, *op. cit.*, pp. 125–30.
131. Wharton, *op. cit.*, II, 525.

NOTES TO CHAPTER V

1. Francis Wharton, *The Revolutionary Diplomatic Correspondence of the United States* (6 vols.; Washington: Government Printing Office, 1889), II, 490–91. See also Franklin to Th. Cushing, February 27, 1778, in Benjamin Franklin, *The Writings of Benjamin Franklin*, ed. Albert Henry Smyth (10 vols.; New York: Macmillan Co., 1905–7), VII, 110–11. (Hereafter cited as "*Writings*.")
2. An interesting and less-well-known discussion of the moral issues of the Franco-American alliance is to be found in *The United States and France: Some Opinions on International Gratitude*, selected, with Foreword, by James Brown Scott (New York: Oxford University Press, 1926).
3. John Adams, *Works*, ed. C. F. Adams (10 vols.; Boston: Little, Brown & Co., 1850–56), II, 516.
4. "J'espere que l'alliance entre la France et mon pays sera éternelle et qu'elle augmentera le commerce et la prospérité de votre ville." Unpublished letter to Messrs. Sube & Laporte, January 12, 1779, American Philosophical Society, Philadelphia. Cf. I. Minis Hays (ed.), *Calendar of the Papers of Benjamin Franklin in*

the Library of the American Philosophical Society (Philadelphia: American Philosophical Society, 1908), III, 517.

5. B. F. Stevens (comp.), *Facsimiles of Manuscripts from European Archives Relating to America, 1773–1783* (24 vols.; London, 1889–95) (hereafter cited as "Stevens' *Facsimiles*"), Vol. V, No. 489 (report of Paul Wentworth).

6. February 12, 1778, in Wharton, *op. cit.*, II, 493.

7. To William Pulteney, March 30, 1778, *ibid.*, p. 527. See also two letters to Hartley, repudiating new peace feelers: January 25, 1779, *ibid.*, III, 31, and May 4, 1779, *ibid.*, pp. 155–56. On April 10, 1779, Hartley replied somewhat bitterly to Franklin's protestations of French magnanimity in the letter of January 25: "All that I will say is this Motives make Magnanimity . . ." (Hartley Papers in the Franklin Collection of the Library of Congress).

8. *Writings*, VIII, 497–98.

9. *Writings*, VIII, 498.

10. *Writings*, VIII, 498–99.

11. *Writings*, VIII, 499.

12. The variety of appointments, replacements, and recalls is rather confusing, and we shall give here some data without which the following can hardly be understood. On March 2, 1776, the Congressional Committee of Secret Correspondence appointed Silas Deane, recently a delegate to Congress from Connecticut, as agent to France with the commission to sound out the French court as to the possibilities of a treaty or an alliance with the United Colonies. Deane also had a commission from the "Secret Committee," later the Committee of Commerce, in order to secure supplies. On September 26, 1776, Congress, having adopted the draft of the Treaty of Amity and Commerce to be proposed to France, appointed Silas Deane, Benjamin Franklin, and Thomas Jefferson as commissioners to the court of France to propose and negotiate this treaty. Jefferson presently declined, whereupon Congress on October 22, 1776, appointed Arthur Lee in his place. On November 21, 1777, Congress recalled Silas Deane, who was held responsible for the inundation of America with French officers and whom Arthur Lee accused of fraud and neglect of his duties in connection with the procurement of supplies from France. In his stead Congress appointed John Adams as commissioner on November 28, 1777. Adams arrived in Paris only after the conclusion of the treaties of commerce and alliance. The dissensions among the three commissioners were such that all of them implored Congress to revoke the joint commission and to appoint a single minister plenipotentiary in Paris.

On September 14, 1778, Congress revoked the joint commission and elected Franklin sole minister plenipotentiary to France. The only state voting against him was Pennsylvania, and "its opposition was due not only to his conservative enemies" but also to others who disliked his having his grandson, William Temple Franklin, as his secretary, since the latter was the son of a notorious Loyalist, Sir William Franklin, royal governor of New Jersey (Carl Van Doren, *Benjamin Franklin* [New York: Viking Press, 1938], p. 608). This congressional move left John Adams without employment in Europe, and he soon returned to the United States. Arthur Lee retained his position as commissioner to Spain to which Congress had appointed him on May 1, 1777, in the place of Franklin, who had held this position from January 1, 1777. However, owing to the unwillingness of Spain to recognize or to negotiate with the United States, neither Franklin nor

Lee ever went to Madrid; Lee was sent back at the border. Franklin's Spanish commission was more or less limited to presenting to the Spanish ambassador in Paris, Aranda, the proposals of Congress for a military alliance in April, 1777.

In 1779 Congress also faced the need of appointing ministers plenipotentiary to negotiate a peace and to treat with Spain. The appointments became the object of party strife. The representatives of "southern planters, northern town workers, and the yeomanry of both sections" (John C. Miller, *Triumph of Freedom* [Boston: Little, Brown & Co., 1948], p. 372) were the Lee-Adams Junto, called after their leading spirits, Richard Henry Lee of Virginia (a brother of Arthur Lee) and Samuel Adams. John C. Meng (*Despatches and Instructions of Conrad Alexandre Gérard, 1778-1780* [Baltimore: Johns Hopkins Press, 1939], p. 101) says: "The Adams-Lee faction, in control of domestic affairs during the early years of the Revolution, had not at first been able to extend that control abroad. The achievements of Deane in France, the respect shown Franklin by the government of Louis XVI, and the utter disregard France manifested toward Arthur Lee had contributed to solidify their resentment against Gérard, Deane, and Franklin. The appointment of John Adams to take Deane's place in Paris had helped to redress the balance of control in their favor. Now they were determined that the negotiation of peace or war, as circumstances might dictate, should be entrusted to men of their choice."

The violent accusations of Arthur Lee and Izard against Franklin, of which more will be said presently, caused a debate in Congress on the recall of Franklin (at that time sole minister plenipotentiary to France) in April, 1779, but on April 22, 1779, the recall was voted down, only Virginia and North Carolina being for it (*Journals of the Continental Congress, 1774-1789* [34 vols.; Library of Congress ed.; Washington: Government Printing Office, 1904-37], XIII, 500).

Arthur Lee, who still held a commission for Spain, was, owing to his suspicious and violently anti-French attitude, objected to by France, and Congress was notified of this opinion (Meng, *op. cit.,* pp. 116-17). On September 24, 1779, it was proposed that John Adams and Franklin be appointed joint commissioners for peace. However, "the following day this suggestion was rejected, when it was decided that a single commissioner would be preferable, in keeping with the principle that Franklin's functions as minister to France should not in any way be intertwined with those of plenipotentiary for peace" (*ibid.,* p. 117). Now John Adams and John Jay, the latter a representative of the other party, the East Coast business interests, were nominated. A deadlock ensued; the foes of Arthur Lee saw their chance and argued that the new functions of minister to Spain did not coincide with those ascribed to Lee and that a new minister ought to be elected, knowing that Lee would not be elected because of French objections. Consequently, on September 27, 1779, John Jay was elected minister to Spain, and John Adams minister to negotiate the peace. Lee was left out and returned to the United States, whereas John Adams for the second time set out for Paris. In this election only John Dickinson, voting for Delaware, cast his vote "either pertinaciously or inadvertently" for Franklin, who had not been nominated (notes of Henry Laurens, in E. C. Burnett [ed.], *Letters of the Members of the Continental Congress* [8 vols.; Washington: Carnegie Institution of Washington, 1921-36], IV, 438).

On the final election of Franklin to the peace negotiations in 1781 see below, pp. 166-69.

13. Burnett (ed.), *op. cit.*, IV, 412, n. 4 to piece 512. Cited from an article by "Q" in the *Connecticut Courant* of September 21, 1779.

14. Samuel Adams to James Warren, March 24, 1779, in Burnett (ed.), *op. cit.*, IV, 207, n. 2 to piece 265.

15. Ralph Izard to Richard Henry Lee, October 15, 1780, *ibid.*, V, 362, n. 5 to piece 420.

16. Burton J. Hendrick, *The Lees of Virginia* (Boston: Little, Brown & Co., 1935), deals in his chap. xi, "The Franklin-Lee Feud" (pp. 262–95), with the London origins of their antagonism.

17. Franklin to the president of Congress, March 31, 1778, in Wharton, *op. cit.*, II, 528. On the complicated story of French secret aid through the fictitious firm of Hortalez & Co. see Samuel Flagg Bemis, *The Diplomacy of the American Revolution* (New York and London: D. Appleton–Century Co., 1935), pp. 35–40, with further references.

18. On the details of the molasses article and its equivalent see Wharton, *op. cit.*, I, 344–46, and Meng, *op. cit.*, p. 83. Meng (p. 310) prints a report of Gérard to Vergennes, September 24, 1778, on the complaints about these two articles which says that "M. Francklin n'est pas épargné dans ces imputations." On the correspondence between Franklin and Izard about this article see Wharton, *op. cit.*, II, 477 ff.; also Izard to Congress, *ibid.*, pp. 498 and 629.

19. Cf. in particular the Franklin biographies by Carl Van Doren (*Benjamin Franklin*); B. Faÿ (*Franklin, the Apostle of Modern Times* [Boston: Little, Brown & Co., 1929]); and E. E. Hale and E. E. Hale, Jr., *Franklin in France* (2 vols.; Boston: Roberts Bros., 1887–88). See also B. Faÿ, *The Revolutionary Spirit in France and America,* trans. Ramon Guthrie (New York: Harcourt, Brace & Co., 1927). Faÿ's exaggerated stress of this point is criticized in Elizabeth S. Kite, "Benjamin Franklin—Diplomat," *Catholic World,* CXLII (1935–36), 28–37.

20. *Writings,* I, 334.

21. Cf. James Parton, *Life and Times of Benjamin Franklin* (New York: Mason Bros., 1864), II, 373–74.

22. The charges of Arthur Lee and Izard against Franklin were discussed in Congress on March 24, 1779 (*Journals of the Continental Congress, 1774–1789,* XIII, 367). Based on a letter from Arthur Lee to the Committee for Foreign Affairs, June 1, 1778, Franklin was charged with withholding information from Lee, his joint commissioner; with showing partiality to his nephew, J. Williams, commercial agent in Nantes, and his friend, M. Chaumont; with having concurred with Deane in "systems of profusion, disorder and dissipation in the conduct of public affairs"; finally, in consequence of a letter of Izard's to President Laurens, he was charged with being "not a proper person to be trusted with the management of the affairs of America, that he is haughty and self-sufficient, and not guided by principles of virtue and honor." Congress dismissed the charges. Lee's incriminating letter is to be found in Wharton, *op. cit.*, II, 600–603; Izard's, *ibid.*, pp. 629–32.

Arthur Lee renewed his charges against Franklin in a letter of December 7, 1780 (*ibid.*, IV, 182–86), stating that Franklin was "more devoted to pleasure than would become even a young man in his station, and neglectful of the public business." Lee accused Franklin of treasonable intercourse with British spies and of preventing French loans or subsidies from being remitted to the United States in order to lead them into his own channels and thus to make immense fortunes. A summary of the consequences of Lee's charges is to be found in an extensive footnote (*ibid.,* IV, 186-88). Lee's letter was read in Congress and contributed to the mission of Colonel Laurens to Paris to take over Franklin's business of procuring a loan from France (see below, p. 299, n. 75 to chap. v). On the battle waged in Congress late in 1780 over the recall of Franklin see chap. v of Irving Brant, *James Madison: The Nationalist, 1780–1787* (Indianapolis: Bobbs-Merrill Co., 1948), pp. 58–69. An account of the Franklin-Lee quarrel critical of Franklin is to be found in Thomas P. Abernethy, "The Origin of the Franklin-Lee Imbroglio," *North Carolina Historical Review,* XV (1938), 41–52. Washington's concern for posthumous attacks on Franklin, probably by Izard, is described in Frederick R. Kirkland, "Jefferson and Franklin," *Pennsylvania Magazine of History and Biography,* LXXI (1947), 218–22.

23. Vergennes to La Luzerne, February 19, 1781, in Henri Doniol, *Histoire de la participation de la France à l'établissement des États-Unis d'Amérique* (5 vols.; Paris: Imprimerie Nationale, 1886–92), IV, 583. (My translation.)

24. Gérard to Vergennes, March 8, 1779, in Meng, *op. cit.,* p. 565. (My translation.)

25. Gérard to Vergennes, July 18, 1779, *ibid.,* p. 794. (My translation.)

26. La Luzerne to Vergennes, December 15, 1780, in Doniol, *op. cit.,* IV, 391. Cf. also Barbé-Marbois to Vergennes, September 19, 1780, *ibid.,* p. 430. See also James Lovell to Samuel Adams, July 10, 1779, in Burnett (ed.), *op. cit.,* IV, 309.

27. The offer of resignation is in his letter to Samuel Huntington, president of Congress, March 12, 1781 (*Writings,* VIII, 220–21). Franklin indicated exclusively reasons of age and health. In a letter to John Jay, April 12, 1781 (*Writings,* VIII, 239), Franklin said that he wanted Jay as his successor. The nature of Franklin's gratification about the refusal of Congress to accept his resignation appears from a letter to William Carmichael, August 24, 1781 (*Writings,* VIII, 294): "I fancy it may have been a double Mortification to those Enemies you have mentioned to me, that I should ask as a Favour what they hop'd to vex me by taking from me; and that I should nevertheless be continued." Cf. a speech of John Witherspoon in Congress (June 11[?], 1781), in Burnett (ed.), *op. cit.,* VI, 117–18, and James Lovell to Mrs. Abigail Adams, August 10, 1781, *ibid.,* p. 174.

28. Cf. John Adams' *Diary,* February 9, 1779 (*op. cit.,* III, 189). A few weeks later, on March 18, 1779, Turgot noted: "Adams est parti ulcéré et jaloux à l'excès de Franklin" (*Œuvres de Turgot,* ed. Gustave Schelle [5 vols.; Paris: Felix Alcan, 1913–23], V, 588). By 1782 Adams had to come to find a kind of grim satisfaction in Franklin's unconquerable popularity: "Luckily, Mr. Deane out of the question, every American minister in Europe, except Dr. Franklin, has discovered a judgement, a conscience, and a resolution of his own, and, of consequence, every minister that has ever come, has been frowned upon. On the contrary, Dr. Franklin, who has been pliant and submissive in every thing, has been constantly cried up to the stars, without doing any thing to deserve it" (to Jonathan Jackson, November 17, 1782 [*Works,* IX, 516]).

29. To Richard Bache, June 2, 1779 (*Writings,* VII, 344). Cf. also a letter to a friend in America, October 25, 1779 (*Writings,* VII, 406).

30. *Writings,* VII, 345.

31. John Adams to Samuel Adams, July 28, 1778, in Wharton, *op. cit.,* II, 667.

32. *Ibid.,* pp. 667–68.

33. *Ibid.,* p. 668.

34. Canada pamphlet (*Writings,* IV, 51).

35. Franklin, Deane, and Lee to the Committee for Foreign Affairs, February 28, 1778, in Wharton, *op. cit.,* II, 508. Franklin, as well as Adams, was at that time still too optimistic with regard to Spanish and Dutch policies.

36. To Samuel Cooper, October 27, 1779 (*Writings,* VII, 408–9).

37. This idea of Franco-Swiss fidelity was apparently first suggested to the Americans by Gérard. Cf. the letter of Franklin, Deane, and Lee to the Committee for Foreign Affairs, December 18, 1777, in Wharton, *op. cit.,* II, 453. Franklin stressed this parallel repeatedly: *Writings,* VII, 102–3 (to Hartley, February 12, 1778); VII, 167 (to Weissenstein, July 1, 1778); VIII, 577 (to Livingston, August 12, 1782). Cf. also John Adams, *op. cit.,* IX, 516.

38. February 27, 1778 (*Writings,* VII, 110).

39. Joint commissioners to Committee for Foreign Affairs, February 28, 1778, *ibid.,* p. 508.

40. Franklin to Vergennes, July 10, 1780, *ibid.,* III, 844.

41. Adams to Gerry, December 5, 1778, *ibid.,* II, 849.

42. Adams to Roger Sherman, December 6, 1778, *ibid.,* p. 852.

43. *Ibid.*

44. Adams to the president of Congress, April 18, 1780, *ibid.,* III, 623.

45. Franklin to the president of Congress, August 9, 1780, *ibid.,* IV, 23.

46. *Ibid.*

47. *Ibid.* "An old Rascal!" was James Lovell's exclamation when he read Franklin's letter and particularly Franklin's intention to "please" the French court. See Timothy Pickering to Rufus King, November 19, 1808, in Charles R. King (ed.), *The Life and Correspondence of Rufus King* (6 vols.; New York: G. P. Putnam's Sons, 1898), V, 108.

48. Wharton, *op. cit.,* IV, 23.

49. Franklin to Livingston, March 4, 1782, *ibid.,* V, 215.

50. Adams to Carmichael, April 8, 1780, *ibid.,* III, 603.

51. Adams to McKean, September 20, 1779, *ibid.,* p. 332.

52. Franklin to Lovell, July 22, 1778, *ibid.,* II, 659. See also an unpublished letter of Franklin to Robert Morris, December 21, 1777, in the Mason-Franklin Collection of the Yale University Library.

53. Reprinted in John Adams, *op. cit.,* I, 649–84.

54. Wharton, *op. cit.,* IV, 23.

55. See above, p. 147.

56. John Adams, *op. cit.,* I, 656.

57. Wharton, *op. cit.,* II, 298. See above, p. 124.

58. See above, p. 126.

59. April 7, 1781, in Wharton, *op. cit.,* IV, 354. See also Franklin to Dumas, September 22, 1778 (after the French alliance!) (*Writings,* VII, 190–91).

60. *Ibid.,* VIII, 501. This attitude is also attested by William Lee, who records Franklin as saying that "it was a matter to be considered whether it was worth our while to ask any of the Courts of Europe to acknowledge our Independence" (note of a conference with Franklin, March 15, 1779; cf. W. Ch. Ford [ed.], *Letters of William Lee* [3 vols.; Brooklyn, N.Y.: Historical Printing Club, 1891], II, 537).

61. October 2, 1780, in Wharton, *op. cit.,* IV, 74.

62. October 14, 1780, *ibid.,* p. 96.

63. November 5, 1781, *ibid.,* p. 829. It is well known that the financial strains which this war brought upon France contributed to the downfall of the French monarchy. Perhaps Franklin was not quite unaware that, as once has been said, he "was bleeding France to death." Franklin, after all, in these years was on cordial terms with Turgot, who had spoken against French participation in the American war because of France's desperate financial situation. Turgot's predictions were in the long run to prove more nearly correct than the arguments of the power politician Vergennes. In the *Works* of Turgot there are many references to meetings with Franklin, unfortunately without any details. See the Index of *Œuvres de Turgot,* ed. Schelle, Vol. V.

64. Franklin to the president of Congress, November 5, 1781, in Wharton, *op. cit.,* IV, 828. Cf. also Franklin to Samuel Cooper, March 16, 1780, *ibid.,* III, 552.

65. November 5, 1781, *ibid.,* IV, 829.

66. To Robert Morris, December 23, 1782, *ibid.,* VI, 160.

67. Cf. also Franklin to Morris, January 9, 1782, *ibid.,* V, 96.

68. Franklin to the president of Congress, July 11, 1781, *ibid.,* IV, 559.

69. The financial crisis in America in 1780, which had contributed to the quarrel between Adams and Vergennes, occasioned Washington's letter to Franklin that America had only the alternatives of money from France or peace with England. Even before John Laurens arrived in France, Vergennes had given way to the urgent warnings of Franklin and granted six million livres as a free gift (see below, p. 164). A convenient summary of French and Spanish financial aid to the United States appears in Bemis, *op. cit.,* p. 93.

70. These ideas were nourished by the reports of Gérard, the French minister in Philadelphia, who suspected that the faction led by Richard Henry Lee and Samuel Adams, grown cool toward France partly under the influence of Arthur Lee's and John Adams' suspicions, was pro-English (Meng, *op. cit.,* pp. 94–95).

71. Soon after the French alliance, Arthur Lee wrote to the Committee of Foreign Affairs that "the balance of European power" must in a few years be in the hands of the United States (April 2, 1778, in Wharton, *op. cit.,* II, 536).

72. January 15, 1782, *ibid.,* V, 112 and 113.

73. Franklin to Vergennes, December 17, 1782, in Wharton, *op. cit.,* VI, 144.

74. Franklin to Vergennes, February 13, 1781, *ibid.,* IV, 255.

75. Congress, through Franklin and through its special envoy, John Laurens, had asked for a loan of twenty-five million livres. The king granted a gift of six millions, to be spent in France under the direction of Franklin, and later "consented to underwrite a loan of ten millions, to be obtained in Holland" (Edward S. Corwin, *French Policy and the American Alliance of 1778* [Princeton: Princeton University Press, 1916], p. 292). The king granted the six millions before Laurens' arrival, which heightened the prestige of Franklin. Corwin says (*ibid.,* n. 12) that Laurens "should be credited with the king's endorsement of the Dutch loan."

76. "Faut-il que des raisons d'État m'obligent à signer ce que je ne pense pas?" Louis XVI is said to have observed. Quoted by Gilbert de Chambrun, *À l'école d'un diplomate, Vergennes* (Paris: Plon, 1944), p. 306. This book, the only full-length monograph of the whole of Vergennes's life, is not satisfactory.

77. Memoir for the Spanish court, July 23, 1777, quoted by Doniol, *op. cit.*, II, 458. (My translation.)

78. Henry Laurens to George Washington, July 31, 1778, in Burnett (ed.), *op. cit.*, III, 356.

79. Vergennes's instructions of March 9 with their bitter complaints of Adams are the immediate background of the famous American instructions of June 15, 1781. They are to be found in Doniol, *op. cit.*, IV, 551–56.

80. Conference of La Luzerne with a committee of Congress on May 28, 1781, in *Journals of the Continental Congress, 1774–1789*, XX, 563.

81. *Ibid.*, pp. 651–52.

82. This is reported in Madison's detailed notes of the debate of Congress on December 30, 1782 (*ibid.*, XXIII, 873). On the arguments against Franklin see also La Luzerne's report to Vergennes, June 14, 1781 (Doniol, *op. cit.*, IV, 622–23).

83. This was the opinion of Thomas Rodney in his letter to Caesar Rodney, June 14, 1781, in Burnett (ed.), *op. cit.*, VI, 120. Thomas Rodney ascribes the election of Franklin chiefly to himself.

The most recent and thorough study of the pro-French instructions of Congress of June 15, 1781, and of the nomination of Franklin and the four other ministers is to be found in chap. v of William Emmet O'Donnell, *The Chevalier de la Luzerne* (Louvain: Bibliothèque de l'Université; Bruges: Desclée de Brouwer, 1938), pp. 117–45. O'Donnell thinks that Rodney's "boastful attitude in his letters, and especially in his diary, gives his statements about himself less importance than they would claim at first sight" (*ibid.*, p. 137, n. 77).

84. December 4, 1780, in Wharton, *op. cit.*, IV, 181. Cf. also Vergennes to La Luzerne, February 14, 1781, *ibid.*, p. 256.

85. O'Donnell, *op. cit.*, pp. 135–36. Sullivan's efforts to get Franklin elected are described in a dispatch of La Luzerne to Vergennes, June 14, 1781, printed in Doniol, *op. cit.*, IV, 621–22. The *Journals of the Continental Congress, 1774–1789* (XX, 628) show Varnum of Rhode Island as nominating Franklin. O'Donnell thinks that "Varnum may have been urged to act by Sullivan or La Luzerne," for in La Luzerne's list of the members of Congress Varnum is described as a friend of Sullivan's and openly attacking Samuel Adams (see O'Donnell, *op. cit.*, p. 136, n. 74).

86. John Witherspoon, according to the notes on the debate of Congress on August 8, 1782, by Charles Thomson, quoted by Corwin, *op. cit.*, p. 302 n.

87. *Diary*, February 18, 1783 (*op. cit.*, III, 359).

88. To the president of Congress, September 20, 1781, in Wharton, *op. cit.*, IV, 717.

89. Franklin to the president of Congress, September 13, 1781, *ibid.*, p. 709. For Arthur Lee's insulting comment on this letter see his letter to James Warren (*ca.* July 23, 1782), in Burnett (ed.), *op. cit.*, VI, 389.

90. Doniol, *op. cit.*, III, 246–47. An important and not yet sufficiently known example of Franklin's close collaboration with the French Foreign Office is the role he played in furnishing material for the anti-British periodical *Affaires de l'Angleterre et de l'Amérique*. See the preliminary report by Gilbert Chinard, "Adventures in a Library," *Newberry Library Bulletin*, Second Series, No. 8 (March, 1952), pp. 225–36.

91. Franklin to Rayneval, March 22, 1782, in Wharton, *op. cit.*, V, 273–74.

92. The indispensable study for this is Bemis' *Diplomacy of the American Revolution.* Corwin's *French Policy and the American Alliance of 1778* is also very helpful. The best studies of Franklin's role in the peace negotiations are to be found in the two chapters on the peace negotiations in Arthur Darling, *Our Rising Empire, 1763–1803* (New Haven: Yale University Press, 1940), pp. 45–98, and in chap. vi of the first volume of Vincent T. Harlow's *The Founding of the Second British Empire, 1763–1793* (London, New York, and Toronto: Longmans, Green & Co., 1952), pp. 223–311.

93. Lord Edmond Fitzmaurice, *Life of Shelburne* (3 vols.; London: Macmillan & Co., 1875–76), III, 248. Cf. Darling, *op. cit.,* pp. 61–62, and Harlow, *op. cit.,* pp. 229–34.

94. "Réflexions," end of 1775, in Doniol, *op. cit.,* I, 245.

95. See above, p. 145.

96. *Journal of the Negotiations for Peace* (*Writings,* VIII, 463).

97. *Writings,* VIII, 497–99. See above, pp. 149–50.

98. *Writings,* VIII, 518.

99. *Writings,* VIII, 518–19.

100. *Writings,* VIII, 513.

101. *Writings,* VIII, 538–39.

102. June 28, 1782 (*Writings,* VIII, 557).

103. June 28, 1782 (*Writings,* VIII, 558).

104. To Jane Mecom, April 19, 1757 (*Writings,* III, 392). Cf. the remarkable significance Franklin attached to this idea in the *Autobiography* (*Writings,* I, 307–8 and 337).

105. *Writings,* VIII, 559. As a similar gesture of confidence for the French, Franklin conveyed to Vergennes confidential communications of Shelburne, intended to reassure Franklin's misgivings about Shelburne's sincerity about American independence, as late as July 24. This move, as V. T. Harlow says, "does him little credit." For this episode see Harlow, *op. cit.,* pp. 271–72 and 277, n. 106.

106. See above, chap. iv, p. 123.

107. *Journal of the Negotiations for Peace* (*Writings,* VIII, 491). Cf. also Darling's comment, *op. cit.,* pp. 52–53.

108. See the next chapter, p. 208.

109. Oswald to Shelburne, May 18, 1782 (F.O. 95/511 [Public Record Office, London]; transcript in the William L. Clements Library, Ann Arbor, Michigan), based on Grenville's oral account to Oswald on May 12 which contributed to their decision to send Oswald for consultation to London. See Harlow, *op. cit.,* p. 253.

110. See above, p. 150. See Franklin's *Journal* (*Writings,* VIII, 498–99). Strangely, Grenville, in a letter to Charles Fox on the same May 14, reported that Franklin this morning "went so far as to say, that when we had allowed the independence of America, the treaty she had made with France for gaining it, ended; and none remained but that of commerce, which we, too, might make, if we pleased" (printed in Lord John Russell [ed.], *Memorials and Correspondence of Charles James Fox* [4 vols.; London: Richard Bentley, 1857], IV, 190).

111. Harlow, *op. cit.,* p. 255.

112. These are known only from Oswald's report to Shelburne of July 10, 1782, printed in Russell (ed.), *op. cit.,* IV, 239–41.

113. See above, pp. 167–68.

114. Jay's report to Livingston, November 17, 1782, in Wharton, *op. cit.,* VI, 48.

115. *Ibid.*, V, 613. For the text of the commission and a detailed discussion see Bemis, *op. cit.*, p. 209.

116. Bemis, *op. cit.*, pp. 218 ff.

117. Jay's report to Livingston, in Wharton, *op. cit.*, VI, 30.

118. *Ibid.*, p. 15.

119. *Ibid.*, p. 14. See below, p. 219.

120. Wharton, *op. cit.*, VI, 15.

121. *Ibid.*

122. Franklin to Cooper, December 26, 1782, *ibid.*, p. 169.

123. Adams, Franklin, Jay, and Laurens to Livingston, December 14, 1782, *ibid.*, p. 133.

124. Jay's report, *ibid.*, p. 23.

125. *Ibid.*

126. *Writings,* VIII, 435.

127. August 12, 1782 (*Writings,* VIII, 580).

128. Jay's report, in Wharton, *op. cit.*, VI, 32.

129. John Adams, *op. cit.*, III, 336.

130. The traditional opinion was expressed as early as March, 1783, by James Madison, who wrote that "in this business" Jay took the lead, Adams followed with cordiality, and "Franklin has been dragged into it" (Burnett [ed.], *op. cit.*, VII, 90 [to E. Randolph]).

131. Franklin to Vergennes, December 17, 1782, in Wharton, *op. cit.*, VI, 144.

132. *Ibid.*

133. Corwin, *op. cit.*, p. 357.

134. *Ibid.*, p. 358.

135. The cabinet of Versailles to Otto, French chargé d'affaires in Philadelphia, August 30, 1787, quoted *ibid.*

136. Franklin to Cooper, December 26, 1782, in Wharton, *op. cit.*, VI, 169.

137. Doniol, *op. cit.*, V, 199.

138. To Livingston, December 5, 1782, in Wharton, *op. cit.*, VI, 111.

139. To Livingston, April 15, 1783, *ibid.*, p. 380. Cf. also Franklin to Morris, March 7, 1783, *ibid.*, p. 277.

140. Franklin to Morris, December 25, 1783, *ibid.*, p. 744.

141. Franklin to Livingston, July 22, 1783, *ibid.*, p. 581.

142. An excerpt of Cooper's letter is quoted in a letter of Franklin to Jay of September 10, 1783 (*ibid.*, p. 686). Franklin sent a copy of Cooper's letter to Vergennes (*ibid.*, footnote).

143. *Ibid.* Franklin sent copies of his correspondence with Jay and Adams on this matter to Congress (*ibid.*, footnote).

144. Adams' letter is given *ibid.*, VI, 696–97 (September 13, 1783); Jay's, *ibid.*, VI, 692–93 (September 11, 1783).

145. See above, p. 171.

146. Jay to Livingston, November 17, 1782, in Wharton, *op. cit.*, VI, 20.

147. Quoted by Bemis (*op. cit.*, pp. 225–26), who says: "This curious language, still dragging in the word *Colonies,* was by no means a clear-cut recognition of American independence. It is doubtful whether even Oswald's new commission to treat with the Commissioners of the United States of America constituted such a recognition beyond recall. Though Europe generally took it as a recognition, the British Government (with the possible exception of the Lord Chancellor) did not

so admit, and it is quite probable that, if the ensuing negotiations had broken down, Great Britain would have maintained obstinately that she had never recognized the independence of the United States."

148. Franklin to Livingston, October 14, 1782, in Wharton, *op. cit.,* V, 812. This reflects a stiffening of the English attitude after the failure of Spanish attempts to conquer Gibraltar in September, 1782.

149. Franklin to Robert Morris, December 23, 1782, in Wharton, *op. cit.,* VI, 160.

150. *Ibid.,* p. 169. (My italics.)

151. To the president of Congress, December 25, 1783, *ibid.,* p. 741.

152. May 12, 1784 (*Writings,* IX, 210).

153. Wharton, *op. cit.,* VI, 741. See also letter to the president of Congress, September 13, 1783, *ibid.,* p. 698.

154. Darling, *op. cit.,* p. 95.

155. Jay to Livingston, December 14, 1782, in Wharton, *op. cit.,* VI, 136.

156. Darling, *op. cit.,* p. 95.

157. Adams to Livingston, July 11, 1783, in Wharton, *op. cit.,* VI, 536.

158. Franklin to Livingston, July 22, 1783, *ibid.,* p. 583.

159. See below, p. 228.

160. Vergennes's policy of supporting the freedom of the seas, of which more will be said in chap. vii, gives a good example of anti-British power politics running under the disguise of disinterestedness. The envoy of Venice in Paris, whose reports about the diplomacy of the American Revolution are very interesting, told the Senate that France had now "uno stendardo che deve piacere a tutti, cioè la libertà dei mari, e l'eguaglianza di una ragione commune per tutte le Nazioni marittime" (report of February 19, 1780, printed in Amy A. Bernardy, "La Missione di Beniamino Franklin a Parigi nei dispacci degli Ambasciatori Veneziani in Francia [1776–1786]," *Archivio storico italiano,* LXXVIII [1920], 247, n. 1).

161. See above, pp. 160–61.

162. Report of Pierre Auguste Adet to the French Foreign Office in 1793, in F. J. Turner (ed.), "Correspondence of the French Ministers to the United States, 1791–1797," in *Annual Report of the American Historical Association for the Year 1903* (Washington, 1904), p. 983, quoted in Louis B. Wright, "The Founding Fathers and 'Splendid Isolation,'" *Huntington Library Quarterly,* VI (1942/43), 181. We follow the translation given in Mr. Wright's article, correcting, however, the translation of *espèce* with "hopes." The translator, apparently, confounded *espèce* and *espoir* and put "human hopes" instead of "mankind."

163. Cf. also the excellent appraisal of Franklin in Harlow, *op. cit.,* p. 238.

NOTES TO CHAPTER VI

1. To David Hartley, February 2, 1780 (Benjamin Franklin, *The Writings of Benjamin Franklin,* ed. Albert Henry Smyth [10 vols.; New York: Macmillan Co., 1905–7], VIII, 5). (Hereafter cited as "*Writings.*")

2. To Jonathan Shipley, June 10, 1782 (*Writings,* VIII, 454). Cf. also IX, 74 (to Sir Joseph Banks, July 27, 1783), and IX, 492–93 (to Ferdinand Grand, March 5, 1786).

3. To David Hartley, October 14, 1777 (*Writings,* VII, 70).

4. To David Hartley, December 15, 1781 (*Writings,* VIII, 349).

5. To Jane Mecom, September 20, 1787 (*Writings,* IX, 612).

6. *Ibid.*

7. See above, p. 106.

8. Burke to Franklin, August 15, 1781 (*Writings,* VIII, 319). Burke requested Franklin to intervene in favor of Burke's friend, General Burgoyne, on parole in England, who was recalled by Congress. See also Burke to Franklin, February 28, 1781 (*Writings,* VIII, 320).

9. To Edmund Burke, October 15, 1781 (*Writings,* VIII, 319). For further details of Franklin's correspondence with Burke during the War of Independence and of Burke's attitude toward Franklin see Dixon Wecter, "Burke, Franklin, and Samuel Petrie," *Huntington Library Quarterly,* III (1939/40), 315–38.

10. Shelburne to Franklin, April 6, 1782 (*Writings,* VIII, 461–62). Shelburne had come to power as Secretary for Home, Irish and Colonial Affairs two weeks before.

11. Oswald to Shelburne, May 18, 1782 (F.O. 95/511 [Public Record Office, London]; transcript in the William L. Clements Library, Ann Arbor, Michigan).

12. *Ibid.*

13. B. Vaughan to Shelburne, August 7, 1782. (Benjamin Vaughan Papers, William L. Clements Library, Ann Arbor, Michigan.) This collection of photostats and transcripts is the most complete collection of Vaughan's letters to Shelburne. The originals of some of them are now in the American Philosophical Society, Philadelphia. Some of these were printed in the *Proceedings of the Massachusetts Historical Society,* XVII (2d ser., 1903), 409–38.

14. James A. Woodburn, "Benjamin Franklin and the Peace Treaty of 1783," *Indiana Magazine of History,* XXX (1934), 225.

15. To David Hartley, February 12, 1778 (*Writings,* VII, 101).

16. To Joseph Priestley, January 27, 1777 (*Writings,* VII, 18).

17. Hartley to Franklin, April 22, 1779 (*Writings,* VII, 306).

18. To David Hartley, May 4, 1779 (*Writings,* VII, 309).

19. To Richard Price, February 6, 1780 (*Writings,* VIII, 9). (My italics.)

20. March 24, 1778 (*Writings,* VII, 122). For similar emphasis on the peculiar injustice and wickedness of this war see *Writings,* VII, 109; VII, 166; and VII, 301.

21. Rush to James McHenry, May 17, 1778, in Benjamin Rush, *Letters of Benjamin Rush,* ed. L. H. Butterfield (2 vols.; Princeton: Princeton University Press, 1951), I, 215.

22. To David Hartley, April 5, 1782 (*Writings,* VIII, 414–15).

23. To David Hartley, January 15, 1782 (*Writings,* VIII, 359). (My italics.)

24. To James Hutton, February 1, 1778 (*Writings,* VII, 99–100).

25. April 2, 1777 (*Writings,* VII, 37).

26. *Writings,* VII, 37 n. Franklin resented this strongly, as appears in a remark he made years later (February 16, 1782) to Hartley (*Writings,* VIII, 383).

27. October 14, 1777 (*Writings,* VII, 72).

28. Cf. George Herbert Guttridge, *David Hartley, M.P., an Advocate of Conciliation, 1774–1783* ("University of California Publications in History," Vol. XIV, No. 3 [Berkeley: University of California Press, 1926]), p. 275.

29. *Writings,* VII, 71.

30. *Writings,* VII, 70.

31. April 5, 1782 (*Writings,* VIII, 414).

32. *Writings,* VIII, 415.

33. *Ibid.* Attempts to arrange for the exchange of prisoners of war and to send some financial support to them fills a great deal of Franklin's diplomatic correspondence in Paris. A large amount of what was achieved was due to the labors of David Hartley. Care for the prisoners was of serious concern for Franklin, as one may clearly discern in perusing his relevant letters. Nothing raised his moral indignation to a higher pitch than when he discovered that one of his agents had cheated him with money received for the purpose of aiding the prisoners in England. For details see William Bell Clark, "In Defense of Thomas Digges," *Pennsylvania Magazine of History and Biography,* LXXVII (1953), 381–438.

34. See above, p. 172.

35. Quoted by A. D. Lindsay, *The Two Moralities: Our Duty to God and to Society* (London: Eyre & Spottiswoode, 1940), p. 40.

36. Oswald to Shelburne, July 10, 1782, printed in Lord John Russell (ed.), *Memorials and Correspondence of Charles James Fox* (4 vols.; London: Richard Bentley, 1857), IV, 240.

37. Interview with Oswald, April 17, 1782 (*Writings,* VIII, 470).

38. E. E. Hale and E. E. Hale, Jr., *Franklin in France* (2 vols.; Boston: Roberts Bros., 1887–88), II, 52. These instructions were the result of Shelburne's conversations with Oswald on April 28, 1782.

39. *Ibid.*

40. *Writings,* VIII, 472. Franklin, as we shall see later in greater detail, on this occasion suggested that Canada ought to be ceded to the United States. This conversation took place on April 19.

41. *Writings,* VIII, 473.

42. Franklin's *Journal:* interview with Oswald, June 3, 1782 (*Writings,* VIII, 527.

43. Russell (ed.), *op. cit.,* IV, 240.

44. See also Shelburne's letter to Oswald, October 21, 1782, in Lord Edmond Fitzmaurice, *Life of Shelburne* (3 vols.; London: Macmillan & Co., 1875–76), III, 282–86.

45. A. B. Darling, *Our Rising Empire, 1763–1803* (New Haven: Yale University Press, 1940), p. 86.

46. John Adams, *Works,* ed. C. F. Adams (10 vols.; Boston: Little, Brown & Co., 1850–56), III, 332 (*Diary,* November 26, 1782).

47. November 26, 1782 (*Writings,* VIII, 625).

48. *Writings,* VIII, 626–27.

49. Francis Wharton, *The Revolutionary Diplomatic Correspondence of the United States* (6 vols.; Washington: Government Printing Office, 1889), VI, 98 (Article V of the preliminaries).

50. The contested question was the right of fishing in the Gulf of St. Lawrence and using the Magdalen Islands and the unsettled shores of Nova Scotia (see Darling, *op. cit.,* p. 91).

51. John Adams, *op. cit.,* III, 334 (*Diary,* November 29, 1782).

52. *Ibid.*

53. *Ibid.,* pp. 334–35.

54. Article III of the preliminaries deals with the fisheries (Wharton, *op. cit.,* VI, 98).

55. To Robert R. Livingston, December 5, 1782, in Wharton, *op. cit.,* VI, 112.

56. *Ibid.*, pp. 112–13. The Smyth edition prints erroneously ". . . while in the ministry . . ." (*Writings*, VIII, 633). See also *Writings*, IX, 22–23.

57. March 23, 1783. Unpublished letter in the American Philosophical Society.

58. Carl Van Doren, *Benjamin Franklin* (New York: Viking Press, 1938), p. 690.

59. To James Hutton, February 1, 1778 (*Writings*, VII, 100). Cf. also a letter of Samuel Petrie, a friend of Edmund Burke, to Burke, reporting a conversation with Franklin a few weeks before Franklin's letter to Hutton; Petrie's letter is dated January 4, 1778, and is quoted by Wecter, *op. cit.*, pp. 326–27.

60. To Henry Laurens, May 25, 1782 (*Writings*, VIII, 506).

61. To Sir William Johnson, September 12, 1766 (*Writings*, IV, 461–62).

62. August 28, 1767 (*Writings*, V, 46). Franklin's interest in westward expansion during the 1760's and early 1770's is to a large extent connected with his participation in the land speculations of the Illinois Company (founded 1766) and the Indiana Company (1767), which developed into the Grand Ohio Company. Franklin took an active part in the negotiations of the latter company to secure the assent of the Privy Council, which was secured, and a royal charter, which came to naught because of the troubles leading to the outbreak of the Revolution. The negotiations about the grant to the Grand Ohio Company—usually referred to as Walpole's Grant—are focused in the *Report of the Lord Commissioners of Trade and Plantations* drawn up by Lord Hillsborough, at that time president of the Board of Trade, opposing the grant, and *Observations on and Answers to the Foregoing Report*, traditionally held to be Franklin's, and included in Vol. V of Smyth's edition of Franklin's writings, but now accepted to be the work of Samuel Wharton, leading spirit of this enterprise (cf. Van Doren, *op. cit.*, pp. 394–99). In 1774 Franklin gave up his share in the Ohio Company but remained interested in land speculations in Nova Scotia. See also Carl Van Doren (ed.), *Benjamin Franklin's Autobiographical Writings* (New York: Viking Press, 1945), pp. 158, 650. Franklin's role in the western land policies of Great Britain is analyzed in great detail by Clarence Alvord, *The Mississippi Valley in British Politics* (Cleveland: Arthur H. Clark Co., 1917), esp. I, 90 ff., 169, 320 ff., and Vol. II, *passim* (see Index of Vol. II).

63. Cf. Marcel Trudel, *Louis XVI, le congrès américain et le Canada, 1774–1789* (Quebec: Publications de l'Université Laval, Éditions du Quartier Latin, 1949), pp. 15–16.

64. *An Account of Negotiations in London* . . . (*Writings*, VI, 330).

65. *Writings*, VI, 338; see also VI, 373 and 383.

66. On the efforts of Congress to bring the Canadians into its fold see Trudel's work. Not the least of Franklin's assets on this mission was his title as "membre de l'Académie royale des Sciences de Paris," a title which was put on the first place of his commission (Trudel, *op. cit.*, p. 72). See also William Renwick Riddell, "Benjamin Franklin's Mission to Canada and the Causes of Its Failure," *Pennsylvania Magazine of History and Biography*, XLVIII (1924), 111–58.

67. *Writings*, VI, 425.

68. *Writings*, VI, 452–53.

69. *Writings*, VI, 454.

70. Cf. Paul Chrisler Phillips, *The West in the Diplomacy of the American Revolution* ("University of Illinois Studies in the Social Sciences," Vol. XI, Nos. 2 and 3 [Urbana: University of Illinois Press, 1913]), p. 25.

71. Edward Corwin, *French Policy and the American Alliance of 1778* (Princeton: Princeton University Press, 1916), pp. 237–42.

72. The best discussion of Vergennes's changing policy with regard to the West is in Corwin, *op. cit.*, chap. x, pp. 217–42.

73. The most thorough examination of this letter is given by Corwin (*ibid.*, pp. 217–32).

74. Wharton, *op. cit.*, V, 88–89.

75. To Robert R. Livingston, March 9, 1782, *ibid.*, p. 232.

76. To Robert R. Livingston, March 30, 1782, *ibid.*, p. 277.

77. Phillips, *op. cit.*, p. 139.

78. Oswald to Shelburne, May 18, 1782 (F.O. 95/511 [Public Record Office, London]; transcript in the William L. Clements Library, Ann Arbor, Michigan).

79. October 2, 1780, in Wharton, *op. cit.*, IV, 75. See also Franklin to Carmichael, January 27, 1780, *ibid.*, III, 476, and Franklin to Jay, January 27, 1781 (*ibid.*, IV, 242), January 19, 1782 (*ibid.*, V, 120), and March 16, 1782 (*ibid.*, p. 244).

80. Russell (ed.), *op. cit.*, IV, 239. Cf. also Vincent T. Harlow, *The Founding of the Second British Empire, 1763–1793* (London, New York, and Toronto: Longmans, Green & Co., 1952), p. 250.

81. Cf. Darling, *op. cit.*, p. 67, and Harlow, *op. cit.*, pp. 229–34.

82. Lord Shelburne to Oswald, July 27, 1782, in Fitzmaurice, *op. cit.*, III, 248.

83. Russell (ed.), *op. cit.*, IV, 241.

84. Benjamin Vaughan to Lord Shelburne, November 5, 1782 (Benjamin Vaughan Papers, William L. Clements Library, Ann Arbor, Michigan). "The question therefore is very short, for the consideration of the American commissioners. It is England & generosity on the one side, or France & consistant politics on the other; this is *their* alternative. England's alternative is still shorter; it is trade & help; or else bagatelles, war & poverty."

85. The good will and the farsighted statesmanship of Lord Shelburne have been celebrated by Clarence Walworth Alvord, *Lord Shelburne and the Founding of British-American Goodwill* ("Raleigh Lecture in History of the British Academy, Read October 28, 1925" [London: Published for the British Academy by Humphrey Milford, Oxford University Press, *s.a.*]).

86. See above, pp. 169–70.

87. On April 12, 1782, Franklin had voiced to Livingston his suspicions in regard to Spain (Wharton, *op. cit.*, V, 300). Now, on August 12, 1782, the design of the Spaniards had been "manifested" (*ibid.*, p. 657).

88. The first news reached London on September 30, 1782 (see Samuel Flagg Bemis, *The Diplomacy of the American Revolution* [New York: D. Appleton-Century Co., 1935], p. 230, n. 9).

89. Darling, *op. cit.*, p. 86. See above, p. 194. The cession of the western lands had been implied not only in Shelburne's letter to Oswald of July 27 but also in the decisions of the British cabinet of August 29, 1782, to conclude peace on the basis of Franklin's "necessary" articles, and it had been incorporated in Jay's definite proposals of October 5, approved by Franklin. To Jay's articles the British cabinet decided to raise objections on October 17 and sent a new commissioner, Sir Henry Strachey, to Paris, to check Oswald's all too "philosophic, that is, pro-American attitude." Strachey and his instructions asserting the British right to the western lands brought a new spirit into the negotiations. Benjamin Vaughan

reported to Shelburne that the American commissioners *"would have been better pleased with a style of confidence, than with a style of bargain"* (Vaughan to Shelburne, November 1, 1782 [Benjamin Vaughan Papers, William L. Clements Library, Ann Arbor, Michigan]). (My italics.)

90. Franklin to Livingston, December 5, 1782, in Wharton, *op. cit.,* VI, 113.

91. Jay to Franklin, September 11, 1783, *ibid.,* pp. 692–93.

92. After the Treaty of Paris in 1763 the few settlements along the Lower Mobile and the Lower Mississippi were organized as the province of West Florida and divided at the Chattahoochee-Apalachicola from the rest of Florida, from then onward called East Florida; the line of 31° north latitude was fixed as the northern boundary. This administrative division explains the recurring reference to "the Floridas" (cf. Bemis, *op. cit.,* p. 96).

93. *Journals of the Continental Congress, 1774–1789* (34 vols.; Library of Congress ed.; Washington: Government Printing Office, 1904–37), V, 770.

94. Resolution of Congress, December 30, 1776, quoted in Franklin's letter to Aranda, April 7, 1777, in Wharton, *op. cit.,* II, 304.

95. Gilbert Chinard (ed.), *The Treaties of 1778 and Allied Documents* (Baltimore: Johns Hopkins Press, 1928), p. 53. (My italics.)

96. Izard to Arthur Lee, May 18, 1778, in Wharton, *op. cit.,* II, 586.

97. *Ibid.*

98. Arthur Lee to Izard, May 23, 1778, *ibid.,* p. 594.

99. *Ibid.,* p. 587.

100. Corwin, *op. cit.,* p. 197. Cf. also Darling, *op. cit.,* p. 20.

101. In his instructions to Gérard of March 29, 1778, almost two months after the conclusion of the alliance (quoted by Corwin, *op. cit.,* p. 197).

102. Instructions to Jay, September 29, 1779, in Wharton, *op. cit.,* III, 353.

103. Bemis, *op. cit.,* p. 229.

104. "Letters of Benjamin Vaughan to Shelburne," *Proceedings of the Historical Society of Massachusetts,* XVII (2d ser., 1903), 421 (letter of December 4, 1782). See also letter of January 18, 1783, *ibid.,* p. 438. This was not the first time that Franklin argued for the surrender of Gibraltar to Spain. See the letter of Grenville to Fox of May 10, 1782, printed in Hale and Hale, *op. cit.,* II, 56, and also the letter of Oswald to Shelburne of June 12, 1782 (Shelburne Papers, Vol. LXXI, p. 52, in the William L. Clements Library, Ann Arbor, Michigan), according to which Franklin explained Spanish desires for Gibraltar by comparing it with the importance Portsmouth assumed for England.

105. Memoir, "West Florida," Paris, November 12, 1782 (Strachey Papers; transcript in the William L. Clements Library, Ann Arbor, Michigan).

106. Cf. Bemis, *op. cit.,* p. 230.

107. David Jayne Hill, "Franklin and the French Alliance," *Records of the Columbia Historical Society,* XXX–XXXI (1930), 165.

108. Bemis, *op. cit.,* p. 197; cf. *ibid.,* p. 201, n. 34.

109. Richard Van Alstyne in his article, "The Significance of the Mississippi Valley in American Diplomatic History, 1686–1890," *Mississippi Valley Historical Review,* XXXVI (1949), 221, rightly emphasizes the continuity of what he aptly calls Franklin's "geopolitics."

110. Congress in its instructions of August 14, 1779, to John Adams stated that "although it is of the utmost importance to the peace and commerce of the United States that Canada and Nova Scotia should be ceded . . . yet a desire of terminat-

ing the war hath induced us not to make the acquisition of these objects an ulti-matum on the present occasion" (Wharton, *op. cit.*, III, 295). When Franklin was named commissioner for the peace treaty, the instructions of June 15, 1781, re-ferred to the earlier instructions of 1779 with respect to territorial questions. Cf. S. F. Bemis, "Canada and the Peace Settlement of 1782–3," *Canadian Historical Review,* XIV (1933), 266–67.

111. See above, p. 190. See also Franklin to Hartley, October 26, 1778 (*Writings,* VII, 196).

112. *Writings,* VIII, 471–72.

113. *Writings,* VIII, 472.

114. *Writings,* VIII, 473.

115. See above, p. 194.

116. *Writings,* VIII, 470. (My italics.)

117. Oswald's journal, August 11 and 13, 1782, in Hale and Hale, *op. cit.*, II, 115.

118. *Journal* (*Writings,* VIII, 527).

119. *Ibid.* Oswald told Franklin this on June 3. Fox's amazement is explained by the fact that Shelburne, when he first got Franklin's paper on Canada in April, showed it to only one member of the cabinet, Lord Ashburton, and kept it secret from all other people (see Hale and Hale, *op. cit.*, II, 51).

120. Hale and Hale, *op. cit.*, II, 53.

121. Franklin's *Journal:* interview with Oswald on May 4 (*Writings,* VIII, 486).

122. Bemis, *Diplomacy of the American Revolution,* p. 230. Oswald reported to the Colonial Secretary, Townshend, on October 2, 1782: "I hope to get clear of the advisable articles, as distinguished from his 'necessary' articles, but as to some of those in my instructions I doubt I shall not [*sic*] succeed" (printed in Hale and Hale, *op. cit.*, II, 169). Trudel (*op. cit.*, p. 210) seems to overlook this indirect reference to Canada and thinks that Oswald's remark in his journal on August 13, cited above, is the last reference to the Canadian question.

123. Bemis, "Canada and the Peace Settlement of 1782–3," *op. cit.*, pp. 281–82.

124. Harlow, *op. cit.*, p. 299.

125. *Ibid.*, pp. 299–300.

126. See now particularly Harlow's book.

127. December 14, 1782, in Wharton, *op. cit.*, VI, 132.

128. Vergennes to Rayneval, December 4, 1782, *ibid.*, p. 107.

129. *Ibid.*

130. Vaughan to Shelburne, November 5, 1782 (Benjamin Vaughan Papers, William L. Clements Library, Ann Arbor, Michigan).

131. Fitzmaurice, *op. cit.*, III, 248.

132. Fitzmaurice, *op. cit.*, III, 248.

133. B. Vaughan to James Monroe, September 18, 1795 (Benjamin Vaughan Papers, William L. Clements Library, Ann Arbor, Michigan).

134. To Thomas Cushing, February 5, 1771 (*Writings,* V, 296). (My italics.)

135. "Rise and Present State of Our Misunderstanding," from *London Chron-icle,* November, 8 1770, under pseudonym "N. N.," in Verner W. Crane (ed.), *Benjamin Franklin's Letters to the Press* (Chapel Hill: University of North Caro-lina Press, 1950), p. 217.

136. *Writings,* VIII, 471. (My italics.)

137. Vaughan to Shelburne, August 6, 1782 (Benjamin Vaughan Papers, Wil-liam L. Clements Library, Ann Arbor, Michigan).

NOTES TO CHAPTER VII

1. This pattern of the three theories of achieving the "harmony of interests" has been developed in Élie Halévy's *The Growth of Philosophic Radicalism* (London: Faber & Gwyer, 1928), pp. 13–17.

2. Reinhold Niebuhr, *Christianity and Power Politics* (New York: Charles Scribner's Sons, 1940), p. 177.

3. Reinhold Niebuhr, *The Irony of American History* (New York: Charles Scribner's Sons, 1952), pp. 36–37.

4. The utmost confusion with regard to the meaning of the term "ideology" reigns in the fields of history and political science. It seems as undesirable to identify the term "ideology" with social or political philosophy in general as to tie it up necessarily with rational disguises for sinister self-interests. We submit a working definition of ideology which does not contest the possible validity of the moral judgments involved and does not try to pin them down as mere disguises or self-deception, although it would not exclude this possibility. This definition does, on the other hand, lay stress on the element of action inevitably involved, which distinguishes ideologies from political philosophies, which latter may exist in the realm of pure contemplation:

"Ideology is a set of ideas and principles presented by or in support of political groups in order to explain their policies to the public, to their opponents, or to themselves, not only or not at all in terms of power, that is, in terms of strength and weakness, success being the sole criterion, but rather in terms of moral right or wrong, using as criterion a moral value claiming universal validity. The exponents of an ideology may—but need not—believe in the principles they set forth."

5. L. B. Namier, "The Revolution of the Intellectuals (1848)," *Proceedings of the British Academy,* XXX (1944), 182.

6. On the search for principles of legitimacy see Gugliemo Ferrero's book on *The Principles of Power: The Great Political Crises of History,* trans. Theodore R. Jaeckel (New York: G. P. Putnam's Sons, 1942), *passim,* and, for their role in the eighteenth century, Albert Sorel, *Europe under the Old Regime,* trans. Francis H. Herrick (Los Angeles: Ward Ritchie Press, 1947), p. 18. This presents the first chapter of the grandiose first volume of Sorel's *L'Europe et la révolution française.*

7. Richard Price, *A Discourse on the Love of Our Country, Delivered on November 4, 1789, at the Meeting-House in the Old Jewry, to the Society for Commemorating the Revolution in Great Britain* (London: Printed by George Stafford, for T. Cadell, in the Strand, 1790), p. 5.

8. *Ibid.,* p. 10. This discourse was the cause for Edmund Burke's writing his *Reflections on the French Revolution.*

9. G. J. A. Ducher, an official of the French Foreign Office during the French Revolution, wrote an article in the *Moniteur* of June 9, 1793, entitled "Nouvelle diplomatie." The expression "New Diplomacy," so common after World War I, has been traced back to this origin by Felix Gilbert, "The 'New Diplomacy' of the Eighteenth Century," *World Politics,* IV (1951/52), 1 and 37, n. 110.

10. Thoughts of international or supranational organization were by no means absent during the eighteenth century, however. See below, p. 222.

11. James Brown Scott, "America and the New Diplomacy," *International Conciliation,* No. 16 (March, 1909), p. 3.

12. Quoted by Halévy, *op. cit.*, p. 170, from a letter of Shelburne's to Jeremy Bentham, March 29, 1789, in *The Works of Jeremy Bentham*, ed. J. Bowring (11 vols.; Edinburgh: W. Tait, 1843), X, 197–98.

13. So does, for instance, that enthusiastic admirer of Shelburne and Franklin, C. W. Alvord, in *Lord Shelburne and the Founding of British-American Goodwill* ("Raleigh Lecture in History of the British Academy, Read October 28, 1925" [London: Published for the British Academy by Humphrey Milford, Oxford University Press, *s.a.*]), p. 20.

14. March 10, 1779 (Benjamin Franklin, *The Writings of Benjamin Franklin*, ed. Albert Henry Smyth [10 vols.; New York: Macmillan Co., 1905–7], VII, 242–43). (Hereafter cited as "*Writings.*")

15. October 16, 1783 (*Writings*, IX, 107).

16. On this topic see the interesting chapter on "Natural Right" in Albert K. Weinberg, *Manifest Destiny: A Study of Nationalist Expansionism in American History* (Baltimore: Johns Hopkins Press, 1935), pp. 11–42.

17. E. E. Hale and E. E. Hale, Jr., *Franklin in France* (2 vols.; Boston: Roberts Bros., 1887–88), II, 112 (Oswald's journal).

18. See above, p. 175, and Franklin to Joseph Galloway, January 9, 1769, in Carl Van Doren (ed.), *Benjamin Franklin's Autobiographical Writings* (New York: Viking Press, 1945), p. 188.

19. *Writings*, VII, 196.

20. Samuel Flagg Bemis, *The Diplomacy of the American Revolution* (New York and London: D. Appleton–Century Co., 1935), p. 173. This appears from a dispatch of Vergennes to Gérard, No. 8, December 25, 1778, discussed in Henri Doniol, *Histoire de la participation de la France à l'établissement des États-Unis d'Amérique* (5 vols.; Paris: Imprimerie Nationale, 1886–92), III, 595–96. The question arose from the tentative efforts of Spain to mediate between the warring countries at the expense of complete American independence. Spain's terms had proposed that the war between England and the United States should end in a long-term truce *uti possidetis;* during the negotiations the United States were to be regarded as independent *de facto* (Bemis, *op. cit.,* p. 172). There is no indication that Franklin at any time accepted the *uti possidetis* formula, which even Vergennes would have been prepared to accept only under the great financial stress of 1781 (*ibid.,* p. 181). Franklin's letter to Hartley two months earlier, and similar statements showing that Franklin thought little of legal recognition by England, as long as independence was a fact and recognized by the other powers, would tend to confirm the correctness of Vergennes's statement to Gérard. Cf. also Franklin to Weissenstein, July 1, 1778 (*Writings*, VII, 168).

21. Franklin's *Journal of the Peace Negotiations* gives ample proof of his anxiety about British maneuvers to impair America's independence. Cf. his letter to John Adams, May 8, 1782 (*Writings*, VIII, 487); his interview with Grenville on June 1, 1782 (*Writings*, VIII, 516–17); his letter to John Adams, June 2, 1782 (*Writings*, VIII, 521–23); his interview with Grenville on June 15, 1782 (*Writings*, VIII, 541–42); and particularly his letters to Livingston, June 28, 1782 (*Writings*, VIII, 556), and to Oswald, July 12, 1782 (*Writings*, VIII, 567).

22. Jay's report to Livingston, in Francis Wharton, *The Revolutionary Diplomatic Correspondence of the United States* (6 vols.; Washington: Government Printing Office, 1889), VI, 14.

23. See chap. vi above, p. 201.

24. Weinberg, *op. cit.*, p. 21.

25. *Ibid.*, pp. 22–23.

26. *Ibid.*, p. 23, quoted from De Jaucourt's article "Conquêt," *Encyclopédie,* ed. Diderot (Paris, 1751–65), IX, 4.

27. *Ibid.*, p. 22, quoted from Justin H. Smith, *Our Struggles for the Fourteenth Colony: Canada and the American Revolution* (New York, 1907), I, 215.

28. *Ibid.*, quoted from E. C. Burnett (ed.), *Letters of the Members of the Continental Congress* (8 vols.; Washington: Carnegie Institution of Washington, 1921–36), III, 476.

29. "Canada Pamphlet" (*Papers,* IX, 65).

30. See particularly Elizabeth V. Souleyman, *The Vision of World Peace in Seventeenth- and Eighteenth-Century France* (New York: G. P. Putnam's Sons, 1941).

31. Many documents and facts relating to Gargaz and his relations with Franklin have been carefully assembled in George Simpson Eddy's Introduction to his edition of Pierre-André Gargaz, *A Project of Universal and Perpetual Peace* (New York: George Simpson Eddy, 1922). This letter, written on February 14, 1779, was reprinted on pp. 1–2 of Mr. Eddy's Introduction. Some interesting details have been added in an article by A. Aulard, "Le Forçat Gargaz et la Société des Nations," *La Revue de Paris,* XXX (September–October, 1923), 45–55. Before addressing Franklin, Gargaz had already written to Voltaire, and it seems that Voltaire replied to him in verses (*ibid.*, pp. 46–47). During the French Revolution, under the Directory, Gargaz was at Toulon and published a revised version of his peace project.

32. Gargaz, *op. cit.*, ed. Eddy, p. 2.

33. *Writings,* VIII, 564–65. It seems an interesting coincidence that on the very same day Franklin presented to Oswald his demands for Canada, for reparations, and for the recognition of England's war guilt.

34. Gargaz, *op. cit.*, ed. Eddy, p. 44. (Translation by Mr. Eddy.)

35. *Ibid.*, p. 12.

36. *Ibid.* This seniority does not mean the length of the reign of a ruling family; the personal age of the respective rulers is meant.

37. Journal of John Baynes, October 2, 1783 (Benjamin Franklin, *The Complete Works of Benjamin Franklin,* ed. John Bigelow [10 vols.; New York and London: G. P. Putnam's Sons, 1887–88], VIII, 418). (My italics.) For an earlier and more "rationalistic" wish for "the Discovery of a Plan, that would induce & oblige Nations to settle their Disputes without first Cutting one another's Throats" see his letter to Richard Price, February 6, 1780 (*Writings,* VIII, 9).

38. Oswald to Shelburne, May 18, 1782 (F.O. 95/511 [Public Record Office, London]; transcript in the William L. Clements Library, Ann Arbor, Michigan).

39. To Ferdinand Grand, October 22, 1787 (*Writings,* IX, 619). (My italics.)

40. December 9, 1775 (*Writings,* VI, 432).

41. An edition in three volumes has been provided by the Carnegie Institution of Washington in its collection of "The Classics of International Law," edited by James Brown Scott; the first two volumes under the title, E. de Vattel, *Le Droit des gens, ou principes de la loi naturelle, appliqués à conduite et aux affaires des nations et des souverains,* contain a photographic reproduction of the first edition of 1758; the third volume under the English title, *The Law of Nations or the Principles of Natural Law Applied to the Conduct and to the Affairs*

of Nations and of Sovereigns, translation of the edition of 1758 by Charles G. Fenwick (Washington: Carnegie Institution of Washington, 1916), contains an excellent Introduction by Albert de Lapradelle.

42. On Vattel's influence in America, which seems to have begun only by 1776 but to have increased rapidly, see Lapradelle's Introduction, *op. cit.*, III, xxix–xxx. By 1780 Vattel's work had become a textbook in American universities.

43. *Ibid.*, p. 7.

44. *Ibid.*

45. *Ibid.*, p. 398.

46. *Writings,* VII, 422 n. On this occasion Franklin also mentions Grotius' *History of the Troubles in the Netherlands,* Book XVI, where Grotius condemns in strong terms the practice of Englishmen escaping punishment for similar injuries done in the East Indies, because no treaty of alliance had been contracted with the people there.

47. To Count Bernstorff, December 22, 1779 (*Writings,* VII, 422).

48. *Writings,* VII, 423.

49. October 15, 1781 (*Writings,* VIII, 319). See above, p. 187.

50. Bemis (*op. cit.*, pp. 131–32) gives an excellent and comprehensive survey of all the issues involved.

51. See also James Brown Scott (ed.), *The Armed Neutralities of 1780 and 1800* (New York: Oxford University Press, 1918). This is a "collection of official documents preceded by the views of representative publicists."

52. The text of this declaration may be found in Scott (ed.), *The Armed Neutralities of 1780 and 1800,* pp. 273–74; also in Wharton, *op. cit.*, III, 607–8.

53. To Dumas, April 23, 1780, in Wharton, *op. cit.*, III, 626.

54. To Torris, May 30, 1780, *ibid.*, pp. 740–41.

55. To the president of Congress, May 31, 1780, *ibid.*, p. 745.

56. June 3, 1780, *ibid.*, p. 761.

57. American Philosophical Society, Philadelphia. See also Wharton, *op. cit.*, V, 606. An earlier hint in a letter to two Dutch merchants, June 8, 1781 (*Writings,* VIII, 263).

58. "Minutes relative to the Freedom of Neutral Navigation, Paris, December 15, 1782" (Oswald to Shelburne) (Shelburne Papers, Vol. LXXI, p. 197, in the William L. Clements Library, Ann Arbor, Michigan).

59. "Propositions relative to Privateering, communicated to Mr. Oswald" (*Writings,* IX, 4).

60. *Writings,* IX, 7.

61. "Minutes relative to the Freedom of Neutral Navigation," *loc. cit.*

62. January 14, 1783 (*Writings,* IX, 4).

63. *Ibid.*

64. May 8, 1783 (*Writings,* p. 40).

65. This treaty was signed at four places on four dates, the plenipotentiaries who had been empowered to treat being scattered in The Hague, Paris, Berlin, and London. John Adams and Jefferson signed with Franklin for the United States. See the notes in Hunter Miller (ed.), *Treaties and Other International Acts of the United States of America* (Washington: Government Printing Office, 1931), II, 183.

66. *Ibid.*, pp. 178–79.

67. To Baron de Thulemeier, February 13, 1785 (John Adams, *Works*, ed. C. F. Adams [10 vols.; Boston: Little, Brown & Co., 1850–56], VIII, 225).

68. To C. J. Ingersoll, July 28, 1814, in James Madison, *The Writings of James Madison,* ed. Gaillard Hunt (9 vols.; New York: G. P. Putnam's Sons, 1900–1910), VIII, 283. There exists an article by Simeon E. Baldwin on "Franklin and the Rule of Free Ships, Free Goods," *Proceedings of the American Antiquarian Society,* XXV (new ser., 1915), 345–57, which is not adequate. Above all, it does not show the political side of the United States and Franklin's interest in that rule during the American Revolution and deals quite inadequately with Franklin's constant efforts for the abolition of privateering and his "reform" of international law.

69. Quoted by Corwin, *French Policy and the American Alliance of 1778* (Princeton: Princeton University Press, 1916), pp. 72–73, from John Durand (ed.), *Documents on the American Revolution* (New York, 1889), p. 62.

70. January 7, 1778, in B. F. Stevens (comp.), *Facsimiles of Manuscripts from European Archives Relating to America, 1773–1783* (24 vols.; London, 1889–95), Vol. XXI, No. 1824 (Stevens' translation). This doctrine of a dual morality, of course, has not been limited to the continent of Europe. Among the Founding Fathers, it found an eloquent advocate in Alexander Hamilton.

71. M. D. B. (Barbeu-Dubourg), *Petit code de la raison humaine ou exposition succincte de ce que la raison dicte à tous les hommes, pour éclairer leur conduite & assurer leur bonheur. À Monsieur B. F.* (1782). On the dedication page we read: "Vous reconnutes dans la première esquisse de ce Petit Code, l'effusion single et naive de votre propre cœur; j'ai achevé de le developper autant que je l'ai pu. ..."

72. *Ibid.,* p. 79. (My translation.)

73. To Benjamin Vaughan, March 14, 1785 (*Writings,* IX, 296 and 299). This letter, containing general reflections on criminal laws and on the practice of privateering, was published as early as 1786 (*Writings,* IX, 291 n.).

74. John Stuart Mill, "A Few Words on Non-intervention," *Dissertations and Discussions: Political, Philosophical, and Historical* (2d ed.; 4 vols.; London: Longmans, Green, Reader & Dyer, 1875), III, 158.

75. Quoted by Hans J. Morgenthau, *In Defense of the National Interest* (New York: Alfred A. Knopf, 1951), pp. 23–24.

76. Thomas Paine, *The Complete Writings of Thomas Paine,* ed. Philip S. Foner (2 vols.; New York: Citadel Press, 1945), I, 30–31.

77. May 4, 1779 (*Writings,* VII, 301).

78. As early as July, 1773, Franklin spoke of offering "to all the oppress'd of other Nations" participation in America's security and liberty (to S. Danforth [*Writings,* VI, 106]).

79. "Comparison of Great Britain and the United States in Regard to the Basis of Credit in the Two Countries" (*Writings,* VII, 8).

80. To Samuel Cooper, May 1, 1777 (*Writings,* VII, 56). See also VII, 408–9.

81. See chap. i, p. 5.

82. To Richard Bache, September 13, 1781 (*Writings,* VIII, 304).

83. To Samuel Cooper, December 26, 1782 (*Writings,* VIII, 648). Cf. also VIII, 602.

84. To Robert Walsh, December 4, 1818, in Thomas Jefferson, *The Writings of Thomas Jefferson, Memorial Edition* (Washington: Thomas Jefferson Memorial Association, 1905), XV, 176. (My italics.)

85. Benjamin Vaughan to Shelburne, January 28, 1783 (Benjamin Vaughan Papers, William L. Clements Library, Ann Arbor, Michigan).

86. *Writings*, VII, 178. See above, p. 158.

87. May 25, 1782 (*Writings*, VIII, 506).

88. Benjamin Vaughan to Shelburne, January 18, 1783 (Benjamin Vaughan Papers, William L. Clements Library, Ann Arbor, Michigan); printed, with slight variations, in *Proceedings of the Massachusetts Historical Society*, XVII [2d ser., 1903], 437).

89. Edmond Silberner, *La Guerre dans la pensée économique du XVIe au XVIIIe siècle* (Paris: Librairie du Recueil Sirey, 1939), p. 268.

90. Gilbert, "The 'New Diplomacy' of the Eighteenth Century," *op. cit.*, pp. 11–12.

91. See above, pp. 106–7.

92. To James Lovell, July 22, 1778 (*Writings*, VII, 176–77).

93. Oswald's report to Shelburne, in Lord John Russell (ed.), *Memorials and Correspondence of Charles James Fox* (4 vols.; London: Richard Bentley, 1857), IV, 240–41.

94. To David Hartley, September 6, 1783 (*Writings*, IX, 88). The failure of the British-American trade negotiations in 1783 is now authoritatively discussed in chap. ix of Vol. I of Vincent T. Harlow, *The Founding of the Second British Empire, 1763–1793* (London, New York, and Toronto: Longmans, Green & Co., 1952), pp. 448–92.

95. March 16, 1783 (*Writings*, IX, 19). Cf. also VIII, 261; IX, 63, 241.

96. To Alexander Small, September 28, 1787. (*Writings*, IX, 616). See also to Benjamin Vaughan, October 24, 1788 (*Writings*, IX, 676).

97. [Richard Oswald] to (Shelburne?), May 6, 1782 (F.O. 95/511 [Public Record Office, London]; transcript in the William L. Clements Library, Ann Arbor, Michigan).

98. July 31, 1782 (Benjamin Vaughan Papers, William L. Clements Library, Ann Arbor, Michigan).

99. To Richard Oswald, January 14, 1783 (*Writings*, IX, 6–7). Cf. also to David Hartley, May 8, 1783 (*Writings*, IX, 40).

100. June 2, 1779 (*Writings*, VII, 341–42). Cf. also to Lafayette, August 19, 1779 (*Writings*, VII, 367).

101. To unknown addressee, December 15, 1787 (*Writings*, IX, 625). (My italics.)

102. To Jan Ingenhousz, February 11, 1788 (*Writings*, IX, 634).

103. To Le Veillard, June 8, 1788 (*Writings*, IX, 657).

104. To Benjamin Vaughan, October 24, 1788 (*Writings*, IX, 676).

105. Cf. Max Huber, "Die soziologischen Grundlagen des Voelkerrechts," reprinted in Max Huber, *Vermischte Schriften* (Zurich: Atlantis Verlag, 1948), III, 87.

106. [December 31, 1776], in *The Deane Papers* ("Collections of the New York Historical Society," Vols. XIX–XXIV, 1886–90), I, 436–37.

107. Thomas Pownall, *A Memorial Most Humbly Addressed to the Sovereigns of Europe, on the Present State of Affairs, between the Old and New World* (London: Printed for J. Almon, 1780), p. 117. (My italics.)

108. John Adams to Franklin, August 17, 1780, in Wharton, *op. cit.*, IV, 35.

109. Paine, *Common Sense* (*The Complete Writings of Thomas Paine*, ed.

Foner, I, 20). See also above, pp. 44, 106.

110. *Comparison of Great Britain and the United States in Regard to the Basis of Credit in the Two Countries* (*Writings*, VII, 6).

111. To Charles de Weissenstein, July 1, 1778 (*Writings*, VII, 167).

112. Carl Van Doren (ed.), *The Letters of Benjamin Franklin & Jane Mecom* (Princeton: Princeton University Press, 1950), p. 265 (May 2, 1786). Cf. *Writings*, IX, 491.

113. To Charles Pettit, October 10, 1786 (*Writings*, IX, 545).

114. To Richard Jackson, March 8, 1763, in Carl Van Doren (ed.), *Letters and Papers of Benjamin Franklin and Richard Jackson, 1753-1785* (Philadelphia: American Philosophical Society, 1947), p. 92.

115. Charles A. Beard, *The Idea of National Interest* (New York: Macmillan Co., 1934), p. 53, quoted from Jefferson, *Works* (Washington ed.,), I, 403.

116. Lord Edmond Fitzmaurice, *Life of Shelburne* (3 vols.; London: Macmillan & Co., 1875-76), II, 330.

117. Hartley to Franklin, May 25, 1782 (*Writings*, VIII, 515).

118. Hartley to Franklin, May 13, 1782 (*Writings*, VIII, 510).

119. To Charles Thomson, May 13, 1784 (*Writings*, IX, 213).

NOTES TO CHAPTER VIII

1. See above, p. 83.

2. Benjamin Franklin, *The Writings of Benjamin Franklin*, ed. Albert Henry Smyth (10 vols.; New York: Macmillan Co., 1905-7), V, 362. (Hereafter cited as *"Writings."*) See above, p. 104.

3. Franklin's marginal comment in *Good Humour, or, A Way with the Colonists* (London, 1766), p. 26. See above, pp. 21-22.

4. Gilbert Chinard, *Thomas Jefferson* (2d rev. ed.; Boston: Little, Brown & Co., 1946), p. 202.

5. *Ibid.*

6. *Writings*, IV, 8.

7. In an interesting German study, Franklin appears one-sidedly as representative of a pacifist trend in early American foreign policy, nourished from Quaker and Enlightenment sources, as opposed to the expansionist trend which was nourished mainly from the frontier. This, of course, simplifies matters too much. See Gertrud Philippi, *Imperialistische und pazifistische Stroemungen in der Politik der Vereinigten Staaten von Amerika waehrend der ersten Jahrzehnte ihres Bestehens (1776-1815).* ("Heidelberger Abhandlungen zur mittleren und neueren Geschichte," Heft 45 [Heidelberg, 1914]), pp. 6, 14, 17, 18. The only two studies of Franklin's political thought which touch upon international affairs stress almost exclusively the internationalistic aspects of Franklin's ideas on foreign policy: Malcolm R. Eiselen's *Franklin's Political Theories* (Garden City, N.Y.: Doubleday, Doran & Co., 1928) and Richard Donald Miles, "The Political Philosophy of Benjamin Franklin" (doctoral dissertation, University of Michigan, 1949), esp. p. 256. A similarly one-sided internationalistic interpretation of Franklin is given in several pamphlets which deal with Franklin's pronouncements on peace, e.g., the Introduction of Nathan G. Goodman to his selection of passages on *Benjamin Franklin on Peace* (Philadelphia: Franklin Institute, 1938), pp. 9-10. One of the most comprehensive selections of Franklin's statements on peace and

war is to be found in Benjamin Franklin, "On War and Peace," *Old South Leaflets* (Boston: Directors of the Old South Work, *s.a.*), VII, No. 162, 225–44.

8. Charles A. Beard, *The Idea of National Interest* (New York: Macmillan Co., 1934), p. 52.

9. Unsigned review of Marcel Trudel, *Louis XVI, le congrès américain et le Canada,* in *French-American Review,* III (1950), 212–13.

10. Gilbert Chinard, "Looking Westward," in *Meet Dr. Franklin* (Philadelphia: Franklin Institute, 1943), p. 137.

11. *Writings,* III, 65.

12. Chinard, *Thomas Jefferson,* p. 396.

13. Dexter Perkins, *The American Approach to Foreign Policy* (Cambridge: Harvard University Press, 1952), pp. 89–92. See also the chapter on "Capitalism and American Foreign Policy," esp. pp. 50 ff.

14. On this see A. K. Weinberg, "The Historical Meaning of the American Doctrine of Isolation," *American Political Science Review,* XXXIV (1940), 542.

15. To John Jay, September 23, 1776, in E. C. Burnett (ed.), *Letters of the Members of the Continental Congress* (8 vols.; Washington: Carnegie Institution of Washington, 1921–36), II, 197, n. 2 to piece 274.

16. Kenneth W. Thompson, "The Study of International Politics: A Survey of Trends and Developments," *Review of Politics,* XIV (1952), 454.

17. *Ibid.,* quoted from Edmund Burke, *Remarks on the Policy of the Allies with Respect to France* (1793), in *Works* (Boston: Little, Brown & Co., 1889), IV, 447.

18. Stuart P. Sherman, "Franklin and the Age of Enlightenment," in the same author's volume *Americans* (New York: Charles Scribner's Sons, 1922), p. 57.

19. Labaree *et al., Autobiography,* 160.

20. Marginal comment in *An Inquiry into the Nature and Causes of the Present Disputes* (London, 1769), quoted in Verner W. Crane, "Certain Writings of Benjamin Franklin on the British Empire and the American Colonies," *Papers of the Bibliographical Society of America,* XXVIII, Part I (1934), 23, n. 51. See also Benjamin Franklin, *The Complete Works of Benjamin Franklin,* ed. John Bigelow (10 vols.; New York and London: G. P. Putnam's Sons, 1887–88), IV, 320. Franklin's copy is in the New York Public Library.

21. Marginal comment in [Allen Ramsay], *Thoughts on the Origin and Nature of Government* (London, 1769), p. 63. For a similar statement see Bigelow (ed.), *op. cit.,* IV, 313.

22. *Writings,* V, 367. See above, p. 99.

23. Unpublished letter, April 14, 1767, to Joseph Galloway. See above, p. 27.

24. Thomas Pownall, *Principles of Polity, Being the Grounds and Reasons of Civil Empire* (London: Printed by Edward Owen, 1752), p. 15.

25. Cf. *ibid.,* p. 95. See also p. 102, where Pownall says how absurd and "how wide of the Scope of true Liberty, are those Maxims of Constitutional Jealousies, Checks, Oppositions, of the Independency of the Powers of Government? For on the Union, Harmony, and Dependency alone of these, is built true and real Liberty." Franklin, with his constant emphasis on the "common good," might well have agreed with this. Cf. also the brilliant and suggestive article by Stanley Pargellis, "The Theory of Balanced Government," in Conyers Read (ed.), *The Constitution Reconsidered* (New York: Columbia University Press, 1938), esp. pp. 47–49.

26. Pownall, *op. cit.*, p. 9.

27. See above, p. 120.

28. Cf. *A True History of the Difference between the Colonies and the Author of the Stamp Act* (March 12, 1778) (*Writings*, VII, 120).

29. *Address to the Public; from the Pennsylvania Society for the Abolition of Slavery, and the Relief of Free Negroes Unlawfully Held in Bondage* (November 9, 1789) (*Writings*, X, 67).

30. Marginal note in [Matthew C. Wheelock], *Reflections Moral and Political on Great Britain and Her Colonies* (London, 1770), p. 44.

31. To Robert Walsh, December 4, 1818, in Thomas Jefferson, *The Writings of Thomas Jefferson, Memorial Edition* (Washington: Thomas Jefferson Memorial Association, 1905), XV, 176.

INDEX

Absolutism, 83, 247

Accountability of rulers, Franklin on, 31–32, 84, 95, 247

Adams, John
and bicameral system, 26, 27
brings order into the legation in France, 152
on British naval power, 155
on checks and balances, 158
correspondence and notes of, 263 (n. 21)
and diplomacy of the big stick, 155–66, 253
diplomacy of, Franklin on, 155–57, 180
diplomatic appointments of, 152, 167, 169, 186, 294–95 (n. 12)
diplomatic dispatches of, 153
on diplomatic negotiations, conduct of, 158
on enmity of neighboring nations, 154
on financial aid from Europe, 161
on Franklin
in Congress, 123–24
his change of attitude toward France, 124, 147
his collaboration in the peace negotiations (1782), 177
his diplomacy in France, 154–56, 159–61, 297 (n. 28)
his intransigence with the Loyalists, 194–95
his reputation, 3
his taciturnity, 123, 172, 291 (n. 100)
testifies to his patriotic conduct, 181
isolationism of, 117–19, 123, 287 (n. 39)
on the myth of the American Revolution, 5
on the Navigation Laws, 123
on the peacefulness of the American people, 243
on the "Plan of Treaties," 118, 123–24
policy of, toward France, 118, 123–24, 154–66, 179, 180
on Swiss-French relations, 155
Thomas Paine's possible influence on, 117–19, 287 (n. 39)
on the treaty with Prussia, 231
and Vergennes, clash with, 156–57, 167–68

on writers of the Enlightenment, 25

Adams, Samuel, 137, 300 (n. 85)
allegedly pro-English, 166, 299 (n. 70)
criticizes Franklin, 150–51
favors "militia diplomacy," 126
favors political alliance with France, 118, 126, 289–90 (n. 71)
member of committee on plan for obtaining foreign assistance, 126
on natural right of acquiring adjoining territory, 221
political stand of, in Congress, 295 (n. 12)
see also Lee-Adams junto

Addison, Joseph, 6, 263 (n. 24)

Affaires de l'Angleterre et de l'Amérique, 300 (n. 90)

Age of Reason, 3, 4, 9, 71, 245, 257

Age of Reason, The (Paine), 25

Agriculture
in mercantilistic theories, 60–61
and prosperity of America, 103–4
significance of, for America's social structure, Franklin on, 56, 60–61, 76, 103–5, 243–45, 251–52
as source of strength, Franklin on, 135
as source of wealth, Franklin on, 105
and world peace, 35, 242–45

Aix-la-Chapelle, Peace of, 40

Albany Congress, and Plan of Union, 25, 52–54, 61, 62, 65, 84, 89–90, 140, 141, 248, 250, 274 (n. 115), 275 (n. 126)

Alembert, Jean Le Rond d', 292 (n. 104)

Alexander the Great, 29–30

Allegheny Mountains, 41, 62, 177, 194, 204

Alliances, changing meaning of the term, 118–19, 289–90 (n. 71); see also Commerce, American; Entanglements, political; French alliance; Isolationism

Ambition, 2, 15, 18–19, 111, 214, 241, 255, 257; see also Glory; Pride

American colonies; see Colonies, British, in North America

American Philosophical Society
established by Franklin, 17
and Jeffersonianism, 22

319

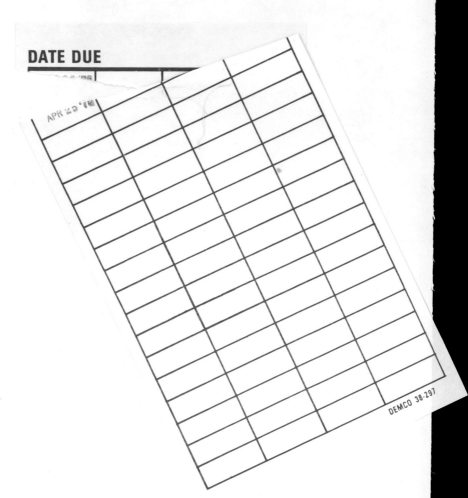